DYED IN CRIMSON

SPORT AND SOCIETY

Series Editors
Aram Goudsouzian
Jaime Schultz

Founding Editors
Benjamin G. Rader
Randy Roberts

*A list of books in the series appears
at the end of this book.*

DYED IN CRIMSON

FOOTBALL, FAITH, AND REMAKING HARVARD'S AMERICA

ZEV ELEFF

UNIVERSITY OF
ILLINOIS PRESS
Urbana, Chicago, and Springfield

Publication supported by a grant from the
Winton U. Solberg U.S. History Subvention Fund.

Library of Congress Cataloging-in-Publication Data
Names: Eleff, Zev author.
Title: Dyed in crimson : football, faith, and remaking
    Harvard's America / Zev Eleff.
Description: Urbana : University of Illinois Press, [2023]
    | Series: Sport and society | Includes bibliographical
    references and index.
Identifiers: LCCN 2022032687 (print) | LCCN 2022032688
    (ebook) | ISBN 9780252044946 (cloth) | ISBN
    9780252087097 (paperback) | ISBN 9780252054105
    (ebook)
Subjects: LCSH: Harvard University—Football—History—
    20th century. | Horween, Arnold, 1898–1985. | Bingham,
    William J. (William John), 1889–1971. | Antisemitism—
    United States—History—20th century. | BISAC: SPORTS
    & RECREATION / Football | HISTORY / United States /
    State & Local / New England (CT, MA, ME, NH, RI, VT)
Classification: LCC GV958.H3 E54 2023 (print) | LCC
    GV958.H3 (ebook) | DDC 796.332/63097444—dc23/
    eng/20220720
LC record available at https://lccn.loc.gov/2022032687
LC ebook record available at https://lccn.loc.gov/2022032688

For my parents and grandparents,
Susan and Scott Eleff and
Annette and Morton Eleff,
with endless love and admiration

CONTENTS

ACKNOWLEDGMENTS

I could not have written this book without the memories and mementos of Jinsie Bingham and Skip Horween. Jinsie made the necessary arrangements with Harvard University Archives to make her father-in-law's scrapbook collection accessible to me. Without these, it would have been impossible to reconstruct crucial aspects of Bill Bingham's life told in this book. Skip invited me to sit with him at Horween Leather Company while he recounted the family traditions and stories passed to him from his grandfather, Arnold Horween. Skip and his son, Nick, also introduced me to his extended family—Stuart Chase, Fred Stow, Fred Stow Jr., and Ralph Stow—who provided important materials for my research and read work in progress. Both Jinsie and Skip shared personal records and encouraged my work. Their trust in me was courageous, and I hope I did not let them down.

Research for this book introduced me to a scholarly literature very different from my usual realm of American Jewish history. The history of American sport is enriching and immense. I navigated the field with the friendships I developed through the North American Society for Sport History (NASSH). Most of the NASSH's very fine researchers and writers are professionally attached to kinesiology departments, sports museums, and print media outlets. I am indebted to them for the kindness they showed in addressing queries offered by an American Jewish historian armed with a scholarly background very different from theirs, as well as an overexuberant love for football. In particular, I am grateful to Lodrina Cherne, Richard Crepeau, Andrew Linden, Andrew McGregor, Ronald Smith, Marcia Synnott, and John Watterson. Finally, among these sports scholars and scribes, I owe much to Kurt Kemper, who read through an earlier draft of this book and made it better. I hope this group will find something novel about my efforts to synergize the histories of American sport and religion.

I also benefited from conversations with my colleagues in the arena of American Jewish history. Kirsten Fermaglich, Daniel Green, and Jeffrey Gurock offered guidance during early stages of writing. Jonathan Sarna is not a diehard sports fan but, as always, supported my research. He urged me to challenge and deepen scholars' understanding of "Americanization." Dr. Sarna's influence may not be as apparent as it is in my other work, but his friendship and mentorship are evident on every page of this book. I grew up reading John Eisenberg's columns in the *Baltimore Sun* and am grateful he took some time to help me now as an adult, discussing the sports history craft and narrative stylings. Friends welcomed conversations with me about the adventures of Bill Bingham and Arnold Horween. They include Dovid Bashevkin, Alex Jakubowski, Jeffrey Saks, Ilana and Adam Stock, and Shlomo Zuckier. Rahel and Yitzi Ehrenberg provided lodging and dinner in preparation for a short archive trip to Harvard Yard. As always, Menachem Butler was a peerless sounding board, friend, and primary source scavenger.

That last point brings me to another debt of gratitude. Historians are rather useless without primary sources. This book drew me to a number of archives and supportive archivists. On all occasions, librarians and directors of special collections were very gracious in facilitating my requests and ensuring that I used my research trips efficiently and profitably. During the coronavirus pandemic, these same institutions and staffs continued to support my work, combing through finding aids and scanning key materials for me. My boundless thanks are therefore dutifully due to the librarians and archivists at Brandeis University, the Chicago History Museum, Harvard University, Johns Hopkins Medical Institutions, the Lawrence History Center, Phillips Exeter Academy, Princeton University, the Skokie Public Library, the University of Notre Dame, the University of Pennsylvania, Yale University, and the University of Chicago.

The University of Illinois Press embraced this book project. Daniel Nassett and Mariah Schaefer identified reviewers best suited to improving the manuscript at various stages of its production. The Press is a field leader in developing and producing books on sports history. Danny and Mariah were partners throughout this happy process. They handed this project off to a very fine production team. I extend my gratitude to Angela Burton, Kevin Cunningham, Dustin Hubbart, Geof Garvey, and Tad Ringo.

I started writing this book as a member of the Touro College faculty and the academic head of its operations in Illinois. Research funding was crucial to the initial stages of reading and writing on this subject. More than that, though, I gained much from the relationships formed during my tenure at Touro and Hebrew Theological College. I completed the final stages of this book as president of Gratz College in Melrose Park, Pennsylvania. I eagerly acknowledge my colleagues, Lori Cohen and Dodi Klimoff, who graciously helped finalize several of the wonderful images in this book. I already owe much to them and everyone at Gratz College. The students, board, staff, and faculty warmly welcomed me to Philadelphia. The students in my "History of Antisemitism" course provided insights that sharpened several ideas in this book and members of Gratz's board of governors, led by Kathy Elias, offered their wisdom on several points covered in these pages. I so much look forward to advancing our college together with a shared and powerful vision.

This book has two origin stories, both rooted in my family. First, my parents, Susan and Scott Eleff. In December 1996, my father drove me and a friend to Memorial Stadium in Baltimore to watch the Ravens defeat the Steelers. It was the Ravens' inaugural season and their first victory over their bitter rival. I've remained a devoted Ravens fan, and my father has generously tolerated my prattling on about Ray Lewis, Joe Flacco, and most recently, Lamar Jackson. My mother nurtured my sports fandom, securing Baltimore Orioles tickets whenever possible. She did even more to ensure that I could write and get the most out of my words. My parents remain a great source of energy and inspiration. I am forever in their debt, even as they continue to derive much enjoyment from the accomplishments of me and my siblings, David, Ben, and Joey. My brothers have done much to make meaning for themselves and the people in their lives. I've been very blessed to grow up with them and be loved by them.

The other genesis of this project dates back a trip to Barnes and Noble. There, my wife, Melissa, surveyed the displayed books and suggested that I find a historical subject that could bring together American Jewish history and popular culture. My in-laws, Marcy and Paul Stieglitz, would have been quick to tell Melissa that her recommendation would yield a sports monograph. This book will not convince my father-in-law that I know all that much about sports. Nevertheless, I hope my in-laws will enjoy this book. Their affection informs the passion that goes into my writing and so much else in our lives.

I am so grateful for Melissa's love and the wonderful ways she challenges me to move onward. She'd say that I don't need much motivation. I say it's because she's the very best sort of inspiration. Melissa and I are raising the most darling children. Time and again, I beseeched Meital, Jack, and Adir to help me untangle and braid the various narratives of this work. They have in certain moments indulged me and on other occasions savvily changed the conversation to topics of interest to a nine-, seven-, or four-year-old. They promise me that we'll return to Bingham and Horween when they are slightly older. There's much to do in the meantime. Being their father is the greatest honor of my life.

Finally, my grandparents, Annette and Morton Eleff, have read everything I've ever written. They constantly asked about the progress of the "football book" and ably discussed with me how the mingling of sport, religion, race, and culture might suggest something important about the American experience. Together with my parents, they are my greatest fans and most constructive and caring critics. It is to them, my parents and grandparents, that I dedicate this book with endless love and admiration.

DYED IN CRIMSON

INTRODUCTION

This is a story about change. Much of it took place on a football field, but its victories transcended sports. It is a tale about young men raised by parents who believed that the Bible prophesied the boundless opportunities promised to their children in the United States. Their actions challenged the patrician culture at Harvard College that suggested just the opposite. The Boston Brahmins who ran the school held that social rank was predetermined, perhaps the only part of the Puritans' Calvinist faith to which their privileged descendants still adhered. The lessons folded into this history anticipated some of the values trumpeted during later struggles on behalf of women and people of color. The import of these later sagas and the decline of Harvard among the football hierarchies have, over time, hidden the present story's significance.[1] Yet, it garnered countless headlines in its moment.

The importance of changing Harvard was on the minds of middle-class midwesterners who never did feel altogether comfortable while studying in Boston's most famous school, surrounded by New England's most privileged. In April 1926, two hundred Harvard College alumni tapped into an indescribable energy source in a rented room in Chicago's Drake Hotel. The president of the local Harvard Club, John Miller, had written to Bill Bingham, the new Harvard athletic director, inviting him to speak among friends in the Windy City. Miller did not anticipate that Bingham would agree to appear at the group's spring meeting. Chicago was a full day's train ride from Boston, and rumor had it that Bingham was inundated with requests to visit about forty Harvard alumni groups around the United States. Chicago did not rank ahead of other, eastern, enclaves.[2]

Miller's invitation to Bingham on behalf of the Chicago Harvard Club was mostly a gesture of gratitude to the athletic director for selecting one of their own to take the reins of Harvard football. He had contacted Bingham's office a month prior when news broke about Arnold Horween's appointment as Harvard's football coach. Horween was not cast from the same mold as prior Harvard Crimson coaches. Horween was an outsider. The Chicagoans, however, adored him. He was one of them. Arnie—the diminutive his friends used for him—was a native son. Born on Chicago's South Side and raised on its North Side, Horween remained northward for the remainder of his life, working for his family's leather company near Wicker Park. His kind fit just fine in a town that had little compunction about elevating the Irish and Polish stock to the upper levels of its political and social establishment.[3]

New England was far more rigid. There, not everyone was so sanguine about the prospect of a Jewish midwesterner assuming the most coveted public position at Harvard, save for, maybe, the presidency of the university.[4] Both "Midwest" and "Jewish" were coded language for outsiders in certain sections of America's most elite social classes. Harvard president Abbott Lawrence Lowell established policies two years after Horween graduated from Harvard College that might have prevented his enrollment had he applied a few years later.[5] In 1922, Lowell introduced admission quotas to undo Jewish "clannishness," the tendency, Lowell observed, to "form a distinct body, and cling, or are driven, together, apart from the great mass of undergraduates."[6]

Then as now, Harvard was much more than a famous college. Harvard is one the major test sites of American social and cultural stature. Who is admitted to the school, who is permitted to teach on its campus in Cambridge, Massachusetts, represent important benchmarks and barriers in American life. The very strong desire of women, faith communities, and ethnic groups to be a part of Harvard College is in large part propelled by a sense that "making it" at Harvard is tantamount to becoming a full-fledged, full-access member of the highest rungs of society and culture in the United States. It marks who is included in the American Dream, privileged to realize the promises of success and opportunity.[7] Both success and opportunity figure heavily in the pages that follow, especially for Jews who, as I will make clear, have measured their own ability to Americanize against acceptance into the nation's leading institutions. On the other hand, a feeling of unwelcomeness at Harvard has been viewed as a signal of sexism and racism. Further, exclusion from Harvard is poignant for America's Jews who interpreted Harvard enrollment quotas as a sign of lingering antisemitism. All the above can also be said of organized sports. The question of who is permitted to play on high school, college, and professional fields, tracks, and courts is very often how the US Supreme Court and the court of public opinion evaluate the strength of barrier making and barrier smashing in the United States.[8] Chicagoan John Miller's curiosity about Arnold Horween's appointment at Harvard was shared by Jews and, frankly, many other stakeholders in the so-called American Dream. Their interest was powered by the centrality of Harvard and sport in determining the red lines of American life.

All these factors are pivotal for scholars of American Jewish history and, as this book argues, for students of all social, cultural, and religious aspects of American life in the twentieth century. The impression of Harvard's Jews matched a growing interwar sentiment about American minorities and, in the case of Jews, spread to other college campuses. A Dartmouth man, for instance, reported that, while the Jews in Hanover were a "mediocre lot," he seemed pleased that he was not surrounded by the "more distinguished" Jews at Harvard who tended to "flock together," never truly assimilating into the campus culture.[9] More diplomatic men at Harvard reasoned that the "proportion of Jewish students at the university is greater than that of any other race. Consequently, the problem of restricting Jews, if it is necessary to restrict, is the greatest."[10]

Chicago alumni thought that a Jewish lad leading the Crimson eleven was a good change for Harvard College. He might even inject some "midwesternism" into the Cambridge, Massachusetts, campus. By this, Chicago's Harvard men meant a certain openness to other people and their "foreign" ideas. John Miller, speaking for his Harvard Club, contended about Arnie that "we feel that he is the best man in the country for the job." Horween respected Harvard's traditions but was unafraid to introduce new strategies and training routines that could raise the Crimson team's prospects. The Harvard eleven had struggled in recent years, a dramatic turnabout from its triumphs in the preceding decade. Miller believed Arnie was well suited to select the very best athletic material on merit and withstand the pressure to draw from the most elite classes. Then again, Miller and his group did not want to dismantle Harvard's ways. The band of Chicago alumni revered Harvard and sang to it, reprising "It's a Way We Have at Old Harvard" to start their meetings. But they also made fun of how their New England friends pronounced it: "Old Hah-vahd."[11] But yet, Chicago's Harvard men did not mind discussions about change at their school, which stood in contrast to the concerted resistance of the Boston and New York alumni.

Horween was a former football captain and one of the most important players on the school's lone Rose Bowl championship team, a squad that outplayed a formidable Oregon squad on New Year's Day 1920. Yet that was not enough to convince many outspoken alumni of his fitness for the post.[12]

The All-American Horween was the product of a progressive private school, a handsome young man with a burly body that betrayed the usual meek and bookish stereotypes of Jewish manliness in that age.[13] He never suffered a loss during his two-year Harvard varsity career. Figuring that some luck did in fact rub off, undergraduates developed a ritual before final examinations, patting Horween's letterman's jacket as he passed through Harvard Yard.

The challengers to Horween's fitness apparently forgot about that superstitious ritual. And opponents disparaged Horween's participation in the seedy nascent National Football League.[14] Even though Horween and his older brother, Ralph, had played under aliases, it was an open secret that the "McMahon" brothers were not some working-class Irish Catholics from Chicago's South Side. They were Harvard-educated athletes, detractors charged, that had sold out and cheapened the integrity of amateur sport. More complicit than most realized, the Horween Leather Company provided the materials to Wilson-Western Sporting Goods to manufacture the prototype footballs that George Halas experimented with at Chicago Bears practices. Many alumni considered all this rather extraneous. Horween was not Protestant, nor was he a Boston Brahmin. On these grounds he was ineligible, fully unfit, to lead Harvard football.

Harvard athletic director, Bill Bingham, was already besieged by opposition before the Horween announcement. He had earlier pledged to give athletics back to Harvard undergraduates and remove the imperious influences of the college's well-heeled alumni. The old guard had to submit, at least publicly, because President Lowell backed Bingham. Surreptitiously, trustees and longtime boosters circulated their resentment of Bingham's posturing in their elite clubs and society gatherings. His selection of Horween further aroused their indignation and contempt. Bingham was eager to surround himself with sympathetic elements and therefore accepted Miller's invitation and made room in his itinerary to visit with his newfound Chicago friends in between a trip to Ohio State and an Easter holiday at Princeton.

Arnold Horween also addressed Chicago's Harvard Club. It was his first occasion to say something in public since the press conference to introduce him as coach held several weeks earlier. He was determined to do better in Chicago than he had performed in Cambridge. His first attempt had provided plenty of fodder for Harvard's incredulous alumni. These were the older guard at Harvard who obeyed a traditionalist creed and were determined to halt the modernist impulses of a rising generation of undergraduates. Speaking before reporters curious about his plan to revive one of college football's first and most successful programs, Horween had started well, promising to rely on tradition. Conservatism was a virtue at Harvard, something Horween knew well from his undergraduate adventures around Harvard Yard, from 1916 to 1920. It was a particular point of view framed around the comfortable sight of massive gates connected to aged bricks with limestone trimming. Harvard men were quite proud of their habits and well-entrenched perspectives on almost every matter, figuring that such an outlook was the very best kind of position. Theirs was a proven formula. Their ranks supplied the United States with its presidents and politicians, industry leaders, and Wall Street bankers.

Horween had not wished to blaspheme in his very first chance. "I am not coming to Harvard to initiate a new football system," he promised. "Harvard football is still fundamentally sound, and it is my intention to build upon the foundations already laid." He had, however, felt required to profit from his post-Harvard experiences. He had tried to remain measured but probably went too far for some Harvard men ready to pounce. "Of course, my connection with the game since my graduation from college has been mostly in the middle west," reasoned Horween, "and I naturally have imbibed what are considered the modern ideas of that section. What I think worth copying of these phases of western football I will not hesitate to introduce."[15] His listeners thought it was too bold, not at all deferential to Harvard traditions. The statement provoked a new round of criticism for Bingham and Horween.

Bill begged Arnie to speak more laconically in this second opportunity at the Drake Hotel. Horween obliged. He made no mention of Harvard's disconsolate position or his plan to revitalize it. Instead, Arnie gave a short speech, thanking the Chicago alumni for their expression of confidence and promising to do his very best for dearest Harvard. He did not commit to any win-loss record, nor did he promise a victory over archrival Yale. This time, Horween warned about any changes to the game plan, expressing doubt about the newfangled forward pass that would eventually elevate his Harvard teams. Still, the roomful of Chicago men read into Horween's remarks and let him and Bingham know it. They were restless, eager to release that energy for the midwesternization of New England Harvard. The press reported how "they voiced it in terms of ancient Harvard yells that shook the chandeliers and with an enthusiasm that clearly indicated they believed Harvard athletics will again rise."[16]

The excitement went undiminished while another speaker, Coach Jesse Hawley of Dartmouth, preached circumspection and predicted that it would be a "difficult task . . . rebuilding Harvard football." The present company could not recompose itself and spoke above the presentation delivered by Kermit and Theodore Roosevelt Jr. on their recent expedition to Tibet and the trove of zoological specimens they had retrieved and deposited at Chicago's Field Museum.

WHEN H MEETS H   By Feg Murray

THOSE "H'S" AGAIN!
HORWEEN VS. HAWLEY —
(HARVARD PLAYS DARTMOUTH
THIS SATURDAY)

JESSE HAWLEY,
FOOTBALL COACH AT DARTMOUTH

ARNOLD HORWEEN
HARVARD'S NEW COACH.

Coach Jesse Hawley of Dartmouth College was an early supporter of Horween's appointment as Harvard's head coach. He initially predicted that it would take time to rebuild the football program in Cambridge. On October 23, 1926, Harvard beat Dartmouth at Harvard Stadium, 16–12. First published in the *Los Angeles Times*, October 20, 1926.

The Harvard Club regained some comportment, finally, for Bill Bingham. Bill had perfected his phrasing to describe alumni relations at Harvard. He described the "new spirit of cooperation between students, alumni, and faculty." Bingham was sure that, together with Horween, new energy and ideas would be "beneficial to Harvard athletics."[17] The prospect sent the crowd into a renewed cheer. Whether interested parties approved of it or not, there was something afoot at America's oldest and most important producer of culture, intellectualism, and leading personalities.

* * *

Harvard's America was reshaped by men who should have had no claim to bending the social arc of Cambridge's most exclusive class: Bingham and Horween, children of immigrants brought up in religious and social traditions that stood outside the New England mainstream. Along with the Irish Catholic football phenomenon Eddie Casey, this group was a collection of outsiders who pierced through to the inside and then did much to complicate the borderlines. They did not intend to influence the center from the periphery. Their foremost interest was to reestablish Harvard football. Bingham and Horween were shaped by visions and versions of America that presumed any man endowed with virtue could rise. This was no doubt the case for Horween in Chicago. Around the beginning of the twentieth century, three-quarters of the city's population were immigrants or immigrants' children. These women and men "saw themselves as good Americans," part of a "patriotic pluralism" that was guaranteed to them by the midwesternism that attracted so many diverse people and provided to them such promise.[18] Their trust in America was taught through faith and family. At Harvard, it played out on fields and in stadiums that displayed notions of courage and manliness in fuller perspective than other arenas of American life.

This aura of open-mindedness supports historian Jessica Cooperman's bold claim that the first decades of the century contain within them the "origins of religious pluralism."[19] The historical personalities in this book seem to have been aware that the United States had, in nuanced ways, broadened the pathways for outsiders to reach the so-called mainstream. Bingham's path initially led him to the cinder track rather than the football gridiron. His was a journey, covered in the first portions of this book, that testified to the best and worst of American class and culture. Bill's surname suggested a line of descent from the Puritans but, as the son of an immigrant millhand, his American credentials began with his own personal bona fides. His experiences redounded to his work as overseer of Harvard sports. As an up-and-coming star football player, Horween trekked to Pasadena and won the Rose Bowl for Harvard. The victory over Oregon in the East-West postseason game restored some respectability for American sports after college athletics had languished during World War I and professional baseball had been dishonored by the infamous fixing of the 1919 World Series.[20]

In the mid-1920s, amid festering nativism and a stark narrowing of what and who could be considered American, Bingham brought Horween back to Cambridge. In turn, Arnold Horween arrived with Eddie Casey, his backfield mate during their playing days. These men instilled a fresh culture at the most important university in the United States.[21] They made "unconscionable" decisions such as selecting the best players, taking no heed of the height of their social standing, the credentials that, for some, had earned them admission to Harvard in the first place. Horween reendowed meaning to erstwhile terms like *honor* and *courage*. He taught his football charges about manhood and detached winning—the expressionless accumulation of bottom-line results—from the animated realization of these noble words. These lessons contrasted with the sentiments of Harvard alumni who viewed winning like wealth: something to accumulate as a marker of success. Bingham as athletic director and Horween as football coach, as partners in the effort, aimed to hand off the game to the players and told the rich alumni that it was not theirs to control anymore.

Determined as they were, Bingham and Horween likely lacked the historical perspective to recognize that their efforts extended far beyond football, to redefine the ideals and character of the United States, for Harvard men and many others. But sportswriters and spectators were very aware of the transformation. Rabbis preached about the brawny and brainy Horween long before they turned their attention to baseball's Hank Greenberg and Sandy Koufax.[22] Journalists praised the efforts of swell Bill Bingham to counterbalance the offensive off-field deeds of sports heroes like Babe Ruth's philandering and Ty Cobb's toxic tongue.[23] For that matter, the All-American Eddie Casey, whose role in this story is not central but still very significant, might still be recollected as one of the all-time great halfbacks, had Harvard maintained its football dominance, part of the Big Three triumvirate with Princeton and Yale.[24] The achievements of Harvard football in this interwar epoch were deemed more American than baseball. The actions of Bingham and Horween were hailed as more patriotic than the Harvard sports heroes who had preceded them.

* * *

Histories of college sports tend to gloss over these names. Scholars have focused on the battles over professionalism in college football, compelled by the roles played by otherwise important historical figures such as Theodore

Roosevelt, Charles Eliot, and Walter Camp, as well as the emergence of the National Collegiate Athletic Association.[25] Historians in search of the cultural meaning of football in the initial decades of the twentieth century have seized on the rhetoric of journalists and enduring—and tragic—icons such as Jim Thorpe.[26] Biographers have chronicled the coaches who designed the architecture of modern football such as Walter Camp, Knute Rockne, Amos Alonzo Stagg, and Pop Warner, as well as Harvard's Percy Haughton, whose tenure at Harvard preceded Horween's.[27] Each of them reveals much about the history of football and its impact on American culture. By refocusing the narrative around Bingham, Casey, and Horween, this book aims to suggest that a pluralistic culture and spirit of fairness and openness played an important role in democratizing football at Harvard. That it happened at one of the most pivotal cultural and intellectual sites in the United States betokens the power and impact of these cultural trends beyond its sprawling ivy campus.

This book benefits from earlier research, especially the work of Marcia Synnott and Ronald Smith. As a historian of racism and sport, Synnott's work has shown the usefulness of athletics to explore deeper meaning and trends in American life.[28] More than any sports historian, Smith has demonstrated the tug-of-war between gentlemanly sportsmanship and the crude determination to win above all else.[29] This work deepens the exploration of that clash between sportsmanship and winning by placing the confrontation in historical context. Earlier scholarship on the subject takes a narrow focus. As a scholar of American Jews and American religion, and as a researcher very mindful of how lived religion interacts with prevailing cultures, I have written these pages to offer a more multivalent perspective. Not just a pivotal change in the history of sport, crucial shifts in social, cultural, and religious aspects of American life forced women and men to reevaluate what they meant when they spoke about success and successful people. Harvard College, then, is a very fitting test site to account for these variables and changed perceptions about masculinity in the United States. The efforts and challenges faced by Bill Bingham and Arnold Horween assume added importance, reflecting a wider effort to define important aspects of life in the Progressive Era and interwar period. Their encounter with the highest classes of New England throw light on boundary making and social possibilities in the United States.

Harvard College was one of the major hubs of college sports—on-the-field play and off-the-field politics—in the decades around the beginning of the twentieth century. Its students, alumni, and leaders struggled with an expectation of a gentlemanly predisposition and a heightened desire to win games. Harvard, for a while, was invested with the former, inheriting that genteel approach to athletics from Europe, particularly from Cambridge and Oxford. Yale celebrated winning and did much of it at Harvard's expense.[30]

Sport separated from decisive competition left many Americans unsettled, especially for the spectators who measured their own worth by the success of the colleges and teams they supported. The British politician James Bryce was very struck by Americans' "passion for looking on at and reading about athletic sports." Bryce noted that sports had become a social investment for the rank-and-file in the United States. "It occupies the minds not only of the youth at the universities, but also of their parents and of the general public."[31] Association with a winner helped the average American occupy a pedestal that, in other realms such as business and politics, only the rarest of elites could attain.

In the United States at the time, sportsmen marveled that the "English seem to play more for the love of sport and less for a desire to beat somebody than their American cousins."[32] In New York, the journalists found it an utter fascination that the English philosopher Herbert Spencer once told a billiards player who had beaten him three times straight that "to play a good game of billiards is the accomplishment of a gentleman: to play *too* good a game of billiards is a sign of a misspent youth."[33] The British complained that an "American athlete can never understand why Oxford men 'throw away their chances' by practising either football or rowing where Cambridge can see what is going on."[34] This English writer mocked the American approach to sport, captured best at Yale. "The winning of a game being the only end that an American player has in view, he subordinates every other consideration to this, and cheerfully relinquishes such old-fashioned ideas as 'style' or 'good form,' or the other shibboleths which have become antiquated in the land of their birth, and are scarcely known at all in new countries."[35]

Harvard was caught in this tension. Some Harvard men clung to their gentlemanly tradition, despite how incongruous it appeared beside other American sensibilities. With a certain degree of hyperbole and a definitive ire for his New Haven counterparts, one Harvard alumnus searched "for any vital book, for any advance in educational method which Yale can claim in the past decade or two." The answer, he found, was that the "modern game of football, developed by Mr. Walter Camp, is the one great contribution made at New Haven in recent years to the world's progress and the intellectual and spiritual uplift of mankind."[36]

Camp's Elis, Blue, or Bulldogs—Yale used all three names for their sporting squads—dominated Harvard's Crimson teams in the 1890s. In time, however, Harvard grew tired of losing for the sake of proper form, especially when it suffered those defeats against its archrival on the chalk-marked gridiron. Harvard had to reorient itself to procure more recurrent victories. In 1904, Harvard alumni started to agitate for "competent management" of the Crimson eleven: "It is not pleasant to be beaten by Yale year after year." Careful not to disparage the gentlemanly honor code, Harvard graduates explained that all they wanted was their "full share of victories"—not the "professional coach" and Spartan stylings of Yale.[37] Winning also meant more ticket sales and revenue.[38] Harvard started to win under coach Percy Haughton, and Harvard feared Horween would alter or altogether dismantle his system. Legend had it that Haughton strangled a bulldog (it was papier-mâché) in front of his players to show them the supreme importance of winning, particularly when matched up against Yale.

Bingham and Horween were heirs to these changes around Harvard Yard.[39] In his running career, Bingham struggled with sportsmanship and winning and suffered from disappointment when he could not live up to Harvard's new and total emphasis on victory. Upon his return to Cambridge, and with more of his attention focused on football, Bingham valued winning but feared that too much was lost in the single-minded path toward triumph. It came at the cost of honor and fairness, Bingham and Horween had concluded. That culture, they feared, secreted beyond the boundary lines of the gridiron, or perhaps it was informed by those forces from outside it. In search of redemption, Bingham and Horween used their power on the football field to teach their charges about the virtues propounded by the Progressive Era that seemed at odds with the token elitism of the Boston patricians who led Harvard, such as President Charles Eliot and his successor, Abbott Lawrence Lowell.

This story, then, is not merely about Harvard athletics. It offers much to consider about outsiders and insiders in American life. From 1880 to 1920, twenty million immigrants settled in the United States, a spike that did much to help double the population to more than a hundred million women and men during that span. Acculturation was no proverbial homogeneous melting pot. Historians have long doubted the Crèvecoeurian myth that the immigrant process of Americanization was singular and simple. To the contrary, ethnic and religious groups deployed multiple methods of acculturation.[40] For instance, the Irish migrants to the United States fashioned institutions that paralleled existing American infrastructures. Their efforts to establish "bricks-and-mortar-Catholicism," as one historian described it, meant religiously sensitive parochial schools, welfare societies, and other "elaborate social networks that facilitated Irish influence within and well beyond the church."[41] The Italian and Polish varieties of Catholic émigrés exercised more tepid approaches to their new American surroundings, doing much more to reconstruct and maintain their Old World homes and habits in the United States.[42]

America's Jews took the most radical path toward acculturation. Jews found something almost spellbinding in Protestant America.[43] The various waves of Jewish migration throughout the nineteenth century bought into the cult of synthesis that moved them to harmonize their Jewish identities with American democracy and its archetypal institutions.[44] Unlike people of color, Jews from Eastern and Central Europe could pose as white. I write "pose" because it was not until the mid-twentieth century that Jews became a part of the white American mainstream. Until then, it was an uneasy path toward a white racial identity. Many Christians considered their Jewish neighbors terminologically different from them, in both their religion and their race.[45] American Jews sought to break down those categories and assimilate. They designated their English-language immersion schools, welfare and labor organizations, and women's and young people's associations as "Jewish Americanization agencies."[46]

Football reflected the complexities of socialization. Several groups used the gridiron to construct independent cultural identities that could match—and often outmatch—the mainstream American equivalent. For example, Catholic leaders established their colleges as alternatives to secular colleges. They deplored social-climbing Catholics for exposing their children to the heresies taught in non-Catholic universities and public schools.[47] Irish Americans—believing that their late marriages and extended bachelorhoods somehow improved their athleticism—seized on sport, encouraging alumni and friends to celebrate the "prowess of the football team" and the "proper sort of institution for the education of Catholic boys."[48] Boston College, Holy Cross, Georgetown, and especially Notre Dame embraced football as a parallel form of Americanization. The Irish's outsized reputation as sportsmen—particularly in professional baseball in the decades around the beginning of the twentieth century—catalyzed the swift embrace of Catholic manliness, even if the American game was not quite the same as Gaelic football.[49] Each of these athletic programs proved that the Catholic social creed could remain religiously firm and just as compelling as American Protestantism.

Knute Rockne's dominant Notre Dame teams set the standard for all other Catholic colleges to compete and hold their own against other footballers, even as other midwestern coaches barred the Irish from their athletic conference, known now as the Big Ten.[50] Owing to this, the Roman Catholic Diocese of Brooklyn in 1919 could not comprehend how, in a time when Boston College had beaten Yale, Notre Dame had defeated West Point, and Georgetown's squad had gotten the better of Navy's eleven, any Catholic young man could enlist at any other university, Harvard, Princeton, and Yale included.[51] And, just as at the college level, it brought Catholic leaders great pleasure in the high school ranks to train their young parochial school athletes to excel in football and vanquish their Protestant public-school counterparts.[52]

Native American schools used football as a tamer form of warfare to strike against their white oppressors and opponents. To elevate the symbolism of their confrontation with the American mainstream, it was common for Native American football teams to adorn traditional Indian headgear and play with a style of wily trickery that rank-and-file whites had long accused them of harboring. Pop Warner's Carlisle Industrial School gained renown for its ethnic pageantry and style, as well as its exceptional play against formidable colleges.[53]

African American colleges adopted a different approach. Some calls to seek integration by competing against and playing for major college teams were drowned out and undermined by low self-confidence and racism.[54] To be sure, each ethnic group formed its own sports leagues that bonded its members together—but these communities also desired to use sport to bridge their communities to others.[55] The painful experiences, accounted for in this book, of Matthew Bullock and William Clarence Matthews competing against severe anti-black prejudices at Princeton and Yale deterred many of the superior athletes who also might have merited enrollment at some of the best universities. Perhaps the finest African American college football player was Fritz Pollard, the first black footballer at Brown University. For Pollard, his teammates in Providence made it more challenging to cope than his opponents did. "I could not get a uniform," was Pollard's example about the coldness within the football team. Pollard credited other outsiders with keeping up his spirits. "I was disgusted and depressed, and ready to quit. But there were a couple of Jewish boys who kept urging me to go back."[56]

These experiences confirmed to African Americans the need to look inward. Around the turn of the century, black schools like Lincoln University in Pennsylvania and Howard University in Washington, DC, did much to assemble a circle of African American colleges and industrial schools that could compete with one another and keep to themselves, away from the white-dominated universities and football powerhouses.[57] In October 1921, when football squads belonging to Roger Williams College of Tennessee and Wilberforce University of Ohio met for a match in Chicago, the local African American press greeted the duel as a landmark competition among "two universities of the Race."[58] A year later, a columnist for that same newspaper described the Howard-Lincoln Thanksgiving showdown as the "game of all games" and that the "social affairs which follow the game will even outrank those given at either New Haven or Cambridge."[59] True or not, the perception among African Americans in this epoch was that their young men and colleges could form their own sport cultures apart from the existing elite white establishment. This book offers an understanding of the variegated process of "becoming American" and the "heterogeneity of peoples"—to draw on two wonderful phrases of historian Jon Butler—and how these cultural forces transformed perhaps the most socially traditional and unyielding institution in the United States.[60] These pages do not explicitly engage these histories but learns from them and contextualizes Bingham, Horween, and college sports within these complex conditions. The complicated relationship between Jews, racism, whiteness, and American culture suggests just how profound otherness is embedded in the nation's history.

* * *

Horween announced his retirement from coaching in November 1930, at a press conference held directly after his Harvard team defeated Yale. "Football can ill afford to lose Arnold Horween," declared sportswriter Allison Danzig, hoping that Bingham could once again convince Horween to remain with the Crimson team. "Arnold Horween is so much bigger than victory, his type is so priceless an asset to the game," concluded Danzig in the columns of the *New York Times*.[61] Arnold Horween had emerged as a symbol of great possibilities even if his background stood out as irregular among Hebrews—a term used at that time interchangeably with Jews—at Harvard or elsewhere. The same was the case for Bill Bingham, raised in an immigrant mill town, able to rise up because of his near-peerless fleet-footedness and unmatched fortitude.

Bingham understood all this and prevailed on Horween to keep going. Horween, however, was unmovable. Equipped with a very satisfactory second option, Bill tapped Eddie Casey to coach the Crimson team. Horween returned to Chicago and his family obligations at his father's leather company. By this time, the friends recognized the impact of their efforts. Some referred to it as the midwesternization of Harvard. They symbolized the patriotic pluralism that seemed more real to Chicagoans than to their counterparts in the Northeast.[62] Others described the changes as the influence of outsiders or foreigners. All this denoted a spirit of pluralism that was before then absent in the most elitist US institutions. The three had redeemed Harvard from its intransigence and helped democratize the United States.

At a banquet convened to celebrate Horween, Bill Bingham vowed that "Arnold Horween will be remembered by the present generation and I hope the legacy will be passed on because of his human attitude to the boys and the game."[63]

These pages are meant to fulfill Bill Bingham's promise.

CHAPTER ONE

THE (CINDER) PATH
TO A BETTER LIFE

Last evening the associates of William J. Bingham, the Y.M.C.A. athlete and superintendent of the Y.M.C.A. gym classes, was presented with a purse and a substantial sum of money at the Y.M.C.A. rooms. All the friends of the young man who are employed in the department of the mill with him were participants in the pleasant affair. The presentation speech was made by Hugh J. Gallagher who spoke briefly of the impression the young man had made with those who had been associated with him and with whom he had grown up. He also mentioned the prowess of the young man on the cinder path and what pride all his friends took in his success.

—"Athlete Bingham Given a Purse," undated news clipping, 1908

In 1908, Bill Bingham was focused on Boston College, not Harvard University. Boston College held a popular track meet for high school–age boys in Massachusetts. Bill departed for the race with high expectations. As a rule, he preferred to run outdoors. Only snow could force them inside, into the Lawrence, Massachusetts, YMCA's small gymnasium. Racing, Bill reckoned, was meant for the outdoors. Besides, that winter season in Boston was much milder than usual. Back in Lawrence, Bill and his band of teenage speedsters would practice on outdoor cinder paths. If the track was occupied, they would trot along the path bordering the Merrimack River in that northeastern Massachusetts town. The temperature on the Friday night in February when the meet was scheduled was just below freezing. No trouble for a handful of mill-town youngsters. The newspapers did not forecast snow. If it did come down, the flakes would not stick. The trouble was that the annual Boston College event had become something of a spectacle at that Jesuit institution.[1] Boston College delighted in showing off its capacious gymnasium on James

Street, supposedly "one of the best equipped around Boston."[2] The lighting on the outdoor grounds was fully unsatisfactory for an evening meet. The Lawrence lads understood that they would be running inside, no matter the weather and no matter how unnatural for a race. It was a calculated compromise to run in front of reporters and recruiters, to perhaps run out of Lawrence and a life of working-class millwork and into a life of greater possibilities. In New England, that dream was best enabled by admission to its leading schools of higher education, Harvard or Yale.

Running did just that for Bill Bingham. Yet Bingham never really departed Lawrence. His running was a representation of his upbringing. In that immigrant town, women and men relied on "mutual dependence and cooperative assistance."[3] Shared labor and a belief in togetherness emerged as core values in Bingham's childhood. They were lessons embossed on the experiences and expressions of those youngsters who trained at the YMCA. Their training focused on hard work and teamwork as a goal and winning as an ancillary purpose, although a likely outcome of determined effort. For Lawrence, the young Bingham emerged as the wholesome symbol of these principles. In due time, as this chapter elucidates, his friends and family dispatched Bill from Lawrence to spread that gospel of merit and accountability to the parts of the United States that tended to privilege family connections and class rather than these blue-collar ideas.

The track team was not oblivious to the importance of victories. The significance was certainly clear before the Boston College meet. It was Dick Fox's team's first major event of the track-and-field season, and much was at stake.[4] It was a chance for every runner to make a name for himself beyond the banks of the Merrimack. All varieties of athletics were sources of commotion in Boston. "There was hardly a Bostonian over seven," recalled one journalist, who had been around enough cities to rate athletics so highly, "who didn't have some avid sporting interest."[5] Fox had heralded his YMCA squad as the most exciting occurrence in Lawrence since Bernie Wefers. More than a decade earlier, Wefers, a middle-distance flier—meaning a running specialist of the quarter- and half-mile varieties—had won several of the midrange runs in the New England Association meet. All of Boston and its surroundings, at least those who followed track, dubbed Wefers the world's fastest human for his record-setting run in the 220-yard dash in 1896. The young racer had identified Lawrence as his home, much to the elation of the Essex County mill town.[6]

But Lawrence would have preferred a champion with better residential credentials. Almost every blue-collared soul in Lawrence looked to the eighteen-year-old Bingham to displace Wefers as Lawrence's favorite son.

Wefers had started to collect his racing accolades in Lowell, where his family had moved after Bernie had finished the fourth grade. For whatever reason, Wefers had been partial to Lawrence, and claimed it while he raced past the competition at Boston College and then at Georgetown. The good people of Lawrence were certainly grateful for that but looked forward to some more indigenous heroics.

Bingham was their chance. Bill was an attractive young man. His Roman nose was positioned at the center of a symmetrical circular face, covered by short, wavy hair routinely parted to the left. Bill's small, dark eyes and thin lips left ample room for his cheeks. His boyish disposition suited a runner competing in the schoolboy competitions. In time, Bill grew into his ears and his jaw squared more, rendering him more handsome. The areas below Bill's eyes were darkened, an indication that he worked hard and was determined. His Lawrence friends appreciated that. Coach Fox subscribed to the prevailing wisdom among running trainers and did not overwork his young men in practices. Bill, however, ran extra laps and busied himself with other activities, such as song performances at the Y and Bible readings at church.

A year earlier, Bingham and his running mate, Roy Welton, had collected sixty medals between the two of them on the cinder path. Four years Bingham's senior, Welton was a long-distance runner and as a junior won the five-mile national championship in Jamestown, Virginia, the year before.[7] Welton was someone about whose sprints the sportswriters routinely wrote he "won with comparative ease."[8] By contrast, Bingham had placed second in the earlier New England regionals, falling to the older and more experienced Mel Sheppard, the eventual national winner of the half-mile trial in Jamestown. Dick Fox had instructed Bingham to stay behind Sheppard, among the middling bunch of runners, until the very last straightaway. Then Bill was to catch Sheppard by surprise. But Bingham, still unseasoned, had timed the ambush late and lost at the tape.

The Lawrence Y team elected the more relatable Bingham captain by unanimous decision.[9] Welton was far pluckier, and more than a little eccentric. In the team photo, whereas Bingham and the other teammates sat with sturdy posture, arms at their sides and with serious dispositions, Welton posed in a reclined position underneath them, sprawled and with an impressible grin. An ungenerous reporter once described the "sickly smile" that Welton revealed to his competition as he passed them by.[10]

Welton was a showboat, an unbecoming feature among the clique that was all-in on the Y's brand of so-called muscular Christianity.[11] By this, Fox and the adults who interacted with the track team—and all other sporting squads—meant that athletics imbued good values like honor and healthiness.

The Lawrence YMCA team, led by Bill Bingham (seated, right) and Roy Welton, reclining in front. Courtesy of Lawrence History Center.

Track taught courage and fairness. Liberal Protestants connected these traits to Jesus, by way of I Corinthians 9:24. Bill particularly liked the first source in which Paul seemed to speak directly to him: "Do you not know that in a race all the runners run, but only one gets the prize? Run in such a way as to get the prize." Running and competing were Christian virtues. Winning was fine but limited to just one victor. The holy men involved in Bill's childhood stressed that it was the willingness to try hard, toward the finish line, that exercised character and mattered most.

But Roy Welton's sportsmanship wasn't bound by the sacred. On the racing track, Roy's figure and costume were unmistakable. At five feet, four inches tall and a matching slight all-around build, he was a curious creature at the head of the racing pack. In addition to the white singlet and dark sash that each YMCA competitor wore during competition, Roy donned a compact wrinkled gray cap. It added character, he figured, but others found it too peculiar and unchristian.

Eighteen of Roy's twenty-two years of life had been spent in Lawrence. Bill was a relative newcomer. Just two years earlier, Bill's parents, Martha and Robert, had packed up their indigent lives and moved from the textile mills of quaint Norristown, Pennsylvania, where Bill had been born on August 8, 1889. The Binghams relocated to the more industrious and rising environs of Lawrence and rented a house on Andover Street in South Lawrence. It was an improvement from Norristown. Their home on Andover Street was much better than the penurious existence that was their forsaken lives in County Down in northeastern Ireland. Their lodging in South Lawrence's Sixth Ward had been secured by Bill Bingham's grandfather, Robert Bingham's father, John Bingham. The eldest Bingham had immigrated to Lawrence at least two decades prior and done well as a laborer in the mills. He also helped his son, Robert, find regular work in a wood mill. Robert Bingham was grateful for it. He was apparently quite respected. In time, after John died at the age of ninety-one and Bill had left for something far beyond the mill life, Robert was promoted to overseer.[12]

Bill Bingham entreated himself to his new environs, even if he was not a true native of Lawrence. At first, Bill enrolled in Packard Grammar School but soon after departed the usual course for high school on the understanding that he was to take evening classes and "assist in meeting the responsibilities that attend a workingman who essays to raise a large family."[13] Usual, that is, by non-Lawrence standards. In that town, about half the population fourteen years old and over worked in the mills.

Throughout night school, during his teenage years, Bill worked at Washington Mills as a sweeper, earning $4.95 for fifty-eight hours of weekly labor in that gaunt and grim complex. It was a modest sum that nevertheless did much to help provide food and shelter for the Binghams and their six young children. Washington Mills was a reliable employer. Established in 1846, Washington Mills was one of the leading wool factories in the United States and the top supplier of worsted wool, a high-quality kind of yarn.[14]

It was grueling employment. Mill workers had to deal with swirling dust and oppressive heat. Poor ventilation and unhealthy doses of carbon monoxide exposure made for very debilitating conditions. The mills tended to drain its residents of energy needed to do much other than collapse for the evening to prepare for the next strenuous day of hard labor. Certainly, millwork did not help with the upkeep of intellectual pursuits. One out of every eight persons in Lawrence could not read or write in any language, an illiteracy rate far worse than the national average at the time. Those who could read didn't do much with the skill, leaving the local libraries by and large unoccupied in the first decade of the century.[15]

But Bill Bingham was far more determined than most of his neighbors. He did not drop out of school altogether. Instead, Bill attended the nascent Lawrence Evening High School, where he earned marks that were, by his own recollection, "good but not brilliant."[16] Soon after he graduated, the evening school would start an ascent to become a top night program for working adolescents, accommodating their busy schedules with solid scholastics, athletics, and even student journalism. During Bingham's attendance, though, boys and girls were offered the most rudimentary sort of education and needed to look elsewhere for the social trimmings of American childhood. Bill spent much time in church; he took up racing and joined the YMCA's glee club, an association that provided Bill with a popular role in the Y's annual much-attended minstrel show.[17]

* * *

Roy Welton did not labor in the mills. His father was a letter carrier. Roy obtained a comfortable position as a clerk in a carpet company in Boston. The twenty-five-mile commute by rail and streetcar was miserable, but the generous wages made it worth all the trouble. Yet it meant that Roy Welton the racing prodigy did not share the oft-grueling experiences of the other boys. Welton's social standing was also a matter of manhood, a popular albeit sore subject in American life.[18] Most of Welton's teammates came from homes headed by former farmers who were in control, as much as anyone ever was, of their lives. Their parents, once self-determining, in self-perception anyway, had been reduced to wage earners. None could number among the self-made men, the likes of John Rockefeller and Andrew Carnegie.[19] Rather, factory labor seemed much closer to the "strenuous life" catchword bandied about by their rugged president, Theodore Roosevelt.[20]

Roy did not fit this mold. Other young men could not ignore his speed and penchant for winning. They also observed that Welton did not appear all that keen on comporting himself on the cinder tracks as the YMCA had instructed its lads. He was too self-assured, self-congratulatory. Bill, in contrast, worked hard, like the rank-and-file and was a prodigy in other intangible ways. He had a knack for winning but did not allow that to define his athletic aspirations, as his Bible lessons had instructed him. He much preferred to be recognized for his accomplishments in the all-important realm of manliness. Bill linked his masculinity to his honor. He had in mind all the preparation and courage poured into each contest as well as the fellowship of competition. The more likable Bill Bingham, then, earned the captaincy while Roy Welton assumed the title of manager, a dignified but second-rate consolation prize for the faster sprinter.[21]

The truth of the matter was that the prevailing wisdom about Welton's race preparation was not a reasonable assessment of Roy's commitment to hard work. While other lads were finding amusement, as Bill once explained it quite vaguely, "in the various places around," Roy was introducing Bill to racing, coaching him and taking an avid interest in his progress.[22] After a long day of work and school, Bill usually arranged to meet Roy at an old horse track in South Lawrence, not too far from Bingham's folks' home. Still, the perception of the person mattered more, and Welton was not about to drop his easygoing façade for the sake of fitting in better with a type. This isn't to suggest that Bill would have changed himself into a more agreeable character had he needed to in Lawrence. His was a very natural appeal.

Years later, Bill Bingham fondly recalled the workouts with Welton. He also recollected his struggles as an upstart runner, competing in nineteen races before placing in the top three, thereby earning a line in the box scores of the Boston newspapers. His twentieth race was, to that point anyway, his finest moment. "I do not think I will ever forget the feeling I had, running from the 95-yard handicap in a mile race at the old Locust Street grounds in South Boston," Bill told a group of young racing aspirants a decade or so later. "I rushed home, tired out, in second place behind Miller, a Harvard runner who started from scratch."[23]

Winning wasn't everything to Bill Bingham. It wasn't the most important thing. Bingham was far from discouraged by the defeat, even with the 285-foot head start. Just the opposite. He was proud of his showing, a determination that earned him more than a modicum of respect and validated months of Rooseveltian hard work and principled failure. "I had been trying, trying very hard, to get through in front in at least one race, and I had the feeling that I could," he said, remembering one of his earliest trial sprints. "At last, even though it was but a second-place triumph, my heart was chock full of joy."[24]

The race committee rewarded Bingham's runner-up effort with a smoker's set, something that resembled an overgrown ashtray. Bill didn't smoke, and so it was, practically speaking, a "thing for which I had no use." Nonetheless, he said, "I do not think any prize I received ever had the appeal in it that the second-place emblem brought."[25]

Bill had qualities that endeared him to his surroundings. He was a brilliant friend, someone who in short order gained the trust of his peers and superiors. He and Roy Welton also got along, even after the protégé surpassed the fleetfooted master as captain and all-around Lawrence hometown hero. In fact, when Welton qualified to compete in the marathon race at the London Olympics in April 1908, it was Bill who volunteered to be Roy's handler, riding a bicycle beside the runner to help keep up a competitive and responsible pace. Welton placed fourth in England and all of Lawrence was "highly elated at the showing."[26]

Running in the Olympics atoned for Roy's more obnoxious qualities. Welton stayed in Europe a little while longer, visiting Scotland and other locales during his sojourn. In the interim, Roy's newly won admirers in Lawrence planned a reception in his honor for a job well done. When Welton returned, his fans were interested to learn that the medal-less marathoner blamed a long morning journey from his lodging to the starting point and a bout of severe cramping that forced Welton to "slow down to a jaunt that was far below my normal speed." Most of all, Roy claimed it was severe nativism that impaired his chances of "fighting it out for first place."[27]

"We were subjected to coarse remarks all along the marathon course," recalled Welton. "At one time I was so incensed by the slurs hurled at me in the marathon run that I thought seriously of stopping and knocking the man down." In that instance, the London fan had reportedly hollered, "You Yanks can't push yourselves in ahead today. This is the Englishman's day." Perhaps tame by the wildness of today's sporting standards, Welton confessed that "I never want to run in England again, for they are the poorest losers on earth."[28]

Back home, the folks in Lawrence were sympathetic and wished to believe that Roy could have performed even better under more even circumstances. But his excuses—there were always some when Welton did not cross the finish line in front—stood in marked contrast to Bill Bingham's behavior. Bill was left off the Olympics squad because the beginning of his racing career collided with that of Mel Sheppard.[29] A star racer for the Irish American Athletic Club in New York, Sheppard ably represented the United States in the London Olympiad, winning three gold medals, one in Bingham's half-mile race. Sheppard had defeated Bingham in each of their matchups, most probably, to be plain, because he was, at that point, the superior athlete. But Sheppard also raced with a certain sort of nastiness on occasion, bumping into his challengers and unbalancing them. After taking out one of his opponents with a sinister sideswipe, a crowd in Philadelphia "swarmed on to the track, and Sheppard was repeatedly struck and kicked by the incensed spectators."[30]

Bill didn't go about his business that way. He ran clean, preaching that mantra to teammates and aspiring racers among the Lawrence children. Several years after moving on from the YMCA, as a guest of honor at the association's annual meeting, Bill credited the Y and the local Episcopalian church for providing him with his start as an athlete and then suggested that it would be only the "fellows of sterling character" who would be able to banish ringers and rid sports of dirty playing.[31] The myth of Bill Bingham had just as much to do with his consistent winning as it did his occasional excuseless losses. More than that, though, Bingham represented a work ethic that people tended to believe was the reason for his first-rate running. His legend was propped up by an unimpeachable commitment to compete with honor, the same way he and his father labored in the wool mill.

Bill's character was why Lawrence held such high hopes for Bingham and his teammates in February 1908. Amid the great expectations in the Boston College gymnasium that evening, the newly installed captain of the Lawrence team lined up among a field of twenty boys determined to cross the tape 880 yards away in 2 minutes or less. That would be the time, insiders figured, to vanquish Henry McGuiness of the South Boston Athletic Club. Sure enough, McGuiness took hold of the race with two laps remaining and probably would have won had he not stumbled fifteen yards before the finish line. Bingham took advantage and passed McGuiness for the medal, earning the coveted L to stitch onto his jacket—a badge of honor for amateur athletes representing their school or city, in this case, Lawrence—and show off to the other boys when he returned to his cramped home on Andover Street.[32]

But Bill wasn't interested in boasting. The papers reported that Bingham's time of 2 minutes and 9 seconds was "considered very fast for the track." He, however, recognized it as a fluke victory. It didn't come to him because of hard work. His time was far slower than what prognosticators figured would be good enough to earn a medal. Had Henry McGuiness not tripped at the final turn, he would have assuredly captured first place, clocking in much closer to 2 minutes even.

As it turned out, the Lawrence youngsters had evidenced much more clumsiness at Boston College during the competition. First, Robert Todd slipped in the 30-yard dash, victimized by the flailing elbow of the young man in the adjacent running lane. Then James Pollard lost his lead in the quarter-mile run on account of an unforced slip. McGuiness's blunder evened the affairs of the evening. The mill town mighty mites figured that all could be salvaged in the coveted relay against the quartet from St. Alphonsus—but it did not work out for them that way. Todd fell once more after a quick lead in the first position. Pollard sped the squad back into competition, making amends for his earlier gaffe. The relay, then, was quite a race until the third runner, Roy Welton, tripped. Bingham was the highly anticipated anchor of the bunch. He hadn't a chance against the errorless squad from St. Alphonsus.

Bill completed the relay with his usual determination, unsure whether the night had concluded in a sinister calamity or sardonic comedy. Upon returning to his buddies at the wool mill, all he would claim was an individual prize caused by an accident. More important, his team had faltered. He was the captain, after all. So, he reasoned, he had faltered.

* * *

Football was not an option for Bill. Only boys enrolled in Lawrence High School—the one with daytime hours—could participate in school sports. This meant that Bill could not play organized football. On the playgrounds and for the Lawrence armory club, Bingham "played a mighty good game" of football.[33] He was known as a sprightly halfback and a reasonable defender. But to advance from the sandlot to the gridiron required formal training and facilities that were standard in New England high schools. The evening program was meant for young people who did not have the time for sports training. Bill reasoned that this was just as well, that he lacked the discipline to improve his footwork and tackling angles to "make it" in football. During his final stretch in Lawrence, the Binghams were slightly more confident about their finances. They decided to send Bill's younger brother, Bob, to Lawrence High, where he excelled as a halfback.[34]

Running became Bill's sport. The track star was a rising treasure in American life.[35] Track running was among the inaugural contests introduced at the 1896 Athens Olympics and, according to Harvard's running trainer, Pooch Donovan, was the "stimulus for a great deal of the track material in the colleges."[36]

Selecting a sport suggested something about a man's societal station. A combination of perception and common sense determined the ranks in sports' sociological caste system. Racing rated behind football but, among the higher classes in New England, running recruited a better pedigree than baseball or boxing. The latter were blue-collar games, thought of as primitive and uncerebral. Football, on the other hand, was a more suitable sport stuffed with ample headwork. Football players studied formations, read defenses and, if they could afford to conduct intelligence, scouted their opposition before waging battle. Football, like all sports, required thick bones and plenty of athleticism. Yet only the sharpest scholars of the game succeeded beyond whatever talent they had for dodging and diving at the oblong ball. Baseball required considerable talent and good instincts to field and run the bases but was not the studious game that football was said to be, at least for the New England breed of intellectuals.

In truth, running was too broad a category to pigeonhole. Racing broke down into levels of studiousness. Smart athletes did not compete in the short 100-yard dash and furlong sprint. Frankly, quipped the pundits, these races were meant for the fast and the brainless. Track-and-field trainers sought the merely quick to run these sprints. There wasn't much thoughtfulness beyond the prerace positioning. Once the coach taught his charge to adopt a proper starting stance and to time his mark, it was up to the racer to speed to the finish line. Some suggested that the mile run, typically the longest race of a track-and-field event, was just as unintelligent as the short dashes. The runner equipped with the most inflatable lungs was usually the man who triumphed, as long as he was not altogether sluggish.[37]

Bill Bingham's half-mile distance was the ideal length for a proud sportsman. In Bingham's time, the field was composed of men of ordinary height and long strides. They were versatile athletes: some blessed with a sprinter's speed and others gifted with "stay," stamina; that is, the ability to push ahead when others slowed their pace. Most trainers figured that stamina was the critical quality, since winners of the more competitive schoolboy races tended to stave off exhaustion and run the final quarter at the same speed—perhaps three seconds slower, at most—as their initial quarter run.

The good half-milers comprehended pace and movement. The first was obtained with experience. After enduring any number of bouts, the successful fliers tended to develop an intuition about when to lengthen stride and reignite for a final burst to the finish. Most track fields loop to a quarter-mile circumference, leaving it simple for the in-progress runner to break down his race into convenient fractions. But the racer also required awareness of his rivals' pace and keeping up with their flares and charges toward the goal. He needed to read the collective gait of the field to move along with the transitions of speed and calculate fatigue to adjust at each juncture of the competition.

Part of pacing was played out in pole position, which is a function of a luck of the draw. The runners stationed on the edge of the track were at a marked disadvantage, needing to angle to navigate around the foot traffic toward the field's inner and shorter perimeter. Strategists like Bill Bingham, who preferred to monitor the initial break of the race from behind to study the competition, did not aspire to patrol the pole at the outset. Instead, he aimed for it before the final straightaway of the competition.

The better runners also subscribed to a theory of the conversation of movements. Drastic arm chopping, for instance, gave off the impression, like the coil springs of a locomotive, that the runner is in the process of an acceleration. That might be, if the thrust of his thighs corresponds to that of his arms. Yet unnatural vertical motions sap needed energy. Much preferred to that deception are gentler arm swings, aimed straight ahead, in reverse correlation to the runner's footwork. Another tendency of hopeful men trailing the leader is to rise on their toes as if preparing to become airborne. The adjustment ruined the steadiness of a racer's gait and shifted his muscles into an unenviable pace. Different bodies were meant to start a gallop at different angles and push faster along straightaways and turns. These were the corrections that track coaches made to their stock to provide a competitive advantage to fast men racing against other fast men.

The mental game of the half-mile along with an ideal length to deploy several strategies along the track rendered it among the nobler and worthier sports in the upper levels of American life.

Bill Bingham was never an exemplar of proper form on the racetrack. He did not contort his face muscles to bend with the wind in front of him.[38] He always raced with a subtle smile. His grin was never wide enough to express an air of overconfidence. It was just enough to indicate to spectators that he thoroughly enjoyed the competition. Likewise, Bill never mastered how to use his shoulders to pump his upper arms in unison with the thrusting of his knees. It wasn't that Bingham's posture and racing movements were all that delinquent. But his mechanics should have limited Bill's ascent, preventing him from reaching beyond Lawrence, to claim a name on the New England running circuit. Bingham, however, had a superior talent. He had the staying power of an Olympian and ran like the quicker men in the shorter dashes. Bill did not need to race like the better runners because he was, frankly, usually the best.

* * *

In June 1908, Governor Curtis Guild of Massachusetts spoke for far too long at the Harvard graduation exercises. It was a sweltering afternoon in Cambridge. Five hundred gowned men, their families, and honored guests were suffocating in Sanders Theatre.[39] The physically uncomfortable moment at Harvard occurred at the same moment as Bill Bingham's ascendence in the racing realm, sending him on a path to an elite boarding school that tended to place its graduates at Harvard College or some other elite university. Aside from that, Bill's constitution could not have been any more different from the one that prevailed around Harvard. Few of the collegians shared much

CHAPTER ONE

with Bill Bingham. In fact, Bingham's best was likely not enough for the upper classes of Harvard. College enrollments in the United States swelled during this period—tripling in size between 1900 and 1930—which meant that schools like Harvard had to be even more circumspect about the type of man (no women, back then) they could accept.[40] Admission to the school meant you were born of rare material. It signaled privilege and stature, qualities that arose from nature rather than learned or nurtured. Its champions counted on Harvard to sort this quality out in their admissions procedures and protect the image of an ideal Harvard man.

Guild's message drew on this theme, but the weather did not assist the governor's knack for elucidation. The crowd seated on the grass of Harvard Yard experienced more reasonable conditions as they watched a procession of tophatted dignitaries march from their buggies to Memorial Hall. Outside they had been protected by overhead layers of tobacco smoke, the shade of the old elm trees and pitchers of lemonade.

The morning social had confirmed to the graduates why they had entered Harvard four years before. Leading figures of politics, industry, and Wall Street held court despite the humidity, recounting tales of their own periods at Harvard. They had pointed out the buildings and landmarks to help jog their memories of the Harvard adventures that had proven so formative. Several of the elder statesmen motioned their fingers beyond the elm trees—alumni would later demean Harvard's decision to cut down the elms in 1914—to Jarvis Field, telling stories of their football conquests of the Elis of Yale. Defeating Yale was a heralded Harvard pastime.

The collegians had paid careful attention, recognizing that graduation would transition them to members of this elite fraternity of Harvard alumni. Theirs was a school meant to cultivate and defend the upper classes of a society besieged by immigrants, suffragettes, and labor unions.

The afternoon ceremony was more stifling than enlightening. Sanders Theatre was cavernous. But aside from the men seated on the stage, the space was overcrowded by the multitudes of people suffering the insufferable atmosphere, sacrificing for a grand rite of passage, a commencement tradition.[41] Governor Guild did not notice his listeners' anguish. He spoke for an excruciatingly long time, especially since his role was secondary, to introduce the main speaker and guest of the occasion, Augustus Wilson. Wilson was the governor of Kentucky and, like Guild, a Harvard alumnus. Wilson, unlike Guild, kept his remarks brief, eager to escape the "savage heat."[42]

Guild redeemed himself, however. First, he praised the school's Crimson football team, "that branch of athletics in which Harvard has been most successful." That was a half-truth. The Crimson had begun the prior season

Percy Haughton made sure to dress like a member of the Boston Brahmin elite. During games, Haughton would also adorn a fashionable straw hat. Courtesy of Library of Congress Prints and Photographs Division.

with seven consecutive triumphs. Then the team wilted, dropping their final three contests: to Jim Thorpe's Carlisle Indians team and then shut out by Dartmouth and archrival Yale.[43] Guild's introductory remarks were interpreted as a prophecy for the hope surrounding the very recent appointment of Coach Percy Haughton. Haughton would fulfill that prophecy, claiming a national championship in his inaugural campaign, the first of four titles in a six-year period, an epoch largely overlooked, probably because it preceded the age of Knute Rockne.

Second, the governor did well to remind the withering crowd why they had of their own volition tolerated the occasion's taxing pomp and insensitive circumstance. "Whatever patriotism of American manhood comes to the fore," trumpeted Governor Guild, "Harvard memory, Harvard ideals, instinctively rise, because Harvard is not merely Massachusetts, Harvard is not merely New England, Harvard is the ideal of America."[44] Guild invoked the gathering's paramount purpose. The huddled privileged masses descended on Harvard to celebrate their version of the United States. The Harvard version of it was, to them, America's most agreeable form.

The message anticipated the rebuttals directed at William Jennings Bryan, who obtained the democratic presidential nomination two weeks later in Denver and ran a losing campaign to unseat Boston Brahmins, robber barons, and other members of the nation's affluent elite. Republicans such as Guild and William Howard Taft, who toppled Bryan to win the 1908 election, adopted labor reforms and changes but also sought to maintain order and income for the upper crust of American life.[45]

Guild concluded his oration, making it altogether plain that the levers of society and power ought to remain planted at Harvard and all that Harvard represented. The women and men seated in Sanders Theatre could readily agree to this, from the entitled New England Puritans to the aspirants, such as Alain Locke. Locke was a young African American man, a son of schoolteachers. He graduated from Harvard College on this occasion and stayed longer to write a doctoral dissertation. Looking back on his acclaimed academic career, Locke once offered that "I am sure it has all been due to Harvard, at least what there has been creditable and productive."[46]

Locke's were terms similar to the Massachusetts governor's message. Guild removed himself from the lectern and the revitalized band played "Fair Harvard." The audience sang along and applauded Guild, forgetting all at once the smoldering heat and the interminable speeches.

*　*　*

Bill Bingham did not yet know the words to "Fair Harvard." The lyrics composed by Reverend Samuel Gilman for the Harvard bicentennial in 1836, which spoke of the "type of our ancestors' worth," would have resonated differently for Bill. His parents and the people surrounding him displayed a workman's comportment. He matched that ethic. His height—five feet and eight inches—was quite normal back then and he towered above Roy Welton. His modest muscle mass developed during the many hours of waving a broom back and forth suggested that Bill Bingham was one of the regular folks of Lawrence.

Bingham was conditioned to handle the brunt of an inordinate load. Lawrence was an exception among the myriad Massachusetts mill towns, most of which originated in the colonial period. Lawrence was a site manufactured by robber baron businessmen. The antebellum industrialist Abbott Lawrence of nearby Lowell organized the Essex Company to petition and purchase unused land along the Merrimack River. Their bid approved, Lawrence commenced plans in 1845 to construct the Great Stone Dam to provide waterpower and direct it into profitable millwork. Word of steady work opportunity spread rapidly. Within a decade, the town of Lawrence was inhabited by sixteen thousand women and men, about 40 percent Irish immigrants desperate to escape the disease and starvation of the Irish Potato Famine. This wave included Bill's grandfather and, eventually, his father and mother, too.[47]

Lawrence remained a community of foreigners, welcoming thousands of durable southeastern European expatriates who were by and large grateful for steady work in the wood and wool mills. By the beginning of the twentieth century, Lawrence counted about eighty thousand residents, seven-eighths of whom were drawn from an eclectic assortment of the foreign-born and their American-born children. The assemblage of backgrounds in Lawrence inculcated a sense of togetherness, at least among the Protestant class. The political players picked on the Irish Catholics. They blamed these "lesser" immigrants when the supply-and-demand situation in Lawrence benefited the mill owners—who deemed lower wages good enough for laborers who, they reckoned, should have been glad to retain their jobs while many others remained unemployed.[48]

The Binghams emigrated from Northern Ireland, the heartland of the Protestant and so-called Orange Irish. Newly settled migrants from Europe brought their churchgoing traditions to the United States and increased the rate of US church membership from 37 percent at the time of the Civil War to almost 60 percent in the first decades of the 1900s.[49] The United States absorbed their religious practices with various levels of tolerance. Bill benefited from his religious heritage in the Progressive Era of Protestant America. No one in Lawrence possessed the sophisticated education or theological training to articulate it in so many words, but tolerance and fairness had become a part of the religious firmament hovering above the mill town along the Merrimack River. The community's pillar, its YMCA, disseminated that message through cooperative sport and play. It instilled a sense of idealism and insistence on upstanding character, especially among the young people who felt fated—or at the very least aspired—to one day leave Lawrence.

The message also came through from Grace Episcopal Church. In the scrapbook that Bill Bingham maintained of his early time in Lawrence, the news clippings and notices included several sermons and articles that preached tolerance, hard work, and manhood as virtues of a good life. These were, to be sure, the religious scruples of the muscular Christianity that the Y and elsewhere devoted themselves to and imparted to its youthful members.

Bill interpreted these values as part of the formula that would remove him from the grind and routine. Almost everyone else stayed in Lawrence, near their families and friends. Life in Lawrence was built for work, not for dreams. Schools were secondary to the busyness of work life, an existence that consumed the time and energies of entire households. The YMCA was Bingham's sanctuary, a retreat from sweeping in the wool mill. Its purpose was to be a Christian refuge, to unburden the hardworking youngsters who set foot into its facilities. Bill benefited from that mission.

Bingham made good on his last season in Lawrence, after the Boston College mishap. In his final competition as the Y's track team captain, Bill won the half-mile race. On short notice, he also was slated to run the quarter-mile contest and won that.[50] It wasn't his usual competition, but the umpires decided that Bingham was still the favored pick and therefore placed a handicap on him. He began from the starting position called "scratch" and soundly defeated the two racers who were granted thirty-five- and twenty-eight-yard head starts. Bill Bingham won that race to grand applause. The cheers had much to do with his running style. Unlike Roy Welton and Mel Sheppard, Bill did not rely on a quick gallop into first place to overwhelm the overconfident competition on the initial lap. Bill's method was to start underwhelming and to overcome the others with doses of paced perseverance and self-determined reliance. The reports of his victories hailed the drama of a good and gutsy comeback.[51]

The applause for Bill Bingham persisted and intensified when the local papers announced that Lawrence's favorite son had been admitted to Phillips Exeter Academy in New Hampshire. Phillips Exeter had a modest record of admitting Bingham's working-class type, if only to prove that its education could reform just about anyone. It was still a rare thing in Lawrence for a working boy to make it into a formidable boarding school such as Exeter. The school was mostly intended for the clique of Bostoners that Oliver Wendel Holmes made known as the "Brahmin caste of New England." Sensitive to how rigid hierarchies could redound quite poorly on American democracy, Holmes wrote that, by "Brahmin," he did not mean "any odious sense." He thought it a "harmless" and "inoffensive" term to describe a "few chosen families" who had descended from the Puritans, were architects of the Republic, and had contributed more than anyone else to American scholarship, making a goodly fortune in international trade after the Revolution.[52] Even as members of these families relocated beyond New England to spread the virtues of their people, "Boston remained their true Hub of the Universe."[53] The invitation to Bill Bingham to attend Phillips Exeter Academy was an offer to join a rung right below the Brahmins, since there was nothing more that could be done to remedy his second-class birthright. The other mill men were terrifically glad for Bingham's plans, figuring that entrance into the elite preparatory school portended a college career and business options well beyond the imaginations of the plain people of Lawrence.

The trouble, they themselves knew, was that Bill Bingham had the right Brahmin-like surname but the wrong attire. Exeter Academy was meant for young men derived from affluence and society. Bill once conceded that "matriculation therein usually meant money, fine clothes, and social position, none of which I had."[54] He wouldn't say it in his own name, but Bill recalled that others wished for him in the fall of 1908 to move to a "better life," beyond the blue-collar existence in the Lawrence mills. Bingham would be one of those lads who "worked his way through."[55] Perhaps his fleetness would earn him some scholarship to mitigate some of the steep tuition costs.

Some support came from home. One evening after graduation from the night school, the other mill laborers surprised Bill with a special presentation of speeches and a purse of thirty dollars. The gift matched the entirety of Bingham's savings, which he had accumulated from waiting on tables and peddling peanuts at the local football games. All the rest of his millhand earnings had been allocated to support his eight-person family.

His friends took turns speaking about Bill's code of honor and the gentlemanly manliness with which the young honoree carried himself. In that ceremony, Bill's friends also presented him with a kind letter, lost for posterity but the contents of which Bingham had memorized and could quote "word for word," even four decades later, as he testified.[56] The whole affair was sentimental. Bingham could not so easily find words when he was called on at the end to respond to all the kindness shown to him. But Bill struggled through, as in a race, and offered his gratitude for so much friendship and decency. He vowed to carry the lessons taught to him by Lawrence and its toughminded inhabitants about fairness, teamwork, and honor with him to the preppy and privileged haven in New Hampshire. Enrollment at Exeter brought Harvard somewhat into view. It hadn't been Bill's goal in running track, but Harvard represented an extreme sort of Americanization that the good people of Lawrence aspired to for Bingham and, by extension, themselves.

Governor Guild could not have imagined Bill Bingham's path toward Harvard, nor would he have likely been inclined to it. Bingham's values that rendered him an exemplar to his fellow mill-town residents did not match the values featured by the affluent Brahmin types. In fact, many Harvard men would have contended that it was their responsibility to convert outsiders to the Harvard way of things. For instance, the final speaker at Harvard's 1908 commencement was a leading judge in the Arizona Territory. Eager for his region to claim full-fledged statehood, Chief Justice Edward Kent admonished the graduating class to broaden its sphere and encouraged the graduates to enterprise westward. "The farther away we get from Harvard," preached Justice Kent, "the more is expected of the Harvard man in spreading the faith."[57] Neither Kent nor Guild would have supposed that in the case of Bill Bingham, it would have worked reciprocally.

CHAPTER TWO

WINNING ISN'T EVERYTHING, BUT IT IS SOMETHING

There is a fervor and a spirt, a cruel depth of despair in
defeat and a corresponding ecstatic elevation in victory,
that no other sports and no other days bring; no Exeter
or Andover man has ever any hope to see those feelings
duplicated when he goes as a member of a college to see
his team play; or, as so often happens, to play himself.
—Laurence M. Crosbie, *The Phillips Exeter Academy:
A History*, 230

Bill Bingham arrived at Phillips Exeter Academy in the autumn of 1908
without much. His Lawrence kinsmen had supplied him with just enough
funds for tuition and housing at the New Hampshire boys' boarding school.
That is, at least for the first couple of months. Bill's was the very last name
read aloud as a roll call of scholarships were announced before Christmas
vacation. He had planned on staying back in Lawrence had his name not appeared on that all-important list. Martha Bingham sent off her son to Exeter,
confident that he could dress respectably, even if his wardrobe was neither
as sophisticated nor as extensive as those of other young men enrolled there.
Martha had urged Bill to attend Exeter, envisaging it as her son's chance to
break the spell of poverty that had plagued her loved ones in the United States.
She recognized that Bill, because of his athleticism, had options.

Among those elite schools was Phillips Andover Academy, located fewer
than six miles from the Binghams' mill town. Andover was another respectable boarding school and Exeter's chief rival in sports and almost everything
else. But Martha had learned that the "best" boys attended Exeter in New
Hampshire. Bill Bingham, the dutiful son, therefore enrolled in Exeter. The
hybrid of Bingham's working-class upbringing with prep school polish throws
light on Bingham's character. Exeter gave Bingham a sport and platform on

which to refine and articulate his cherished values of fairness and teamwork. Phillips Exeter also taught Bill about the usefulness of winning, even if it was far more celebrated on a football field than on a cinder track. Back in Lawrence, Bill was taught to eschew it. Dick Fox and the pastors who lectured to Bill in Lawrence preached that too much cheer over victories distracted from the workmanship that Jesus or any other higher order wanted from human beings to gain from sport. Phillips Exeter provided a different perspective. Victories qualified hard work and offered a stage to set an example that could not be accomplished through a second-rate performance. Bill's ascent at Exeter showed both to Bill and to the elites who ran the preparatory school and studied there that the accumulation of all things associated with success could be parlayed into principles freighted with higher meaning.

* * *

Exeter was unlike any place Bill had experienced. His friends and family trusted that he was up to the task. His mother was especially confident. Martha Clyde Bingham had taught Bill to be resourceful. The Clydes had migrated from Ireland in 1865, when Martha was just six years old. Her family was caught in a cycle of destitution, like so many working-class Ulster Protestants looking for something better in America, especially after the Great Famine in the 1840s. Boston and Philadelphia were popular destinations for these emigrants, and their surrounding townships were an even better fit for the poorest of these people.[1] The Clydes belonged to this latter beleaguered group. Martha had endured hardship, spending her childhood and then some of her adulthood working to help feed her family. Her obligations delayed marriage.[2]

In 1888, Martha married Robert Bingham, just before her thirtieth birthday. But married life did not solve Martha's troubles. Robert Bingham's family shared much of the backstory of the Clyde clan. Without an education and the connections to gain the needed economic traction, Robert and Martha Bingham struggled before relocating to Lawrence. Even with Robert's steady job in the mills, the Binghams' financial burdens, with seven children, were considerable. Add to that the death of their fifth child, Samuel, at the age of four. Heartbreak notwithstanding, Martha remained resolute, taking on small jobs—though in census questionnaires she gave her occupation as "wife"—to supplement her husband's income and raise her blue-collar family.

Exeter also appealed to the Binghams because of its open-mindedness to their kind, who were outsiders to the dominant ethos of New England Yankeeism. This culture privileged a type of orthodox British Calvinism brought to the New World by early Puritan pioneers, featuring particular forms of churchgoing, traditional styles of preaching, and, above all, an inflexible theological postulate of predestination: certain people were born fated to be saved and headed for heaven while others, no matter what they did in life, were condemned to damnation, for eternity. Exeter exercised more openness, which did some good for Bill Bingham.

Bingham was able to overcome the disconnect between his religion's cool approach to winning and Exeter's emphasis on the accrual of victories. After all, it wasn't that Exeter Academy was faithless. To the contrary, the school aimed to cultivate a deeply devout environment. Its leading student association was the Christian Fraternity, founded in April 1856. The purpose of the group was to "hold a prayer meeting," to "kneel and ask God in prayer for divine guidance and direction."[3] The fraternity held social programs like a YMCA branch and even mulled the possibility of converting into one in 1899. Phillips Exeter—and Andover, too—liked to boast about their all-male faculties who modeled a devout, gentlemanly behavior for their students.

But Exeter's brand of open-minded piety differed from that of its rival school, Andover, founded by Samuel Phillips Jr. in 1778. Like the group that had broken away from Unitarian-leaning Harvard College sometime later to form Andover Theological Seminary, Samuel Phillips's all-boys school was committed to a more rigid kind of Calvinist tradition. Samuel Phillips's bylaws mandated censure of any faculty or student who espoused the "erroneous and dangerous doctrine of justification by our own merit." By this, Andover had had in mind the covenant of works, or the ability for man to merit a blessed life by obedience to God's word. Orthodox Calvinists fervidly rejected the so-called New Lights teaching against predestination, considering it an outright misreading of the Bible. Samuel Phillips and his coreligionists believed that people were born fated to be saved or condemned, and nothing could be done to change that.[4]

No wonder, then, that Harvard College had enjoyed a stronger relationship with Exeter. Samuel's uncle, John Phillips, chartered Phillips Exeter Academy in 1781. He built a modest two-story wooden schoolhouse and opened its doors two years later. In September 1783, fifty students piled into a Mr. Thurston's class on Latin. The schoolhouse remained the main campus building for nine years, before being replaced by a bigger structure and removed several years down the road to become a dwelling for senior administration. The elder Phillips had provided substantial funds to jump-start his nephew's school in Andover and monitored it closely in hopes of duplicating Samuel's efforts. The two had exchanged correspondence and shared much in their philosophies of schooling and the business of education. Their opinions diverged on several important points, however.

Foremost, the Phillipses parted ways on religion, or rather religious narrowness. In his personal life, John Phillips also subscribed to salvation by faith. Unlike his nephew, however, Phillips could not reject others' Christian creeds and, therefore, in his school's constitution, swapped out Samuel Phillips's religious rejectionist stance for a general statement of Trinitarian belief. Religious openness, to a range of Protestantism anyway, remained important at Exeter, long after John Phillips's death in 1795. A course in theological instruction had been discontinued in the mid-1800s and another in sacred music was made available for "those who desire it." Exeter's flexibility, though, was not the same as laxity. Each pupil was still expected in regular chapel services and every school headmaster was to belong to the Calvinist tradition, defined however broadly.

The same spirit imbued Bill Bingham's life at Exeter. At that moment, Christ Church was led by Reverend Victor Haughton, a fixture on Exeter's campus. Haughton was a ranking minister in New Hampshire and among the Anglican faithful throughout New England. Bill Bingham encountered him this way. Upon touching down in New Hampshire, Bill "became prominent in Y.M.C.A. and religious work also."[5] He maintained a clean attendance record at chapel and at church. It was a formula that had worked for him in Lawrence, as did regular churchgoing.

His punctuality made an impression on Exeter's instructors who happily appointed Bingham residential proctor of Dunbar Hall, where the youngest Exonians lived. The appointment permitted him to cease waiting on tables. Not that waiting on tables was beneath him. The residency supervisory paid significantly better. The position also elevated Bill's social rank. Exeter typically plucked its pool of residential proctors from the most well-heeled New England families. Bill never disguised himself as one of that type, but the proctorship obscured Bingham's low economic standing from those who might have cared about it. The Exeter brass notified Bill of his appointment as he was packing to return home for the Christmas intersession, when he was unsure whether he had enough funds to return to school once classes resumed.[6]

In November 1908, just months after entering Exeter, Bingham attended Father Haughton's Thanksgiving sermon, a dissertation on how "good, honest, godly lives" come about through examination of Jesus's character and teachings. Inspired by Progressive Era ideas of hard work and self-improvement, Haughton described the "Christian call" as a determined effort to become more literate in the Bible.[7] Haughton warned that the relative peacefulness to which his parishioners had grown accustomed generated a tendency to overlook the practice of their faith. Enduring the exigencies of war and crisis required worship and religion-seeking. Without it, Haughton alleged, American Protestants verged on complacency and downright theological ignorance, interpreting the Bible, as so-called liberals were wont, as sociological recommendations rather than visions of righteousness. Bill Bingham was caught up in Haughton's descriptions of Jesus, of emulating him with hard work—the "Great Teacher, the Great Example"—as a strategy to bring about salvation.

With some ecclesiastical bias, Haughton advised seeking guidance of ministers to show the way forward, for "duties at home and in the world of business." In a tone that rang like the New England boarding school's own educational philosophy, the Christ Church rector begged for a balance of liberal and adaptable life lessons and a semblance of obedience to a higher wisdom and to those who espoused it. Exeter's longtime headmaster, Harlan Amen, once described Exeter as a "company of youths who came to school because they would have an education, of whom diligent labor was expected, and who never thought to question the value of the studies prescribed, [and for whom] discipline was a simple matter."[8] The message must have resonated with Bingham. Bill pasted the printed version of Haughton's sermon in his scrapbook as a token to recall why he and his mother had decided on attending Exeter in the first place.

* * *

Another decided difference between the origins of Exeter and other boarding schools was the priorities given to considerations about the makeup of the student population. Both Exeter and Andover faced competition for the most exclusive groups of proper Bostonians. The emergence of these "Saint Grottlesex" schools, as they were called—shorthand for Lawrenceville (founded in 1883), Groton (1884), Hotchkiss (1892), Choate (1896), St. George's (1896), Middlesex (1901), and Kent (1906)—remained much smaller than Exeter and reinforced the New Hampshire school's mission to support the less-than-proper New England families.[9] John Phillips had understood it as his faith-bound responsibility to share Exeter's education and religious program with a wide pool of students fourteen to thirty years old.

Phillips believed that to get the most out of education it was crucial to remove young men from their indigenous environments. The town of Exeter was quaint. In 1790, the population was 1,722. Hardly a metropolis itself, Andover, Massachusetts, held a total of 2,863 women and men. As part of Boston's metropole, however, Andover's modest tally was joined to 175,000 people. Exeter was more than doubly distant from Boston—fifty versus twenty-four miles—and much more rural. For John Phillips, Exeter was meant to rise as a campus of stately school buildings and dormitories amid the sappy New Hampshire woodlands, far away from the influence of the less-than-enlightened. "Enlightened" applied to pupils of all classes. Phillips's largess was meant to pay, at least in large part, for the tuition and board of "poor children of promising genius."[10] Exeter priced tuition at $2 in 1802. It remained a reasonable fare at $12 a half-century later.

This last principle was trickier to maintain, if less persistent in the annals of the school. The Exeter trustees in the back half of the nineteenth century had forgotten the planks of the school's founder and succumbed to an elitist sort of attitude that had come to betoken much of New England culture. By the 1870s, tuition at Exeter Academy had already risen to $60 per annum and was therefore limited on the whole to wealthy families who could afford the private schooling for their sons. This, despite the fact that Exeter possessed a considerable nest egg and was "altogether the best-endowed institution of its class in the State of New Hampshire, if not in the country."[11]

Exeter's founding principle was restored just in time for Bill Bingham. It was Harlan Page Amen who returned the school to John Phillips's vision. Under headmaster Amen, Exeter grew from 191 students in 1895 to 463 by the time Bill matriculated at the school. Amen also improved the campus's facilities. Some students missed shady elm trees dotting "every green and grassy plot," as one oft-sung "Academy Hymnal" had described it.[12]

In Amen's first year on the job, Exeter had opened Peabody Hall as a dormitory fit for budding scholars, a four-story brick structure with marble trimming. Each suite contained two bedrooms and an adjoining study. Then, to accommodate the influx of students, Amen had persuaded Exeter's trustees to convert a series of warehouses into the Merrill Buildings, colonial-style, white-marbled edifices replete with balustrade balconies protruding beyond large windows. The construction also gave a reason to knock down a large barn on campus, removing one of the final vestiges of the wooden, agrarian-minded campus that John Phillips had set into motion a little more than a hundred years prior. Under Amen, Exeter was to punctuate its place as a bastion of learning by looking the part, better than Andover or any other school close to its sophisticated pedigree.

Amen's designs had a definite purpose. He tended to speak aloud about Exeter's "realization of the democratic spirit with which it was founded, of having both the rich and poor boys who were students meeting on common ground."[13] He did so by raising tuition to a hundred dollars for those who could afford that formidable figure, so that he could underwrite the costs for those who certainly could not. Still, the "common ground" to which Amen referred tended to mean that the poor boys had to conform to the sensibilities of the wealthier Brahmins of Boston and the balance of New England's white Protestant culture. Stratification at Exeter declined, but differences among the students there remained.

Bill Bingham was definitely different, in ways that he would own up to decades after departing the preparatory school. The written record of Bingham's Exeter tenure glosses over it: "He immediately became popular through his straightforwardness and faithfulness and there is probably no student who has ever been so respected by faculty and student body as 'Bill' Bingham."[14] Most of Bill's Exeter friends were the well-to-do sort and could afford to lounge around. Bingham could not. He was busied with odd jobs, selling peanuts at ball games, soliciting himself as an available local photographer. He hustled, hard. That's what running track had taught him. Throughout his time at Exeter, Bingham cleaned rooms for extra income. From the moment Bill Bingham rose in the early morning he was on the go and, in his own idiom, he "made good with bang." Once better initiated to campus life, Bill and a roommate opened a laundering service, a chore that dutifully reminded Bingham of his distance from the more affluent rank-and-file.

* * *

That Bingham came to Exeter as a racing sensation was an odd thing. The athletes ruled the school—typically, if not always, the football stars. In Boston, the Saturday evening newspapers would make it to the newsboys on the streets before evening so that the masses of interested readers could read the football scores in the prep school and college ranks. It was a homegrown manifestation of the favorite American pastime: winning. The father of modern football, Walter Camp, understood this all too well. "The American people worship success," wrote Camp about triumphs on and off the gridiron, "and reward it with an extravagance beyond that exhibited by other nations."[15] In the United States, competition, contrived on a playing field or, say, in a political or economic field, can solve a lot more than in Europe. Such contests are welcome, "designed to upset the social order and reposition us in that new order."[16] European life is freighted with rigid caste systems, and family lineages tend to matter much more than individual achievement. *Revolution* is a dreadful word in the vernacular of the respectable classes of Europe.

Women and men living in the United States, a nation founded on the proposition of revolution, worship the generalship and soldiering of the brave men who revolted in the past on their behalf. Football is for them a wargame that helped them relive the sentiments of patriotism. They also believe that football taught good American economics and its attendant virtues. Theirs is a nation built on the well-known proposition of Max Weber that a "Protestant ethic" produced virtue and honor. Long before Weber, Cotton Mather preached to colonial Americans that one ought to find "some settled business" in order to "glorify God by doing of good for others and getting of good for himself."[17] Mather and other Puritans saw "material success as a sign of the diligent performance of the callings which God assigned all men," even as they feared wealth as a "temptation to sin."[18] The harder one works, the more evident that one had "won." Affluence became the signature indicator of success and winning in the United States. It was certainly an easier commodity to calculate than, say, character, a quality that many eighteenth-century women and men used to describe this-worldly achievement.[19] Benjamin Franklin, who published an essay of adages called "The Way to Wealth," was one of the first to try to transform wealth from a vice to a victory. Throughout the 1800s, Americans debated whether success ought to be quantified in finances or whether it was still sufficient to describe it in less tangible terms, such as the "desire to be something in the minds of others, to gain respect, honor, social power of some sort."[20] In time, however, the latter method proved far too vague. By the 1910s, Americans spoke about "keeping up with the Joneses" and made the accumulation of things a contest of status and station.[21]

Of course, certain quarters were invested in an older order. Oliver Wendell Holmes, for instance, agreed with the general sentiment that "of course everybody likes and respects self-made men" and it was a "great deal better to be made in that way than not to be made at all." At the same time, Holmes was quick to express his position that "other things being equal, in most relations of life I prefer a man of family."[22] By this, Holmes meant someone of his traditional New England stock, preferring that native son over an immigrant or a descendent of one who had managed to pull himself up by his bootstraps. These were very important exceptions. For everyone else, many Americans were willing to disrupt the status quo. But even the more open-minded in the United States were unwilling to yield to a new challenger when "he" was a "she," or when that contender looked or spoke in a manner that was out of step with establishment ways.

Winning at something somehow proved a lot, particularly in the Progressive Era around the turn of the twentieth century. Theodore Roosevelt reclassified Manifest Destiny as the "Winning of the West." A popular writer, William Makepeace Thayer, published a text for schoolboys called "Ethics of Success and Men Who Win." The renowned lawyer Louis Brandeis wrote about the winners of the business world.[23] During World War I, it was of the utmost importance that the United States "tell all the people on earth what

President Wilson was saying about the war and what the aroused American people were doing to win it."[24]

The theme of winning was present in every corner of American life. The theater aficionados talked about how to best recruit a company of actors to "turn out a winner."[25] A Roman Catholic author hoped to inspire young boys and girls to do the work of Jesus by developing an indomitable "will to win."[26] He and other religious writers invoked a kind of social Darwinism, even among the many who found the scientific findings a contradiction of their faith. Even this, though, separated European traditionalists from their counterparts in the United States, William Jennings Bryan notwithstanding. Next to the Bible, the most influential book in American life was Darwin's. In the Catholic camp, the Rev. John Augustine Zahm, a scientist and faculty member at Notre Dame, defended Darwin and biologist Jean-Baptiste Lamarck, congratulating them both for having "stimulated investigation and spurred on progress in a manner to win the admiration and extort the plaudits of the most indifferent and phlegmatic."[27] Father Zahm's word choice—to "win"—to describe Darwin's success in garnering attention, of course, was no happy accident or coincidence.

Evolution was another reason Americans took to football. The rules were still under negotiation, everyone eager to emancipate it from English-style rugby. In 1880, a collection of college captains met in New York to eliminate the rugby scrum. The scrum involved interlocked competitors from both teams bullying one another for possession of the pudgy ball. The captains did not care for that odd-looking spectacle, enacted to restart play after the ball had been removed from the field.

From then on, American football players lined up on opposing sides of a line of scrimmage. Both sides had the goal of moving that line to their advantage. The shorthand initial iteration of rules stipulated that an offense of eleven men—led by the quarterback, the first ball handler to begin each play—had three opportunities to advance the oblong ball five yards. The offense was to accomplish this goal with clever blocking—back then, called "interference"—and stout running. The forward pass was not allowed until 1905. If successful, the offensive squad was rewarded with a new set of three tries called "downs" and attempted to repeat its successful five-yard advance until it reached the goal and scored a touchdown or drop-kicked a field goal above the posts. Back then, a field goal was worth more points than a touchdown. The defense was also composed of eleven footballers. Its task was to halt the march of the offense, tackling the ball carrier to the ground (or dislodging and recovering the ball altogether) to stop the play and force the offense to use another one of its allotted downs. If the defense prevailed, that team took over on offense and control of the egg-shaped ball and attempted a campaign of its own to advance and score. Same stipulation: three downs to convert five yards, onward toward the goal line. In 1887, teams agreed to set the game time at 45 minutes per half. Other elements, like kickoffs and punting, were important but this was the gist of football. The game's allure to the American mind was its simulation of warfare. The game assigned defined roles for offense and defense. To players and spectators, the disciplined running and block formations and dogged rushes resembled a consecrated Civil War battlefield like Gettysburg or Antietam.[28]

Like warfare, strategies and the rules of engagement have changed. Blockers were permitted to be ahead of the runner in 1888. A year later, referees started to wear stopwatches to add more precision to the game. A fourth down was eventually added to aid the offense and the number of yards needed to restart the series of downs was increased to ten to support the defense. Reforms were made to the length of the match and the size of the field. At one point, college athletic heads enhanced the rows of parallel gridiron chalk with perpendicular lines to form a checkerboard. The addition, however, proved an uninspired decision, overly cumbersome to the players and onlookers. Then there was the matter of inflation. The point value of a touchdown steadily increased and the impact of a field goal was mitigated by a reciprocal decrease. Teams started to substitute players more often but were not allowed to return the replaced players to the field after the swap was completed. The most pivotal innovation was the 1905 addition of the forward pass. The change added an aerial aspect to the sport, not coincidentally just as the US War Department debated the formation of the Air Force. The forward pass was approved in very limited situations that depended on the field position and juncture of the game. It was instituted after considerable negotiations by a variety of interested parties, including President Theodore Roosevelt.[29]

The fluidity of football rules resonated with Americans. It became their self-made sport. Football challenged contestants to demonstrate courage and ingenuity, to outthink and outmuscle the opposition. It satisfied those searching for a place to exercise honor, generalship, and sportsmanship. It provided others with a quest for success, to win above all else. The Darwinian social changes to the sport signaled an opportunity to claim a place among the fittest. For those averse to the disruption of constant rule changes, debates about football provided a chance to push back against change in defense of an older regime, even as that group had in some earlier period revolted against an earlier epoch for the sake of something new.

Football was a polarizing sport. The elite preparatory schools craved it.[30] In February 1905, Headmaster Amen had declared his full support for amateur football. He admitted that the game was brutal but maintained that there were "elements which can be modified or eradicated and still leave to us a manly, courageous sport."[31] Developing a model of masculinity packed with honor and discipline was Exeter's ultimate priority. Amen's advocacy was intended to defend football against the charges levied by Harvard president Charles Eliot. Months earlier, Eliot had unfavorably described the sport as something like "driving a trade, as winning a fight, no matter how"—qualities undeserving of honor. For years, Harvard's leader had tried to ban football, or at least severely minimize its presence on campus. Eliot's protests did not accomplish their goals at Harvard, nor were his admonishments received at Exeter, perhaps Harvard's best feeder school. Amen argued that at Exeter it was surely not "forgotten that football is a game which calls for mental as well as physical training and can be made a strong moral force in both school and college life."[32] He extended that logic to all amateur sports, like baseball, rowing, and track. Football, particularly, though, was "too good a game to let go."[33] Winning remained integral to Exeter and punctuated the school songs trumpeted from the bleachers:

> Old Ex'ter's sons may truly boast of a grand and glorious name,
> For Ex'ter's men are sure to win all honor and highest fame,
> Hearts, proudly loyal to thee, do cheer thee on thy way,
> So onward once more and show again, that we will win to-day.[34]

Amen's sentiment for sport might have struck students as somewhat unusual. He was a little man and hardly evinced an athletic proclivity. To those around him, Amen exuded a nervous energy, always quick-moving and lacking the deliberateness and fortitude that he and others at Exeter routinely preached. The headmaster's occasional speeches during morning chapel meetings were forceful, and he was much beloved and respected for exhibiting an austere sincerity. Amen's public remarks from the podium beside his usual place on the rostrum of the chapel were described by one observer as "graceless" and, by students, as "clumsy."[35] Still, his efforts and commitment were peerless, and so, despite his shortcomings, Amen was regarded as a father figure and someone who could rightly speak about the import of manliness and sport.

What was it about football? College men adored the sport, as did the graduates of Harvard, Yale, and other schools who sought instances to prove that their alma mater was better than their rival's. On the whole, professors were not really sure how to treat football. A number of the older gentlemen among the faculty liked to quote from Horace Bushnell's published remarks delivered decades earlier at a Phi Beta Kappa lecture at Harvard. "Work and play," the Congregationalist minister had declared, "are the universal ordinance of God for the living races; in which they symbolize the fortune and interpret the errand of man. No creature lives that must not work and may not play."[36] Some took to it as their students did, without the muscular Christian tones that Bushnell had anticipated. Others contracted bouts of envy, discomforted by that attention paid to a game instead of instruction. The fiercest opponents like Charles Eliot disdained football altogether, finding its brutality and popularity subversive to their educational project.

Endicott Peabody, founder of the most elite boarding academy, Groton School, was an important man on Eliot's side. Peabody was the whistle-blower who had informed his former pupil, Theodore Roosevelt, of rumors alleging that Harvard men had figured out ways to cheat and foul without getting caught by the umpires. "The teaching of Foot-ball at the Universities is dishonest. There are all kinds of abuses connected with the game which should be remedied," he reported to the US president. Peabody demanded that "this fundamental dishonesty calls for immediate treatment."[37] The result was Roosevelt's series of meetings that led to football reform and the formation of the National Collegiate Athletic Association (NCAA). Once formed, the NCAA invited Peabody to address its committee at an annual meeting. "Our traditions are bad," railed Peabody.[38] "In America, it is victory—and especially victory over the institution which is our special rival; if we fail to accomplish that, the season is counted a failure."[39]

Most other preparatory schools did not have these qualms over the grid-iron game. On the whole, educators aligned with a religious faith of any sort were still very committed to the tenets of muscular Christianity. They remained convinced that sport yielded desirable forms of virtue. The preparatory schools had an easier time containing football, even leveraging it to their academic purposes. Harlan Amen credited athletics with supplementing the broader educational vision at Phillips Exeter: "Earnest study and manly conduct." Football's focus was on the individual. To develop him, train him for a noble life, which matched the mission of the prep school. "The Phillips Exeter Academy insists first of all," Amen once declared, "on honest labor. The day's work must be done." He drew a line to the "ancient New England community," the Puritans that is, who had held learning in high esteem, even if "but few among a poor and frugal people could hope to attain it." The total educational system at Exeter, suggested Amen, ensured that "every boy, high or low, rich or poor," could be made into a sophisticated man as long as he "showed actual performance." The trick was obedience.[40]

Headmaster Amen asserted that football increased self-reliance and self-control. These outcomes were sought in the classrooms as well. Some, not necessarily the headmaster, alleged that football had a way of doing it better than in the classroom. The bleachers at Exeter's Academy Field had room for five thousand spectators. Every seat was filled when Andover's squad came to New Hampshire, and the other games were well attended, too. The fans learned the same self-help lessons through osmosis; at least Amen wished to believe that.[41]

Football, packed with its warfare allusions, inspired a kind of discipline that other sports could not, but one that jibed with the broader drive of the New Hampshire school. The law at Exeter was that "the Academy has no rules—until they are broken." Embedded in the school's mythology was that Exeter's reputation to cultivate a particular breed of manliness was the feature that had led Abraham Lincoln to enroll his son, Robert, in the school in 1860. Lincoln had traveled to New England to deposit his son at Exeter, just after delivering his remarkable address at Cooper Institute in New York. According to the legend, Exeter's vision of American citizenship made a deep impression on Lincoln. This, and several meetings with Republican leaders in New England, convinced him to become, upon leaving New Hampshire, a presidential candidate.

Sport, then, was important, even vital, at Exeter. Football prime above the others. The managers and coaches to the student athletes served in no small way like Amen himself, whom the young men referred to as "Pop" more often than "Mr. Amen." The paternalism and manliness at Exeter became a symbol of the school's principles of faith.

Take one memorable incident, recalled by one of Bill Bingham's classmates. On the morning of an annual Exeter-Andover football game, Headmaster Amen stood on the rostrum in front of, by this point, some five hundred students in the chapel. "I watched Pop dart toward the lectern," remembered a young Exonian. The behavior appeared odd, even for the peripatetic Amen. "He exploded with the force of an H-bomb the single thought which possessed him—'Beat Andover.'" The principal then pounded the wooden podium, summoning an energy that reddened his face and jerked his head up and down so that his eyeglasses flew off the bridge of his nose. "When he went back to his seat, breathless as was the audience, we went wild with enthusiasm. We thought he was great."[42]

But Exeter wasn't all that great. In fact, Amen's chapel-time theatrics were the product of exasperation. From 1905 to 1913, Andover had defeated Exeter in every annual contest, and the score, typically, was not very close. During those darkened eight seasons, Exeter had tallied just 11 points. Andover held its rival scoreless in six of those matchups. In Bill Bingham's freshman year, for example, Andover won by a shutout, 12–0 in what was reportedly a well-fought and close game. Exeter blamed the loss on significant injuries and unfair umpiring, but the complaints were to no avail.[43] After much anguish, the curse was lifted in 1913. Former star football player Tad Jones returned to campus to coach Exeter. Just as important to Exeter's changed fortune was the departure of one of its rival's favorite sons. Andover's splendid half-back and kicker, Eddie Mahan, had fulfilled his coursework, graduated, and departed for Harvard College. Determined to do his part on the eve of the Andover game, Harlan Amen stayed up late to prepare his chapel speech. He never showed up for the contest. Amen had suffered a debilitating stroke while crafting that sermon and died shortly after Exeter won, 59–0. No one informed the students until after the game. The celebration was canceled to mourn Exeter's leader and its greatest football fan.

The long losing streak had placed other activities into greater focus. The gridiron shortcomings gave impetus to launch a debate team at Exeter in 1906. Exeter had defeated Andover thirteen of fifteen competitions between the two schools. Still, Exeter's decided dominance in those faceoffs paled against the excitement that sport inspired.

* * *

Other sports did not feature football's gamesmanship. Ordinarily, then, a fine runner such as Bill Bingham could not have emerged as prominently on Exeter's gridiron-crazed campus. Track, and practically every sport except baseball and football, was not given much support before the school's soured football fortunes. Back in 1878, Exonians had petitioned for a gymnasium, a "commodious building, in which the muscular Christianity of Phillips Exeter Academy will find every appliance dear to the true born athlete."[44] The students pledged to raise five dollars apiece during summer vacation and returned to school with a purse of about $300. The student-driven track-and-field movement had obtained a foothold among the pupils in nearby St. Paul's in Concord, New Hampshire, and gained some traction in other eastern private schools. Midwestern students inaugurated annual field days at Shattuck School in Faribault, Minnesota, and in some other places, but it was generally presumed that if alumni provided support for a national competition, the meet would "undoubtedly be won by the East."[45]

The argument remained hypothetical because alumni did not invest in track. The sum generated by the Exeter students to construct their gymnasium was insufficient to move alumni to cover the remainder. Students got heated when they learned of an endowment pledged to the English Department when, "if some of the money had been invested in a gymnasium[,] it would have been disposed of to an infinitely better end."[46]

The school tried to placate students by building a running track under the main recitation building, but the place was too dark and too close to a furnace. Exeter constructed a new gymnasium in 1886 and added a cinder running track two years later. Before then, long races were held on the rough turn around the lower campus. Then, Exeter students had agitated without much success for a new track house, complaining that the present facility "can hardly be called better than a mere shed."[47] The small shack was not all that well ventilated or well lighted. Amen had refused to draw from his discretionary funds to support a new space, although he did do some campaigning among alumni to raise money for the track players. Then again, alumni were smitten with football, and some others with baseball. Thousands showed up for football games, even larger numbers for the Exeter-Andover contests. Baseball drew more modest numbers, but the turnouts for it were very respectable.[48]

Track did not receive its due. Exeter alumni rarely returned to campus for track meets. Sometimes several hundred showed for the annual event with Andover. Just before Bill Bingham arrived at Exeter, the old track house was renovated to serve as an infirmary, leaving the nonfootballers without any place to dress or store their belongings. On the other hand, Bingham's class was the first freshman crop to use the newly erected Plimpton Playing Field for baseball, tennis, and running. The new complex certainly signified a reorientation of priorities. But all things considered, it was an inauspicious place and time for Bill Bingham to arrive and change that air of preppy privilege at Phillips Exeter Academy.

* * *

Exeter had been on the market for a young hero for some time before Bill Bingham's arrival at the New Hampshire campus. Marshall Newell was Phillips Exeter's last chosen son. He had grown up a farm boy from Great Barrington, a small town in western Massachusetts. Samuel Newell was a prominent lawyer and wanted his son to study classics and become a person of significant sophistication. The younger Newell entered Exeter in September 1887. Marshall was a faithful student, remembered for his religious work with the other Exeter fellows along with his creditable schoolwork and ability on the football gridiron. He didn't seek to get involved, not at all needing to be present in others' affairs. Just the opposite, Exeter students and faculty members sought out Marshall to improve their own lots. Newell was an inspiration to younger students in all areas of Exeter life, and then to his peers at Harvard College, where Marshall added a fine crew career to his trove of athletic accomplishments. Football accrued him the most fame. A "glance of his eye and a grasp of his hand" made just about anyone understand why Newell was reportedly one of the best tackles who ever played amateur football. "No opponent could charge him with unfairness. In football and in everything else he was 'square' in the fullest sense of the word." After graduation from Harvard, Newell traveled to Ithaca to coach Cornell's football team and then came back to New England to become assistant superintendent of the Boston and Albany Railroad.[49]

The legend of Marshall Newell was raised by tragic circumstances. He was walking along the train tracks in the early evening of Christmas Eve in 1897. Working an unenviable shift and taking the place of a family man, the bachelor Newell was headed toward his office in Springfield, Massachusetts. He had raised his coat collar to protect him against the severe New England winds. That, along with the unusual gustiness of the weather, had impaired his vision. An engine struck Newell, killing him at the age of twenty-eight. He became a sainted New England–style martyr for unfulfilled potential and an unreachable standard for boyhood virtue.

Newell's friends published a memorial volume to mourn and pay tribute to "one of Exeter's most noble sons." Caught up in the zeal to recall that grand Exonian, more than a few eulogists in that memory book compared the lessons of Newell's life to the early demise of Jesus of Nazareth. Not about to let Newell's death be in vain, an inspired Exeter classmate commissioned a full-sized image of the fallen hero to hang above the gymnasium's east-side door. Other friends, moved by similar tributes at Harvard, arranged for a fund to build a new boathouse—initially supposed to be a track house—in Newell's memory.[50]

Exeter became aware that Bill Bingham could become the school's next savior at the annual Faculty Shield Meet. The competition had become a tradition at Exeter, part of daylong festivities and concerts, held on Washington's birthday. The event attracted alumni throughout New England and was the single occasion when running outshined football. Spectators were particularly keen to watch the 600-yard meet and senior John Paul Jones. Jones was a celebrated mile-runner, Cornell-bound and a future Olympian.[51] Bingham lined up next to Exeter's famous athlete. The 600-yarder was neither Jones's nor Bingham's preferred contest. Bill had come in second in a preseason run several weeks earlier, eliminated by inches because of an extreme handicap granted a junior varsity runner from Yale. Jones was touted for his long-distance runs but was nonetheless the favored racer to capture the middle-distance Faculty Shield title.[52]

Neither racer demonstrated much skill other than speed. Like the rest of the field, both young men took off with the sound of the pistol and hurried toward the tape ahead of them. Bill won, clocking in at 1 minute, 15⅕ seconds. His prolonged spurt produced a remarkably fast time, a school record that earned Bingham a coveted E to stitch onto his jacket. Most onlookers were more fascinated that the relatively unknown freshman had toppled the usually redoubtable and sterling Jones. The defeated runner was stunned, as was Coach George Connors. Realizing he had something special in the Lawrence-raised newcomer, Connors penciled in Bingham for the same sprint several days later at the Boston Athletic Association meet. Not wanting to disappoint, Bill won again. He finished several seconds behind the time he clocked to beat Jones at the prior 600-yarder, likely because no one else in the field had pressed him to drive himself any harder.[53]

Bill caught on sensationally at Exeter. The scions of the New England aristocracy and lordly fortunes elected him president of the freshman class. "It isn't what a fellow has," a report declared about the venerated Bingham, "but what he is that really counts. It isn't what he can buy, but what he can do."[54] The youthful fascination with Horatio Alger and the other boyhood symbols of self-made effort—likely concocted to "reflect the craving for stability in a society in the throes of transformation" during the Progressive Age—had, at least during the fleeting age of adolescence—overcome their parents' New England patricianism.[55]

It wasn't all about virtue and the Protestant ethic. Winning as a discrete measure of success mattered more now. Bingham was doing much more of it than his football counterparts. To his church friends, Bill sermonized about sport and gentlemanliness. He credited track, football, and baseball with having the wherewithal to produce a "well-developed man." He spoke of the Exeter-Andover rivalry as mutually beneficial, transcending final scores, wins, and defeats. "If one was physically, mentally and socially thorough, moral thoroughness," he preached when the pulpit was sometimes ceded to him as a student of prominence, "would be sure to follow." Liberal Christians like Bill liked to use *morality* as a substitute for loaded Protestant terms, to make sure they did not offend anyone's denominational sensibilities. "Having these qualities meant the possession of the best of all things," trumpeted Bingham. "Good character."[56]

Then again, Bill liked to win. He was good at it. Bingham became more punctilious about noting and underlining his saved clippings of articles that proclaimed his victories. His scrapbooks started to feature more captions below photographs indicating his racing times, lane assignments, and other details of his first-place finishes. Earlier images from his Lawrence competitions were accompanied by scribbles of who else had ran in the race. The shift from his earlier upbringing in Lawrence was subtle. The 600-yard victory made him feel self-made. The experience somewhat spoiled him, registering to him as a justification for his rise in social rank rather than an indication that his virtue and hard work had prevailed for him. What's more, despite success in the 600-yard race, Bingham liked the half-mile run better. The extra 280 yards provided more runway for Bill to exercise his terrific stamina and persevere against other, quicker but less durable runners. He didn't dare complain to George Connors. That sort of insubordination wasn't part of Bill's psychological constitution. What is more, Bill was sure that his coach recognized that he was best suited for the 880-yard race. George Connors wanted to work with him for some time before he recommitted Bill to his preferred half-mile run.[57]

Winning at the preparatory-school level required more precise calculations. In Lawrence, Bill had clinched his best time in that heralded half-miler against St. Augustine. That personal best of 2 minutes, 1 second, was sturdy enough for YMCA racing meets but would not suffice against Andover or other schoolboy opponents. He would need to shave off another second, at least, to win against the more elite and prepared competition. Connors cautioned Bill that he "possesses so much speed"—enough to oust John Paul Jones in the shorter sprints—but tended to waste most of that fleetness in the opening turns of the race. He admonished Bill that he had to "cut your own pace," and place more faith on his stamina and conserve more speed for the final steps of the contest. That wisdom put Bill in much better stead.[58]

Exeter boasted a fine squad for track and field. The trio of Bingham, John Paul Jones, and Fred Burns, who had lately transferred to Exeter from Boston Latin, set the pace for Exeter. Jones handled the long-distance race. Coach Connors counted on Burns to score points in the shorter sprints of 100 and 220 yards. Bingham represented Exeter in the half-mile competition, occasionally standing in for the less traditional 600-yarders. Exeter was shakier in the throwing and jumping competitions. Connors prayed that the runners would carry the rest of the team, as long as the others posted respectable numbers in the other field contests.

* * *

Bill excelled as a middle-distance runner. George Connors had counseled Bingham to lean on his good conditioning and begin each meet in somewhat unremarkable fashion. The coach made sure that Bill remained behind the first group of leaders, to let the overambitious runners in the field set the pace for the first lap and a half. Bingham never lingered too far behind the lead cluster of racers, however. He used his position to study the puffs of dust emerging beneath the leaders' shoes. He waited for more of it to kick up, an indication that the racers in front were starting to shorten their gait, slog their legs, and dig into the sawdust underneath them.

It was not the most rigorous science. Still, it served Bingham well as an approximation to time his final burst, when he stepped it up, "running the other men off their feet" with a remarkable thrust of clinching speed. He deployed that strategy to vanquish the Harvard College freshmen, crossing the tape in record fashion, the first New England schoolboy to run the half-mile in under two minutes. His finishing time was three-fifths of a second ahead of the prior record holder, William McVicar of South Boston, whose 880-yarder in 2 minutes, 1⅕ seconds had held up as the record from 1904.[59]

Runners got two chances to win at a meet. They competed for individual victories against the field of racers. Bill usually lined up beside a half-dozen other young aspirants, some from his own Exeter clique. This was a winner-take-all competition and just the single quickest racer to cross the finish line was declared victor. Track was also a team sport. Athletes accrued points for their schools, scaled for the top three to complete each race. The school that accumulated the most combined points after all the competitions won the meet. A runner who earned a couple of points for a third place showing could provide the needed tally for his school to overcome the rest of the pack. In contrast, a speedster might take a race but ultimately partake of a defeated school's losing effort if the rest of the team didn't assemble enough points.

The touted threesome could not race all of Exeter's contests. To Bill's chagrin, Worcester Academy won the Harvard interscholastic track meet in May 1909 and Exeter came up second. Bingham's individual performance at Harvard Stadium of 1 minute and 59 seconds bested the national schoolboy mark achieved by Princeton's H. E. Manvel a dozen years earlier. To preserve that individual accolade, Bill saved his number 7 from the Harvard event and a newspaper clipping that announced him as "one of the most promising track athletes in the history of the academy." Still, the loss in the overall competition left a lingering sour feeling.[60]

Bingham balanced personal success and Exeter's collective shortfalls. Later that month, Exeter fell to Andover, in a score of 49–47. The Exonians were favored by a small margin against their archrival. Prognosticators figured that the speedster Burns would collect the points for the 220-yarder and John Paul Jones would tally for the mile run, but R. G. Hopwood of Andover rallied in the very final stretch of the 220-yard dash to topple both Fred Burns and Exeter team captain, Tom Cornell.[61]

The forecasts of victory had pleased Bill. The projections were an unwelcome jolt of expectations for John Paul Jones, however. Jones hadn't beaten Andover in the long races before and, despite his overall success, he was unlettered at Exeter. On the trip to Andover, Bill observed that Jones was "not in any too good spirits." Bingham turned toward Jones. "I hope you get your gold medal today," he wished aloud. Jones responded, "Bill, I don't care for the gold medal. I am after the five points for my school."[62]

Bill rehearsed the exchange many times after that. "I knew then I had met my ideal athlete for he considered himself subordinate to sport and wanted to do something for his school. From that time on I tried to put into effect the same spirit Jones had displayed."[63]

John Paul Jones's lesson positioned a team spirit above individual triumph, but it still placed winning above all else. It was not the message delivered at the Lawrence YMCA, nor was it the thoughts that bounced around while Bill trained along the Merrimack River with fun-loving Roy Welton. The natives of Lawrence welcomed winning but never stated it quite like Harlan Amen or John Paul Jones. When he reflected on it, Bingham's conversation with Jones drew from familiar tropes of muscular Christianity, coalesced with rugged American-style competition. Jones, like all Exonians, spoke of a shared spirit, full of friendship, courage, and Protestant honor. If done right, that formula manifested as winning. That was the discrete "something" that both young men wanted to do for their beloved school.

Jones delivered. But the upset of Burns in the short run meant that Andover led by four points entering the final event, the half-mile. To leave Andover Academy's Brothers Field victorious, Exeter needed to place first and second in the race. Bingham was sure to win. Burns was rendered unavailable, struck moments earlier by a teammate's errant hammer throw. The blow from the powerful twelve-pound hammer shattered Burns's shoulder blade while he was plotting a strategy with his father. Jones was spent from his long-distance triumph. He had proven all but useless for any race under a mile but stepped into Burns's lane just the same. Three young men lined up, sure to secure the overall meet for Andover. One of them, Sam McCulloch, tested Bill, establishing a very fast rate but then "succumbed to the kill pace."[64] Bingham overcame the brazen runner. He drew out of the fading sprinter's stride and galloped ahead by two lengths. Bill broke the tape first, but two Andover racers, Hayes and Hubbard, finished second and third. Hubbard finished inches ahead of Jones. Exeter's season ended, downed by Andover. Bingham won and lost, feeling much more of the latter.

* * *

Coach George Connors received considerable credit for the individual rise of the half-miler Bill Bingham. The English-born Connors was a small, handsome man. Standing next to Bingham, Connors was a full head shorter. He typically dressed in a three-piece suit and a curve-rimmed fedora. Connors removed his jacket at practice, usually carrying a pistol to fire in the air to trigger the start of a scrimmage. Connors's appearance was a marked contrast to the scholars and headmaster of Phillips Exeter, who sported straight collars, long coats, and bow ties and concealed their faces in thick beards. His younger-looking, clean-shaven face appealed to the Exeter students, as did his more relatable attire, especially to the young men from homes of more modest means, a part of that portion of society who had more use for short coats than high-class New England robes.[65]

Connors was raised in a small house on London's East End. His backyard was adjoined to the Prince of Wales Running Ground. The track was a premier spot for Britain's most promising racers. As a small boy, Connors cut a hole in his parents' fence so that he might watch the competitions. Before long, Connors started to run, ingratiating himself to some of the younger sprinters. Connors wasn't the fastest runner, but he was determined and well-conditioned. The older runners shared their workout techniques, showing Connors that speed was just one aspect of a good racer. He and others recognized that Connors could preserve a goodly amount of "stay." Connors ran two hundred long-distance races along that East End sawdust track and earned considerable fame for a solid effort for the Ashley Belt race. The walking race was grueling. Participants maintained a quick pace for twelve hours a day for six days. Connors finished second to George Littlewood, who already held the world record for the race. Connors settled in the United States to compete in long-distance races, including a 568-mile effort at New York's Madison Square Garden. All told, he logged 2,277 miles of running in his career.

Connors's transition to trainer and coach was a seamless one. More reliable revenue than competing for prize money, Connors earned a fine reputation for helping cyclists and boxers improve their stamina and outlast the opposition. He coached track at Cornell University and then left the school with Pop Warner to condition the eleven enrolled at the Carlisle Indian Industrial School. At each stop, Connors trained his charges in the art of stay. At some point during his Carlisle sojourn, Connors was noticed by a member of Phillips Exeter's Western Alumni Association and cajoled into working with the young men of that preparatory school.

Exeter racers were to fare well under Coach Connors. But he arrived at New Hampshire with unrealizable expectations. In his first season, the previously mediocre team placed first in the 1901 Harvard Interscholastic. Exeter also beat Andover in the annual May match, 61–43. The following year, Andover edged the Exonians. In the final event, Kinney of Andover tossed a hammer 145 feet, 7 inches. The throw was a school record and earned the

With much attention paid to conditioning and training, George Connors elevated Bill Bingham's racing career at Phillips Exeter. Photograph first published in *Exonian Supplement*, February 8, 1922, 1.

deciding points, 53–51, in favor of Andover. Some students credited Connors with pushing the Exeter squad beyond its natural talents—what Connors called the "proper limit"—but others held the miracle-working coach accountable for any loss, especially to its archrival. In succeeding seasons, Connors-led teams won at Harvard once more and twice in the Boston Athletics competition. Still, George Connors was supposed to do better for Exeter.

Connors made good at Exeter in Bingham's sophomore campaign. John Paul Jones had graduated, now a scion of top-ranked Cornell and tapped to become the "greatest distance runner of the age," though he never did live up to that grandiose billing. Fred Burns had recovered from the grisly shoulder injury and Coach Connors had a group of hopefuls to select from during the preseason tryouts. But Bill Bingham was the top sensation, even in losing. For instance, he assumed his position in a race in Mechanics Hall to defend his title in the 600-yarder at the Boston Athletic Association (BAA) meet. For the prior four weeks, Bill had been suffering from a grip of bronchitis, and rumor had it that he had returned to Lawrence to recuperate and skip the event. He showed up for the race nevertheless and stayed competitive for the first lap around the track but then had to give up. When he quit the race, the Exeter contingent gave Bill one of the greatest ovations ever witnessed in Mechanics Hall, all in "admiration of his grit." Withal, Exeter won the BAA competition.[66]

Boston was Bingham's only failure of the season. Bill had grown several inches and amassed more muscle since his inaugural Exeter year. His circular face and chin had become squarer and more chiseled, providing a more mature appearance. Connors paid special attention to Bill, helping the young man refine his craft and conditioning. Bingham continued to start out his race with a medium gait, allowing more aggressive racers to hold the early lead. Connors taught Bingham patience, to develop an instinct of when to pull ahead, when the competition started to flag. No one in the schoolboy ranks could preserve the tank of energy that Bill Bingham brought with him to the final stretch of the half-mile. Bill excelled in the stretch to the finish line, as long as he stayed true and on pace in the first turns of the run.

His method was how he punished the Harvard freshmen in the half-mile. Then Bingham and his Exeter teammates conquered the fields at the interscholastic competition at Yale and Harvard. Bill set a new mark in the 880-yarder for the competition in New Haven and equaled his record at Harvard, despite running on a slower and heavier track. Bingham was in a class by himself.[67]

As always, the season's final competition was the Exeter-Andover meet, this time held in New Hampshire. The Exonians remained in control for most of the day. Andover, however, hurdled its way back into contention with victories in consecutive jumping competitions. Before the final two races, the cheerleader bellowed into his megaphone and announced, "If we get first in the half-mile and the broad jump, we win the meet."[68] Most Exeter fans were alarmed, not realizing that the score was so close. The announcement reminded the Exeter faithful of the prior year's dismal finish.

Exeter won the broad jump to allay most concerns. Then Bingham trotted to the starting point. All of Exeter rose to him, clapping and waving, expecting Bill to "do things."[69] This would be his greatest race.[70] Bingham waved his hand to acknowledge the cheering schoolmates. The students wanted that half-mile run and for Bingham to cap that revitalized racing season. One lap in, Bingham galloped into third place, seven yards behind the leader. In front were Matt Hayes of Andover and an Exeter teammate. The seven-yard handicap was a good deal more spacing than Bill Bingham surrendered in the opening turns of the half-mile. Some even feared that Bingham was still recovering from the illness that had beset him earlier in the season.

Connors knew better, having taught Bingham much about the dramatics of competition. Bill closed the gap. "There he goes! Good for old Bill!" the home crowd cheered.[71] The Exeter students suddenly remembered the theatrics of Bill's game, shouting "Now he is getting his stride." "Watch him!" cried another Exeter stalwart.[72]

Bill moved into first place, gliding ahead of Andover's Hayes toward the final curve. Bingham overpowered the field until a hundred yards from the finish. Hayes recovered the lead, something no one had ever done against Bingham. Bill caught sight of Hayes's auburn hair whipping around in the lane beside him. Surprise swept over Bill's face, a look very visible to the focused spectators, not one still seated on the bleachers.

Bill became indignant. He stretched his stride and rose, as if on tiptoe. He crossed the finish, about six yards ahead of the Andover opponent. His time was clocked at 1 minute, 58⅘ seconds. Bill had shaved off more than a second from his schoolboy record for the half-mile, clocking in against Andover at 1 minute, 57⅖ seconds. It was a new national schoolboy record. "Everybody but the Andoverites went wild, and all the fellows, even before the meet was ended, rushed out on the track, and did the snake dance around it."[73]

The box of Exeter fans rooted for their hero, detaining him on the track to offer their adulations. Coach Connors was already perched atop a student's shoulders. Another sturdy young man awaited Bill to hoist Bingham to celebrate with Connors . But before that, Bingham turned to his fallen rival. He lifted his hand to the staggering Hayes. He had come closest to defeating Bingham during that sophomore campaign. "It was a great race," Bill said in congratulations. Hayes nodded in affirmation, releasing Bill Bingham to celebrate the triumph with his adoring friends.[74]

Bingham's final two years at Exeter were like an extended victory lap. By the end of it, he was an imposing figure within the New England track scene. Since entering Phillips Exeter, Bingham had grown three inches taller and added fifteen pounds to his frame, mostly muscle. Bill's teammates voted

ANNUAL
TRACK MEET
EXETER
—vs.—
ANDOVER

AT EXETER, N. H.
May 30, 1912

EXETER . . . 71
ANDOVER . . 25

Captain Bingham   Captain Tilton

Long before his final year at Phillips Exeter, Bill Bingham was the headlining track star. Courtesy of Phillips Exeter Academy.

him track captain, a title that warmed up his family back home in Lawrence, where he confirmed that he was mostly the "same Bill Bingham" who had inhabited that mill town. The newspapermen in Lawrence boasted that Bill was "one of the best captains Exeter has ever had."[75]

Just before the race, a schoolmate from Paris, Texas, wired a note to Bill urging the young man, "Don't forget that the word defeat has not yet been known in your vocabulary so take your all-time records with you into the game. The eyes of all Paris are on you and we will expect a wire tomorrow night announcing good news."[76] Winning was paramount. It justified Bingham's standing and the values he had become known to represent. Bingham broke the Phillips Exeter record for the 1,000-yard run. Against the Harvard freshmen, Bill replaced Fred Burns, who had strained a tendon, in the 100-yard dash. Bill won that one, too.

It was an unchallenged opinion that "Bingham is probably the most popular boy in the school and is connected in every way with all phases of school life."[77] In this quotation, the other Exeter men were marveling at Bill's uncanny knack for broad appeal. At Exeter, he was president of the Christian Fraternity and a member of the Golden Branch Literary Society. He was a studious learner, a member of the Kappa Delta Pi Fraternity and recipient of the Yale Cup for achievement in athletics and scholarship. Bill possessed a deep, husky voice that made him a natural for the Exeter glee club. He also managed the Exeter football team because Connors forbade his disciple from actually playing that rougher sport. Bill transcended type for each identity and made his own mold—and did so without conceit. He was voted Exeter class president and was asked to serve as the marshal at commencement, a role so coveted that, in accepting it, he passed up trying out for the American Olympic team that competed in Stockholm in 1912.[78]

* * *

Winning and religion complemented each other for Bill; he was Exeter's prophet. The millworkers in Lawrence deemphasized the relationship between faith and victory. Phillips Exeter Academy and its pious supporters took a very different approach. Too reserved to be an overzealous Bible-thumper on campus, Bingham made a deep impression as a reliable young man, full of courage and dignity. For many New England faithful, he was a downright saint. The Christian press described Bingham as a "fine example of a student combining athletics and Christian work."[79] It wasn't at all infrequent for ministers from New Hampshire to Vermont and southward into Massachusetts to preach from their pulpits about Bill Bingham. They liked that, on one occasion, Bill returned to the Lawrence YMCA to address the issue of ringers—street athletes recruited from outside the student body who tainted the amateurism of sport—and the importance of "fellows of sterling character" to get involved and rid athletics of seedier elements. Bill taught his listeners that winning was something worth coveting, a signal of solid effort and sound commitment. Whether he was consciously doing so or not, he was proselytizing a different virtue about sport than what he had learned as a younger boy. The press approved and looked forward to the next stage of Bingham's track career. "He is the sturdy type which wins in the world after college days," offered one pious pundit.[80]

The Boston sportswriter Tom McCabe described Bill as a real-life Frank Merriwell.[81] Concocted in 1896 by Gilbert Patten, Merriwell was a dime-novel sensation, a superhero before comic books were a part of the American childhood pastime. Frank Merriwell was invented for a purpose, namely, to teach boys to become better men. Young boys collected the serial adventures of Merriwell's adventures at Fardale Military Academy and then at Yale.[82] Like Bingham, the fictional Merriwell was not one of the usual middle- and upper-class boys who attended the imaginary Fardale or the actual prep schools whose purpose was to train future political and business leaders.

Despite his plebeian background, Merriwell performed well on his entrance examinations and Fardale, like, say, Exeter Academy, desired a handful of young men from the society's lower ranks to show the overprivileged how self-improvement could elevate just about anyone.

Instead, Merriwell changed Fardale. He did so with sports, particularly with baseball. Merriwell transformed the conditions at Fardale into something that better reckoned with the ruggedness that those adolescents required to become honorable men. On the diamond, Captain Merriwell "gave the word for every move."[83] The opening and oft-rereleased issues of the Frank Merriwell sagas stressed that even among the older cadets, Merriwell was "obeyed with a promptness and precision that told how utterly his men relied on him and were confident that he was the proper captain."[84] Frank Merriwell's many later adventures at Yale College taught lads about courage and virtue, values that allegedly went missing among the overly nurtured softhearted children raised among the American elite.

Newspaper writers figured Bill would choose Yale after graduation, because they had absorbed the Merriwell comparison. After all, Merriwell was credited with restoring the youthful American soul, just in time as the "spirit of democracy was dying out at Yale," as Gilbert Patten wrote.[85] In Patten's words, New Haven was less "status conscious" than Harvard. Bingham had performed much like Merriwell, those around him had figured, in Lawrence and then at Exeter. If he was, as the papers claimed, "an inspiration to Young America," then perhaps this was the United States described in dime comic books.[86] But Bingham hadn't declared his college plans, at least not publicly. Yale was the traditional destination for Andover men. Exeter sent most of its sons to Harvard. Back in 1883 when Exeter celebrated its centennial, Harvard's Charles Eliot stood before the crowd and cheered for the "long line of excellent scholars which the academy has sent year after year to the University."[87]

The more reliable reports revealed that Bill had remained undecided about his collegiate plans until a few weeks before graduation. Then the Exeter faculty awarded him the Teschemacher Scholarship, endowed by a longtime Harvard patron, and meant to subvent the tuition of an Exeter alum admitted to the Cambridge school. The venerated Exeter fullback Charles Brickley had received the prize a year earlier in 1911 and was at that moment an even more adored footballer at Harvard than he had been in New Hampshire. Bingham, of course, had won more than Brickley at Exeter. The professors bestowed the prize on Bingham unanimously. Headmaster Amen declared that Bill "has been the greatest influence for good at Exeter since the days of Marshall Newell."[88] Newell, after all, had matriculated to Harvard, where the school eventually built a boathouse in his name. Bill chose Harvard as well. Upon his departure, Exeter furnished a proper track house.[89]

CHAPTER THREE

AMERICANIZATION, THE JEWISH TAKE ON SUCCESS

> Arnold Horween, as president, piloted our perilous way
> through the Freshman year. He was once a profound student.
> Nothing was too great for his titanic brain to attempt. He
> paused at nothing. Impossible was facile to Arnold. With an
> indomitable will, he would accomplish anything. . . . Splen-
> didly endowed with Nature's best gifts—a giant's frame, a
> superman's brain—he will make his school famous. There
> is a bit of a gladiator, a bit of a genius, a bit of the Caesar, a
> bit of a Morgan, about him.
> —*The Parker Record* (1916): 15

In 1893, Chicago hosted the World's Columbia Expedition, which opened in May. It was a great boon for the midwesterners who had overcome a small legion of bidders from New York and Washington, DC, to hold the six-month affair. It was no small thing to serve as the site of a world's fair. In 1876, the Centennial Exposition in Philadelphia had been the first world's fair in the United States. The Centennial Exposition had attracted 10 million guests—a very respectable number for that time—and introduced them to new inventions like the sewing machine, the typewriter, and the telephone. Four years before that, the Exposition Universelle in Paris had pulled in some 30 million visitors, who entered the fair by passing through the newly constructed Eiffel Tower. Summoned to impress on an international stage, the Chicago World's Fair welcomed more than 25 million visitors to the convention grounds. The Chicagoans displayed some very practical inventions like the dishwasher and an early version of the modern zipper. Most visitors to the event, which marked the quadricentennial of Christopher Columbus's New World voyage, were most taken aback by George Washington Gale Ferris Jr.'s new amusement contraption, eponymously branded the Ferris wheel.

Isadore Horween did not pay much mind to the 264-foot "Chicago Wheel."[1] Instead, his attention stayed glued to the "Leather and Shoe" displays on the ground floor of the Manufactures and Liberal Arts Building. A coterie of companies from France, Germany, Japan, Mexico, and Russia exhibited their wares, eighteen in all. The United States, however, was calculated to be on grand display. The world's fair organizers had intended to showcase their domestic firms. More than forty US leather companies exhibited their products to boast their Yankee genius. There and then the young man recognized a fortuitous path to Americanization.[2] Isadore transmitted his faith in the possibilities of acculturation to his children. He was unaware of how other regions and people in the United States were far less eager to provide pathways for outsiders to find their way. On this score, to put it in Brahmin terminologies, the House of Horween and the House of Harvard, where Isadore's sons, Ralph and Arnold, would in time enroll, could not have differed more fundamentally.

* * *

Up until his visit to the Chicago's World's Fair, luck for Isadore was in short supply. The twenty-four-year-old Horween had just arrived in Chicago. He was an immigrant from a Ukrainian village near Mogilev, now in Belarus. There, Isadore endured a most challenging childhood. He was the son of poor and pious Jews. His father had died when Isadore was fourteen, leaving Isadore's poor mother to support her son and daughter by raising chickens and peddling their eggs. Figuring her son could use a proper profession, Isadore's mother indentured him as an apprentice to a tanner who had come to town from some German province, likely from Bremen.

The leather artisan taught Isadore to prepare shell cordovan. It was grueling labor to produce this durable high-end leather. The tanning formula was invented by the "ancient Orientals" and shared with Europeans in Spain.[3] Master tanners in Constantinople, Smyrna, and Aleppo made the best variety of shell cordovan leather. In the 1880s, everything about the production of this hand-shaved leather was primitive. The lad took care of the tanner's goats, sheep, and horses. The best cordovan was made from horsehide. The "shell" was the muscle beneath the hide, the choicest selection being the rump of the horse.

The process required patience and focus to carve the shell out of the animal. Horween learned to assiduously run a blade just right to reveal that very dense layer of fingernail-like substance buried under the horse's hide. The entire section needed to remain whole because the muscle does not naturally stick to the hide, and there is no good way to glue it back together. Horween scrubbed the hindquarters in the nearby Dnieper River and then trimmed and dehaired it. Before wintertime, Isadore dug pits in the ground to bury the hides with shredded bark and sand because Ukrainian tanners lacked the proper wooden vats to curry them. When available, Horween prepared the currying liquor from the traditional formula of tree bark, mimosa, and chestnut. In the spring, he dug out the hides and shaved them. It was a physical and methodical process that involved handiwork without the benefit of modern machines.

For Isadore Horween, leather making was Sisyphean. He had mastered the skill and routinely completed nearly all the steps to manufacture and sell handmade leather. But he never profited from his efforts—someone else, his master, reaped the benefit. Isadore received a wretched compensation, and he used most of that to help support his mother and sister who were not very good egg saleswomen. In four long years, Isadore was unable to save the funds to purchase his own cattle or hides. Perhaps as Albert Camus had imagined of the cursed mythical king of Ephyra, Isadore Horween took solace in the refining of his talent.

Conscription released Horween from his burdensome apprenticeship. He served in the czar's military for five years. When he was released to return home, there wasn't much for him on the outskirts of Mogilev. His mother had died shortly after Isadore received his draft papers, and his sister had continued to struggle for food. But there was Rosa Rabinoff, a girl just a year his junior, from the more affluent side of town. Rosa was educated and excelled in the natural sciences. Horween understood that Rosa was a class above his social stock. She should have been an unattainable match. Desperate to secure the courtship, Isadore offered to take a chance and desert from the Russian army, but Rosa convinced him to remain in his post and complete his military commitment. In 1893, the unbetrothed couple and the rest of the Rabinoff clan traveled to Hamburg and then to the United States by way of the River Elbe. In the United States, Isadore Horween stood a better chance of accumulating some luck.

Rosa must have believed in him. Aware of some relatives in the Middle West, she recommended that they settle in Chicago. The Windy City had a reputation for taking in greenhorns and acquainting them with a productive rhythm to American life. Chicago was a city dominated by ethnic cliques and was thought of as more forgiving of accents and the customs of a foreigner's way of life. Upon touchdown at Castle Garden in the New York Harbor, they traveled westward. The Rabinoffs moved to a small house on Sedgwick Street, close to Lincoln Park on Chicago's North Side. Rosa lived with her father and stepmother—her mother had died when Rosa was a small child—and her half-dozen small siblings. Isadore settled on the South Side. The Rabinoffs and Horweens remained apart from Chicago's West Side, the first- and second-settlement destinations of about a quarter-million immigrant Jews and their children. For decades a modest Jewish enclave existed on the North Side—but it hardly compared to the robust Landsmanschaften that incubated in the Maxwell Street and Lawndale neighborhoods of Chicago. Then again, in Chicago Isadore had little use for his father's brand of Orthodox Judaism, the dominant form of the faith on the West Side. He believed in some higher order but, with little compunction, abandoned the rituals of his religious heritage.[4]

Horween remained resolutely committed to the Jewish people all the same. When he became a man of means, Isadore donated to relief funds to support Europe's Jews after World War I and contributed to a building campaign for the Chicago Hebrew Institute. He sat on several executive committees to support Jewish migrants as well. Still, the United States had become Horween's faith. Isadore's holiest possession was his US naturalization papers executed in July 1898 that formally emancipated him from "every foreign prince, potentate, state or sovereignty whatever, and more particularly all allegiance which he may in anywise owe to the Czar of Russia of whom he was heretofore a subject."[5] The document testified to Isadore Horween's conversion to American society and served as the bedrock of a creed that instilled within him some hope—although he would never have phrased it this way—that he and his family could transform from Jewish immigrants to white Americans.

That's how Isadore found himself and a friend—he needed help navigating through the English signage and directions—at one of the most spectacular spectacles in nineteenth-century American history and joined the millions visiting the sites of Chicago's Columbia Expedition. A month or two after he had settled in Chicago, Horween traveled to the fair to get inspired about his new American life. There, he stood beside Exhibit 95. With probing intensity, Horween studied the arranged cowhides on display belonging to Eisendrath W. N. and Company. Standing behind Isadore was the Prussian-born Nathan Eisendrath. Eisendrath noticed the young man's posture and the way he studied the exhibit. Isadore's movements suggested that he knew how to evaluate top-grade leather. The leaders of the leather industry had capitalized on the wave of migration to find cheap help. Eisendrath saw that this young man was different, however. Isadore's robust frame and thick forearms indicated that he could lift and flip the hides without much struggle. Eisendrath also observed that Horween had been speaking to his companion beside him in Yiddish. Fluent in that Judeo-German language, Eisendrath interrupted the two young men.

"That's very nice leather, isn't it?" began Eisendrath.

"Yes, it's good," confirmed Horween. "But I can make better."

"Well, if that's so then you better come see me Monday morning."[6]

Horween impressed Eisendrath. Isadore started in the factory two days a week. In between, Horween and Rosa attended school to learn English—they rehearsed Shakespeare together—to get along in their new American environs. In line with the vogue of that age, Isadore purchased a handsome suit and sported a well-groomed mustache. Figuring it to be more American, Rosa began to introduce herself more routinely as "Rose." She bought a few stylish dresses and wore her long dark hair in an elegant bun. Both played an active role in the Self-Culture Club, an outfit founded by a younger element of Russian-born, mostly Jewish immigrants.[7] It was a part of the same self-help spirit that would arrest the attention of the Binghams in Massachusetts and of so many other hopefuls standing on the sidelines of society. Rose and Isadore romanticized about the possibilities of American life. Jews, at least one historian has surmised, were a group particularly taken by the "American gospel of success."[8] In Chicago, the women and men of the Self-Culture Club eagerly learned American customs, holding regular meetings in some rented quarters in Wicker Park to "study the constitution of the United States and its history." In addition, the Self-Culture Club organized lectures on American colonial life and popular home décor.

Isadore Horween's fortunes started to materialize in short order and with tremendous promise. Horween was promoted to foreman, a rank that finally earned him Rose's hand in marriage in 1895. Eventually, Eisendrath elevated Isadore to general manager of the leather plant. With each promotion, the Horweens jumped to residences with increased social status. First to a small brick cottage on the North Side. Then to a more elegant flat on the middle-class Orchard Street in Lincoln Park. Eventually they upgraded to a fine home on the 4200 block of North Sheridan Road. In 1905, Isadore started out on his own, establishing I. Horween and Company. He purchased an L-shaped red brick factory on Chicago's Goose Island. Horween was grateful to Eisendrath and the two men remained cordial. Horween rented a modest facility and hired a couple of Irish workers to operate machines for trimming the hides. Still doing much of the wheelbarrowing and currying, Isadore also supervised production and handled all purchasing and distribution.

Isadore was a self-made man, an example of the American dream.[9] Other migrants aspired to labor hard so that their children might benefit from English-indoctrinating schools—eventually college, maybe—and surrendered their own personal visions for success, however defined. Isadore managed both. He elevated himself from a hireling wage earner to a manager and then proprietor. He was accountable to just himself, a striking image of the masculinity that the most powerful men in the United States envisaged for themselves. Horween produced all kinds of leather, but his choicest wares were the shell cordovan he had learned to produce in Eastern Europe. Isadore augmented the formula to produce an even softer leather that was still as durable. He sold it to manufacturers of the classiest footwear, wallets, and belts. In time, shell cordovan made him positively rich when his reputation reached General John "Black Jack" Pershing. A letter that still pridefully hangs in the leather factory's office relates how another officer had "walked into General Pershing's office wearing said riding boots, and these riding boots took General Pershing's eye."[10] Pershing, the commander of the American Expeditionary Forces in World War I, commissioned Horween to furnish riding boots for his men as they rode the Western Front in combat with the Germans. His cordovan line was Isadore Horween's contribution to the leather industry and, in some measure, the great American cause in the war.

* * *

Rose and Isadore Horween's sturdiest American foothold was their two children. Ralph was born in 1896, Arnold in 1898. Rose pushed her sons to absorb the best of American culture so that they would not be misconstrued as immigrants. She arranged for Ralph to learn to play the violin and Arnold the piano.[11] The latter once imagined that he would grow up to become a composer. Rose was no doubt inspired by her entrepreneurial younger brother, Max Rabinoff, an opera impresario who had a considerable hand in organizing the Chicago Philharmonic Orchestra. Rose ensured that both lads practiced their music for an hour each morning. Most of all, their schooling was paramount. Rose enrolled her sons at the private Francis W. Parker School, about a mile from their home in Lincoln Park.

Francis Parker was a prodigious product of the Progress Era. In October 1901, the philanthropist Anita McCormick Blaine founded the Parker School in the spirit of its namesake education reformer and of the likeminded philosopher John Dewey. Dewey was an adviser during the school's earliest planning stages. The impetus for establishing the school was the removal of the liberal Chicago Institute to the University of Chicago campus on the South Side, leaving the north siders without a progressive sort of school. To absolve its deed, the university loaned a large plot on Webster Avenue in a leafy Lincoln Park neighborhood, very close to where the closed school had been located. Blaine donated the funds to construct a colonial-style brick mansion with handsome copper trimming and ample field space flanking the structure and even more behind it.[12]

In the Progressive Era, the child-centered school was a hallmark of democracy and Americanism. The philosophy entailed lots of student-run

Rose, Ralph, Arnold, and Isadore Horween. Courtesy of Skip Horween.

plays, field trips, and group work. Students tended gardens and engaged in crafts. Play period was always held outdoors, even in the frosty wintertime. Parker class clubs were self-governing, though with teachers to coach and oversee the organization. The school began with about 150 students and there was a waiting list for Chicago families of all kinds to enroll at Francis Parker. Parker attracted a goodly number of Jews who anticipated what their coreligionist Horace Kallen would in a dozen years from then describe as a "melting pot" of American ethnicities.[13] For instance, counted among Arnie's classmates were Bill Greenberg, Margie Greenbaum, and Morton Marks to go along with the McCormicks, Fieldses, Piries, and Armours. Rose Horween considered herself very fortunate that her oldest child began in the inaugural kindergarten classroom.[14]

The Parker School was the Horweens' community and creed. At Principal Flora Cooke's school, the purpose of all learning was to inspire wholesome

American civics. Both Horween brothers in the third and fourth grades, respectively, participated in a schoolwide investigation into the history of Chicago, exploring the village-turned-metropolis through the vantage points of all its settlers, appreciating the democratic spirit with which Native Americans first imbued it. The curriculum bespoke a culture of pluralism that Parker had preached and maintained as a counterpoint to the more ancient private schools on the East Coast. That theme pervaded the duration of their schooling. The morning exercises at the start of Arnold's senior year led with a passage from the Gospel of Matthew to teach the paramount importance of self-government.[15] On the following day, the all-school assembly centered on the timeless messages of the Hebrew Bible for the "children of the future" and "serving for models for lawmakers."[16]

Francis Parker's progressive character appealed to the Horweens. Arnie's kindergarten class learned to read in a most memorable fashion. After the tedious process of stitching together consonants and vowels into words, the teacher, a Miss Phillips, introduced wonderful stories about Eskimos and walruses. Years later, the pupils recalled drafting pictures of Eskimo dogs and sleighs. After a heavy snowfall, Miss Phillips trained the children to build a "really-truly Eskimo igloo," near the swings and fit the entire class inside.[17]

The students made looms and wove rugs dyed with cranberries and onions harvested in the school's gardens. When Parker pupils studied the Greeks, they constructed a replica of the Parthenon. When the curriculum dictated British history, the students staged Shakespeare in nearby Lincoln Park. Arnold Horween's fourth-grade class built a bridge to prove their mettle in woodworking. Back then, Arnie was a "fat, woolly, rolly little cherub" and that the bridge was strong enough to hold him and four unidentified classmates was a testament, the children agreed, to the strength of their construction project.[18]

Arnie's physique changed by high school, just as "boys and girl friends had all become young men and women."[19] The boys, like Arnie Horween, "had all begun to think of things other than lessons and base-ball." His friends who had "avoided girls as they would the plague, became dance mad." The youthful mingling tended to be tame, and whatever trouble the youngsters plunged themselves into could be "blamed," reckoned student opinion, on "Arnold's car—it was the greatest enemy to the class welfare that was ever encountered. It was his motor that led us all astray."[20]

Perhaps the most Americanizing agent at Francis Parker for the Horweens' purposes was sports. Ralph and Arnold loved athletics. The boys and their mother preferred them to spend most of their time tossing a ball in the backyard. Arnie learned to play from the older Ralph and his buddies. Arnie could watch someone perform an action or a movement on the field and replicate it on the spot. Much later in life, he decided to take up golf because other leather industry executives did business on putting greens. Horween had never swung a golf club before that time. Once he took up the sport, he could shoot par in short order.

It was unusual for Francis Parker to facilitate competitive sports. The school lacked the competitive inclination, that fascination with winning, that fired up the private schools that caught the attention of Harvard, Yale, and their like. The school matched the impressions of its benevolent founder, Anita McCormick Blaine, who, after attending a Chicago-Michigan college game in 1905, told the University of Chicago president that while she did not care at all for the brutishness of its players and fans, she did marvel how the footballers on both teams drilled "so magnificently" and "so valiantly."[21] Francis Parker's in-house historian reported that the "school was against competition, and as a result, Parker athletes were known not so much for their success at winning games as for their effort and undying spirit."[22]

Parker teachers promoted sport insofar as athletics contained a capacity to foster character. They allowed the annual seventh grade baseball game, for instance, to persist, even though the contest unfairly pitted the Francis Parker boys against the girls. Far less accustomed to the game, the young ladies did not stand much of a chance. The boys' team "beats them or makes it exceedingly difficult for the girls to win." Yet Francis Parker excused all this since sport was also a sexless "test of the ingenuity, strength, courage, endurance, and prowess of the players and engender[s] respect for these qualities in others."[23] The faculty made sure to prize these qualities above the final score in all cases of Francis Parker sporting competitions.

An exception was the short-lived Horween epoch at Francis W. Parker School. The school had Isadore Horween to thank for its first-place fortunes. His sons were not so much bent on winning; it was more the case that they were determined to excel and acquire talent. Winning was just a consequence of this strong combination, like Theodore Roosevelt and other manly exemplars had confirmed to Isadore upon touchdown in the United States. The elder Horween wasn't a sportsman, but he understood hard work. From his diligent studies of good American living, Isadore recognized the value sports had for his sons in their local climes. He taught them to protect their own honor, even it meant fisticuffs and an occasional shiner. The brothers starred in baseball and basketball. The local papers often produced a box score and a brief recap of hardwood contests that tended to read "Francis Parker School trampled University School, 30 to 7, on the winner's floor yesterday. Pain and the Horween brothers were the stars." After the reported Charles Pain and

The 1915–16 Francis W. Parker School football team, led by captain Arnie Horween, gripping a football in the center of the photograph. Courtesy of Chicago History Museum.

NICKNAME	ADDRESS
"Arnie"	4213 Sheridan Road
AGE	LUCKY COLLEGE
Eighteen Falls	Harvard

ARNOLD HORWEEN, as president, piloted our perilous way through the Freshman year. He was once a profound student. Nothing was too great for his titanic brain to attempt. He paused at nothing. Impossible was facile to Arnold. With an indomitable will, he could accomplish anything. Lately he has been resting on laurels already won, resting for next year's struggle (for the survival of the fittest theory is in fullest blast at Cambridge), and the startling tendencies of his earlier youth have been somewhat modified and abated. Splendidly endowed with Nature's best gifts—a giant's frame, a superman's brain—he will make his school famous. There is a bit of the gladiator, a bit of the genius, a bit of the Caesar, a bit of the Morgan, about him. Mathematically he is a wizard. He is (or rather thinks he is) a socialist. And he is a musician. We once thought he would be a composer. He plays a piano "like a streak." Arnie is also an Ajax, an Atlas, a Hercules. He has been active in the back-field since almost prehistoric ages, when he came to us in kindergarten, a fat, woolly, rolly little cherub. He is the mainstay of our athletic department. At his whim games have been lost and won. This year he was captain of both the foot-ball and basket-ball teams. In the play he is impersonating Claudius, the king. Withal he is quite human, most anxious to do others a good turn, and is much beloved by all of us.

"Why, man, he doth bestride this narrow world like a huge colossus."

Arnold Horween's yearbook profile in the 1916 edition of the *Parker Record.* Courtesy of Chicago History Museum.

Ralph Horween had graduated, it was Arnie who captained the basketball team. His play proved decisive in a low-scoring win against Hebrew Institute, 25–24.[24]

The brothers Horween favored football above all, the sport of choice in Chicago since the 1890s.[25] In the autumn of 1914, Ralph was chosen captain of Parker's football team, and he and Arnie shared the backfield. Theirs was a motto that bellowed, "Everything to help and nothing to hinder."[26] The younger brother's football prowess redounded to the effectiveness of the entire team and made Ralph appear much better on the high school gridiron. Arnie captained the squad in his final season at Francis Parker, leading public opinion to prophesy that "our football team should be better than ever."[27]

Arnie Horween was Francis Parker's favorite son. He was class president and secured the role of Claudius in Hamlet, the senior class's play of 1916. His friends celebrated the nearly 200-pound, broad-shouldered sportsman with a "giant's frame" and lauded what they evaluated to be a "superman's brain." The yearbook editors gushed that "there is a bit of a gladiator, a bit of the genius, a bit of the Caesar, a bit of the Morgan, about him." He also possessed a determination, an "indomitable will." He was Parker's champion. "At his whim games have been lost and won." His schoolmates believed so much in him that "he could accomplish anything," unless he slacked and lost concentration, which actually occurred and led to a rather mediocre academic performance in his senior year. Like the biblical Samson, Horween "could carry only five men through the line and all that sort of thing." He persevered, unstopped by a painful sore shoulder, a broken nose, and a bad ankle in his final football season at Francis Parker.[28] Most of all, Arnie Horween was very likable. He remained "quite human," despite his celebrity, "most anxious to do others a good turn, and . . . much beloved by all of us."[29]

All this and Ralph's good grades—particularly in the natural sciences— convinced Parker's coach, Perry Smith, that Harvard College was a reasonable goal for Arnold Horween. Harvard mostly attracted New Englanders. The college recruited from New York and other eastern cities and a fair number from the West Coast. Young men from the Middle West "much preferred Yale."[30] But several years prior, Smith had suited up on Percy Haughton's Crimson team. Smith was an unremarkable footballer by Crimson standards. But his recommendation carried some weight in Cambridge. What is more, Coach Smith's younger brother was enrolled at Harvard and arranged for Ralph to stay with him on a visit to Boston.

Arnie felt most comfortable following in his older brother's footsteps. Naturally, then, Arnold Horween was also Harvard-bound. Almost all the thirty-one graduates in Arnie's senior class matriculated in a college. Higher

Photograph of young Ralph Horween in 1920, shortly after
graduating from Harvard College. Courtesy of Fred and Ralph Stow.

education was in vogue in all places in the United States, but it was especially
encouraged at Francis Parker. A half-dozen young Parker ladies gained admission to Vassar College and another student was admitted to Radcliffe. A
handful of the young men entered good local schools like Northwestern and
the University of Chicago. Three others prepared for Cornell and the "anti-
German, anti-pacifist" Keith Macaulay appeared a grand fit for his school of
choice, West Point.

Ralph Horween had been the first Parker student to matriculate at Harvard. As it turned out, Ralph did not need the added support from his football
coach to gain admission to Harvard. Upon learning of his scores, Parker's
principal dashed off a short letter to the Horweens to inform them that their

eldest had scored highest honors on Harvard College's entrance examination.[31] Harvard officials were also made aware that Ralph represented good material for the Harvard Crimson football team. These academic feats did much to improve Arnie's chances to enroll in Harvard, especially after his somewhat subpar scholastic scores. That he was a better athlete than his older brother rendered it all the more certain that he would, in due time, join Ralph in the Crimson backfield.

* * *

The Horweens arrived at Harvard directly after a protracted period of controversy about its athletic programs. To its students and alumni, Harvard football was much more than a game. Sport in general at Harvard College was inspired by the virtue-building muscular Christianity that had migrated from England. In the 1870s, for example, Harvard students invited the British writer Thomas Hughes to present his speech "Muscular Christianity and Its Proper Limits." More than five hundred young men descended on Massachusetts Hall to listen to Hughes preach on "patience and thoroughness" and to encourage resistance to the pitfalls of gambling and pay-for-play professionalism.[32] In June 1905, President Theodore Roosevelt addressed a gathering of Harvard alumni and spoke of the importance of football. The Rough Rider admonished nevertheless that "it is a bad thing for any college man to grow to regard sport as the serious business of life." Sports was not intended to translate into a career, at least not directly. To the rugged Roosevelt, football was meant to teach valuable lessons to future leaders of politics, industry, and culture. As Roosevelt explained, the gridiron game was much more than victory-filled seasons and triumphs against Yale or Princeton though "I wish to see Harvard win a reasonable proportion of the contests in which it enters," admitted Roosevelt. Its proponents claimed that the sport refined the very masculine conceptions of honor and virtue. "I should be heartily ashamed of every Harvard athlete," trumpeted Roosevelt, "who did not spend every ounce there was in him in the effort to win, provided only he does it in honorable and manly fashion."[33]

Ten years earlier, Oliver Wendell Holmes had delivered similar remarks to Harvard upperclassmen. His subject on that occasion had been faith and honor. To make his point, Holmes had taken up the value of all athletics, asserting that "I rejoice at every dangerous sport which I see pursued." Broken necks and "sword-slashed faces were a "price well paid for the breeding of a race fit for headship and command."[34]

Holmes's and Roosevelt's comments came during a pivotal moment. Harvard Crimson supporters had urged Roosevelt and other sports enthusiasts to combat the antifootball sentiments of Harvard President Charles Eliot. Eliot had ranked as a Harvard athlete and a supporter of muscular Christianity, even though he himself was not all that devout. "The ideal student," Eliot once told his trustees about the better Harvard man, "has been transformed from a stooping, weak, and sickly youth into one well-formed, robust and healthy."[35] Yet Eliot feared that football was freighted with elements much more disastrous than other sports, such as rowing and track, which were better suited, so he claimed, to build character. In September 1904, for instance, Eliot had offered that there was nothing "honorable" about a game of "barbarous ethics" and "warfare."[36] He otherwise described it as something like "driving a trade, as winning a fight, no matter how"—qualities undeserving of honor.[37] Eliot found football vain. "A game that needs to be watched," he scorned, "is not fit for genuine sportsmen."[38]

For years, Harvard's president had tried to ban football, or at least minimize its presence on campus.[39] Eliot demurred at President Roosevelt's question, "what matters a few broken bones to the glories of football as an intercollegiate sport?" Often comparing it to a battlefield, Roosevelt assured that it was surely worth it for the athlete to sacrifice and suffer to experience some of the manliest of virtues. Anything short of this was an abject surrender of the most recognizable masculine cues, a forfeiture of the father-son bond, even. At the Harvard Club in Washington, DC, Roosevelt told likeminded sportsmen that he would "disinherit" a son who was too cowardly to compete on the gridiron.[40] Rumor had it that Roosevelt had once called Eliot a "mollycoddle," the worst kind of Rooseveltian slur.[41] Eliot probably did not mind the slur all that much. He once said aloud that the most important skill a college president could possess was a "capacity to inflict pain."[42] In some respects, Eliot and Roosevelt represented a generational divide at Harvard, probably the most pivotal gridiron site in the United States. Harvard was the most sacred of the "Big Three" schools—Princeton and Yale being the others—that cultivated football around the beginning of the twentieth century.

Eliot was an assistant professor of mathematics in July 1860 when the Harvard faculty banned the annual freshman-sophomore football scrimmage. In defiance, students conducted a funeral for their beloved game, burying a football in a casket beneath the playing field. The junior class led a subdued singing of dirges and a bout of wailing against their teachers.[43] But for quite a while, that was that for football in Cambridge.

Roosevelt's experience at Harvard in the 1870s was very different. In 1871, Eliot, now elevated to Harvard's top executive position, begrudgingly allowed a group of students to reinstitute campus football. Three years later, Harvard started intercollegiate play against a squad from McGill University in Montreal. In November 1875, Harvard shut out Yale, 4 to nothing.[44] A year later, young Teddy Roosevelt traveled with friends to New Haven for the Harvard-Yale rematch. Yale prevailed, to the chagrin of the teenage Roosevelt. He wrote to his mother about his trip to Connecticut, complaining that the Crimson lost "principally because our opponents played very foul."[45] In his political career, Roosevelt remained a staunch supporter of collegiate football, doing much to bring university presidents and football leaders together in 1905 to reform the rules, add the forward pass, decrease brutality, and organize the National Collegiate Athletic Association, better known by the initials NCAA.[46] Eliot still protested that the "spirit of the game, however, remains essentially the same." Among other objections, Eliot lamented an "extreme recklessness" inherent in football.[47] Others were better mollified by the rule changes and broke ranks with Harvard's president.

* * *

The bulk of the Harvard faculty could be plotted somewhere between Eliot and Roosevelt. For one thing, Harvard professors had no patience with the invariable injuries and infrequent fatalities associated with the rough game. In 1884, the Harvard Athletic Committee, worried about students' safety, temporarily suspended intercollegiate football and continued to monitor and suspect its usefulness for several decades. President Roosevelt's actions in 1905 were a response to Harvard's intentions to abolish the sport altogether. "If the game does not stand the test," said one observer about calls for rules reform, "it will be rooted out completely at Harvard."[48] The geologist and anti-Darwinist Nathaniel Shaler supported Eliot's position, that football neither enlightened nor evolved its young men. "In watching for a quarter of a century the tide of youth which sets through Harvard College," claimed Professor Shaler, "I have paid a good deal of attention to those cases in which there has been a manifest retardation in the mental development."[49]

Some faculty members, however, spoke about football's code of honor. With Roman emperor Vespasian's Colosseum in mind, members of the Harvard Athletic Committee supported the construction of a new stadium that could inspire athletes and spectators to revere the mental calculations and physical competition of the sport, even as they feared injuries and football's problematic interference with students' studies—teachers' prime personal and professional business with the undergraduates. George Santayana conceded that athletics was far more Spartan than the university-amenable Athens. Yet this famous Harvard philosopher also supported football and other sports because "in them [is] a great and continuous endeavor, a representation of all the primitive virtues and fundamental gifts of man."[50] One historian put the matter in terms that were more comprehensible to the less philosophically minded who were much more attuned to the language of American success: "On football fields young men were training themselves for that larger game of business and life where secular 'salvation' was at stake."[51] Written with evident masculine tones, Santayana and other sympathetic voices expected the student athletes to best determine how the sport could complement the broader goals of Harvard's man-making moral project.

At the center of the debate was the question of honor. It started to stir long ago. Around the time of the Revolution, Americans had developed and held tightly to a code of honor and virtue that stood for ethics and conduct. They interchangeably deployed "honor" and the more religiously endowed "virtue."[52] Both meant living a fair, thoughtful, and loyal life. Though the culture's grip on that code loosened in the early nineteenth century and became in some sense limited to white Protestant men, an allegiance to honor remained a most becoming cultural trait at upper-class schools like Harvard College.[53] In the post–Civil War era, Harvard intensified its emphasis on furnishing "honorable men," a thread that ran through the late-nineteenth- and early-twentieth-century rhetoric and writing of President Eliot, Dean LeBaron Briggs, and Professor William James.[54]

Football called for discipline and a work ethic, virtues of supreme value in the industrial United States. The sport taught honor, reifying the abstract concepts and obtuse formulations of the scholarly mind. Football was dominated by the sons of the influential classes. Upper-class children could afford to invest time in an amateur sport that did not at that time yield opportunities for professional and semipro pay-for-play leagues. They were by and large the young men who attended the preparatory schools and colleges that could afford to furnish fields with goalposts and hire referees to umpire football matches. By contrast, the working and middle classes could collect the necessary equipment for discipline-honing baseball, even if that meant a stick for a bat and sheets of wood in place of rubber bases constructed to stay in place.[55]

It was no secret that the upper class viewed football as the ultimate pedigree-pumping contest. Taking in a game at Harvard, spectators were apparently aware that the same young men bashing their shoulders against one another would one day become "either Secretary of State, Ambassador to England, Japan, Germany or Russia, or even Chief Executive of our country." The will power and courage taught on the field in the eleven-on-eleven contests would help these children of the elite emerge as fine "captains of industry, heads of corporations, financiers, lawyers and men of science."[56] Some might have hoped that the "center-rush on the football eleven may be the son of a billionaire" and the "quarterback may be a chap who is working his way through college by chopping wood and making fires," a conceivable scenario at Yale or Princeton, which might welcome athletic young lower-class men who could help their teams win for that reason alone.[57] But this was still rarely the case at the Boston Brahmins' Harvard College.[58]

Some detractors were among the affluent class. They refused to believe that football developed virtue and viewed it as an unethical and unseemly influence that distracted from the cultivation of honor on the college campus. In their view, the high-class audiences in football stadiums tended to degenerate along with the gruesome hard knocks on the field. In the impressionable bleachers, college students and alumni transformed into "as near an approach as possible to an elemental type of civilization."[59]

In his 1904 presidential report, Charles Eliot sought to preserve honor and ethics for students by stomping out a game that, to his mind, induced trickery and a penchant for rule breaking. Eliot rejected parallels to military codes and comportment—an arena that everyone at the time agreed inculcated honor. Eliot also demurred when football advocates compared the heroic maiming and injuries sustained in battle with the scars obtained on the gridiron. The bulk of those latter injuries, he said, were inflicted by athletes "disabling opponents by kneeing and kicking, and by heavy blows on the head and particularly about eyes, nose, and jaw."[60]

Eliot was not alone in this point of view, at Harvard or elsewhere, particularly among the devout. In the 1890s, several faith-based colleges banned football on the grounds that "athletics run mad on college culture and public morals."[61] Likewise, Shailer Matthews, dean of the University of Chicago Divinity School, blamed the "boy-killing, education-prostituting" sport as one of the major ills imperiling his school.[62] Keeping abreast of the Chicago football scene and siding with other local ecclesiasts, Rabbi Tobias Schanfarber denounced football as a cult and a distraction from traditional forms of religion and worship.[63] A hearty supporter of most other sports, Schanfarber wrote frequently about the American Jewish contribution to athletics and was particularly pleased that the Jewish "contestants for football honors can not so easily be counted."[64]

Others suggested just the opposite, that their game promoted a healthy conception of honor. Boston's Joseph Lee, often called the father of the modern playground, described the virtue of teammates linked by a "common consciousness, with a completeness hardly found in the associations of later life."[65] President Roosevelt and other sculptors of early-twentieth-century American manliness seized on football as a sport that tested the mettle and fortitude of a college man. Sports, theorized one contemporaneous commentator, replaced the closing of the American frontier, or at least a "partial substitute for pioneer life."[66] Adherents of these positions also counted among them religious leaders who were convinced that football contributed to a Calvinist ethic. President Charles Thwing of Western Reserve in Cleveland was a Harvard alumnus who credited football with teaching gentlemanly self-restraint. The Congregationalist-trained minister dubbed the football player a modern-day Nazarite, the biblical ascetic who exercised virtue and temperance. The football player embodied power and control, "taking and giving hard knocks without swearing or without a tear."[67] Thwing described the football field as a "small ethical world," comparing the lines marking every five yards to "white lines of moral distinctions."[68]

* * *

The tension over football and honor at Harvard kept the game in check. In December 1884, the Harvard faculty determined that "in all of the games the manifestation of gentlemanly spirit was lacking." They disapproved of instances of fist fighting in the Yale and Princeton games and the preponderance of one-sided matches that belied any semblance of fairness and competition. Their findings were sufficient to suspend football at Harvard for the 1885 season.[69]

Apparently, the philanthropist Henry Lee Higginson blamed Harvard's rivals for the rough-and-tumble football gamesmanship. In June 1890, President Eliot invited him to deliver a Harvard College commencement speech, a reward for donating a large plot of land. The Civil War veteran had determined to honor fallen comrades by dubbing his donation "Soldiers Field." Higginson remained loyal to Harvard even though he had dropped out of the college to travel to Europe in pursuit of an ill-fated career in music. Upon his return, Higginson enlisted in the Union army but was wounded in the war. His consolation was a position in the family's investment banking business, a role in which Higginson excelled quite significantly. Before four hundred students and alumni, Higginson entreated future Crimson footballers to use the new field in the very same honorable spirit that their forebears had, and, borrowing from the prophet Isaiah, be a light unto their competition, to boot. "The Princeton and the Yale fellows are our brothers," said Higginson. "Let us beat them fairly if we can and believe that they will play the game just as we do."[70]

Higginson's gift catalyzed plans to construct a full-blown stadium for its football team and its fans. This first modern collegiate stadium in the United States was massive, boasting reinforced iron and the staying power to rival any sacred church or temple. This and other signs of football mania rendered it all but impossible for Eliot and other ardent opponents to vanquish the burly sport.[71] Many students and alumni agreed that the game was far too ruthless. Still, they did not care for the one-sided Eliot-sponsored reforms that would induce "men in the American colleges to play lady-like games."[72] To the contrary, the risk of injury was part of imparting "courage and manhood." Harvard men reasoned that, "if a boy is ever to get away from his mother's apron string, he must take his chances against other boys."[73]

A goodly number of students preferred brutality over emasculation. In 1901, a quarter of Harvard undergraduate newcomers—the incoming class numbered 550 young men—tried out for the freshman football team. Two years later, enthusiastic alumni dedicated Harvard Stadium on top of Soldiers Field amid grand fanfare. Eliot refused to fundraise for it. The inaugural game in the new facility between Harvard and Dartmouth was watched by a "great mass of humanity." An onlooker in favor of the visiting team was struck by the "magnificence" of the building and the moment, suggesting that the stadium "itself [is] worth a trip from Hanover to see."[74] Still, some teachers, such as philosophy professor Josiah Royce, determined the new edifice to be excessive and to imbue the campus with the wrong sort of atmosphere. "Harvard Stadium is an admirable place," quipped Royce, "when it is not too full of people."[75] All in all, though, Harvard men celebrated the gridiron sport no matter what their president and faculty felt about football.

But there were limits to Harvard's brand of gamesmanship. Theirs was a British-derived devotion to fair and honorable play above winning. Opponents found this posture "annoying," interpreting it as an "unmistakable air of self-satisfaction or smug self-righteousness."[76] Truth to tell, that smugness worked for a while. In the earliest years, the Crimson dominated most of their competition. From 1874 to 1900, Harvard football's record was an impressive 201 wins, 36 losses, and 8 ties. The Crimson struggled mightily, however, against its bitterest adversaries. In that same period, the Crimson tallied a record of 3-16-3 against Yale and underperformed at a 3-11-1 clip against Princeton. Most of those rivalry games were not close matches.

Yale played to win. Walter Camp was Yale football's founder and the enduring godfather of the game in New Haven. To his mind, a "real man" might have to "tear out the grand central ganglion of his nerves before you could make him enjoy losing."[77] Harvard, Eliot, and Harvard's meager football program were "soft" and "boyish," claimed Camp.[78] He advised his players to exercise sportsmanship but not at the cost of growing accustomed to defeat. "When you lose a match against a man in your own class, shake hands with him," wrote Camp. "Do not excuse your defeat; do not forget it, and do not let it happen again if there is any way to prepare yourself better for the next match."[79]

Harvard Stadium's east wing under construction in 1903. The reinforced concrete structure was the first large-capacity college sports complex. Photograph first published in I. N. Hollis, "Origin of the Harvard Stadium," *Harvard Engineering Journal* 3 (June 1904): 96.

Fortunately for Camp, Yale rarely lost. The Elis—Yale went by this shorthand name of its founder or the Blue long before settling on Bulldogs as its permanent nickname—record from 1872 to 1909 was 324-17 and 18 ties. From 1890 to 1893, Yale outscored its opponents 1,265 to zero. To sustain that culture of dominance, Yale hired coaches—the first among colleges—to assist their amateur student athletes.[80] And though unpaid himself and never the official coach, Camp continued to mentor his beloved Yale squads and their coaches. He preached comparisons to Napoleon's military strategies, introduced heavy doses of powerful running plays, and developed situational defensive formations. The old-fashioned Camp did not care for the forward pass conjured up by western outfits like Notre Dame and the University of Chicago. Instead, his Yale teams relied on preparation and toughness to solidify their winning brand.[81] Camp's strategy far outpaced the Crimson's unimaginative running-style play, described as "stupid mismanagement which is too much the rule at Harvard."[82]

The Blue's dominance over the Crimson downright infuriated Harvard. Camp's win-above-all-else rhetoric and the record to prove it betrayed the gentlemanly sort of athleticism that both Harvard and Yale prided themselves on. Of course, some were desperate for Harvard to topple Yale. "I want Harvard to play the part which belongs to her in the great drama of American life," once declared US Senator Henry Cabot Lodge. "I want her to be filled with the spirit of victory."[83]

Still, most Harvard men were not as eager for a winner if it meant surrendering its consecrated character code. Exertion was not genteel. "To walk to the boat-houses and row upon the river requires effort," the press once reported about regatta competitions in Cambridge. "Therefore there is little general rowing among Harvard students."[84] Winning meant a little less to the aristocratic New Englanders, the kind that eschewed the Darwinian implications of social upheaval and retained their standing because of class and status. Their attitude matched the British position. "The tone of Boston society was colonial," wrote historian Henry Adams, a direct descendent of Puritans and two US presidents. "The true Bostonian always knelt in self-abasement before the majesty of English standards; far from concealing it as a weakness, he was proud of it as his strength."[85] About the rest of the United States, Adams unkindly alleged that "America contained scores of men worth five million or upwards, whose lives were no more worth living than those of their cooks."[86] Theodore Roosevelt offered much of the same. In the White House, the president was overwhelmed by the preponderance of self-made men of undistinguished origins and underwhelmed by what those men had to say to him. "I am simply unable to make myself take the attitude of respect toward the very wealthy men which such an enormous multitude of people evidently really feel," confessed Roosevelt in a private correspondence. "I am delighted to show any courtesy to Pierpont Morgan or Andrew Carnegie or James J. Hill, but as for regarding any one of them, as for instance, I regard Professor Bury, or Peary, the Arctic explorer, or Rhodes, the historian, or Selous, the big game hunter (to mention at random guests who have been at the White House not long ago)—why, I could not force myself to do it, even if I wanted to, which I don't."[87]

Yale had become much more cosmopolitan. In 1800, New England elites made up 87 percent of Yale College. A hundred years later, that quotient was reduced to about half the student population. New Haven liked to believe that the "main stream of American life was flowing through Yale." Its in-house historian reported that "symbolically and pragmatically Yale was the poor boy's Harvard.[88] That much, at least, was the given impression. Harvard was for the heirs of the Brahmins. "Yale was a school," it was alleged, probably with the Rockefellers and Mellons in mind, "for the sons of the new rich of America's gilded age."[89] Harvard exemplars such as Charles Francis Adams had "known, and known tolerably well, a good many 'successful' men—'big' financially—men famous during the last half-century; and a less interesting crowd I do not care to encounter. Not one," continued Adams about the breed more typical at Yale, "that I have ever known would I care to meet again, either in this world or the next."[90]

One writer chided that if Harvard was Athens, then Yale provided its students a "Spartan simplicity of life," bolstered by Camp's "anything to win" policy and questionable "character."[91] Other Harvard students regretted the harsh tones of that editorialist but did not deny his findings or opinions.[92] Among the faculty ranks, the European-born George Santayana visited Yale and could not help but note the pervasive "crudity and toughness" that stood in great contrast to the British universities and, of course, to Harvard College. In step with other observers, Santayana noticed that "divisions of wealth and breed are not made conspicuous at Yale as at Harvard."[93] The Harvard philosopher anticipated that Yale would cure itself of these ills but that it would take the New Haven school some time to self-correct along the lines of the "studious and athletic life in England."[94]

The pursuit of victory assumed several forms. Both Yale and Princeton did more to recruit elite prep school athletes to join their football programs. In one instance, all three schools vied for the athletic services of Jim Hogan. Hogan was a standout at Phillips Exeter and a coveted right tackle. He passed his entrance examinations to attend Harvard and was guaranteed some scholarships to decrease the burden of the school's tuition. Nevertheless, Hogan eventually chose Yale in 1900 because at Harvard "no definite promises would be made." Such deals flouted the sanctity of athletic amateurism on college campuses. One commentator chalked the result up to the nefarious notions of "commercialism" that plagued the sport and benefited certain squads around the beginning of the twentieth century.[95] Harvard was not completely immune to such notions, of course. Like other universities, Harvard and its alumni boosters were sometimes guilty of putting amateur athletes through colleges with "loans." The papers reported far fewer instances of this flagrant abuse of collegiate amateurism in Boston, however, and far more cases of, say, baseball players booted off the Harvard nine for pay-for-play summer league competitions.[96]

Fair and safe play was also a factor in determining the premium placed on winning. In November 1880, Harvard and Yale played in a downpour. The Harvard players complained that their opponents had tried to drown them in the deep puddles that had accumulated on the field. The referee did not believe the accusation, but Walter Camp later admitted that the charge was "not without some ground."[97] In November 1894, the Crimson's and the Blue's blood-drenched bout required nine substitutions from injury or ejection. The more neutral reporters from New York claimed that Harvard was the superior team on that occasion but got terribly rattled after a muffed punt fifteen seconds into the game. Out of utter frustration, a Harvard man gouged a Yale opponent in the eye, drawing, quite literally, first blood. The rough-and-tumble Yale captain, Frank Hinkey, retaliated by breaking a Harvard man's collarbone. The Elis' mauling of the timider Crimson team just worsened from there.[98]

Yale was, however, civiler than Princeton. Like Yale, Princeton coveted winning more than fairness and honor. For example, Ellen Wilson testified to the forlornness of her husband, Princeton president Woodrow Wilson. He was supposedly crestfallen after the Princeton Tigers lost to the Pennsylvania Quakers, an "overwhelming football calamity."[99] To keep winning, the Tigers had a reputation for bending the rules and taking shots when referees were unable to catch them in the act.[100] Sometimes they did so from outright prejudice. In 1903, for example, it was believed that Princeton had broken Dartmouth's Matthew Bullock's collarbone on one of the very first scrimmages of the game. Bullock was an African American standout and graduate of one of the best preparatory schools in New England. Another African American, William Clarence Matthews, was Bullock's high school friend and a popular man around Harvard Yard.[101] Himself the victim of Yale roughness, the Crimson player was more than a little bothered by Bullock's injury, especially since a third childhood friend played quarterback for Princeton.[102] The vexed Matthews confronted Princeton's Tommy Burke, a white man, soon after learning of Bullock's fate.

"You've changed, Tommy, since you were at Andover," cried Matthews.

"What do you mean, Matt?" asked Burke.

"At Andover you used to say that race or color does not count; it is the stuff in the man."

"I stand by that now," Burke replied.

"No, you don't. Princeton doesn't believe it, and I'm afraid you have absorbed Princeton ideas." Matthews then referred to the intentional injury done to Bullock and added, "You put him out because he is a black man."

"We didn't put him out because he is a black man," Burke replied with indignation. "We're coached to pick out the most dangerous man on the opposing team and put him out in the first five minutes of play."[103]

Matthews left the conversation without the confession of racism he sought. But his interlocutor had said enough to the Harvard footballer to render conclusions about the measures Princeton took to stay atop the college gridiron hierarchy. But neither was Harvard's record of openness and fairness immaculate. Stakeholders existed who would have liked the Crimson to exercise some of the strategies of its rivals. Harvard mostly resisted on the grounds that its brand of football stood for something more honorable than winning games.

* * *

In 1875, Lucius Littauer joined the fledgling Harvard football squad. Littauer had also rowed in a regatta or two. He was one of the few Jews around Harvard Yard and was eager to prove his social mettle.[104] He often reminisced later about his athletic accomplishments as an undergraduate. Littauer considered sports an important part of collegiate culture and one that had shaped his life after Harvard. Athletics and academics, for him, seemed to coalesce to form a well-rounded and loyal member of American aristocracy. Writing to other Harvard graduates in the alumni club, Littauer mourned the death of a young classmate who represented the Harvard ideal of sports and sophistication.[105] Before advancing toward a decorated career in business, politics, and philanthropy, Littauer, committed as he was to collegiate athletics, returned to Harvard College to reunite with his beloved Crimson as the football team's "umpire," something akin to a part-time manager.[106]

The number of Jewish Harvard collegians picked up around 1900, just as a tidal wave of Jewish migrants settled in their new world.[107] In 1880, the Jewish population totaled 250,000 women and men. By 1900, that figure had spiked to a million and further increased until immigration restrictions halted resettlement from Eastern Europe in the 1920s.[108] In 1907, Jews totaled 60 of about 2,000 undergraduates on Harvard's campus. Ten years later, the Hebrew "race," as Jews were referred to back then, at Harvard tallied 250.[109]

For education-minded Jews, Harvard's high status in American life became a benchmark of acculturation.[110] Many also credit President Eliot's cosmopolitanism for broadening Protestant-infused Harvard. Under Eliot's watch, more and more Jews and Catholics enrolled at Harvard. Eliot deleted Latin from the admissions requirement, a subject untaught in the public schools. A fairer, merit-based admissions process convinced some young Eastern European Jewish extracts that, if they could refine their English and suitably perform on entrance examinations, they too could attend the "rich man's college."[111] Upon Eliot's retirement, the Harvard student body was 9 percent Catholic and 7 percent Jewish.[112] Several members of the faculty would have liked to have seen the numbers reversed. Nathaniel Shaler approved of the Jewish work ethic he had observed around Harvard Yard and invited several young Jews to supper at his home. He did not feel the same about the Catholic students, either the Irish or the Italian variety. Theirs was a form of Christianity to which Shaler could not subscribe. Catholic students were incorrigible, unwilling to drop the "faith or the tools of their forefathers."[113]

Harvard's Jews were not bullied as they were at other colleges. In New Jersey, F. Scott Fitzgerald remembered how some of his fellow Princetonians "filled the Jewish youths' bed with lemon pie."[114] Eliot was aware of the welcoming spirit that he had fostered, acknowledging it to a professor of German concerned about the "Hebrew difficulty" in the dormitories. "It is doubtless true," Eliot asserted, "that Jews are better off at Harvard than at any other American college; and they are, therefore, likely to resort to it."[115]

But on the whole, Jews did not secure the usual footholds for social climbing at Harvard. Rather, the school's growing group of Jews obtained a reputation for clustering among themselves, a quality that set into motion an attempt to establish a Jewish quota at Harvard, as I will discuss later. In 1906, a small band of Harvard undergraduates formed the Menorah Society for the "study of Jewish History and Culture." Though their platform was broadminded and eschewed the aggrieved narrowness of their parents' ethnic faith, the Menorah young leadership encountered steep opposition to their efforts from their fellow students.[116]

The opposition was nativistic. Many of the Eastern European Jewish immigrants and their children who attended Harvard were poor and hadn't the time or financial wherewithal to properly engage in campus life. Free time and social hours were opportunities for them to scramble back to the city and earn some money to help cover tuition and housing. They appeared nothing like the small group of better-heeled American Jews of German origin who had adapted to Harvard norms and then generously underwrote philanthropic causes having to do with the college.[117] The new and more visible breed of Jewish Harvard undergraduates, explained one commentator, typically "live at home, eat a pocket lunch on the college campus, and leave the university grounds to earn the money for their tuition by night work." This commentator therefore surmised that these were the main reasons for the Jewish lack of acculturation to Harvard's social standards: "Many retain the gregariousness born of life in the Pale, and remain only half-assimilated."[118]

Harvard Yard offered Jews little to do. Undergraduate clubs and societies were closed to them, impelling the emergence of the Menorah Society and other clusters that other undergraduates found clannish. In both Harvard and Yale, Jews were, on the whole, denied membership in college fraternities because they were not typically the "football captain or the track champion."[119] Exclusion was particularly painful since fraternities were the "ready-made organizations" on college campuses that foster "student initiative."[120] Others deflected the cries of antisemitism. One promising Harvard-trained lawyer called for his coreligionists to offer a pass to his alma mater. Alfred Baensch likely paid no mind to one Boston Brahmin's complaint and fear that an influx of European immigrants—Jewish or otherwise—in Crimson athletics would further distance Harvard clubs from the gentlemanly form of English sportsmanship.[121] These outlier claims, for Benesch, did not match the historical record. He argued that Jewish students earned scholarships and won academic honors and prizes. That none of the sixty or so of his Jewish classmates had distinguished themselves in sports was not, as far as Benesch could tell, a matter of "racial or social favoritism."[122]

But the Jewish absence from athletics had to do with more than just energies and attention diverted elsewhere. Their invisibility on the football field and other sports symbolized a barrier to Jews' quest for acceptance and the outright effectiveness of its Americanization. Were Jews not virtuous? Could they not harness the sort of honor and masculinity that was linked to the usual football rhetoric on campus? William Cameron Forbes had his doubts whether they could, preferring Protestant stock to lead his football squads. "Football is the expression of the strength of the Anglo-Saxon," wrote the one-time Harvard Crimson coach. "It is the dominant spirit of a dominant race, and to this it owes its popularity and its hopes of permanence."[123]

Just the same, Jewish pundits offered excuses for the dearth of their football accomplishments and overall pitiful participation in the elite college sport. It did not bespeak a paucity of honor, they said. One Jewish man believed that his coreligionists required more time to adapt to the manly ruggedness of football. After all, this writer presumed from a deep influence of Darwinian eugenics, the "religious and political persecution to which they were subjected in later times destroyed their desires to measure athletic prowess with the Gentiles."[124] Then again, one Jewish journalist confessed, engaging in athletic competition may well have been a fully futile effort. His people, he feared, were just not an "athletic race."[125]

All such claims were dubious and had no effect on Jewish attention to sports. In fact, most immigrants understood the importance of athletics in American culture. Especially the youth, as historian Oscar Handlin maintained, were constantly "preoccupied with the events of the world of sport within which were played out the vivid dramas of American success and failure."[126] Football tended to animate such feelings, and in grand fashion. Jews took an interest in the football primers produced by Yale's Walter Camp and Harvard's W. H. Lewis.[127] They cheered for their kinsman, Phil King. Correctly or not, American Jews assessed the diminutive Princeton quarterback and reckoned that in the 1890s there was "hardly a better foot-ball player in the country."[128] The Jewish press followed King's subsequent coaching career at the University of Wisconsin and took an interest in some personal items such as his November 1904 engagement to Miss Jeanette Harris.[129] Later on, these same journalists fawned over other Jewish football stars like Dartmouth's "giant," John Marks and Pennsylvania's Israel Levine, a "Quaker hero," despite a "stocky" shape whose "features bore unmistakable signs of his Semitic ancestry."[130]

What is more, the Harvard-Yale football rivalry figured quite prominently into a belles-lettres serial distributed in several Jewish periodicals. In this fictional account in *American Israelite*, a young woman from Baltimore with ties to Boston struggled with her predicament in the Yale section of the grandstands: "After all, what was Harvard to her? Her father was a Baltimorean, educated abroad; her brothers Johns Hopkins men; why should she feel herself a traitor because she was watching the Yale-Harvard game from Yale seats, the guest of a Yale man, a blue flag in her hand?"[131]

Jews had more than just an inkling of the importance of Harvard football in the top tiers of American life. The prejudices and circumstances of their lot and luck in Cambridge made it an ambitious goal to appear between the painted goalposts of Harvard Stadium. Ralph and Arnold Horween were not aware of much of this; their identities hewed more closely to the progressive-minded Francis Parker schooling than a substantial Jewish upbringing. As sons of immigrants, the brothers understood what admission to Harvard represented to Rose and Isadore Horween. Ralph and Arnie were also cognizant of how much the pluralistic values—they tended to describe it as midwestern—that had been inculcated in them differed from that of the New England prep school graduates who made up the lion's share of Harvard students. The Roosevelts, Whitneys, Beaumonts, and other rank-and-file collegians in Cambridge, Massachusetts, were reared to maintain sturdy barriers to their interior social and cultural spaces that the Horweens were never taught to observe. A positive performance on the football field went a long way toward breaking down those barriers. Ralph and Arnold entered Harvard confident that they could leverage athletics to that end, to their own personal gain. Using it any further, for the sake of a broader purpose, as Bill Bingham had figured out at Exeter, was not at all in their plans. Yet their coreligionists were not about to let that symbol of Jewish Americanization pass them by.

CHAPTER FOUR

WINNING FOR WINNING'S SAKE

It is not pleasant to be beaten by Yale year after year, but life
is worth living even under those conditions. All Harvard
men want to win our full share of victories, but, after all,
the ultimate end of athletics is not to defeat Yale. If it were,
then the employment of a professional coach would be wise.
College sports are carried on for the purpose of benefiting
the men who take part in them. If we can get all the good
that should come from these contests, and, in addition, win
rather more than half of the events with Yale, well and good.

—"Professional Coaching," *Harvard Graduates' Magazine*,
September 1903, 32

In the autumn of 1912, Harvard College began its 277th year with a promise
to redouble its spirit of openness. The Brahmins had always been at the
forefront in certain arenas. President Charles Eliot opened Radcliffe College
for women in 1879. The all-female college in Cambridge, Massachusetts, appeared after Mount Holyoke (1837), Vassar (1865), and Smith and Wellesley
(both 1875) started to enroll students. Radcliffe was the first, however, to
ensure that the bulk of its teaching was handled by college-trained professors.

Richard Theodore Greener graduated as the first African American from
Harvard in 1870 and soon after served as dean of the law school. Harvard
started to admit blacks with more regularity in the 1890s, W. E. B. Du Bois being among the prominent alumni from that period. African Americans were
welcome in all college classes and as members on the newspaper staff and in
the clubs, a situation that impeded interest in Harvard for many potential
young Harvard men from the South. Eliot noticed that African Americans
were most welcome on the sports field, "on account of their remarkable
athletic merit."[1] Openness had its limits, however. The college remained a
citadel of New England wealth and did not want to absorb peoples who
might pose a challenge to that profile. Admitting groups that through their
appearance—meaning, nonwhite and nonmale—would not amount to a

threat to the establishment was a safe gesture on Harvard's part. Even then, the heads of the Cambridge school maintained certain racial checks. As in most places, Harvard discouraged African Americans from residing in the dormitories and entreated social distancing, seen from a present perspective as an abhorrent disposition.

Harvard College was also open to varieties of faith. Harvard was a Protestant school and had in a quasi-official manner aligned itself to liberal brands of Christianity. In 1881, Harvard maintained a ministerial staff from five different denominations to hold a variety of chapel services. It was a testament, lauded Eliot decades later, to the school's "liberality as regards opinions, its devotion to ideals, and the preciousness in its sight of individual liberty."[2] In Boston, a group of Irish Catholic men founded the St. Paul's Catholic Club in 1893. Eliot was no strong admirer of the Catholic faith—during his narrowminded youth, Eliot had declared that he had hated Catholicism like "poison"—or their parochial schools, but he much preferred that able students enroll at Harvard than, say, the nearby Jesuit-run Boston College.[3]

A newspaper profile of the Harvard newcomers in the autumn of 1912 welcomed its largest class to that date, about five hundred students.[4] The group was diverse, at least in the context of that time. A few came from China and a handful from France. It was the first time Harvard accepted a young man from South Africa. The Andover football phenomenon, Eddie Mahan of Andover Academy, headlined the Catholic cohort. Eddie was the youngest of eleven children born to Irish immigrants.[5] His father Patrick was a Civil War veteran and a busy member of Natick's municipal inner workings. Each of Patrick and Julia's children spoke with a brogue, softening their vowel pronunciations like a quintessential Irish transplant.

Theirs was a proud heritage. Eddie's older brother, Charles, joined the New England priesthood. But excepting Archbishop William Henry O'Connell, Eddie was the best-known and most beloved Irish Catholic in New England. He was handsome, affable, and polite. He played every sport at Natick High School and excelled in the ones that counted most: football and baseball. At Andover, Mahan overpowered Exeter on the gridiron and usually beat his rivals on the baseball diamond. It helped his cause that sport was one avenue in which the Irish and the Brahmins had something in common. "The two groups do not associate to any extent," recalled a Boston sportswriter, with some hyperbole. "They are divergent in politics, religion, and most other ways, but they are very much alike and they have an unavowed admiration for each other which boils down to the standards of toughness each sets for itself."[6]

The Exeter faithful adored Eddie, too. They had realized, before Mahan's Harvard coaches did, that Eddie was the "greatest football player God ever

Eddie Mahan posing for a dropkick, adorned in a US Marine Corps sweater. Mahan was the leading member of a fraternity of Harvard undergraduates and alumni who enlisted during World War I. Courtesy of Library of Congress Prints and Photographs Division.

made."[7] He was a Jim Thorpe–like figure, able to compete and captain the baseball and football teams and possessed of enough speed to run with some of the sprinters on the track squad. Thorpe himself once offered the thought that "Eddie Mahan of Harvard was the greatest football player I have ever seen."[8] The Carlisle Indian and Olympic star affirmed that Mahan "had everything." In due time, the undergrads and alumni at Yale and Princeton also recognized Eddie's greatness. Unlike the more generous Exeter fans, the Crimson's main rivals jeered him for spurning their overtures in favor of Harvard. Eddie chose Harvard, and that gave the Crimson a better chance at winning.

All the foregoing helps explain how an Irish immigrant's son could make good at a New England institution such as Harvard College. Like a growing number of undergraduates in Cambridge, Eddie Mahan did not possess a Brahmin pedigree. It mattered a little less at that point within the halls of Harvard, for winning's sake. Bill Bingham had learned that, as well. He just did not count on it being such a difficult lesson to master.

*   *   *

Bill Bingham wasn't Eddie Mahan. Eddie's grades were better than Bill's. The latter's Bingham family lineage was bereft of affluence. His Episcopal Protestantism was an everyman's heritage that Harvard could not hold over their more closed-minded rivals in New Haven and Princeton. What's more, Mahan competed in more popular sports. Football, no matter how much President Eliot had complained about it, was chock full of honor and values that pervaded the school's very spirit. The football and baseball teams made money besides. Meanwhile, the expenses of training and transporting the track-and-field squad was, considering modest ticket sales, a breakeven effort.

Track was a secondhand sport at Harvard. Observers found it missing heft and depth in key realms like discipline and sportsmanship. They determined that racing, hurdling, and hammer throwing lacked the dimensions of every position on the football field. The Harvard eleven was a miniature military brigade, led by a general into battle and highly trained in athletic warfare. The track meet was a team competition, but still, aside from the relay, the runners did not run cooperatively. Formalized intercollegiate foot racing began in July 1873 as a sideshow for the intercollegiate regatta in Saratoga Springs. In it, three men ran a two-mile race before the annual boating battle. On that inaugural occasion, D. E. Bowie of McGill University won the sparsely attended competition. A Cornell runner came in second and an Amherst man did not bother to finish the race. Lackluster as it was, the regatta committee figured that the meet did not enjoy proper publicity. Hoping to improve the allure of the regatta, organizers added five track events to the rowing affair. Harvard competed in 1874, but it was reported that the "result clearly demonstrated that we are greatly in need of an active athletic association."[9]

Running and dashing gained interest from then on within the college ranks. It had a sizable foothold at the club level. The biggest star in the realm was Lon Myers, a Jewish lad from Virginia, who carried the Manhattan

Athletic Club and held most of the national records for short and middle distances during the final decades of the nineteenth century.[10] College track and field picked up speed as well. But Harvard remained at a distantly low ebb, probably because its racers trained on a poorly maintained dirt track at Jarvis Field. Unhappy with the embarrassment and delinquency of a Harvard endeavor, President Eliot added a five-lap cinder track to Jarvis Field in 1879. Improved facilities at Holmes Field in 1884, Soldiers Field in 1900, and Harvard Stadium in 1904 increased the chances of the fleetest-footed Harvard men in intercollegiate competition.[11] The alumni also covered the costs for a professional trainer, starting in 1881. Better-prepared Harvard teams won championships in the 1880s and 1890s. Other programs at Cornell and Pennsylvania recruited finer material and invested in better training grounds, by comparison, and outclassed Harvard in the first decades of the twentieth century. Harvard remained complacent about its steady success against Yale, always scheduled at a season's final meet. Then the Elis bypassed the Crimson racers. By the time Bill Bingham entered Harvard, curious students wondered aloud, he later recalled, "What is the matter with the Harvard Track Team?"[12]

* * *

Harvard initially rejected Bingham. The decision made Phillips Exeter look quite foolish for bestowing on Bill the coveted Teschemacher Scholarship, meant for a Harvard-bound graduate. It also did not redound well to Exeter that its greatest living alumnus was also a Harvard reject. Beside himself, Harlan Amen trekked to Cambridge and met with LeBaron Russell Briggs, the longtime Harvard dean. Amen pleaded with Briggs to reconsider Bingham for Harvard, asserting that Bill was the "kind of a man they ought to have in their institution."[13] Briggs was a prominent figure in the NCAA and a strong supporter of Harvard football, a sport that generated considerable revenue and donations from well-off alumni. Amen assured Briggs that the Exeter scholarship and Bill's hard work would cover the whole of Bingham's tuition. Briggs, not wishing to lose other suitable Exeter men to Yale, acceded to Amen's cajoling. Bingham arrived at Harvard Yard and unpacked his belongings alongside his college roommate, Eddie Mahan, formerly of Phillips Andover Academy.

Harlan Amen was right. Bill made friends with the rest of the Harvard newcomers and did well enough in his classes. Most of the richest young men from the highest patrician rungs of New England—the ones who had graduated from "Saint Grottlesex" preparatory schools and least likely to warm to a plebian such as Bingham—lived off campus, south of Harvard Yard. These were the sons of millionaires who were trained to calculate whom they could bring home to their families or introduce to their sisters. A roommate, they figured, needed to satisfy those criteria. This class therefore preferred to live apart in the private luxurious, electricity-infused suites in the so-called Gold Coast of Harvard College. They left the less-gilded campus dormitories—some had no central heating or plumbing above the basement—to the "mediocre" stock—a situation that Bill and other Exeter men much preferred.[14]

The Harvard freshmen voted Bingham over Mahan for class president by a lopsided tally, 278 to 161 votes.[15] The election confounded the upperclassmen, who had anticipated that the younger men would follow the tradition of appointing for its class leader the captain of the freshman football team. Mahan was a swell-enough man. He reminded Coach Percy Haughton of Charles Brickley. Charlie had matriculated at Harvard from Exeter a year earlier. Like football captains before him, Brickley had been elected class president and led the freshmen on the gridiron. Mahan was faster and funnier than Brickley. He probably would have secured the freshman vote any other year. Bingham's instant popularity, however, won out. Just as at Exeter, Bill proved, without much trying, that he could fit in with almost every undergraduate and represent the very best of every Harvard student. The other young men recognized a spirit of selflessness in Bill. Bingham's determined perspective appeared very natural and admirable, almost football-like, to the Harvard collegians.[16]

Bingham was also noticed by William Donovan. Like most everyone else, Bill called the track coach "Pooch" Donovan—Donovan's first name was a treasured secret among those in the know around Cambridge. Donovan was Natick's favorite Irish son before Mahan came along and made them forget Pooch's racing heroics and footwork on the local high school's offensive line. Like Bingham, Donovan prepared for college at Phillips Exeter. In New Hampshire, Pooch once got into a thicket of trouble for taking money to line up for Georgetown. From time to time, he also raced against horses—the spectators did not know that the steeds were broken-down racehorses—in a "death-defying spectacle" for some of P. T. Barnum's circus performances.[17]

Pooch tapped Bill as the freshmen's track captain. This decision was much easier for Donovan than it had been for Dean Briggs. In amateur racing circles, Bill Bingham was a well-known commodity. He was a winner. His record at Exeter surpassed Pooch Donovan's and almost everyone else's. Bingham won his first Harvard contest "without extending himself" and did much the same for the balance of the season.[18]

Donovan worked Bingham hard, pushing Bill to run on the Harvard gymnasium's wooden indoor tracks. Donovan needed Bill for his usual half-mile race and, without a competitive alternative, to run the quarter-mile sprint as well. Harvard also used Bill for the freshman relay race. Bingham obliged, as was his wont. He drilled himself so thoroughly on the smooth indoor board tracks that he ruined the arches of his feet. A few years later, the condition confused physicians, who tried to discourage Bill from enlisting in the World War I on the grounds that he was flatfooted. The army's medical staff, without testing his speed on the cinder path, determined that Bingham was much too slow for the battlefield.[19]

In truth, Donovan overextended Bingham that first year at Harvard. Bill's freshman team was upset at Soldiers Field in the final meet against Yale, 56–47. Harvard had defeated Yale in the relay earlier in the season and expected to produce a strong showing in the medley competition. Bingham did not disappoint in that first contest against the Crimson's archrival. He contributed to Harvard's scoring for the half-mile trot. He "easily outclassed the rest of the field."[20] It was Bill's teammates who had underperformed, vanquished by a lesser Yale team. He still shouldered some blame, not just because he was the captain. Bingham was scheduled to compete in the quarter-mile race just as Donovan had planned it. Then he reconsidered when Bill declined to line up because he was "rather used up."[21] Yale won the race and parlayed that into a victory in the overall meet against its rival.

* * *

Bill Bingham completed an undefeated season for the final time in his running career. The only blemish was a failed attempt to start a laundry service with Charles Brickley, which caused the Exeter alumni to suffer some serious financial losses. The material Bill had faced among his freshman campaign was mediocre, probably a level or so weaker than the stock he had confronted during the prior year as an Exeter flier. Bill masterfully overcame the handicap of learning to run a new race: the quarter-mile. The 880-yarder was an ideal distance for him. The strategy first taught to Bingham by Dick Fox in Lawrence seemed to still work out. He got off a beat slower than the competition, staying back to assess their speed. Then he overpowered them, turning it on with plenty of slack on the course to make that signature move to the front of the pack. The shorter race limited his time for observation and a change of pace. Bingham was certainly better suited to run the half-mile than Harvard's middling incumbent Francis Capper. Pooch Donovan had no one good enough to run the quarter-mile and therefore moved Bingham to the 440-yard competition.

Sportswriters were delighted by the prospect of watching Bill Bingham compete in the quarter-mile. Cornell, the reigning power among the track

Like Bill Bingham, Ted Meredith of the University of Pennsylvania grew up in blue-collar conditions. He emerged as Bingham's major collegiate rival and defeated him each time they faced one another. Courtesy of University Archives and Records Center, University of Pennsylvania.

schools, possessed several fine runners at that distance. The best of their lot was Clement Speiden. Yale's Val Wilkie was another formidable runner. Wilkie had earned a reputation and some revenue racing middle distances in the New York Athletic Club's summertime events on Travers Island.[22]

Then there was Ted Meredith of the University of Pennsylvania. Prognosticators hailed Meredith as a "worthy rival" for Bingham.[23] Neither had absorbed a defeat in prep school competition: William J. Bingham at Exeter or James Edward Meredith at Mercersburg Academy. "In the next three years," one journalist prophesied, "they should provide some races that will be worth seeing."[24] Another predicted that "it would be interesting to see these two fliers come together. They are," he concluded about the pair, "about the fastest freshman performers that were ever enrolled at a college."[25]

Bill Bingham entered Harvard determined to vanquish Ted Meredith, probably the only schoolboy runner better known than Bingham. His experiences at Phillips Exeter had refined his penchant for winning. Before then,

Bill had never made racing about winning, but that Meredith's high station among the elite collegiate runners was, to Bingham, a sore and personal matter. Bill had a hand in the creation of the Meredith myth.

The Merediths were from the small Pennsylvania town of Elwyn, situated two dozen miles from Philadelphia, which must have appeared otherworldly to Elwyn residents like James Hauxwell Meredith. The senior Meredith was an "open air man," a descendent of farmers. James raised crops and trained horses. James might have been a formidable sprinter in his youth had the sport taken root in the period immediately after the Civil War. To make up for this, James started a running club as an adult. The Meredith family tradition had it that their grandfather, William Meredith, had held a reputation for fast running in England. William Meredith was Catholic and therefore not part of the British mainstream. He did not participate in formal sports such as rowing, competitions reserved for England's more elite stock. William's exploits were evident on the playgrounds and were nothing quite official. Fortunately for his descendent, track had gained traction by the time Ted was a youngster.[26]

Ted's prospects began a bit dimly. He was a small child. Then, as a teenager, the young Meredith developed broad shoulders, strong limbs, and a deep chest. James trained his son—Ted was one of two Meredith sons, of seven children overall—the same way he did horses. Ted Meredith ran with his chest puffed out and his head cranked far back. His posture resembled the contortions of Mel Sheppard, the gold medalist who had bettered Bingham in 1908 and emerged as the Olympic darling of the United States in the London games of that year. Ted idolized Sheppard. He even stretched his face—the sight of it looked somewhat odd with Ted's dark eyebrows and thick hair—in the final seconds of a race like the once-peerless Sheppard. That Meredith ran like Sheppard was not an accident or fanboy obsession. James Meredith once explained that he taught his child prodigy to run like a racehorse.[27]

Ted Meredith gained a modicum of fame during his lone year at Mercersburg Academy. The school is in Pennsylvania's Cumberland Valley, along the edges of the Allegheny Mountains. Coach Jimmy Curran had recruited Meredith from Williamson Trade School, where Ted had been training to be a bricklayer. Meredith gained some acclaim as a Williamson footballer, once intercepting a pass "far behind the goal line, and galloped to our only touchdown," recalled a teammate about Williamson Trade School's mediocre eleven.[28] Mercersburg Academy was only interested in Ted's track work, however. At the academy, Meredith won the quarter-mile and the half-mile at the schoolboy event at the University of Pennsylvania, which was Williamson's best showing at the regional program.[29]

Meredith excelled at Mercersburg under Curran's more human-centered training regimen. Impressed by the young man's prospects, Curran entered Meredith in the Olympic tryouts in Boston. Curran recalled that "every one of the experts told me I was making a mistake." The judgment error related to Curran's decision to register Meredith for the 800-meter race. Experts knew that the "most experienced middle distance runners in America" competed in that race, including Mel Sheppard. There was one important absentee. Bill Bingham was not present. He had turned down the invitation to overtake Sheppard in order to attend commencement exercises at Phillips Exeter.[30]

Meredith won the first heat against the former-Exeter-star-turned-Cornell-standout, John Paul Jones, and then lost the second round to Sheppard. No one expected Meredith to compete with the vaunted Sheppard. The newspapers had envisioned a very different storyline. The sportswriters were frankly disappointed by Bill Bingham's absence, figuring that the latter stood a good chance at redemption from the earlier London tryouts four years prior to topple Sheppard once and for all. The biggest of the big shots, Sheppard advised the committee members to bring Meredith on board on the grounds that the younger man could push Sheppard to run faster. He could be all the difference in his quest to beat the Germans, not to mention the chance to set a world record. In fact, it was Ted Meredith who beat the 800-meter record in Sweden that summer, clocking in at 1 minute, 51 and 9/10 seconds. The upstart Meredith spurted past Sheppard on the final turn. Bill Bingham's replacement, then, won gold. Sheppard took second place and received the silver medal at the Stockholm Olympics.[31]

Bill Bingham was far too Christian to admit to envy. He also had much to fall back on. Upon returning to Harvard for his sophomore year, Bingham received more votes than any other Harvard man—including roommate and varsity halfback, Eddie Mahan—for membership to Delta Kappa Epsilon, the school's most select fraternity.[32] Membership in "Dickey" (from the fraternity's acronym, DKE) signaled social status, and meant that the rich men in the Gold Coast suites along Mount Auburn Street could now happily introduce an initiated member to their sisters.[33] Bingham was also a member of the glee club, in those days a most respected extracurricular group. Bill found meaning in the Episcopal Church. Yet Bingham was troubled that Meredith of the Blue and Red Pennsylvania team had risen, in part, because of his interrupted track schedule.

It did not encourage Bingham that he was the focus of a much-more-visible Harvard track squad, and that his teammates and fairly everyone passing through Harvard Yard wanted to see him get the better of Meredith on the racing paths. "I haven't seen a runner in the whole chop of the last few years who has the knack of negotiating the corners that Bingham has," Pooch Donovan related to interested readers in Boston's local press.[34]

Bingham and Harvard started the season grandly. Eddie Mahan joined the relay team that beat Boston's athletic association's group. Bill took the baton from Mahan with a three-yard lead at the end of the second lap. Bill extended the margin beyond repair by the time he handed the stick to the captain and anchor, Bill Barron.[35]

Bingham also took on Boston's Tom Halpin in the short-distance race. At the 100-yard mark, Halpin caught up to Bingham, reaching to Bill's elbows. "I simply had to run then, if ever," Bingham told the crowd about the surprise of seeing a competitor that close to him after the first stretch of the run. "Had Halpin ever passed me I guess it would have been off."[36] Bingham ended up winning the race by ten yards. Bill then outdueled the Yale competition in the 440-yarder by about sixty feet. His finishes earned him a coveted H. The newly minted letterman set a record for Harvard-Yale relay contests.

The intercollegiate springtime portion of Harvard's running schedule was much more challenging. Mighty Cornell beat Harvard, 75 to 41, in their faceoff. Bingham took the quarter-mile race, but the decision turned out to be rather close. The Cornell man closed the gap in the final hundred yards but lost to Bill at the tape.[37]

The alumni hailed Bingham, reminding the young man that "you work best when conditions are hardest."[38] Dean Briggs, now something of a track fan, wrote a note to Bill with "belated congratulations on your work at Cornell."[39] The well-regarded Prohibitionist preacher Reverend Amos Wells seized on Bingham's exciting finish in a written sermon that Bill clipped and saved in his scrapbook. Wells reported to his listeners and readers that, like Bingham, "we are runners, every one of us, speeding toward competitive goals. Of a hundred civil engineers, one reaches the presidency of a great railroad." He beseeched his fellow Christians to follow in faithful Bill's cinder path and to "trust himself to the great Judge, whose eye is keen for the inner as well as the outer merit, and who will award an adequate prize for every honest endeavor."[40] The message: God makes winners.

Bingham didn't need much faith to defeat his next opponents, Oxford's fleet band of runners. He marched to the starting position of the quick-paced 220-yard dash and won. Bingham persevered against a competition that had more practice at this distance and against a strong and hampering wind blowing against him in his first-ever race at that short length.[41] After Oxford, though, Bingham could have used some more prayers against Yale's Vallean Wilkie in the dual meet in Cambridge. Bingham was "probably the greatest disappointment" for the Crimson in an afternoon full of Harvard misery and Yale triumphs.[42] Bill would have preferred to race in his much more natural half-mile, especially since Captain George Brown had made a name for himself in the 880-yarder by defeating John Paul Jones of Cornell and would be far too much for Cappers of Harvard.

In the quarter-mile, Pooch Donovan had instructed Bingham to break out of the gate with speed and to forbid others from setting the early pace, as he had lately grown accustomed to doing in the half-mile. It was a different strategy that did not make use of Bill's racing intuition. It did not work. Wilkie launched out in front of Bill. Bingham tried to recuperate but the course was not long enough to catch the Yale man. Bingham lost by about three yards. The defeat was Bill's first since he had entered Phillips Exeter and the high-stakes and high-class world of the New England patricians.

* * *

Harvard wanted winners in the Age of Bingham. The sea change began on the football field. In January 1904, sportswriter Casper Whitney reported that Harvard alumni had started to agitate for "competent management" of the Crimson eleven. "It is not pleasant to be beaten by Yale year after year." Careful not to disparage the gentlemanly honor code, Harvard graduates explained that all they wanted was their "full share of victories"—not the "professional coach" and Spartan stylings of Yale.[43] Whitney reported that the alumni could not have it both ways. To produce a successful squad, Harvard required a full-time coach and needed to do away with the longtime "graduate coach," a part-time position filled by recent alumni with extra time on their hands. The Crimson needed strategy and discipline, someone to drill the team at practice and refine technique. Whitney frankly welcomed the move, fatigued by the "crass stupidity" that had overcome the Bostonians' football squad.[44]

Harvard did not budge, and Yale won. Once again, Whitney called on the Crimson to "establish a system" so that winning would not be a "matter of occasional chance." In the 1904 season, Harvard underwhelmed, tying Dartmouth and suffering defeats to Pennsylvania and Yale. Whitney demoted Harvard from the "Big Three," slotting the Crimson as the fifth-best collegiate team at season's end, behind Yale, Penn, West Point, and Princeton.[45] Some students were still satisfied with the mediocre season. As steadfast sports purists, they felt that the invigorated efforts to defeat Yale and its other rivals were "slimy" and had drained Harvard athletics of fun and gentlemanliness.[46] But many more Cambridge collegians had apparently come to see things quite differently.

The Yale defeats had caused a "certain loss of manhood."[47] Harvard courted Bill Reid on the hunch that he could beat the Elis. Reid had done exactly that as a Harvard player in 1898 and as an unpaid graduate coach in 1901. The school offered him a handsome salary to do it.[48] Since Reid's graduation, Harvard had not scored a single point in matches against Yale.[49]

Reid was not a Boston Brahmin. He had represented a new kind of Harvard athlete. He had won for the Crimson and did all he could to accomplish that task. His attitude had not elevated Reid's standing among the undergraduate elite, but he did not care all too much about his social station.[50] He had played football and baseball—and did very well in both. As a sophomore in 1898, Reid had scored twice to help the Crimson to the rarest of their football routs of Yale. He was also a standout for the Harvard nine, starting at catcher for each of his four years in Cambridge. Reid's baseball prominence placed some of his misdeeds in the sports pages. On one occasion, Reid had moved beyond the basepath to needlessly knock over Princeton's backstop. Observers ranked it one of the "dirtiest pieces of ball-playing," leaving Reid with a decidedly un-Harvard reputation, which required rehabilitation.[51]

Reid won a lot at Harvard. In two seasons as football coach, his Crimson team marched to a 30-3-1 record. Reid accomplished that record through hard work and a repudiation of the British-borrowed athletic ethic that had pervaded—to his mind, plagued—Harvard Yard for decades. Though he would not openly flout it before the Harvard faculty, Reid disregarded the "English system" and its gentlemanliness as a "handicap."[52] Far less interested in honor and virtue, Reid emphasized victory as the most central purpose of football competition. It was a Yale approach to athletics. Just as his players took the field before his first game against Williams College, Reid made it known that what counted was the outcome of the contest: "Williams has come down here to-day not to tie you fellows, but to beat you and she expects to do it. Are you going to let a small college come down here and do anything of that kind? If you are, we might as well stop now as any time."[53] This was something new at Harvard.

Becoming numbered as one of the nation's best coaches was not Reid's goal.[54] Beating Yale was most important to him. That season finale defined, in retrospect, the entire success of all the preceding games. Reid calculated rest regimens for his athletes during the season to ensure a squad at full strength for the Yale match, always scheduled at the end of the football campaign. He scouted the Elis in New Haven and sought coaching advice from Michigan's Fielding Yost, University of Chicago's Amos Alonzo Stagg, and even the New Haven legend himself, Walter Camp. To his efforts, most of Reid's players responded with vigor.

Some undergraduate athletes remained on the course charted by earlier "virtuous" Harvard men. The Crimson coach could not fathom how one of his students preferred to do well in calculus rather than put in some extra practice hours. "I don't care how much of a student a fellow cares to be at other times," observed Reid in condemnation. "I don't see how a man can help feeling that hardly anything is more important than to beat Yale."[55] Most pledged to Reid to "do my damnedest to lick Yale."[56] This was the new honorable speech around Harvard Yard.

The sportswriters credited Reid for his team's "well-rounded form" and ranked the Crimson the second-best team in the nation. But Reid didn't beat the top-rated Yale eleven. As consolation, Casper Whitney credited Harvard for "point[ing] the way that sportsmen should conduct themselves on the field of contest," an honor code that the win-at-all-costs Yale still severely lacked.[57] This code of conduct, though, did not matter at all to Bill Reid.

The condition of sport at Harvard, pushed along by Coach Reid, was changing. Harvard no longer privileged that gentleman's creed as much, at least in comparison with winning. Reid's banter was his own undoing. His two losses to the Elis haunted him, rendering Reid's return to the Harvard gridiron a failure.[58] Despite beating everyone but Yale and Penn, the sentiment around campus was that "Reid had two years to bring out a winning team at Harvard and did not do it."[59] Reid quit, but his players did not mind all that much. His one-year replacement, Joshua Crane, was a man without credentials. His uninspired charges lost to Jim Thorpe's Carlisle Indians and were held scoreless by Dartmouth and Yale. Crane departed after the season, leaving the university to continue its search for a "football leader who would mean as much to Harvard as Walter Camp does to Yale."[60]

Crane's successor was Percy Haughton. Haughton was a Harvard two-sport legend, unmatched as an outfielder and punter. His past play and considerable coaching experience seemed to excuse his mediocre, non-Boston Brahmin pedigree, or was enough for Harvard, on the insistence of Captain Francis Burr, to give Haughton a chance after Bill Reid's unspectacular two seasons. Haughton "arrived at Harvard at the psychological moment"—and transformed Crimson football.[61] Haughton was a winner. In truth, the "Haughton System" resembled Reid's. Haughton studied Reid's coaching journal and grafted those materials onto his own formulations and formations. Haughton drilled students in practice, preaching precision and Rooseveltian "strenuousness."[62] He was a consistent personality. The coach concluded each speech with "Let's go to work."[63] During practices and games, Haughton always exhibited a "talent for picturesque profanity."[64]

Haughton was an intelligent student of the evolving sport. He improved on Walter Camp's football planning. One particular difference was the way Haughton had elevated the quarterback position. Camp once described the quarterback, quite pedestrianly, as the "middle rusher's assistant."[65] In truth, Camp valued the quarterback, considering him like a field coach, recommending that other coaches "select for your quarter-back material as much brains as can be found in any of your candidates."[66] Yet Camp's Yale quarterbacks did not contribute all that much to the physical aspects of the game. The quarterback took the ball from the center, who was crouched down on the scrimmage line. Then he handed it off to one of three runners typically stationed in the Yale backfield. The quarterback in the Walter Camp era of Yale football never rushed forward with the football, nor did he block for anyone else lined up behind him.

Camp's more substantial contribution was his role in emancipating American football from British rugby. Camp abhorred what he perceived as a randomness in the English game. It lacked structure: a beginning, middle, and end to each segment of the game. Camp had figured into nearly every discussion about rule changes, sorting out a "position for every player and a duty for every position," as opposed to the English "mass of men with no definite positions."[67] Camp also had a say in slimming down the ball. Under his direction, football morphed the bulgy rugby orb—measuring 27 inches around in the middle—to a slenderer version, about 21 inches in circumference. Haughton and that newer generation of college football minds found more roles for the other men on the gridiron, spreading them out along the width of the field. Camp usually had most of the footballers bunched together, near the center of the field, ready to push an inevitable mass of men forward toward the goal line, in search of a new set of downs. It was a more primitive version of the "guards back" formation that Penn had developed in the 1890s.

Harvard had a variety of lineups, but nothing too complex. Under Haughton, the football team worked with a playbook made up of a handful of formations. Most of the time, Harvard lined up in an unbalanced "tandem formation," meaning a quarterback behind center, and two runners, a halfback and a fullback, staggered behind him. The Crimson's best maneuver was a wheel shift, a play that required an interior lineman to rotate to the other side of the center. No matter how many times the Crimson ran the protocol, the strategy tended to confuse defensive coverages. It forced the opposition to choose whether to slide over to the overloaded side or stay put. The quarterback was the field general, selected for his "warp of long training and a woof of common sense."[68] Even when the rules were changed to allow it, Haughton did not stroll the sidelines. He never barked plays to his quarterback. He trusted his players to make the correct call at the line of scrimmage. To signal that decision, the quarterback chanted a double series of

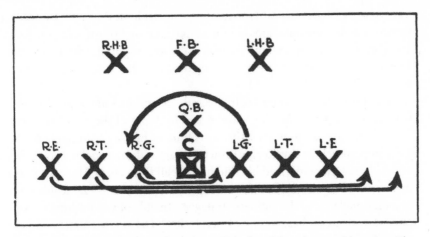

Harvard's "wheel shift" was perhaps Percy Haughton's best-known formation. The play required the left guard to shift to the right side before the snap to create an unbalanced formation. According to the quarterback's signal, other blockers also "wheeled" to the right side to interfere on behalf of the runner. First published in Herbert Reed, "Football Problems of 1911," *Metropolitan*, November 1911, 18.

four numbers, with a break of two beats between the double-timed cadences. The first number indicated the formation selected for the play. The second called out where the halfback was meant to run: even numbers for the long side of the offensive line; odd numbers for a run to the short end. A 1 and 2 meant to rush to a hole on either side of the center. Haughton's men knew how to change it up if the defense happened to figure out the number codes.

Runners raced with deception for Haughton. Haughton had borrowed the hidden ball technique from Pop Warner's Carlisle Indian teams. Each spring, Percy Haughton "summoned his wife and several other ladies to the practice field and spaced them in front of the Harvard team."[69] The quarterback practiced taking snaps from the linemen, feigning handoffs to decoy runners and sliding the ball clandestinely to his chosen backfield rusher. Haughton did not end the exercise until the women were thoroughly stumped. Then, at a subsequent practice, Haughton would test his players' ball-faking skills again against "big, but very smart dogs, who had been carefully trained in the fine art of chasing a football." Haughton ended the practice once the quarterback had outsmarted the canines.[70]

Haughton developed a sophisticated scouting report. To prepare for each game, Haughton dispatched Crimson scout Reggie Brown to study the opposition. The former Crimson back had catalogued every play made in the Harvard-Yale rivalry since the Bill Reid era. On Saturdays, Brown perched himself at the top of Harvard Stadium near a telephone. From that altitude, Brown scanned the field, looking for weaknesses on both sides of the line. He relayed those impressions via telephone to Haughton, who issued the advised adjustments to the team, placing trust in every word and suggestion Brown offered him.[71]

Haughton also relied on Lorin Deland. Deland had never played football but had a genius for it. Deland was a Brahmin of the very first order and had the freedom, monetarily, to volunteer himself in support of the Crimson cause. Whereas Reggie Brown had aptitude that coalesced with his athleticism, Deland derived his skill in football from chess. He was a chess master and authority on the Napoleonic Wars. These intellectual acquisitions together made Deland a ruthless strategist, capable of vanquishing his opponent, with an application of violence. In 1892, Deland invented the "flying wedge," a blocking configuration so tight that a tackler could not penetrate it. He developed the wedge play after the collegiate rules committee revised the regulations to permit blockers to rush forward before the start of the play. Deland's formation leveraged that presnap momentum. College coaches deemed the play too dangerous to the defenders, however—in fact, President Grover Cleveland suspended the Army-Navy game fearing the brutality of the play design. Coaches therefore made it illegal a year after Deland had conjured it up for Harvard.[72]

Haughton and Brown submitted plans for the upcoming game to Deland. Deland reviewed them and narrowed the contingencies for Haughton's players. He identified the precise formations that had the most promise. Haughton realigned routes and blocking assignments, if he deemed it to be warranted.[73]

Other teams criticized Haughton for his scouting activities. They decried his methods as unfair. He had rigged the system, taken the gamesmanship out of football, at least from the point of view of the college athletes, and replaced it with espionage. Haughton had gone too far, they complained. Percy Haughton reacted by expressing sorrow for the opposition, believing that either their priorities were misguided or that their schools simply lacked the requisite level of genius alumni with a splendid background in military history.

Haughton's strategic methods, intelligent defense, and determined kicking propelled Harvard to an undefeated 1908 season—including a 4–0 defeat of Yale that even Charles Eliot had to admit was "very satisfactory."[74] Haughton much preferred the low-scoring contests, making the game one of field position. He often coached his halfbacks—he liked to stock his team with fast runners who also posed as able kickers—to punt the ball away on first or second down to catch the defense by surprise and pin the opponent deep, near its goal line. The purpose was to exhaust the adversary. In that

The Flying Wedge play, developed by Lorin Deland, which Harvard introduced in a losing effort against rival Yale. The photograph depicts the Harvard players bracing for impact on November 19, 1892, at Hampden Park in Springfield, Massachusetts. First published in Parke H. Davis, *Football: The American Intercollegiate Game* (New York: Charles Scribner's Sons, 1911), 278.

era, substitutions were restricted, permitted only at the start of each period. Haughton drilled his players to endure. Harvard was almost always better conditioned than the other team. Haughton's Crimson squads tended to wait until the final minutes of the game and then pounce on the fatigued material on the other side of the scrimmage.[75]

Winning changed the mood around Harvard football. Before his second season, the coach had, in one pundit's estimation, "recruited better players than appeared on Yale field for the first time."[76] It helped Haughton's cause that Charles Brickley, Hamilton Fish, Tack Hardwick, and Eddie Mahan chose his program over the competition in New Haven and Princeton. Haughton was, as Hardwick recalled it, the "idol of a boy's intense hero worship."[77] Haughton relied on allegiance. "If he told us to jump off a cliff one hundred feet high," once explained Hardwick to a sportswriter, "all fifty of us thought he'd catch us. And every man would take the jump. He is a hard man, but a great one."[78] The coach liked to think that he won recruits with sermons comparing football training and the sport's All-American toughness to a business work ethic.[79]

Haughton believed he had a talent to "take a bright student with a reasonably good physique and teach him the physical part of the game." That, he surmised, was simpler than to "take a man who has all the physical equipment but is not mentally up to the task."[80] The preparatory school students came because Harvard was winning. In return, Haughton celebrated their efforts. "I am proud of the men who worked shoulder to shoulder in bringing about Harvard victories. The list is a long one," Haughton would state after several years of tallying wins. "I shall always cherish the hearty co-operation of these men who gave their best for Harvard."[81] He imagined that this was good training for life beyond Cambridge. It was fine preparation for successful lives, a loaded term that Haughton tellingly equated with the "avid test of a championship game."[82]

That spirit defined the whole of Harvard athletics and probably had much to do with a similar culture festering at one of its top feeder schools, at Phillips Exeter Academy. "Winning" and "success" had animated Bill Bingham throughout his time at Exeter. Like Percy Haughton and his football program, Bill was a superb winner. That is, until he lost. Losing was blasphemous. Bingham's fall to Val Wilkie rendered him an apostate, at least in his own mind. Bingham's defeat at the Yale meet also deflated the hype around his intercollegiate competition with Ted Meredith. No one expected Harvard or any other squad to overcome the better-balanced Cornell team. Ted Meredith of the University of Pennsylvania toppled Bill Barron of Harvard, not Bingham, at the tape. The newspapers ran a superb image of Ted bowling past Barron, arms extended to clear himself from the pack. The journalists in light derbies stationed on the green inside track, one with a thick mustache like Theodore Roosevelt's, focused squarely on Meredith. A step behind Barron was a University of Michigan runner Phil Jansen taking it all in. Bill Bingham was still farther back on the left side, his vision obscured by the traffic of runners in front of him. He came in fifth, crushed, just behind Wilkie of Yale.[83]

* * *

Bingham spent the summer on a ranch in an unincorporated section of Wyoming, tutoring aspiring young school-age cowboys in lessons that had little bearing on their rural lives. The boys appreciated Bingham's Christian teachings but saw no use for his tutoring in reading and mathematics. What they wanted from Bill was reports of the Boston Braves. During the first half of the baseball season, in spring, George Stallings's Braves ranked at the very bottom of the National League. Summer changed things. The Braves rarely lost from then on. No one knew what it was that had jump-started the Miracle Braves, but stellar pitching and solid all-around play by middleinfielders Johnny Evers and Rabbit Maranville carried Boston to the pennant. "Everyone wanted to talk about the Braves with me when they discovered I came from Boston," remembered Bingham. "Cowboys," he remarked with irony, "almost worship the Braves."[84] The local newssheets chronicled the sensational climb, and Bill was about the only man within many miles who could read the columns to the anxious children. Bingham departed Wyoming certain that the youngsters "know as much about the team as the fans right here in Boston." Bill started back eastward before the end of the season. How the children learned and received the excitement of the Braves' World Series triumph over Connie Mack's favored Athletics is unknown.

Bill started out his third campaign at Harvard revived. If the Braves could do it, then why not him? Bill Barron had graduated, elevating Bingham to relay anchor. In that pivotal position, Bill engineered a comeback, putting on a full head of steam after the second turn to defeat the Massachusetts Institute of Technology. He strode in front with three inches to spare before the tape to help Harvard retain bragging rights among the Cambridge-area intellectuals. Bill was also pleased by the presence of Westmore Wilcox Jr. on the track team. Wilcox also played baseball and football at Harvard, where he proved his speediness. Wilcox handled the quarter-mile run, leaving a delighted Bingham to reserve his full attention for the half-mile race. In one early-season 880-yard contest, in fact, Bill jumped ahead of eight racers in the final lap of the Irish-American games in Boston, another victory to add to his collection. Bingham made a similar comeback against Cornell as well. He did not need to employ much drama to defeat Yale.[85]

But Bill could not beat Ted. First it was the Harvard-Pennsylvania relay in February 1915. Bingham grabbed the baton a second or two behind Meredith at the armory grounds in Hartford, Connecticut. The head start was enough for the Red and Blue racer. The standout runners were even until the final turn, but the steel-legged Quaker crossed the line an inch ahead of the Harvard anchor. The reports credited Bingham's dogged effort for pushing the "fastest man in America" to lead Penn to a collegiate relay record. That was no help to Bill, but he did generate some optimism from the defeat. Bingham had outrun Meredith on the last lap, something that he prayed would portend in the head-to-head arrangement in May.[86]

Two months later, Bill aimed at redemption at the intercollegiate meet in Philadelphia. It had rained earlier in the morning, but no one was claiming that the track was slow. Bill ran well, at first. He let Meredith set the pace and passed the Pennsylvanian on a turn. Bingham led for the first three-quarters of the half-mile race. Then Meredith caught him. His view of Meredith on the brink stunned Bill, causing him to lose all his speed. He ended up crossing the finish line in seventh. His explanation for the dispiriting showing was colored by self-resentment. "It was not in me to run in a race like that today."[87]

Bill was crestfallen. The sportswriters had anticipated much better competition from him. Some prophesied that the Harvard man would finally overcome Ted Meredith. Before the meet, the columnists had rehearsed the two runners' qualifications. Bingham stood at five feet and ten inches, slightly taller than Meredith. Both weighed about 155 pounds, but the Penn star seemed to carry more of it in his powerful shoulders and thighs. The reports reviewed Meredith's bolting speed and Bingham's genius in reigniting his second effort. Most of all, commented one writer, "both men are alike in being able to respond in a drive."[88]

Ted Meredith knew all this. To a journalist, Meredith confidently confessed that, while he had no real rival in the quarter-mile—he won that, too—he had considerable concern for the longer race. "Bill Bingham of Harvard," he said, identifying his only formidable challenger. "I have run 'em all, but you never know when you have Bingham beaten. He is the gamest runner I have ever tackled on the cinder path."[89] Meredith had studied up on Bingham's running style and very deliberately held some speed in his reserves to surge forward in the final stretch. They hailed it as a victory for Ted Meredith's brains over Bill Bingham's legs, a turn of phrase that irritated all aspects of Bill's Christian manhood, the core sensitivities of most of Harvard's young scholars.[90]

* * *

Bill did not preserve the newspaper clippings of the miserable loss to Ted Meredith. The sole mention of the unhappy affair in his beloved scrapbook is in a six-page letter from his old teammate, Bill Barron. Barron, now a partner in a major investment firm, had called Bingham's resident hall to offer proper congratulations on becoming captain of the Crimson's track-and-field team. Bill was in no mood to receive calls, and so Barron sent along his felicitations by mail. "You are the type of man that we are all proud to know," the former Crimson captain reminded Bingham. Barron sensed that Bill was wallowing. He sympathized, explaining that he had gone "through exactly the same unpleasant experience. Running fairly well on Friday, only to find on Saturday that I was hopelessly not there." Barron urged his friend to "absolutely obliterate" the recollection of the race and think forward, or at least "try reading this note over, Bill."[91]

The trouble was extreme expectations. Harvard's honor code was by this time tightly fastened to notions of winning. The change had much to do with football and Percy Haughton. In eight gridiron campaigns, Coach Haughton's record was 71-7-5. He racked up three of those seven losses during a final lackluster 1916 season. During Haughton's reign, the journalist Grantland Rice announced that "Boston was the sporting capital of America."[92] A collection of sportswriters crowned Haughton's 1910, 1912, and 1913 Crimson teams "national champions." More important still, Haughton's Crimson surrendered but twice to Yale.[93]

Harvard and Yale faced off at the close of their seasons in November. The two campuses still call it "The Game."[94] The railroads marked the date and made sure to arrange for many more railcars on the weekend of a Harvard-Yale contest. So crucial was The Game that the Yale athletes sometimes resorted to heaven for support in the annual tilt. In 1907, on the morning of the Harvard game, quarterback Tad Jones woke up "stale," far too weak to perform against the Crimson. "I had no strength," he told of his Samson-like experience. "I went to my room and prayed for it, and when I came down ready for the game, my strength had returned, and I was ready to play hard."[95] Other young men appealed to the devil instead. "Come around this end, you yellow dog," the Elis were wont to razz the Crimson quarterbacks, "and I'll break your neck in eight pieces."[96]

Haughton was neither pious nor diabolical. He figured that the reason past Harvard elevens under Bill Reid underperformed against the Elis had more to do with nervousness than a dearth of Crimson talent. He therefore developed a ritual to ease his men into the finale. He arranged for the team to relocate on the Thursday prior to the Yale competition, "planted in some secluded spot where we were all alone," recalled a former Crimson footballer. If the game was to be held in Cambridge, then Haughton would rent a block of rooms at "some country club anywhere within 25 or 30 miles of there to be away from the tense atmosphere that always pervades the student body." If scheduled at New Haven, Haughton had a preferred spot in New London, a town "sleepy enough to lull one to sleep in the closing days of autumn." Harvard arranged for a troupe of vaudeville actors or some other distracting entertainment for Friday night, designed to keep the players' "minds occupied."[97]

That was as personable as Haughton got. His on-field demeanor was cruel. At practice, Harvard's coach was a "tyrant and drove, cursed and manhandled players."[98] In coaches meetings, Haughton did not let anyone share an idea that hadn't been raised with him first. He preferred to remain aloof from all persons associated with the Harvard eleven. Everyone agreed that Percy Haughton was a polarizing figure, and in complicated ways. "He was feared, admired, and loved," said LeBaron Russell Briggs. "There was nothing neutral about him and his feelings were expressed either in friendship or hostility."[99]

Haughton's military-type discipline created an awe-inspiring spirit about him. Some students resented it. "A few players hated Haughton but a big majority liked and respected him," recalled Eddie Mahan. "Personally, I hated him at first but got to like him and found him a good friend."[100]

Harvard's football warriors based their manhood on the outcome of games, a validation of the brute and hard work displayed on the field. Some still preferred to talk about honor. "If Jesus had gone to the Yale-Harvard game I think he would have much admired the Spartan courage of these men," once sermonized Reverend A. B. Williams to the five hundred women and men sitting in the pews of his East Boston church. The Harvard-advantaged affair defined muscular Christianity for all of Cambridge. Jesus "would have been glad to find that the players were not all tutti frutti, chocolate éclair, champagne Charlie boys," concluded Williams.[101] In 1914, Harvard vanquished Yale by a tally of 36–0. It was the first game played at the newly constructed Yale Bowl in New Haven, and halfback Eddie Mahan decidedly owned it on that occasion.[102]

Eddie Mahan captained the 1915 football team. That squad was not as perfect as Haughton's team had been one year prior. Eddie blamed himself for a midseason blundering bout against the Cornell Big Red at Harvard Stadium. Chuck Barrett was Cornell's best player—one of the best in the nation, actually—and punished Harvard early in the contest, converting a Mahan fumble into a touchdown for the Big Red. That was about it for Barrett, however. In the third quarter, he crashed into Mahan. Barrett was knocked out for the remainder of the tilt. Mahan stayed in the game. The wobbly Crimson footballer fumbled multiple times and threw an interception when he lined up at quarterback. The Cornell defense held up and prevented Mahan's offense on each drive, stymieing a comeback attempt. The Big Red capitalized just enough, shutting down Mahan and Harvard 10–0.[103]

It was Harvard's first loss in 1,442 days. Reggie Brown, Harvard's star scout, faulted Haughton for reducing the play selection to just three or four formations. The Harvard strategist, Lorin Deland, had recommended otherwise but Haughton wished to conceal something so that Princeton's spies would not be able to obtain a better handle for the Tigers' upcoming bout with the Crimson. Haughton planned to do the very same thing against Pennsylvania State. Deland asked Haughton to reconsider for the Cornell game. Brown reluctantly sided with Haughton, since both men "did not think Cornell much superior to Penn State."[104] As usual, Deland, the chess master and military scholar, turned out to be right.

The more practical journalists sympathetically offered that "Harvard was merely due" for a loss.[105] Mahan, however, blamed himself. He cried after the loss, consoled by Haughton. Winning was everything. Mahan had abided by the dictates of muscular Christianity: he played hard though injured. But that was no longer how Harvard judged its footballers. Haughton reminded Mahan of his many other victories and individual performances. Yet Eddie knew better. Haughton himself had preached far too much about victories and undefeatedness for Mahan to reorient his perspective. "I wish to goodness I could go back and play just one game over," reflected Mahan shortly after graduation. "The score of that game will haunt me all my life long. This game has been a nightmare to me ever since. Every time I think of football that game is one of the first things that comes to mind."[106] The defeat stung Haughton and Pooch Donovan, who trained the football team each autumn before the track season started in the winter. The weekend of the Cornell debacle was the most downcast Pooch had ever been.[107]

The loss redoubled Mahan's and the rest of Harvard's resolve, their conviction to win. "We know what it is to be licked," Captain Mahan told his teammates, "and we'll be damned if we'll be licked again." The Crimson decidedly beat Penn State, Princeton, and Brown.[108]

Then the Yale game. The Elis weren't very good. "Yale has had a poor team all season, but they have come back now with a rush," cautioned Haughton at a rally attended by 1,500 undergraduates and alumni. "They're all right now, you can bet. Football is a haphazard game, in which it doesn't take such a great break in fortune to win or lose a game," Haughton reasoned, no doubt still sore over Cornell. "No two games are the same." Mahan, suddenly taciturn, backed up his coach. "About this Yale game, I want to say that we haven't won it yet."[109]

A late-season return by Bob Bingham generated some optimism at Yale. The Yale faculty diplomatically called his absence a matter of "scholarship restrictions," having to do with poor classroom performance. The younger Bingham brother was a very fine athlete, the leader of the Exeter football team that had broken the Andover hex the year after Eddie Mahan had graduated from there. Bob chose Yale rather than enter Harvard because, quite reasonably, he wished to "make good without any help." The fleet halfback desired to "win honor and glory by his own ability and not because his brother is a famous runner."[110] He wished to be a self-made man just as Bill had been. Bill's friends, understanding quite well that he rarely pushed his religion on anyone, liked to claim that the only evangelizing Bingham did was a failure: to convince Bob to come to Harvard. Yale Coach Tom Shevlin badly needed Bob Bingham back. He had contended sometime before then, on several occasions, that Percy Haughton wasn't all that much. Shevlin apparently, to quote from the man himself, "didn't give a rap" about Harvard's vaunted system. The Yale man held that football was truly a game of warrior men engaged on a gridiron battlefield. No system or series of formations could overcome physical preparedness and a genuine passion to win.[111]

Both campuses delighted in paraphrasing Abraham Lincoln, crying that the "house of Bingham was divided this afternoon."[112] Bill was head cheerleader for the Crimson, and after Bob fumbled and surrendered possession to Harvard, Bill made it clear that he aligned himself with his fellow fans rather than family. Bill cheered loudly for Mahan and the rest of the team, exuding a "boundless joy."[113]

Mahan starred and got some help along the way, particularly from his understudy, Ralph Horween. At Francis Parker in Chicago, Ralph was a bruising runner but without all that much speed. That model did not fit well within the Haughton system. Harvard preferred smaller and speedier halfbacks to line up behind the quarterback and take the pitch downfield. But, after a decent tryout from Horween, Haughton offered Ralph a spot on the squad. The coach figured that Horween could be a fine backup fullback and an above-average kicker. In practices, Haughton directed Ralph to dropkick and punt with Eddie Mahan, the best of Haughton's prodigies.

In time, the underclassman's stock climbed. Haughton and his junior coaches had to admit that Ralph Horween was the "best line bucker Harvard has" and "can be developed satisfactorily."[114] Until the Yale game, Horween mostly appeared on the field as a substitute, as in the irrelevant final minutes against the overmatched Carlisle Indians, who wound up losing to the Crimson, 29–7. Against Yale, Haughton surprised the Elis by bringing in Ralph to play on the offensive line. He dropped many Yale defenders on that November afternoon, bowling them over so that Mahan had clear lanes to do his damage. In one of the more sensational plays of the game, Horween played the decoy. Harvard quarterback Don Watson faked a pass to Ralph, who sold Yale a bill of goods for a hefty price. Horween swept toward the sideline, barreling forward in search of an angle to move upfield. Meanwhile, Watson faked another throw to All-American Dick King, who played the charlatan on the other flank. The Yale defenders darted to both sidelines, figuring that tackling both Horween and King would cut down the insurrection. In fact, Eddie Mahan, who started off behind everyone in position to boot a dropkick, held onto the football, claiming for himself a clear lane up the middle for the third touchdown of the occasion. The reports gave Horween's chicanery all the credit for the sensational score. In all, Mahan tallied four touchdowns. Harvard won, 41–0.[115]

Bill Bingham led a happy throng of Harvard men in a snake dance under the goalposts. The Yale men endured watching the rite of triumph, the penalty for representing the losing team. Bingham started an urgent call for Haughton to reappear from the clubhouse. It was the greatest onslaught against Yale, at the hands of the Crimson or otherwise. Haughton had been more than a little irked by the Yale coach's earlier comments about the former's contribution to Harvard's winning culture. Later, Haughton wrote an elaborate essay, detailing precisely how his efforts to cultivate discipline and toughness had factored into Harvard's dismantling of the Elis. In the immediate aftermath, however, he was too giddy to gloat. "Well, just now I haven't much to say," began Haughton, mounted on the stadium's terrace railing. "This is the happiest moment of my life, and that as I haven't had a chance to congratulate Eddie Mahan yet, I think I'll hurry right in and do so."[116] Haughton then disappeared into the locker room. He extended his hand to Mahan, an honorable farewell after three years of winning varsity service.

* * *

For Bill Bingham, Ted Meredith was the football equivalent of Yale. That his track mates voted Bill captain after the end of his junior season at Harvard was no solace. The campus newspaper praised him. "There is no questioning the fact that Bill will make a good leader of the Crimson forces. He has the personality, the track ability and the knowledge of how to get the best out of his men."[117] Dean Briggs, by now a full convert to Harvard running, begged Bingham to "please take my hearty congratulations on your captaincy and my best wishes for the track team."[118] Harvard alumni in high standing sent along their good wishes, promising Bill that "you will appreciate more keenly than you possibly can at present how much Harvard has done for you."[119]

It was an open secret that Bill was hurting. He was overwhelmed in disappointment after losing so middlingly to the Quaker sprinter. In private correspondence, the editor of Harvard's alumni magazine pleaded with Bill to stop focusing so drastically on the defeat. "Don't take things too seriously," he pleaded. "It is evident that human nature does not turn against a man simply because he cannot rise to the greatest of heights all of the time."[120]

Bill thrived on being good at all things. It was precisely what had accorded him such wide appeal. He was an everyman, and therefore a peerless self-made man, even in comparison with Harvard heroes like his roommate, Eddie Mahan. By most accounts, Mahan was the very greatest football star to don Harvard's crimson colors. All told, that meant that Mahan was rated slightly above Charles Brickley and, of course, the legend himself, Percy Haughton. Eddie Mahan, then, was better than anyone else at a very specific role at Harvard: football star. Either William James or George Santayana—maybe Ralph Waldo Emerson, if one framed him that way—was Harvard's utmost philosopher. In his moment, however, Bill Bingham transcended a particular type.

This everyman trait required more than a modicum of courage. A couple of examples reflect this. Once, Bingham joined the other Crimson athletes in rapping the crew team for their elitism at the expense of hard play. Many undergrads were said to have secretly rooted against the Crimson crewmen. The crew was often defeated by six to ten boat lengths because it was "composed of eight of the finest men in the university," Bill commented sarcastically.[121] His remark insinuated that the team was made up of Gold Coasters, frivolous sons of millionaires. No one besides Bingham had deigned to state the general opinion for the record. "This is just the spirit that we undergraduates interested in Harvard sports resent," announced Bingham to a room full of fellow students, at a meeting intended to address a very different matter. "If the crew is to be composed of men who embody the principles of fellowship, and whose rowing ability is of secondary importance, it should not row on the water as a Harvard crew, but as a crew of good fellows." With his word, the Harvard rowing team was reformed and repopulated with "better" men. The complacent Brahmins were replaced by talented athletes capable of upholding, as Bill put it, "those principles carried out in other Harvard sports."[122]

Others liked to remember the embarrassed expression on Bingham's face when he had refused to accept a drink at a club meeting. The affair was for one of the elite fraternities, attended by many Harvard men—students and alumni—whose social networks and net worth could open much for Bill's future business prospects. "Faithful Bill," however, refused alcohol on social and religious grounds. Bingham had figured that he and his piety had effectively surrendered his social capital among that collection of significant men. He was therefore relieved and surprised to spend the subsequent morning surrounded by delegates of that group, praising Bingham for his resolve, wishing that they too had done likewise.

These were the foundational myths of Bill Bingham's Harvard fame, rehearsed time and again in the autumn of 1915, Bill's final year at Harvard. Bingham had spent the preceding summer in rural Texas, preferring an escape not much different from his Wyoming sojourn, far away—geographically and culturally—from the white-collar-tarnished conversations that he routinely heard in all sections of Harvard Yard. He admired the rough-and-tumble men who raised cattle and were altogether ignorant of society's latest trends. Bingham believed competitive sports was a helpful approximation of that spirit. It certainly was not the real McCoy, however.

The decidedly un-Harvard experience did not diminish his standing in Cambridge. To the contrary, Harvard seniors voted Bill first marshal at the forthcoming commencement exercises. Once again, Bill outdueled Eddie Mahan, 276–259.[123] The recognition was considered the highest honor at the graduation ceremonies. The Boston newspapers reported that the vote was the closest in many years and supposed under a headline that read "Bill Bingham a Self-Made Man" that his candor and background had pushed him above Mahan.[124] There was at that time a festering incredulity about claims of "successful" and "self-made" men. Critics charged that "success" had been altogether detached from how Puritans such as Cotton Mather had described it—in terms of an attainment of Heaven-bound virtue and good Protestant character. "The truth [is] that success is the natural reward of industry," complained one writer, aware that this rhetoric suggested more about the nostalgia of the erstwhile Gilded Age's rapid economic growth and entrepreneurialism than the half-promises of the Progressive Era and limited labor reforms. "This theory of success deceptively inculcates the idea that social conditions permit the rewards of industry to find their natural objects."[125] But for those associated with him, Bill Bingham seemed to restore the sacredness of the Protestant ethic. The press feted Bingham in the verbose subheadline, which stated, "Harvard's 1916 First Marshal, Class President and Track Team Captain is working his own way through college and has made a remarkable record as a leader and an athlete."[126]

Bingham appreciated the accolades. Judging the situation from his Lawrence upbringing and the muscular Christianity of his YMCA youth, the tribute amounted to the finest reputation he had hoped to procure. Nonetheless, winning had some time ago attached itself to Bingham's sense of worth. Bill's final year at Harvard was his last opportunity to vanquish Meredith. He had two chances: the team relay and the intercollegiate program that closed out the track season. Meredith's Penn squad, on the heels of several poor races, defeated Bingham's in the dual relay at New York's Madison Square Garden. Both team captains were positioned as anchors; Meredith received the baton several lengths behind Bingham. The Pennsylvania flier caught up and then let up a little, just as he had done the year prior. The maneuver sent Bingham into his full stride a moment before he would have liked. Meredith capitalized, finishing just ahead of Bingham. Bill fought for every inch on Harvard's behalf but ended it beaten.[127]

Bingham had one more opportunity. The forty-first intercollegiate competition was held at Harvard Stadium. The final contest of both Bingham's and Meredith's amateur running careers was observed by 15,000 spectators, an indicator that the young racers had done much to elevate their sport. Bingham pressed from the start, undesirous of Meredith controlling the tempo of the half-mile race. Bill hoped that the aggressive move would catch

Bill Bingham (first row, center) and Harvard's 1916 track team accomplished much during its season but could not defeat Pennsylvania and Ted Meredith. First published in *The H Book of Harvard Athletics, 1852–1922*, ed. John A. Blanchard (Cambridge, MA: Harvard University Press, 1923), 533.

Ted by surprise, knowing by now that the Penn man approached their races with studious research of Bill's tendencies. Meredith kept up, spurt for spurt. The other less-worthy racers trailed, the closest some eight yards behind. The pair were even at the quarter-mile mark. Neither man had ever galloped so strongly at the start. Bingham and Meredith crossed the tape together. Compelled to pick, the judges determined that Meredith's shoulder was the first human matter to pierce through the flimsy barrier. Both finished under the time of the prior record holder, Dave Caldwell of Cornell, who had set the standard several years before at 1 minute, 53⅖ seconds. Bingham's 1 minute, 53⅕ seconds was the best race of his career. Unfortunately for him, Meredith's 1 minute, 53 seconds even was the new college record. Bill would have been a world beater, all agreed, had it not been for Ted Meredith.[128]

Bingham had failed by his own standard only. Everyone else anticipated great things from Harvard's real-life Frank Merriwell. Some encouraged

Bingham to join the Boston Athletic association track squad. He pondered the possibility but ultimately felt far too ashamed to line up against the likes of Val Wilkie and Ted Meredith. The New York banker Thomas Lamont recommended that Bill join his firm at 23 Wall Street. Lamont, like Bingham, was an Exeter and Harvard alumnus—there's a library bearing his name on the southeast corner of the Harvard campus—and took an avid interest in Bingham's development at both institutions. Bill confided to Lamont that he wanted the "simple life" he had discovered in northeast Texas, just along the Oklahoma border. Bill was "quite sure that the rest of my life should be spent there." Lamont disagreed, informing Bingham that for a "man of your temperament and capacity for work, I think the chances are still wonderful"; if not with Lamont, then to "land something in Boston or in New York."[129] Bill was hardly eager to sit in an office. That was not the path of a self-made man, no matter how rich he could become. Bill participated in the June 1916 graduation rituals at Harvard College. He led 15,000 graduates and friends in cheers. He sat among them as Evan Howell Foreman, the designated class orator, praised the graduates for instilling a particular culture at Harvard. "We are now beating Yale simply from force of habit," boasted Foreman.[130] It was not Foreman's intention to slight Bingham. Bill knew that. Yet he could not help but experience the pain. The speech also reinforced Bingham's resolve to retreat to self-imposed exile in Paris, Texas, to work as a banker or maybe as a rancher.

Bill preserved some mementos from the commencement, such as a swatch of his sash and the ribbons bestowed on him as first marshal. He pasted them beside the last newspaper clipping on his running career. The sportswriter Howard Valentine wrote the final entry on Bingham the track runner in the sport pages. "Bill Bingham Is Through," the headline declared. "But for one factor," wrote Valentine, himself a former running standout before the epoch of Sheppard and Meredith. "Bingham would be hailed as a world beater, and that factor is James Edward Meredith."[131] The writer had meant for the syndicated column to applaud Bill's efforts. "Bingham's experience is a forceful illustration of the fierce competition that has brought the intercollegiate meet up to its present standard."[132] Instead, Bill glued it into his scrapbook like a mark of Cain. That intercollegiate standard was not Bill's measuring stick. In his own estimation, Bingham had failed to make good on all the expectations made for him. Shortly after graduation, Bill Bingham traveled Texasward. He had convinced himself that his new home was the "garden spot of the world."[133] But Bill knew his Bible far too well to believe that. Cain's family, after all, had been banished from the Garden of Eden.

CHAPTER FIVE

FOOTBALL, THE ULTIMATE WARGAME OF LIFE

All concerned plainly show the mental and physical stress
of the campaign, but a bond of sympathy is aroused wherein
the power of the will predominates. All gloom is discarded,
and in place of joy the mental attitude of the players is poised
between full recognition of the enemy's strength and a grim
determination to win.

—Percy D. Haughton, *Football and How to Watch It*, 116

Eddie Casey was the new dauphin prince of Harvard football. The Crimson had dispatched Eddie Mahan and Billy Murray to court Casey, then a student at Phillips Exeter. Princeton had also comprehended the "worth of a star" and sent their own Irish Catholic representatives to meet with the preparatory school prospect.[1] Similar Irish connections had formerly been relied on to lure Mahan, who possessed at one time a "predilection for Yale."[2] In Harvard's case, both young men sent to recruit Casey came from Natick, Massachusetts. Mahan was Harvard's greatest runner. Murray had played alongside Casey on the Natick High School's state champion team. Murray was a hard-running quarterback and Casey played a bruising halfback. The combination was supreme. In 1911, Murray and Casey had accounted for ten touchdowns in Natick High's 101–0 demolition of Wellesley High School.[3] In a span of four 1911 games, the Natick squad had accrued 282 points while shutting out their opponents.[4]

Casey's "two pals" managed to spirit him away from Princeton.[5] It was another win for Percy Haughton's Crimson in an age when Harvard did a lot of winning, even if that meant a break from several previously tightly held Harvard traditions: a loosened relationship with rival Yale and its further embrace of non-Protestant football prospects, for instance. Seen in the broader historical sweep, the change within the New England gentlemanly culture was rather radical. No one in Cambridge seemed to notice, however, amid all the Crimson's football triumphs.

The recruitment to Harvard had gone a lot better than the previous one to Andover. Casey's decision to prepare at Exeter had defied the attempts of both Murray and Mahan to convince Eddie to join them at Andover. In New Hampshire, Eddie Casey was part of a burgeoning juggernaut. The reports boasted that Casey and the Exonians "could compare with any college eleven to-day." In 1913, with Casey and under the leadership of Coach Tad Jones, Exeter defeated Billy Murray's Andover team, 59–0, avenging several years of misfortune, a fulfillment of Harlan Amen's dying wishes.[6] The following year, Casey's final campaign at Exeter, the Casey-captained team traveled to Andover's Brothers Field and vanquished their rivals, 78–7.[7] That Exeter team also ran over the freshman teams of Dartmouth, Harvard, Penn, Princeton, and Yale.[8]

The Harvard suitors were not denied by Eddie a second time. Natick prided itself on breeding the best stock for Crimson sports: the "cradle of gridiron heroes."[9] The Caseys and Mahans had grown up on Natick's East Street. The street stretched the length of two football fields. The Mahans lived on one side and the Caseys on the other. Pooch Donovan had set the precedence for Natick athleticism. The first football star was George Casey, the twelfth of Ellen and James Casey's fifteen children. George was seventeen months older than his brother Eddie, and there was a sibling between them. George and Eddie Casey learned to play football with Eddie Mahan. The future Harvard runner had played quarterback on the local high school team. The Caseys took their cues from Mahan. Eddie Casey lined up at receiver. George played halfback and was also responsible, from time to time, for catching passes from Mahan. George was not as smooth at football as his younger brother. Eddie Casey had a way of allowing the football to settle in his arms. George's method was more stilted. He waited for the throw and secured it with his fingers. This worked for George Casey, but in the process of controlling Mahan's hurls, George mangled the top digits of the second and third fingers on his hands. He departed Natick on a football scholarship at Boston College. George lettered in his sophomore season but his "meatgrindered" hands did not hold up for him in the upperclassmen stages of his college career.[10] Natick's Irish immigrants were therefore more honored in the college careers of Eddie Mahan and George Casey's nimbler younger brother.

Eddie Casey's admission to Harvard did not receive much attention from America's Irish Catholics. Then again, neither did Mahan's. Ten years earlier, the Catholic press had noted "four or five strongly Irish names among the list of the Harvard football players" and boasted that "great institutions of learning must have athletes and they know what race abounds in such."[11]

But in the 1910s, Catholic colleges had emerged as good competition for the erstwhile football powers. Georgetown, Boston College, and especially Notre Dame proved to their Catholic constituents that they could create their own parallel programs and compete against the very best. They could do this, as Knute Rockne, himself a convert to Catholicism, explained it, because their brand of football was transmitted "from God."[12] These schools and their football teams were "defenders of American Catholicism's honor."[13] Just as they had pushed for parish parochial schools instead of public schools, then, Catholic leaders stressed that Americanization did not have to be tantamount to assimilation. The Catholic way in the United States was to furnish its own institutions, bigger and better than the Protestant incarnations. Imbued with this moxie, the newspaper of the Diocese of Boston candidly complained about the "Callahans" and "Brickleys" who renounced Catholic colleges in favor of Harvard and Yale.[14]

George Casey took the Catholic route, settling in at Boston College. Eddie Casey did not follow suit. He enrolled in Harvard. Eddie overcame an injury-plagued season on the freshman squad, preparing in the autumn of 1916 to take over Mahan's vacant spot in the varsity lineup. Percy Haughton's Crimson material lacked experience. Just four upperclassmen, including Ralph Horween, had earned a coveted H, an emblem sewn onto a jacket or sweater that signaled participation in a game against rival Yale. The popular Casey was the "most important newcomer," someone the Harvard fans expected great things from.[15] He was crucial to the Crimson's pursuit of Harvard's new status: winning, especially against the Elis.

* * *

Harvard wanted to win. The school had grown accustomed to it. The college and its supporters recalled how "Harvard felt a certain loss of manhood in not winning a single football game with Yale in the eighties and only two in the nineties."[16] President Charles Eliot's crusade against football hadn't won everyone over, or even the majority of Harvard. Still, his opposition reminded others of the potential perils of overemphasis. In 1903, the head of the college's athletic committee, Ira Hollis, reviewed the campus culture and concluded that the drive to beat Yale and the Crimson's other rivals had taken a toll, that "we have succeeded in developing a war game wherein it is the business of each side to take every possible advantage."[17]

Harvard was let loose once A. Lawrence Lowell took over for Eliot. Harvard's longtime president did not care much for his successor. Appointed professor of Science and Government in 1898, Lowell had been a vocal critic of Eliot's pandering to the Brahmins. Eliot had separated himself from traditional New England thinking in some respects, but not in the ways that were important to Lowell. The opposition was quite unexpected, especially from the growing pool of Boston elites—rather than traditional scholars—who made up Harvard's faculty roster. Eliot had refused to furnish new dormitories, but Harvard's wealthiest sons were not at all keen on residing in outmoded facilities. More of them, then, took up residence in the fashionable Gold Coast lofts, away from the resident halls and the busyness of Harvard Yard. Lowell also blasted Harvard's curriculum. He had urged Eliot to compel students to focus on a major area of study, as undergraduates do today. Lowell was not the first to point out the pointlessness of Eliot's Harvard curriculum. "Better than a college education," recommended John D. Rockefeller, "is the training that a boy gets in the technical schools that have sprung up all over the country."[18] That Rockefeller still donated to Harvard was sufficient for Eliot, who, like many other New England patricians, paid no significant attention to the opinions of neophyte elites such as Rockefeller and his band of robber barons. Lowell despised the current educational climate at Harvard in which students progressed through college by enrolling in unchallenging introductory courses in a smattering of fields, never elevating the rigor of their coursework and reducing Harvard to a "faculty of larks and cinches."[19] Lowell knew about this condition better than most. His general course on US government registered more than four hundred students each year.

All this made Lowell something of a renegade among Boston's patricians. He was derived from one of New England's most authentic classes and castes. His ancestor, John Lowell, born in 1704, was the first of the Lowell clan to enter Harvard College. His son, also John, graduated from Harvard in 1760. George Washington himself appointed this Lowell to the District Court of Massachusetts. All told, A. Lawrence Lowell was sixth in an unbroken chain of Harvard graduates. Money was something taken for granted among the Lowells. His father, Augustus Lowell, was so wealthy that, when he died, "seven bonds of the treasurers of great corporations were found in his tins" that were otherwise unaccounted for in his ledgers.[20] His mother was a Lawrence, a family that traced itself to Sir Robert of Ashton Hall in Lancashire, England, allegedly knighted by King Richard I. Through marriage, Lowell was related to the most affluent classes and families such as the Higginsons, Bigelos, Cabots, Coolidges, and Roosevelts.

Lowell's pedigree made it impossible for Eliot to prevent Lowell's ascendance. Upon learning of Eliot's decision to step aside in 1909, one trustee frankly conjectured to another board member that this "means Lawrence

Lowell as President of Harvard."[21] Lowell kept his word about pulling back from Eliot's way of doing things at Harvard. He built four new freshman dormitories and abolished the patrician Gold Coast enclave: He forced all incoming students, regardless of social station, to live on campus on what was called the South Yard. Lowell also rearranged the courses of study at Harvard and applied rigorous structure, leaving alumni to complain, sometimes bitterly, about the scholastic expectations placed on their sons once they, like their fathers, matriculated at Harvard College.[22]

Lowell also undid much of Eliot's presidential managing of intercollegiate athletics. Lowell preferred to keep university presidents out of football rule negotiations, insisting that Percy Haughton always accompany him to meetings with the Yale and Princeton brass.[23] Yale's Arthur Hadley had insisted that, despite his affiliation with Walter Camp, he could not "delegate the responsibility regarding the safety of football." President Hadley wrote to President Lowell, "I sometimes find myself compelled to do things in a different way from that which is dictated. I am afraid that I know too much about football."[24]

Lowell wasn't an athletic ignoramus. In his Harvard athletic prime, Lowell was something of a track star. This was an image he liked to recall in his addresses, particularly to Harvard alumni. In 1875, Lowell had won the half-mile against Harvard's various nemeses. His best time was 2 minutes and 9 seconds, several steps slower than the eventual and more brilliant records achieved by Bill Bingham and Ted Meredith. Like those later runners, Lowell's "long legs and barrel chest and calculated breathing seem to have put him in a class by himself."[25] Yet Harvard's president did not care all that much about football, nor did he wish to govern it as an act of policing American culture.

But Lowell appreciated what the sport did for Harvard, how football ticket sales provided sufficient revenue to support all the other athletic programs and then some. He was also aware of the perception that the "youth of America is attracted to a university which has a strong football team."[26] Lowell found the notion nonsensical and would have been relieved that it was an undergraduate at Illinois and not at Harvard who had uttered that "sports supply that college spirit in this country which at European institutions of learning is made up in atmosphere."[27] Yet Lawrence Lowell countenanced football better than Charles Eliot had because he was frankly more pragmatic about college life. Lowell invited Yale's Hadley to Harvard to sit with him in Soldiers Field when Yale was expected to win. Sport in the abstract, he figured, was good for the Harvard students as well. Before Henry Lee Higginson donated the land for the stadium, Lowell told the philanthropist that athletics was one way to ensure that "heroism is developed."[28]

The support for Soldiers Field anticipated a much more public turn against Eliot. Harvard's athletic committee approved a plan to construct Harvard Stadium on Soldiers Field. Eliot had refused to fundraise for the horseshoe-shaped ferroconcrete structure. But the alumni offered money and the engineering faculty provided the designs, which evoked the Greek amphitheaters and Roman stadia. Even if some leaders regretted the high costs to build the sports complex, most of the supporters were glad to see Harvard Stadium feted in architectural journals and magazines as the first such sports arena on a university campus and a magnificent collegewide effort. It symbolized just how out of step Charles Eliot had found himself around Harvard Yard at the twilight of his presidential tenure.[29]

Lowell made it plain that he did not wish to continue Eliot's campaign against sport. In a casual rebuke of Eliot's stance on the matter, Lowell once expressed to a crowd of alumni that "my own experience is that athletics do not seriously interfere with study; that the men who play on teams and do not work would do the same in any case." According to Lowell, "the games are a means for the alumni to enjoy themselves."[30] Lowell's was not the high praise of sport that Theodore Roosevelt might have offered—Lowell didn't like him either—but it did indicate his willingness to tolerate football as long as he was correct in his assessment, that it would not disturb the other portions of Harvard life.

Timing also mattered. Lowell did not need to engage in the philosophical tug-of-war that Eliot had engaged in. In the latter's time, scholars had liked to debate the merits of sport in terms of morals and honor, words that meant a great deal to Harvard teachers and students. That was by now a bygone era. Gone were judicious learned supports of college football such as those of William James, who died in 1910, and George Santayana, who retired in 1911.

Lowell's speeches did not confirm to Harvard undergraduates that he was in their corner on football. They remained "uncertain of his attitude," claimed Lowell's biographer, "toward intercollegiate sports."[31] But Lowell took the path of least resistance on nearly any matter that resided beyond his core principles. On the basis of this posturing, and despite Lowell's harshness toward Brahmin elitism, Harvard College, "in the eyes of the rest of the country, more than ever, identified with Boston's Back Bay."[32] (The Back Bay was the Boston neighborhood most closely associated with New England's "old money.") Lowell preferred to align with his rich alumni rather than antagonize them. The Harvard collegians ought to have noticed the fact. Lowell removed himself from the politics surrounding football, leaving Percy Haughton and his disciples to conjure up a Yale-like culture of winning above all else. Eddie Mahan had accomplished so much of this for Haughton and Harvard. Eddie Casey, the next one up, was supposed to do the same.

* * *

The commotion around Eddie Casey's promotion to varsity from the freshman eleven stirred up comparisons between the fleet backer and Mahan. Sportswriters opined that Casey possessed a "Mahan style" of shifting in the open field and reversing course in search of a running lane. Like Mahan before him, Eddie Casey was "rated as one of the hardest men on the team to down."[33] Both halfbacks had a knack for "skirting the ends," to race to the edge of the field, then to motor down the sideline toward the goal. In preseason drills, Casey "showed up well" and "handled himself like a veteran."[34]

Some pundits supposed that, on an evaluation of running alone, Eddie Casey was the "equal if not the superior of the departed Mahan."[35] He did things that no one else had tried on a football field. Casey weighed just 155 pounds, far slighter than other Haughton running prodigies. To compensate for his size, Eddie spun in place to whirl past the tackler. Galloping toward a defender, Casey timed his arm extension just right, to stiff-arm the opposing footballer to the ground. He also had a talent for catching passes, a skill cultivated on Natick's East Street that forced Coach Haughton to diversify his conservative running-heavy playbook. Casey had an instinct for the aerial pass, able to "catch the ball on the run," sometimes one-handed, then "continue to speed without slowing up to fix the ball."[36]

An accompanying football intuition made Eddie something of a wunderkind on defense. Casey could not tackle, at least not with his arms. He had sustained a badly injured shoulder participating in tackling drills on the Harvard freshman squad and could not stretch his arm on defense to corral a ball carrier. The defect might have retired a regular athlete from the gridiron, but the shoulder malady did not impair Casey's offensive play, which was superior and badly needed. Players had to remain on the field for offense and defense, since the rules approved substitutions between quarters, not between downs. To keep his place in the lineup, Casey developed a defensive motion called "Indianizing." Indianizing meant that to stop an offensive player, Casey lunged his body across the runner's legs, upending his forward progress and forcing the offensive player to the ground. The timing and angling had to be precise. Casey rarely missed his target. Princeton's Bill Roper hung an image of Eddie Casey's full-body hurl in his locker rooms to inspire his own eleven to perform their own mental calculations of speed and contact. The caption underneath Roper's poster read "The Perfect Play."[37]

The comparisons between Mahan and Casey had also taken place back in Natick. "I couldn't let old man Mahan have anything on me," James Casey narrated about his son's rising stock. "We have fifteen children each, and now with my Eddie proving to be as good a football player as his Eddie, I guess we're even."[38]

Others thought they knew better. "Casey is not the valuable man Mahan was, because he cannot kick."[39] Eddie Mahan was a very fine dropkicker and punter, a skill he had learned from his Harvard backfield predecessor, Charles Brickley. In Haughton's system, the offense liked to keep options open, to punt or attempt a field goal if the defense was unprepared. An unexpected punt could sail and bounce a great distance without someone assigned to receive it. The football could travel from one goal line to the other, pinning the opposition deep in their own territory, saddled with far too much field to march through in a passing-cautious era of college football. The strategy afforded Mahan with contingencies upon receiving the ball, leaving the other team fully unsure about how to defend him. Eddie Casey freely admitted that Mahan "had everything in all departments of the game."[40]

Percy Haughton cajoled Brickley and Mahan to return to campus and tutor Casey in kicking drills. But kicking was not Eddie's genius. He had an "unusually short stubby foot."[41] Casey resigned to always trail his friend Mahan. "When I went back to receive the ball, no matter what motions I might have made to give the semblance of getting off a punt," Casey recalled of his own limitations, "the opposition always knew that I couldn't kick one."[42]

Haughton was determined to keep a viable kicker on the field at all times. He lined Ralph Horween beside Casey on most downs. Ralph did not feature the qualities that Haughton preferred for his backfield stock. Horween was plenty capable of "bull-like rushes" and was equipped with "powerful shoulders" designed to tear "hole after hole" in the defensive line.[43] Haughton appreciated Horween's talent. Ralph was a "heavy man."[44] At 179 pounds, Horween's weight compared with that of the men along the offensive line. Haughton favored lining up two runners near the quarterback like the Mahans and Caseys, who could break loose for a large gain. Haughton also recognized that Ralph's defense was dubious.[45] Nonetheless, he was the best kicker on the squad after Mahan graduated.[46] He therefore found a permanent place in the Harvard backfield beside Casey the halfback and Billy Murray the quarterback.

Harvard underwhelmed during that 1916 campaign, but only because success, more than ever, was defined by victories. The expectation was just not very sustainable, especially after Brickley and then Mahan graduated.

The Crimson lost to Yale, unseated by Coach Tad Jones. Jones, it turned out, had a knack for football redemption. Three years prior, Jones had, with Eddie Casey in the backfield, broken Exeter's losing streak against Andover and was determined to accomplish much of the same for his alma mater in New Haven. Jones was the same Yale quarterback who had, in the pre-Haughton era, prayed for the strength to vanquish Harvard. He had been successful back then, too. The defeat to the Elis in the season finale was enough to spoil an otherwise successful Crimson season. Harvard never did capture the usual rhythm of a Haughton-coached team. "Poor Old Harvard," as one commentator phrased it, performed sluggishly against Colby College, winning 10–0, in the season's opening game.[47] Two weeks later, the Crimson lost, 7–3, to Tufts. Harvard had boasted a forty-one-year stretch of undefeated football against its Tufts neighbors in nearby Somerville. Haughton's eleven rebounded in a mighty romp of North Carolina, 21–0 and then avenged Eddie Mahan and the prior year's squad by dealing a 23–0 shutout of Cornell.

The Cornell game raised the nation's attention on Eddie Casey. Since there was no radio broadcast, the newspaper reports described his long touchdown run, how he broke through the line of scrimmage by dodging two or three Cornell defenders and then slipped past another four men on his ascent to the end zone. On another play, Casey spun around "no less than six or seven Cornell tacklers." The sportswriters on hand did their darnedest to convey Casey's brilliant change-of-pace running, how he swayed his body to evade the defense and then knocked down another defensive back with a straight arm into the fellow's chin. Cornell managed to cut Casey down just before the goal line but were far too exhausted to push back Ralph Horween on the ensuing play, a plunging touchdown to seal the victory for Old Harvard. Casey and Horween sat out the final quarter of the contest.[48] Afterward, Haughton publicly offered Horween a congratulatory handshake, an "unprecedented proceeding for the stoic Haughton so early in the season."[49]

The accolades were forthcoming. The newspaper writers anointed Eddie Casey the "best halfback in the game." He "doesn't crush the line like Mahan or Brickley," but Casey's "peculiar twisting motion baffles tacklers." "The Cornellians," it was reported, "are of the belief that he has a double jointed frame."[50] Ralph also garnered attention, particularly after the Princeton game. The best team Harvard had faced off against all season, Princeton made things rather intolerable for Billy Murray. The Crimson quarterback fumbled several times, a recurrent feature of his play that had rendered him something of a culprit and hindered the Harvard team all season long.[51] Horween covered for the beleaguered Murray, delivering several long-distance punts, and booting a field goal for the game's only score.[52]

Yale mattered most. Neither Haughton nor Casey was present in Cambridge when Brown University and Fritz Pollard lined up against Harvard one week after the victory against Princeton. The Crimson pair had traveled to New Haven with Harvard scouting expert Reggie Brown to observe the Elis. The assignment was part of a standard strategy for Haughton, who liked to rest his starters in the season's final stretch and focus on Yale. Brown alumni routinely complained that they would "prefer to see Haughton's first-string players used against us, but so long as substitutes are sufficient to 'turn the trick' for Harvard, we do not see that Brown has adequate reason for complaint."[53] In this instance, however, the absences left the Crimson reeling against the All-American Pollard, but Harvard's loss was a consequence, collateral damage, of its determination to keep something in reserve in order to defeat its archrival.[54]

Scouting and psychological gamesmanship sometimes started quite early. Eddie Casey had traveled to Connecticut a few months earlier, before the season opened. Several of the Yale footballers had invited him to a private club in New Haven. The goal was to shake Casey's confidence. It was an odd display of a culinary contest of masculine sensibilities. Yale's Tim Callahan ordered a slab of steak. The waiter asked the brawny lineman how he would like the meat prepared. "Raw and ruddy, please!" responded Callahan.

Captain Cupe Black ordered next. "Bring mine running with gore!"

"And how will you have your steak, Mister Casey?" asked the waiter. Casey feigned a look of surprise by the carnal production.

"Don't bother to do any carving," answered the Harvard man. "Just run the steer in here and I'll take a cut at him as he goes by." The Elis then dropped the theatrics and ordered their meals in a more conventional fashion. Casey would not be intimidated.[55]

The Yale Bowl was filled with fans on November 25. "Gentlemen!" thundered Coach Tad Jones to his players in the locker room while 77,000 fans waited in the boxes and bleachers outside. "You are now going to play football against Harvard. Never again in your whole life will you do anything so important."[56]

Jones knew just how to contain the former Exeter halfback. He had purchased better equipment for practice. He had also brought with him to New Haven George Connors, Bill Bingham's track coach, from Exeter to improve the Elis conditioning. The two men had insisted that all varsity players needed to stop smoking, at least during the season. This was Connors's way of introducing "stamina" and "stay" to the football vernacular. All autumn long, Jones had abused his Eli charges with endless series of drills designed to produce more disciplined tackling to cage the allusive Casey.[57] The Harvard-Yale game proved Jones's prescience. The so-called Crimson Crash rushed twenty-two times and gained just forty-five yards, suffering a broken nose for his effort.[58] Casey's sole highlight did not count for Harvard. In the second period, Eddie slipped into a hole in the defense and skirted to the left side of the field. He twisted clear of three defenders and then sidestepped two other Yale tacklers. Casey raced seventy yards for a touchdown, leaving behind him a pile of diving Yale tacklers.

The crowd broke into pandemonium. The Yale devotees shrieked in horror. The Bostonians cheered with tremendous elation. No one could hear the umpire's whistle as Casey galloped toward the goal line. Referee David Fultz then halted the volume, explaining to both teams that he had called a holding penalty, negating Casey's score. Eddie's run "would have been immortal in Harvard football." Instead, the play was "converted into a mere incident of a hectic game."[59]

Yale won, 6–3. It was New Haven's first conquest at Soldiers Field in five years. There was "no question about the Jones machine doing such a stunt good and properly in the big game."[60] Eddie Casey lamented that too much was placed on him and his fine talent for catching the long passes. "We used long and longer forward passes, even in our own half of the field, in order to produce a scoring play. Anything went—anything by which we could get a touchdown and win the game, for a touchdown would surely win it."[61] "In all the games which I remember," wrote Percy Haughton, "I do not recall a more disastrous penalty."[62] Yet Haughton offered no alibi for the "disastrous season."[63] To Walter Camp, the Harvard coach conceded that the Crimson's dominance over the Elis was "due to a great measure to Yale's unsound methods. But this year it was Greek meeting Greek—and the 'Big Fellow' won."[64]

* * *

The Yale defeat was Haughton's last football game patrolling the Harvard sideline. Sportswriters figured that Haughton, despite the loss, was in good shape to restock his Crimson squad. None other than Grantland Rice reported the consensus opinion that, led by "Eddie Casey, Ralph Horween and Horween's kid brother, who is a star, the backfield will be up to the Mahan and Brickley standard."[65] Arnold Horween had earned a reputation on the bruising freshman team. The younger Horween weighed 198 pounds, even heavier than Ralph and than half of the Crimson offensive linemen.[66] Arnold was the freshman standout, "said to be better than his more illustrious brother." He was president of his class and popular at local dances. On the football field, Arnie ran with much more speed than Ralph and "shines especially as a defensive player."[67] Powered by Horween in the backfield, the

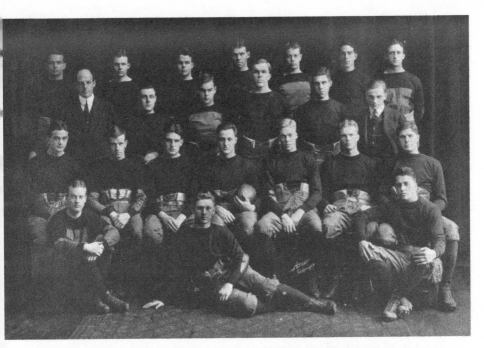

The 1916 Harvard Crimson team was led by coach Percy Haughton (third row, on the left) and featured the running talents of Eddie Casey (fourth row, second from right) and Ralph Horween (third row, second from left). First published in *The H Book of Harvard Athletics, 1852–1922*, ed. John A. Blanchard (Cambridge, MA: Harvard University Press, 1923), 429.

Crimson yearlings had stomped the Yale freshmen, 21–6.[68] Arnold recorded two touchdowns, and it reportedly "took an average of three Yale freshmen to stop Horween."[69] Horween's gridiron exploits and his campus popularity made up for his struggles in the classroom. His midyear marks during his freshman year placed Arnie on probation:

Chemistry I	E
English A	D+
German 1c	D
History I	E
Philosophy A	D+

Dean Lawrence Mayo clarified for Horween and his parents that an "E" represented a failure and that the young man required mostly Cs to continue at Harvard. Mayo was a Boston Brahmin of the first rank and understood how Horween's availability stood with the school's alumni. Far too invested in Harvard's superiority in gentlemanliness, Dean Mayo would not have considered doctoring the student records, as other colleges—Princeton and Yale, for instance—allegedly had done, but kindly recommended that Horween seek tutoring from the brainy members of the Phi Beta Kappa honors society.[70] The young man took the suggestion to heart. Horween raised his grades and was restored to good standing in the college. The feeling around campus was that Arnie was one of those "all around chaps," someone who could be helpful to Haughton and Casey in a quick rehabilitation of the Harvard eleven's dominating reputation of late.[71]

Other factors removed Haughton from Harvard football. About the only obstacle that could halt Horween and Harvard was World War I. The rumors about suspending the 1917 football season started in March.[72] The Harvard student newspaper reported that "activities in the University are continuing very much as usual, although the tension of the situation has caused interest in everything but military organizations to lag."[73] Then, in April, Congress heeded President Woodrow Wilson's request and declared war against the German Empire.

Harvard men supported the war effort, even if many had opposed A. Lawrence Lowell's public push for Woodrow Wilson to involve the United States in European affairs. Eleven thousand Harvard students and alumni enlisted. Most trained for reserve duty, particularly those underclassmen whose age did not meet the minimum for compulsory conscription. Some deployed overseas, and almost four hundred of Harvard's sons perished on the European battlefields.[74]

By June, every member of the Crimson eleven had entered "some branch of military service or ambulance work." Patriotism and pragmatism dictated the trend. Percy Haughton and Walter Camp had preached that football was an "ultimate wargame." World War I was an actual war. Ensign Ralph Horween was one of the first, joining the naval coast reserve of the Boston Navy Yard in nearby Charlestown.[75] Soon after, Eddie Casey reported to the Boston Navy Yard as a promising seaman.[76] Owing to the paucity of veteran athletes crossing through Harvard Yard, students regretted that "there will not be much of a team this year, as Harvard teams go. The team will have none of the polish of a smooth war machine." Harvard administrators decided that no official season would be played, especially because Percy Haughton had also volunteered, assuming the rank of major in the Chemical Corps. Instead, freshman coach Wingate Rollins headed the Informals, an unofficial Harvard football team, a moniker that Captain Arnold Horween resisted for its connotations.[77] This moniker was reportedly a concession to President

Wilson, since everyone had freely admitted that the "college football ranks were literally shot to pieces."[78]

Harvard organized the Informals for students registered for the Reserve Officer Training Corps (ROTC). The ROTC program drilled student cadets for six hours a day, making good use of Harvard Stadium.[79] The Informals competed against military camps. Matches against other collegians were considered unbecoming and a disgraceful distraction from their nation's commitment to toppling the Central Powers in Europe.[80] Football was sidelined, but not without some resistance. For example, Professor George Johnson reminded the readers of a Harvard alumni magazine that football games were "expressions of loyalty" and that "winning games was an entirely wholesome aim in athletics."[81] The Harvard alumni president, however, was flabbergasted by Johnson's insensitivities. "Professor Johnson urges this argument with no special reference to a period of war; but the truth that underlies it is precisely as applicable in war-time as in peace. The worthiest loyalty now is the highest loyalty of all—the loyalty to the great cause for which especially the young men of athletic capacities are laying down their lives."[82]

Some held out hope for the most sacred of Harvard football rituals. Yet, New Haven athletics had been decimated just as much as it was vanished from Cambridge. A tally revealed that 121 of 138 lettermen at Yale from the whole of the 1910s had contributed in some meaningful way to the war efforts. In October, Coach Tad Jones announced that "probably the most that can be done with the upperclassmen is to let them hold scrimmages among themselves."[83] President Lowell waited to render a decision about the annual Yale meeting but eventually called that off as well.[84]

Horween and the Informals shut down their first opponents. He scored two touchdowns as Harvard bullied Dean Academy. "Horween showed as the prize of the Crimson backfield" and was needed only for the first two periods.[85] At Soldiers Field, the Informals trounced the army men at the Bumpkin Island Naval Reserves and the First Marine Heavy Artillery. Withal, the Informals played at a standard below Haughton's coaching pedigree.[86] The replacement players were not varsity caliber. Horween was the sturdiest member, weighing in at 206 pounds. The Informals' competition was much less impressive. The hearty Informal captain plunged through defensive lines, gaining sizable yards, sometimes rattling off sequences of eight-yard rushes. "It was only when the opposing line was massed against him that he was stopped with less of a gain in his rushes at the center of the line."[87] Stiffer competition awaited. The Informals did not earn a point in its final four contests, including a scoreless draw against Camp Devens, a team without experienced footballers but well coached by none other than Percy Haughton. Horween led the Informals in scoring, with four touchdowns and five field goals during the seven-game season. Arnie completed the semester at the Boston Navy Yard, reuniting with Eddie Casey and Billy Murray.[88] The Navy Yard lost only its final match, a scrimmage against the Newport Reserves that, according to Walter Camp, "called together perhaps as many former university stars as have been collected in a single contest."[89]

World War I engulfed the following season, as well, leaving football "almost but not quite dead at Cambridge in 1918." This time, the track and football trainer Pooch Donovan assembled a starless team to compete against the Tufts College Students Army Training Corps as well as Boston College's and Brown's student cadets. The best footballers were stationed on army bases or fighting overseas. Others were stranded at home, awaiting orders for military service. Arnold Horween was part of the latter group. Never a scholar student like Ralph, Arnie reported to a Harvard administrator that "I have not been loafing." Back in Chicago at the tannery, Horween related, "I have been helping Dad make cordovan leather for army officers' shoes and leggings."[90]

Military football turned out to be quite a draw, "furnishing the inspiration and practical knowledge of the sport."[91] It popularized the game well beyond college campuses, convincing a number of entrepreneurial veterans to professionalize the sport after their college careers had closed.[92] More than ever, Americans were driven to win. The war had reinforced the state of mind in which there were winners and losers. Judgments of political rightness or justification were handled by armistices and surrenders. It was sensible that this perspective would redound to sport, which very naturally produced a glorious winner and a downtrodden loser. Football was reduced to this bottom-line perspective, and all the other qualities of the sport were advanced or tolerated for the sake of a win-or-else—frankly Yale-like—attitude. The experience of so-called war football also sent Horween and Casey back to Harvard Yard, desirous of more official victories and determined to avenge the Crimson against the Elis and think of other possibilities for football glory.

* * *

"I see Eddie Casey's coming back," remarked one spectator to another at the tennis championships in Forest Hills, New York, piquing the curiosities of a nearby journalist. Both men found tennis rather unexciting.

"Casey?" responded the other gentleman. "What league is he in?"

"Don't you remember that game called football the boys used to play?"[93]

Football and its Crimson variety returned after Germany and the Allied Powers signed the Treaty of Versailles in June 1919. The Cambridge men had to manage the gridiron without Harvard's winningest coach. Percy Haughton had entered a brokerage firm and purchased stock in the Boston Braves.[94] Still, Haughton did not altogether leave Harvard football. He remained on a football advisory committee to support his successor, Bob Fisher. Fisher did not look like Haughton. He didn't have Haughton's sculpted physique. He wore circular bifocals like a college professor and tended to dress more formally, even at practices, than college football coaches and trainers.[95]

Bob Fisher was very much qualified to lead the Crimson. He was an All-American lineman on an earlier iteration of Haughton's Harvard teams and was keen on replicating his mentor's vaunted football system. Harvard had preferred other men with more experience in running Haughton's system, but none turned out to be available for the post. Fisher was still a very fine selection, especially for a program seeking to maintain its culture of winning and Haughton's method of management. Fisher had been Haughton's first recruit in 1908. Back then, Fisher, just out of Phillips Andover Academy, had interned for Haughton when the latter worked in a downtown Boston firm. "He told me he had passed his examinations for Yale and after having a talk with him I persuaded him to go to Harvard," recounted Haughton about Fisher. "He won a place on his freshman team and other honors each year. Had he gone to Yale he would have been lost to Harvard and Yale probably would have beaten us." Haughton once remarked that Fisher was a "man whom I consider my son."[96] The Haughton disciple selected other Harvard men as assistant coaches and invited the master back to Soldiers Field to help prepare for the Yale contest, an incident that led to speculation that Haughton had truly never left Harvard at all.[97]

The return of Harvard varsity football brought with it some intrigue. Seniors Ralph Horween and Eddie Casey were both swell candidates for the captaincy. Because of the wartime interruption, Arnie had not yet earned his H for participation in a varsity-level Yale game. The Harvard Athletic Committee deferred to the student council on the decision to letter its wartime athletes. The students decided against it, a vote that, to an extent, disqualified Arnold Horween's rise during World War I to Crimson stardom.[98]

The Harvard players wisely avoided political conflict between Ralph Horween and Eddie Casey by electing quarterback Billy Murray captain.[99] More controversial was Fisher's decision to restore Ralph to the backfield alongside Casey, inserting the younger Horween at the center of the offensive line. Arnie made the decision somewhat easier for Fisher by returning to campus in substandard shape for football. Arnie had pitched for Harvard's baseball nine in the springtime and was worn down by a lame arm. He was operating during the preseason drills without the same speed and power he had evidenced for the freshman and Informals teams.[100]

Fisher's eleven started out strong. The Crimson shut down Bates College, 53–0. Eddie Casey scored two touchdowns. For one score, Casey glided to the left sideline and then cut back into the field for forty-two yards. All told, Harvard defeated Bates, Boston College, Colby, Brown, Virginia, and Springfield by a total of 179–0.[101]

Harvard's only misstep occurred in Palmer Stadium against Princeton. The Tigers were not expected to pose much of a challenge to the Crimson. The pundits teased that "Princeton has quite some distance to go before it can hope to give Yale and Harvard a battle."[102] Coach Bill Roper used the doubters to his team's advantage, telling his Tiger eleven that "they are not the mutts that people thought they are."[103]

Princeton bruised Harvard. "We went into the contest and found Princeton had a completely rejuvenated team," recalled Eddie Casey. "All of the supineness they had shown earlier in the season was gone, and they were at us quickly like very real Tigers. It was a rather rude shock for the Harvard players, who were expecting a tough enough battle, but hardly expected to be rushed off their feet."[104] The Tigers marched eighty yards for a touchdown on its first possession, the longest drive on Harvard in a very long time. The Crimson was listless, manhandled by a smaller opponent. Ralph Horween dropkicked the ball above the uprights in the third quarter, but Princeton equaled that by scoring a kick in the same period. With a 10–3 advantage, the home team received a chant in the final minutes of regulation, "Wow, Wow, wow, hear the tiger roar."[105]

Harvard hadn't materialized much of an offense and their men were injured. Ralph Horween had separated his shoulder and Murray, besides playing poorly, had been badly roughed up by the Tigers. Arnold Horween was molested by the Princeton defenders. He remained in the game on account of Ralph's injury and Harvard's need to line up several men in the backfield. Things were so desperate that Fisher replaced Billy Murray with his substitute quarterback, Babe Felton. Felton rewarded Fisher, tossing a series of passes in the last seconds to Eddie Casey. The final hurl was a touchdown, rallying Harvard to an unexpected and unsatisfying draw with Princeton.[106]

That Eddie Casey had saved the Harvard football season on the eve of the Yale rivalry game was beyond doubt. Although he did not figure too much in the newspaper box scores, Arnold Horween revitalized his stock during that Princeton bout. Fisher had struggled to find Horween playing time, especially at his most valuable position as a line-bucking rusher. He was a satisfactory offensive lineman and the third-heaviest Harvard man on the team. Arnie was also a stellar defender, but Harvard did not need help on the line of scrimmage. Horween never did complain about his position on the field or on the occasions that he was substituted off it. He knew his worth. Despite his slow start, by the conclusion of the Princeton game, Horween was regarded as "one of the most valuable men Harvard has."[107]

Both Horweens were sore upon their return to Harvard Yard. To prove the ableness of his condition, Arnie made sure to be seen around campus "to make light of the muscle bruise he has on his back."[108] Ralph was in worse shape. Even if they had been healthy, Harvard men were unsure about the upcoming Yale contest. "Opinion is evenly divided among the students," wrote the local newspapermen, whether "the muscular Chicagoan will replace his brother Ralph."[109] Despite their condition, Fisher's Crimson would be favored against the Elis. The latter had suffered losses to Boston College and Princeton. Coach Al Sharpe lacked the athletic material and the inspiration to accomplish what his predecessor Tad Jones had done three years earlier to spoil Harvard's and Haughton's season.[110]

Arnie started beside Casey in the Yale game. The official word was that Ralph was too badly hurt, available only as an auxiliary player in case of a needed field goal. In fact, Ralph did sub into the game to execute a forty-two-yard dropkick, persevering against the harsh resistance of a gusty southwest wind. Yale's Jim Braden matched that with a fifty-three-yard boot, a record at that time for kicks in a Harvard-Yale contest. Felton's pass, a piece of deception that started out as a quarterback draw, to Eddie Casey, was the deciding score in the match. Arnie Horween received considerable credit for his heady plunges and several strips at the expense of the Yale runners, including a forced fumble when the Elis were on the threshold of the Harvard goal line.[111]

It was quite something to beat Yale, particularly after the Elis had upset Harvard in 1916 and after two years of military interruption. Eddie Casey had delivered, ranking among Brickley and Mahan as Harvard's greatest runners. Casey could not dropkick, but then his forerunners, such as Eddie Mahan, could not catch the oblong ball as he could. He received due praise for his role in preserving Harvard's season against the threats of Princeton and Yale. The sportswriters dubbed him an All-American, just like his Crimson predecessors, an award the modest Casey did not "think much of."[112] He was not much acknowledged, however, by Irish Catholics in Boston or elsewhere. The Catholic press in Boston, controlled tightly by the archdiocese, had long since, to quote the official diocesan newspaper, "grown rather sick of the cheap gabble and whispered gossip about great players of popular games."[113]

Other Catholic-sponsored newspapers commented from time to time on football, but usually on "their teams." The Catholics' football squads included Boston College, Fordham, Georgetown, Holy Cross, Marquette, Santa Clara, Villanova, and, of course, Notre Dame.[114] The last was recognized in 1919 by one Catholic journal as deeply deserving of "championship honors" and did not mention Casey's Crimson.[115]

American Jews, on the other hand, were moved to rapture by the Horweens' role in Harvard's reconquest of Yale. They shared in Isadore Horween's personal sentiments. Isadore had never seen his sons play on the gridiron. He had some business to attend to in the East, so he humored Ralph and Arnie. According to family lore, Isadore had arrived at Harvard Stadium quite late. Upon entering the stands, Isadore was greeted by a thunderous welcome: "Horween! Horween!" The timing was uncanny. "That's marvelous," said Isadore to the usher directing him to his seat. "How did they know I was here?"[116]

Isadore understood very well why Harvard chanted for "Horween." It satisfied him as he took it in again as his second son finished Harvard College. He and Rose had done it, lived out an American dream, in real life. Harvard—and the United States, by extension—had absorbed the Horweens and certified their self-made social standing.

Jews celebrated the newfound examples of "Jewish brawn," as they giddily slipped the rumor that Arnold Horween was in line for captain next season, after his brother Ralph as well as Murray and Casey graduated. Jews supposed that the Boston Brahmins had softened. Harvard's was now just a formidable quasi–New England Protestant bunch, not at all the Waspy brand of the United States that tended to incite discomfort among Jews. That Horween hadn't figured as integral to the Crimson's victory as had Eddie Casey was of no great concern to America's Jews. The Boston Jewish press, for example, produced a banner headline exclaiming "Horween Brothers Triumphed for Harvard."[117] They did so, recalled one memoirist, "as if to prove that a boy who worshiped on Saturday could still be a terror between the goal-posts to old-stock youth who went to church on Sunday."[118] More important, still, Jews seized on that all-important measurement of winning to track their rise in the American social stratosphere.

Back in the Horweens' hometown, Chicago journalists, indicating the close-knit nature of their community, reported on the "sons of Mr. and Mrs. Isadore Horween." With an air of bias, the Jewish papers claimed that "football critics attribute Harvard's triumph to their versatility."[119] Another took it further, attributing "Harvard's triumph at the Harvard-Yale game to the brilliant playing of two Jewish young men."[120]

In the largest Jewish hub, New York, commentators begged their coreligionists not to make too much of the Horweens' performance, especially as a marker that Jews had reached a new plateau of acceptance at Harvard or elsewhere. They did not believe that the Brahmins had changed all that much. "We are equally aware of the fact that no coach will jeopardize his chances for a victory because he does not like a boy's face, or name, or religious belief."[121] But most American Jews wanted to believe that the Horweens of Harvard represented something more than a university's total devotion to winning. "Jewish football players are coming to the fore," declared an Israelite down south in Dallas. Harvard's triumph, this pundit alleged, was a "victory"—a choice word indeed—for the entire "Jewish People."[122]

* * *

The Harvard-Yale game had been the climax of America's football season since the sport had obtained a foothold on college campuses. It was one of the best-regarded annual affairs in New England. Included among President Lowell's papers in Harvard's archives are many requests from university presidents, politicians, and well-to-do men in search of tickets to the yearly rivalry game. One of the more compelling solicitations was written by Daniel Moore Bates on behalf of his promising son. Charles Theodore Russell Bates was preparing at Middlesex School in Concord. His ancestors were all "staunch Harvard men." The elder Bates conceded that he himself had settled for a step below Harvard's peerless rank when he had enrolled in the Massachusetts Institute of Technology. To rectify that mistake, pledged Bates, "my boy expects to follow in their foot-steps," meaning, no doubt to Lowell's delight, the lad's more intellectually gifted forebears. But the young Charles, it was made clear, had also taken up an interest in Princeton. There was much pressure, then, on the senior Bates to redirect the lad to Harvard, something he believed would be much easier if his son could experience the thrill of the Harvard-Yale game.[123] The letter-writer politely asked for a ticket. "Unfortunately," responded Lowell, "it is impossible to give them to boys intending to come to Harvard, much as we should like to do so."[124] The stadium, explained Lowell, could seat only some thirty thousand spectators and, between students and privileged alumni, no spaces were available.

The Harvard-Yale contest remained a sacred closing ceremony for the autumn sport calendar, even as other football programs such as Chicago, Notre Dame, and Pittsburgh upended the hegemony of New England's big three. Another challenge to the high station of "The Game" was the invention of the collegiate postseason. In 1902, officials running the Rose Parade in Pasadena, California, tried to add a postseason football contest to their New Year's Day

Harvard-Yale tickets were hard to come by during the presidency of A. Lawrence Lowell. This stub gained entry to Arnold Horween's last contest for the Crimson in 1920. Courtesy of Harvard University Archives.

event. The group consisted of many easterners hoping to market their new West Coast climes. By showcasing football in their warm winter season, they figured, more Americans might consider a western relocation. Relying on the prevailing culture of winning, a victory for the West at the expense of the East would present California life as that much more appealing.[125]

The plan backfired. Michigan's 47–0 rout of Stanford in the 1902 "Tournament East–West Football Game" proved that the West Coast was unprepared to make itself a riveting regional contender. The organizers of the Rose Parade prudently replaced football with chariot racing. In 1916, Pasadena officials once more striped the grounds of Tournament Park for a football "championship." By this time, western football had vastly improved. Walter Camp now recognized its collegians in his annual All-America teams. East Coast newspapers inserted game summaries and box scores in their sports columns. The elevens for Washington State and Oregon were so good, in fact, that they shut out Brown and Penn, respectively, in the 1916 and 1917 Rose Bowl tilts. In response, the bludgeoned easterners claimed that the multiple-days' travel to reach Pasadena had sapped their players' energy. The enervated footballers could not fairly perform at the Tournament of Roses. The excuse appeared plausible enough to retire the postseason event, preserving the Harvard-Yale game as the major finale of the college football season.[126]

That's why, perhaps, the most pivotal person at Soldiers Field for the Harvard-Yale game in November 1919 was not a player in that contest. Seward Simons Jr. sat among the fifty thousand spectators that filled Harvard Stadium. Most left very satisfied with the Crimson's 10–3 triumph over its New Haven nemesis. Still, two young Harvard fans departed despondent, along with the soured band of Eli faithful bound back to New Haven. The first was a girl whose pigtails were cruelly snipped off by the mischievous Harvard undergraduate sitting behind her. The other was Simons, that delinquent with the overaggressive scissors and a penchant for playful pranks. The police arrested him for the act, charging the Pasadena native with "mayhem."[127]

Simons's father was a Harvard alumnus and a successful California lawyer. He traveled back to his alma mater to plead his son's case. Simons Sr. was also a member of the Tournament of Roses athletic committee and tasked with reenergizing the annual New Year's football competition. The Rose Bowl could not, however, recruit an East Coast power to Tournament Park for two straight years, on New Year's Day, 1918 and 1919. The official reason was that formal football had been canceled so that the strongest men could enlist to help the Allies in World War I. But no college team wished to make itself vulnerable to the western football powers after witnessing Brown's and Penn's poor performances before the war.

There was ample pressure to resume the Rose Bowl. An avid football devotee, President Woodrow Wilson recommended temporarily releasing the most superior athletes from military duty. He reasoned that "such a celebration would not interfere with the government's war activities."[128] University leaders disagreed. Servicemen had competed in place of college players in 1918 and 1919. But the lineups of former college stars stripped of their college branding did not have the same appeal as college teams. The concerned Seward Simons Sr. worried that the tournament would once again replace football games with odd spectacles like chariot racing and tent pegging. On one New Year's, the committee featured a racing showdown between an elephant and a camel.[129]

A lot was at stake. Simons Jr.'s legal troubles gave the elder Simons an idea to revive the sport. It made good sense to court the Crimson. Harvard offered a particular pedigree unrivaled by any other American institution. Crimson footballers and their classmates produced the longest legacy of US senators, industry captains, and Wall Street bankers.

Simons went for it and tossed his Hail Mary. He suggested to Harvard's leadership that the Rose Bowl was just what the school required to jump-start an underwhelming and probably overly ambitious endowment campaign. Harvard's A. Lawrence Lowell set a target of $16 million. In today's amounts, that would equal $235 million. Simons claimed that Harvard needed to expand its base to reach that figure. "None of Harvard's graduates has ever seen their school play in the West," contended Simons. "They need something to arouse their old interests. Why not send the football squad to Pasadena?" Simons theorized that the Pacific-bound team could make strategic stops along the railway to greet fans and western alumni who would be "stirred up" to see the 7-0-1 Crimson players.[130]

Harvard had demurred several earlier invitations to play postseason football. It was a cardinal rule in Cambridge that the football season ended with Yale. Yet the alumni were willing to break a precise tradition of the Yale ritual for the sake of procuring another triumph on a grand scale. "There was a great division of opinion at Cambridge as to whether it was wise to send them," recalled Thomas Lamont. "At one time I was accused of urging the matter too strongly, but it seemed to come out all right."[131] All right, because Harvard won.

The Harvard faculty argued that the ten-day winter recess was not long enough to support the trek and recuperation time for the students to prepare themselves for the spring semester. They also balked at the overemphasis on athletics to the detriment of scholarship. Mostly, though, adding to the season's ritual was a kind of sacrilege.

Simons anticipated all this. He reminded Harvard officials that the school had stretched Christmas break by five days that year and downplayed the recently lopsided Harvard-Yale contests. "What's more, you don't have to worry about a thing," concluded Simons. "We'll provide the stadium and even line up another team as an opponent. All you have to do is come."[132] Harvard was impressed. Lowell needed the cash and was pleased by the westernizing strategy. The professors eventually came around.

Fears of a national coal shortage due to miner strikes almost caused a false start.[133] In mid-December, the unions negotiated a better deal for the miners but the Brahmins were not yet sure about a post-Yale contest to end the football season. Harvard eventually signed on, however, willing to forsake tradition the sake of fundraising. In addition, a Crimson victory would signal how far along, beyond Yale, the school had come in manufacturing Haughton-style winners. The Rose Bowl organizers were overjoyed. Seward Simons Sr. also managed to strike up a deal for his son, restoring Junior's good name at the university and among the Boston authorities.[134]

The rest of the preparation and execution for the Rose Bowl was routine. In short order, Simons secured the University of Oregon's Webfoots to represent the West in the Rose Bowl. (A half-century later, the football team changed its name to the Ducks.) Coach Shy Huntington led the Webfoots to a surprise shutout over the favored Penn Quakers on New Year's Day 1917. Among the nascent Pacific Coast Conference, "Oregon was the smallest of the lot and," suggested its athletic director to a friend, "we must depend on our brains primarily to lick the other fellow."[135] Against Penn, the little-known Webfoots "set a trap for Pennsylvania and they played into our hands."[136]

Oregon obliged Simons's invitation. After all, the 850 miles from Eugene to Pasadena was a breezy trip in comparison with the 3,100 miles from Boston. Tapping Oregon elevated interest in the Rose Bowl for eastern fans seeking to avenge Pennsylvania's demoralizing defeat. It also excused the committee for bypassing the Washington State Cougars—though Washington State's coach admitted Oregon had the better team—who had beaten the Webfoots back in November in Portland. Against the Webfoots, Harvard knew to come better prepared and better rested.[137]

Likewise, the Crimson was not unknown to Oregon. Oregon representative C. N. McArthur had attended the Harvard-Yale game. Congressman McArthur was a passionate regular lobbyist for including his local boys in Walter Camp's All-American teams. He had little to say about the "Harvard team outside of Casey who is dangerous because of his speed." The politician remained confident in his home squad, writing in a personal letter to Walter Camp that the Crimson "showed flashes of real football but lacked in consistent attack."[138]

McArthur undersold the abilities of the rest of the Harvard eleven. He probably shared his impressions with Oregon coach Shy Huntington, who had starred as a player in the Rose Bowl defeat of Penn. Huntington also tried to squeeze information out of a Yale player, offering him cash and fare to Eugene to counsel him. The young Yankee refused, declaring that he would not help the scout. He stood with Harvard, united with a usual nemesis in the East's looming battle with the West.[139]

The 1920 Rose Bowl was developing into much more than the scheming Simons had initially intended. The faceoff between Harvard and Oregon featured competing football strategies and cultures. Bob Fisher trained his Crimson players according to Haughton's Harvard system. The western team reckoned that the East played far too subdued a game and overthought it. The Webfoots played smashmouth football, a less elegant design than the brainy boys of Harvard. They counted on the brawny shoulders of halfback William

"Bad Bill" Steers, an All-American and member of the Mare Island Marines replacement team that competed in the college-less Rose Bowl of 1919.

Still, Oregon did not plan to win on grit alone. The Webfoots subscribed to the newfangled notion of throwing the football. The forward pass had been illegal until 1905. For a short time, a throw was not allowed to travel more than twenty yards downfield. A dropped pass resulted in a fifteen-yard penalty and, if untouched by any player on the throw, it was treated like a fumble or automatic turnover. The stiff repercussions of an imperfect pass-and-catch coupled with the general tendency to stick to tradition rendered the forward pass a rare thing among the eastern colleges. The board of elected rule makers were disinclined to change. The rulebook was meant to hold innovation in check to protect the integrity of the sport.[140]

Throwing the ostrich-egg-shaped leather ball became a fad in the unbridled hinterland, popularized by Pop Warner's Carlisle Indians and then further westward by Knute Rockne's Notre Dame teams and Amos Alonzo Stagg's at the University of Chicago.[141] Warner had claimed it was first introduced by Fielding Yost of Michigan. But Warner also claimed that "Yost also invented everything else in the game—including the football."[142] In any event, The first coaches and trainers at Oregon were disciples of Stagg's Chicago passing method. They hazarded to pass the football judiciously rather than always running it. The attitude reflected the risk-taking activists who challenged the social status quo and dared the men in charge to push the limits of the "Progressive Era." In kind, Oregon's untraditional game plan was not something that Harvard had encountered in its undefeated regular season.

The contest was freighted with so much more than what the newspapers billed as "When East Meets West on Gridiron."[143] It was shaping up to become a clash of cultures, a competition between elegant traditionalism and undaunted innovation.

* * *

The whole affair was designed for the sake of publicity and pageantry. Reporters followed Harvard along the protracted journey, printing travelogs in a variety of newspapers. The train lugging thirty-five Harvard players, coaches, and trainers pulled out of Boston's South Station's Track 13 on December 20, 1919. After some delay, the team made it to Chicago on Day 2. There, Harvard alumni toasted the young sportsmen. Their words were "well calculated to stir up the athletes to a realization of just how serious is this coming game with Oregon in sight of Harvard men the world over."[144]

Fans positioned themselves along the train platforms during the journey, waving to the two cars carrying the Crimson players. On each occasion, the

HARVARD SQUAD STARTS
FOR COAST AT 2 TODAY

First Crimson Football Outfit to Cross Continent in Good
Shape to Play Oregon—Students Plan Big Sendoff
—Stopover in Chicago Tomorrow

Newspapers covered the Harvard Crimson's westward trek to the Rose Bowl with
great anticipation and imagination. This illustration from an unknown source
depicts the curiosity about Harvard's travels to uncharted territory. Courtesy of
Harvard University Archives.

collegians, dutifully obeying Coach Fisher and the other chaperones, took a break from their never-ending bridge tournament and saluted the Harvard supporters throughout the Middle West.

On Day 3 of the cross-country trip, Fisher arranged for a travel stop in Omaha so that the team could practice. He pushed them hard in Nebraska, reckoning that the fine dining and extended sitting had weakened the footballers. Everyone sweated through the drills and exercises, except for Eddie Casey, who had been laboring with a severe cold since departing from Boston. In Wyoming, the temperamental locomotive temporarily stalled.[145] The waitresses at the Green River station begged to meet the famed footballer, Eddie Casey. Day 4 was Christmas Eve. As the engine conductor distracted the Harvard men, showing off some sights in San Francisco, team managers set up a Christmas tree and laid out plenty of presents meant for small children. That generated some merriment and lots of laughter.[146]

The passenger train pulled into Los Angeles on Day 6. They were reminded of the stakes by a telegram from Massachusetts governor Calvin Coolidge, admonishing the eleven that "Massachusetts knows you are game, believes you are superior, and hopes you will win." The message was published in the press. Tellingly, many newspapers either omitted or separated Coolidge's final sentence from the earlier portion: "There is a victory in doing your best of which no one can deprive you."[147] That wisdom was no longer in keeping with football or Harvard values.

Coach Huntington's Oregonians had been stationed in Los Angeles for more than a week, owing to severe cold and snow in the Northwest. Upon arrival, Harvard's athletes hobnobbed with heavyweight champion Jack Dempsey and Douglas Fairbanks, the "King of Hollywood," at Robert Brunton Studios, now the site of Paramount Pictures. The team was grateful to Fairbanks for the introduction to Charlie Chaplin and politely invited the two renowned actors to sit among the mix of Harvard fans at the New Year's Day matchup. Other Harvard faithful were on their own to purchase tickets from scalpers at $25 a seat.[148]

Seward Simons Sr. also seized the moment full of celebrities and the best-known US college. The Tournament of Roses added ten thousand seats to accommodate a respectable thirty thousand spectators at the event. Most were piqued by the curious appearance of Harvard on the West Coast but were committed Oregon enthusiasts. Harvard's fans numbered in the hundreds, a sizable portion traveling from San Francisco and San Diego.[149]

Stops were pulled. The parade preceding the game featured automobiles, not horses. Simons's committee arranged for two propeller planes to fly low, just above the stadium. The first swooping airplane deposited a football connected to two long streamers: a red one for Harvard's colors and another, lemon-yellow, to represent Oregon's. The same colors bedecked the north and south goals. The other airplane dropped the game ball into the waiting hands of the players and umpires stationed below. The stunt thrilled the patrons but frightened Pasadena officials. They promptly met in special session to ban low-flying aircrafts in the city's airspace.[150]

The game, played during a humid afternoon, was a good one. Harvard's and Oregon's defenses did not disappoint. The first quarter featured forced fumbles and a volley of punts. Oregon neutralized Eddie Casey and managed to block the recuperated Ralph Horween's field goal attempt, regaining possession at midfield. On the play, Horween fell to the ground and landed on his bad shoulder. He was removed to the sidelines and was replaced by Freddie Church.[151]

The Webfoots displayed more than a modicum of moxie. On one play, the Oregon quarterback feigned an injury, prone on the ground. "In just a fractional second," remembered Eddie Casey, the Oregon man snapped back the ball, the Oregon backfield leaped into place and the whole play caught the Crimson team off its guard."[152] The thirty-yard-gaining trick play was a result of Oregon's close relationship with Amos Alonzo Stagg, the University of Chicago coach who had invented the hidden-ball trick, a "most un-Christian" stunt.[153] Despite the garnered momentum, Oregon's march was curtailed. Arnie Horween's tackling halted the Webfoots' assault at the start of the second period to mitigate the damage. Horween "proved the most stalwart of the team on the defensive."[154]

Oregon's best player, Bill Steers, had to be helped off the field after he was "madly tackled by Arnold Horween."[155] At halftime, several Oregonians chased down Horween on his way to the locker room. They warned Arnie that they "would get him in the second half for the way he had tackled Steers."[156]

"Why not do it!" declared Horween. He raised his arms with closed fists. The Webfoot footballers balked and continued along.[157] A western writer remonstrated that "Arnold Horween should be ruled off the turf." Others found it hard to believe that Steers was that hurt, sensing that it was "one of those questionable 'I'm hurt!' plays."[158] Indeed, Steers had recuperated well enough to return and sail a dropkick between the goalposts. 3–0 Oregon.

Harvard then traded in its playbook for Oregon's. Animated by the daring western style, Murray lobbed consecutive passes to Casey, who was normally surehanded though he had committed a costly fumble earlier in the contest. Arnie Horween and Casey carried the ball hard into Oregon's linemen while Jack Dempsey realigned Ralph's collarbone. It turned out that the understudy, Freddie Church, came up with the big moment. Likely the only athlete faster than Eddie Casey, Church received a direct snap and swung to the left sideline for a thirteen-yard touchdown. Ralph was still too injured to attempt the extra point, and so younger brother and emerging hero Arnie kicked the ball between the uprights. 7–3 Harvard.[159]

Oregon's quid pro quo came on its subsequent drive. Steers could manage to complete only a single pass during the contest, and so the Webfoots resorted to hard running. Steers powered toward Harvard's end zone. He might have won the day had it not been for two determined Harvard defenders who caught up to him and knocked him out cold along the sideline. Oregon removed the wobbly Webfoot. Steers was relieved by the smallish Skeet Manerud, who kicked another three-pointer before halftime. 7–6 Harvard.[160]

Oregon liked its chances in a close game. Out West, football experts had predicted that Harvard "would crack wide open after two periods of real red-blooded football against the husky lumberjacks of Oregon." But Pooch Donovan had trained the Harvard eleven for the most brutal of conditions. Donovan preached "all the ideals of courage and intelligence." Certainly, this wasn't how Fisher was trained to speak under Haughton. Pooch, however, was cut from an entirely different cloth. He was proud of the "manly material" on display in Pasadena, especially Arnold Horween, who appeared to grow stronger in the final minutes of the contest.[161]

Many absentee Harvard fans back East cheered the Crimson on. The faithful assembled at the Harvard Clubs in Boston and New York, dressed in fine attire. Radio, though, was still an experimental medium. Harvard did not install microphones in Soldiers Field until 1924.[162] On Forty-fourth Street in Manhattan, a telegraph operator translated the incoming wires from Pasadena into dramatic sentences. He plastered the game notes onto large blackboards and moved a football-shaped placard back and forth along another board outfitted as a football gridiron.[163]

The makeshift arrangement represented the absolute height of long-distance sport spectatorship to date. The crowds—which included Percy Haughton and Theodore Roosevelt Jr.—appreciated the effort, anxiously awaiting the rapid and suspenseful reports. "Hey, stop that ball!" the fans shouted as Oregon took it deep into Harvard territory. "That's far enough, quite!"[164]

A journalist witnessing the whole scene testified that, when Church scored, "this was no longer a club room; it was a segment of the Stadium at Cambridge at the supremest moment."[165] Upon learning of Bill Steers's unfortunate injury, the scorekeeper in New York relayed that his counterpart in Boston had asked the wire operator in Pasadena "whether the delay is due to the fact that they are burying Steers." Some Harvard fans cheered while others prayed for "Bad Bill" to recover—after the conclusion of the contest.[166]

The third quarter produced no scoring. Neither did the fourth, but it did yield uncommon drama. The night was nearly wrecked for all those in favor of Harvard. The surefooted Steers remained sidelined. His substitute, Manerud, booted a short dropkick. The Rose Bowl scorekeeper hastily placed a 9 next to Oregon's name. The operators in Boston and New York did the same. Then referee George Varnelli, an Oregon native, signaled that the kick had sailed wide of the post. Still 7–6 Harvard.

The Crimson returned to the offense and relied on Arnie Horween to absorb the balance of the game clock. He lumbered—some might say "smashed"—downfield. He stopped at the opposing goal line, not wishing to run up the score, as time expired. "We'd have made it if we had needed to make it," explained Horween.[167] The writers declared that the East had finally won the Rose Bowl. The local press in Boston beamed, announcing that the "Harvard victory is not only for itself but for all Eastern football."[168] Much was made of Eddie Casey, who had played in his final contest for the Crimson and "will go down in the record books as one of the greatest football players ever turned out by Harvard."[169] Eddie might have stayed at Harvard. He opted, however, for a "war degree," a dispensation offered by the college to count army service as college credit. But Casey had met Anna Louise Cusick, a Radcliffe student, at a class dinner and was anxious to wed and begin his professional life. Anna had not missed a game in that last season and "watched with admiring eyes as 'her Eddie' smashed through the opposition teams, cheering lustily every gain he made."[170] Anna and Eddie married in 1921, very content with how Harvard had turned out for Casey.

President Lowell and Harvard officials were very pleased. The Pasadena affair had raised its stature in the West and clinched the Crimson's claim to the top of the football rankings, to the chagrin of other powers, like Rockne's Notre Dame team and the Fighting Illini under the tutelage of Bob Zuppke. To mollify Yale, Harvard vowed about postseason play that "once will have to do."[171] It did not much matter anymore, because the Harvard Crimson had triumphed. This, then, was the fulfillment of Percy Haughton's winning legacy passed on to Bob Fisher's championship football team and Harvard College.

CHAPTER SIX

HORWEEN VERSUS MCMAHON AND THE RISE OF THE NATIONAL FOOTBALL LEAGUE

For years, the colleges have been waging a bitter warfare against the insidious forces of the gambling public and alumni and against overzealous and short-sighted friends, inside and out, and also not infrequently against crooked coaches and managers who have been anxious to win at any cost, and victory has not been completely won. And now along comes another serious menace, possibly greater than all others, viz., Sunday professional football.

—Amos Alonzo Stagg, "To All Friends of College Football," November 1, 1923

On January 20, 1920, Harvard made Arnold Horween football captain by unanimous decision. "I am very pleased at the results of the election," said Bob Fisher. "Arnold has the personality, is a hard worker, knows the game and has a natural genius for leadership."[1] Horween's climb was an odd occurrence at Harvard. "It is very difficult for an individual to rise to an outstanding position without the aid of a reputation as a 'prep school' athlete," wrote Harvard student journalists. "Horween, coming from a little-known institution in the middle-west, became the star of one of the best Freshman teams that has ever worn the Crimson."[2] His ability to overcome his doubtful high school credentials—certainly, no one who calculated a school's worth from its football standouts would have known much about Francis Parker on Chicago's North Side—was a testament to Arnold's extraordinary personality. He was one of those amiable men, like Bill Bingham before him, who attracted friends and followers. He was "one of the best-liked fellows at Harvard" and was described as "just a great big, good-natured kid."[3] Horween rated as a member of social clubs such as the Hasty Pudding Club and the Institute of 1770. He was president of the Owl Club, a secret society that held not-so-secret meetings on its premises on Holyoke Street. He was also inducted into Delta Kappa Epsilon, that high-status-signaling fraternity that accepted only the most promising students, athletes the caliber of a Bill Bingham or an Eddie Mahan.[4]

Horween's elevation was also a credit to his great playing in the Yale and Oregon contests. His defense had earned Horween the short-lived nickname "Eagle Rock."[5] His association with the image of America's signature feathered fowl betokened Horween's rise among America's most respectable classes. About the only thing going against Arnold was his academic record. Never able to repeat his more scholarly scores during his high school years at Francis Parker, Horween always teetered on the brink of academic probation. "I take it that you are familiar with all the facts of Arnold's case," wrote Isadore Horween to the Harvard dean's office on his son's behalf. "You know how important it is for him to get in good standing with the college. For him to be dismissed from school now would be little short of a calamity. It certainly would be disgraceful."[6] Harvard never broke the rules for Horween—nor did Isadore's request for them to commit an infraction—but the college ensured that Arnie had the right tutoring aptitude around him to pass his examinations.[7]

The Jewish press had predicted Horween's rise and heartily celebrated the "first Harvard man of the Jewish faith to be so distinguished."[8] Jews in the United States desired acceptance into the mainstream, and Horween's captaincy signaled to them a form of Americanization that they had urgently sought. "The successful triumphs of our young men in athletics give the hearty satisfaction that they are not only able to accomplish such achievements, but that their generous Christian comrades recognize their merits sufficiently to choose them voluntarily as leaders."[9] By contrast, Catholics and blacks at this time were keener on building institutions that paralleled the Protestant white majority rather than assimilate into the establishment.

Jews, of course, possessed their own cliques. The overall goal, however, was a type of cultural absorption. Unlike Bill Bingham's or Eddie Casey's experiences with the Anglican and Catholic establishments, Arnold Horween didn't have much to do with Harvard's Jewish clubs.[10] But they noticed him, rating him among the very best Jewish footballers in the nation.[11] The closeness of Horween's connection to the American Jewish community was of no mean importance to the group. America's awareness of Horween's Jewishness was all they had cared to consider. He fulfilled a very particular model of Americanization that appealed to America's Jews. His Harvard acclaim touched on their desire to gain entry into America's leading Protestant institutions.

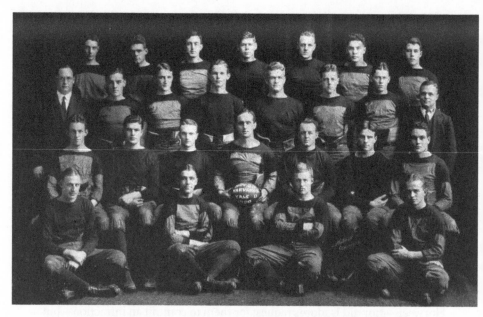

Captain Arnold Horween (center) shows off the game ball after the close of
an undefeated 1920 season and victory against the Yale Elis. Coach Bob Fisher
appears on the left of the third row. First published in *The H Book of Harvard
Athletics, 1852–1922*, ed. John A. Blanchard (Cambridge, MA: Harvard University
Press, 1923), 437.

The arena of higher education had no greater exemplar than Harvard. And
sport presented no higher stage than the football gridiron. Jews from New
York to Los Angeles, Detroit to Texas, boasted that Arnold and Ralph were
"football stars of the first magnitude."[12] Even the New York newspaper that
had cautioned against making too much of the Horweens after the Yale bout
submitted to the fanfare. Horween occupied a supreme place on the social
ladder since, in the phrasing of that Jewish weekly, "college athletes are worshiped, for there is that vein in the American blood, especially among the
younger generation, that bursts out in appreciation of physical prowess."[13]

The conversation about the emergence of Arnold Horween therefore anticipated the later commotion around Hank Greenberg and Sandy Koufax.[14]
In addition, Horween's fame among American Jews for his Harvard football
stardom stands in contrast to his post-Harvard career. Upon graduation, Horween returned to Chicago and played professional football for the Cardinals
under the pseudonym "McMahon." Fearful of the implications of joining a
startup and socially shabby organization like the National Football League,

Arnie and Ralph Horween played under a banner of working-class Irish Catholics. To the public, Arnie's Jewishness was therefore a contested thing. Whatever gains he and his coreligionists had made in the arena of white America was not to be damaged by his athletic avocation. It was symbolic of the complexities of Jewish life, mediated by unique forces of Americanization and fears about growing antisemitism.

*   *   *

Some felt that Horween's high stature in American Jewish life was undue, but not because of his religious affiliation. For instance, Isadore Brown read about Arnold Horween in the pages of a New York Jewish weekly, where an entry on Horween appeared as part of the special feature "Who's Who in American Jewry."[15] The editors had furnished a directory of those it considered famous Jews, sorting them into categories. An undergraduate at Syracuse University, Brown confessed that the section on Jewish athletics "appealed most to me." He was floored—"it fills me with pride," he gushed—that "Horween of Harvard is of Jewish stock." Brown reveled in his coreligionist's accomplishments. But he also begged the Gotham newspaper not to overlook another Hebrew hero. Brown dutifully pointed out Joseph Alexander of Syracuse, a three-time first-team All-American lineman.[16]

Brown was right to tout Alexander's achievements. The son of Russian immigrants, "Doc" Alexander was bound for medical school and would, in the not-too-distant future, find time to work as a physician while playing lineman and then coaching the New York Giants of the nascent National Football League. Alexander possessed a unique combination of brains and brawn that nourished American Jewish self-confidence. Yet Horween had Harvard, and that counted for much more to millions of Jews shaken by the festering presence of antisemitism in the United States and in search of a particular form of Americanization.

That Harvard had Horween was crucial for the success of its 1920 campaign. He was the team's leading scorer and its defensive pillar. Against nine opponents, the Crimson allowed scoring plays to just seven challengers. Princeton, however, managed a pair of touchdowns against Harvard in a 14–14 draw. Horween "doubtless felt the effects all through the game of a severe twist of the neck that he suffered early in the afternoon."[17] Harvard's captain was too impaired to play much of a factor on offense, which limited the Crimson's scoring potential and better chances of an outright defeat of the ferocious Tigers.

Centre College was the other team that had tallied points against Horween's eleven. Centre was a small school in Danville, Kentucky. Quarterback

Bo McMillin played a hard game against the Crimson, continually advancing on the vaunted Harvard defense. In Cambridge, few likely knew that McMillin was a twenty-six-year-old gambler who had failed most of his undergraduate courses during that senior year. No one at Harvard knew that McMillin should have been ineligible, nor could anyone have known he was a few formative years older than the Crimson backs.[18] In the second quarter, on a fourth-down play, McMillin pulled the ball into his chest rather than punt it to Harvard, a precarious decision with his team positioned on Centre's 30-yard line. McMillin sailed the heavy ball thirty-five yards to Lefty Whitnell. The defense had never seen a football—much denser than the ones used today—fly that far in the air and therefore did not bother to cover Whitnell so far in the distance. The receiver ran the remaining thirty-five yards of the field for a touchdown, the second for Centre in that contest. These two occasions were the first in which the opposition had scored two goals against Harvard since the onset of the Percy Haughton era.

Horween calmed his teammates and restored order. Arnold was responsible for two touchdowns of his own and an interception, leading the Crimson to a 31–14 victory. After the game, Horween approached Centre's locker room to offer McMillin the game ball as a keepsake for his personal effort.

"To the victor belongs the spoils," reasoned McMillin.

"You deserve it," protested Horween. "You are the greatest backfield player I ever saw."

McMillin demurred. Moved to tears, the footballer turned Horween down on the grounds that Harvard had won the game and was earmarked for the trophy.[19] McMillin vowed, "I would be back next year to win the pigskin." McMillin did just that, portending a less auspicious period in the post-Horween Crimson era.[20]

Horween's graciousness paralleled Bill Bingham's sportsmanship at Exeter when he congratulated Matt Hayes of Andover before celebrating his great racing triumph with his Exonian classmates. Horween's gesture also evinced a subtle change in Harvard football, a "long way in advance of the old orthodox Cambridge game." The claim betrayed Fisher's football upbringing and suggested much more about the ingenuity of his eleven. Crimson attempted sixteen passes against Yale in the season finale. The strategy surprised Yale and coach Tad Jones, even though the newspapers had predicted that the game "will be replete with varied forwards."[21] Jones had returned to New Haven, as the last grid general to have defeated the Crimson, then under the tutelage of Percy Haughton. Jones had been content in his new life in Seattle, part of a well-to-do shipbuilding business. Yet his employers were Yale men and they insisted that Jones return to New Haven. His bosses covered the expenses of his augmented salary for the sake of their beloved Elis.

Harvard completed nine of those passes, setting up a number of field goals by Horween and sophomore halfback Charles Buell. Harvard defeated the Elis in the Yale Bowl, 9–0. "A few years ago," conjectured a sportswriter, "anyone who had suggested at Cambridge that forward passing down in your own half of the field was a sound and logical method of attack would have been told that he was not wanted on Soldiers Field."[22]

Then there was Arnold Horween's pregame ritual. Before kickoff, Horween huddled the starters. They bunched together, their hands clasped out of sight in the center of the mass of men. In the huddle, Captain Horween "said a few words to them that made their hearts almost come into their throats, as each one felt the pressure of the hand clasp of the player that was to fight beside him."[23] Then the group broke, prepared as ever to fight for Harvard and one another. These were moments that restored concepts such as honor and virtue to the gridiron game at Soldiers Field in a time when most others under the spell of Percy Haughton focused on the dry facts of wins and losses.

The routine appeared much too sentimental for the sterner Haughton system of comportment and play. Haughton's teams did not rely on pep and emotion. His was a method that counted on precision and poise. The players carried out Haughton's game plan. The footballers executed successful plays because that was how they were drawn up, not because they willed it to a happy completion. The non-Haughton departures were Horween's radical innovations, but Coach Bob Fisher allowed them. On the football field, Arnold Horween could do no wrong. The Crimson remained undefeated in Horween's last season. He remained a winner throughout his tenure with the freshmen. Arnold Horween also stayed unblemished with the unofficial Informals and had never surrendered defeat while stationed in the varsity backfield.

To boot, Horween, in that career-capping season, never lost the coin flip to determine possession and goal position at the start of a football game. He was almost mythical, a source of energy previously unknown to Harvard Yard. The Harvard collegians who encountered him on campus shook Horween's hand or rubbed his letterman's jacket (some dubbed him "the Lucky") before a major examination, to gain an advantage "in the tilt against the academic bugaboo."[24] Walter Eckersall and most other pundits placed Arnold Horween on their first All-American teams at fullback.[25] Walter Camp, ever the traditionalist football man, put Horween on his All-American squad of reserves, unwilling to elevate Arnie above Notre Dame's George Gipp, a decision that anticipated by two weeks Gipp's apocryphal last will and testament request of Knute Rockne to "win one" for him.[26]

* * *

Horween's Harvard triumphs carried direct consequences for Bill Bingham. Bill had uneven experiences during his self-imposed Harvard exile. His happiest development during that sojourn was his marriage. In May 1917, Bingham had married Miss Florence Patee. Bill and Florence had met while he was at Harvard College. Florence had been attending finishing school in Boston, where it was fashionable to be introduced to Harvard men. Her father, Henry Patee, was a scion of a hotel family. He added to his inherited wealth in land speculation. Patee had moved his family throughout the Midwest, finally settling in Billings, Montana. Florence had been raised with a respectable amount of furnishings. Her only childhood misfortunate had taken place while she was on vacation from school, summering with her family at her grandmother's home in St. Joseph, Missouri. Florence had been driving an automobile that had a defective steering gear. The car had careered over a six-foot embankment. Florence and her friend in the front of the vehicle were thrown from the car and suffered minor injuries. Another young woman, a "Little Miss Burns," had been seated in the back and turned over with the heavy automobile, killed, rather horrifically, in the sad episode.[27]

The trauma had remained within Florence, making her a cautious risk-taker. After Bill graduated from Harvard, he moved to Paris, Texas, without having married Florence. Florence had returned to her family's home in Montana instead, waiting for Bill to "make it good" in business. Bingham suffered a false start in Paris. He relocated to Quanah, Texas, known best as a stop on the Fort Worth and Denver Railway. The Texas Panhandle reminded Bill of his ranch work in Wyoming. In Quanah, Bill found peace and work at a local bank. The manager instructed him to discard his ink, since the Quanah ranchmen strictly used pencils, the rationale for which initially alluded Bill. Ranchers were honest men, and for good reason. "I used to wonder why checks were not forged," recalled Bingham, "until a big cattleman told me one day that they still carried guns in Texas."[28]

Bill patriotically enlisted in the military once President Woodrow Wilson brought the United States into World War I. Before doing so, Bingham "telegraphed to Miss Patee," pleading with her to make an exception and consider a "war marriage."[29] Florence obliged and made arrangements for a small wedding at an Episcopal Church in St. Joseph, perhaps in hopes of receiving her dead friend's posthumous blessing. Bill promptly joined a

Harvard alumni unit and sailed for France to drive an ambulance. Florence departed for Lawrence to stay a few weeks with Bill's parents and then back to Billings to wait for Bill's return from Europe.[30]

War was both amazing and dispiriting to Bingham. To Charles Townsend Copeland, Bingham's poetry professor at Harvard, Bill expressed the great bravery of the US aviators who ascended to the heavens to face off against the Germans. He marveled at their fine skills, comparing that talent to the football acumen of his good friend, Eddie Mahan. Bingham, self-depreciatingly, wrote that he was good for the ambulance unit rather than the Air Service because "an aviator must be clever. I could never play football at Harvard because I was not clever."[31] A year into his service, Private Bingham was promoted to captain. Bill did not understand the cause of his advancement. He tried to inform his superiors that it was a mistake, that the commanding officer had bollixed him with some more deserving Bingham. A friend removed that idea from Bill, insisting that a challenge to the order would result in court-martial.

That wasn't the most unfair event that Bill observed in Europe. Bingham was deeply affected by the battle scenes. He wrote to his family's pastor in Lawrence, repeatedly reporting to the reverend of the "hell on earth" in the trenches of France, on the banks of the Meuse River. He guarded his German prisoners and noticed that a number of them had etched on their belts the words "Gott mit uns" (God with us). If in fact God was with the enemies, preached Bingham to Rev. Arthur Moulton, then "you have lost one member from your fold, for this is not the God I have learned to love at my mother's knee."[32]

Bingham returned to the United States with the throngs of surviving young men, unsure now what to do with themselves. Bill reasonably collected Florence from her parents' home. The couple moved to Texas, determined to make a life there. As he told Thomas Lamont, the rich Harvard man who wanted to employ Bingham on Wall Street, "I was quite sure that the rest of my life should be spent there."[33] Bill and Florence started a home in Paris, Texas. Bingham thought he could advise other war veterans how best to use their army pensions and used his local contacts to start a savings department in a small bank.

It did not last long. Florence was unhappy. The veterans preferred to do other things with their pensions than keep them in a bank vault. The Binghams packed up their belongings and left Texas, finally, for the East Coast. The couple had departed "so hurriedly that there was not an exact understanding of what he was going to do." Rumor had it that Bill was returning to Cambridge to become a professor, but his Texas friends "couldn't associate him with the idea of horn spectacles and a stack of books and the other things which pertain to a college professorship in the popular mind."[34]

The truth of the matter was that Fisher's and Horween's rapid success had compelled Harvard alumni to push for change in other sports. Track had lately suffered through a disastrous season. According to the news reports, "some of the graduates took the Crimson defeats much to heart and decided that it was time to begin to build up what would be eventually a winning organization," on par with the Harvard eleven.[35] Hiring Bingham was the obvious solution to their troubles. Bill Bingham ended his exile and returned to Harvard. He moved to Belmont, a town in the western suburbs of greater Boston. Bill spent most of his time four miles away in Cambridge. His decision to settle in Belmont was based on an uneasiness about living too close to Harvard and being overly engrossed in the school's drive for winning. Having followed Harvard in the sports pages during his absence, Bingham had ably detected the cultural change around Cambridge. Bill did not like it. He communicated his feelings to friends as he relayed the news of his return in correspondence. The altered attitude around Harvard reminded him of the conversations he had had before coming up short again and again against Ted Meredith, before losing made him much more aware of Harvard's unceasing desire to win.

* * *

As for Arnold Horween, he was not as invested in Harvard. His mood was never affected by ebbs and flows of Boston Brahmin life. After graduation, he returned to Chicago to join his father and Ralph at the Horween Leather Company. Ralph had entered the business a year earlier and spent time in Germany to learn about the chemical processes of tanning. Isadore never said so directly, but his sons intuited their father's desire for them to join his business. The brothers eagerly filled their free time with football. Rumors that Arnold Horween was interested in professional football started to reach the newspapers in February 1921.[36] The professional teams had started up in the Middle West. Football had settled well in Chicago, first among high school lads and then at the University of Chicago and Northwestern University. In less structured ways, neighborhood cliques formed prairie teams to compete against one another for ethnic superiority. In the summer of 1900, Chris O'Brien had established the Morgan Athletic Club. Made up of working-class Irish Catholics, this South Side group from the Stockyards was designed to keep young men occupied with sport and reduce the available time left over to get into trouble. O'Brien was a painting contractor and had a number of at-risk youth under contract for various jobs.[37]

The team had evolved with the professional game. O'Brien reformed and renamed his squad several times, joining the Chicago Football League before establishing the much more ambitious American Professional Football Association, the first incarnation of the National Football League. By then, O'Brien was the owner of the Chicago Cardinals, one of the sturdier handful of professional football teams in the Middle West.[38]

O'Brien took his Cardinals franchise very seriously. He wanted to win, even at the cost of more reliable profits. He recruited Paddy Driscoll, the brightest star among the professionals besides Jim Thorpe, from the Hammond Pros in Indiana and started to make arrangements to play home games at Comiskey Park. Driscoll had made a name for himself at Northwestern, ending the Evanston school's bad fortunes against Amos Alonzo Stagg's University of Chicago teams. He was disqualified from amateur collegiate play after he played third base for the Chicago Cubs in June 1917. Driscoll knew the consequences of playing professional sports but took his chances, at the time in need of cash to help feed his family. His reputation had increased as George Halas's backfield running mate on the Great Lakes Naval Training Station team during World War I, a group that won the Rose Bowl a year prior to Horween's Pasadena triumph. His experiences suggested to Driscoll, an all-around athlete, that he could make a good living on the fledgling professional football circuit. Hammond paid him $75 per game. O'Brien offered Driscoll $300 to suit up for the Chicago Cardinals. For that pay, O'Brien convinced Driscoll to coach the men, as well.

The Cardinals preceded the Bears in Chicago, the latter having been relocated by George Halas from Decatur, Illinois, in 1921 after purchasing the team, originally the Decatur Staleys, from Eugene Staley. Halas made the team his own a year later when he dropped the Staleys moniker in favor of the Bears, an image inspired by the well-established Cubs baseball team.

The Horweens approached the Cardinals about playing for their team. O'Brien's was a surer option, even though the Bears played much closer to the family's leather factory, at Wrigley Field. The Cardinals battled at Normal Field on Chicago's South Side and then moved into Comiskey Park in 1922. Arnold and Ralph appeared in Chris O'Brien's office and made their case to the Cardinals' management.

"We want to play," they said. The brothers believed that statement would be enough to secure a position. "We didn't need the money," recalled Ralph. "We did want the sport of it, the sheer fun of it."[39]

"Who might you be?" queried Paddy Driscoll.

"I'm Arnold Horween; this is my brother, Ralph. We're pretty good, I think."

"Good Lord," gasped Driscoll. "Not the Horweens? Why, that's fine. We'll play you up. Why, I've got newspaper friends that'll—"

"No, you won't," interrupted Arnie. They had already considered this contingency. "We'll be McMahons. We want to be anonymous. We don't want publicity, and we don't want a whole lot of money. We do want to play football."[40]

The Cardinals agreed to report Arnold to the sportswriters as "A. McMahon." He first played under that Irish pseudonym in October 1921 against the Rock Island Independents at Normal Park. McMahon displaced Driscoll at quarterback, permitting the latter phenomenon to settle into his more natural halfback position. Driscoll was a short and slender man, weighing about 150 pounds. He maneuvered sprightly, ably jostling between defenders. Horween had known the type, having grown accustomed to Eddie Casey's athleticism back at Harvard College. Two years later, Driscoll handed off coaching duties to Horween too.[41]

Ralph appeared as "B. McMahon" several weeks later. Driscoll was perhaps the best dropkicker in the nation, topping greats like Eddie Mahan and certainly eclipsing the likes of Ralph Horween. Ralph's brother therefore spent a good number of plays at fullback, sometimes shifting to the offensive line.

The Horweens were not the first Jewish athletes to hide behind an Irish pseudonym. It was common for boxers to conceal their identities. The public considered rank-and-file boxing a decidedly ruffian sport, meant for working-class men without much recourse other than to batter and bruise another man in a ring. To avoid embarrassment and for the sake of their families' reputations, Jews and Italians assigned themselves Irish cognomens, an indication of how other immigrants juxtaposed themselves against Irishmen. Popular perception was that the "majority of the Jack O'Briens and young McCoys are Hebrews."[42] One editorialist opined that the grandfather of J. B. Choynski would have "hanged his head" at the sight of Choynski, then a nineteen-year-old boxer, competing in an "arena where mostly the scum of society congregate."[43]

Take, for instance, the very greatest American Jewish boxing champion. Benjamin Leiner assumed a rather indistinguishable alias, Leonard, to avoid the detection of his parents and friends living on New York's Lower East Side. Leonard could not remain underground, however. He had a tremendous talent for crushing people his size and became the lightweight champ. Once crowned, Leonard was outed as a Jew, but he no longer felt the need to hide that identity. He had made it, and his community had embraced him for his sportsmanship and service in World War I. The highest-ranking pugilists acquired favorable attention, and "it is only after a boxer has achieved any kind of fame that the sports become interested in the history of the man and ascertain the fighter's correct name."[44]

Only the boxers who had risen to the top, at which the athlete was admired, or at least dissociated from mere thuggishness, could shed his codename. Sometimes reaching the highest pedestal was not enough. The middleweight champion Tommy Ryan refused to be unmasked from his Irish cognomen. The press had outed Ryan as the Jewish-born Joseph Youngs. But Youngs would not relent. "Tommy Ryan is a Hebrew, yet he has repeatedly denied that he is a representative of the race."[45]

Arnold Horween's ruse was an indication of the low condition of professional football in the 1920s. It was regarded as seedy and altogether beneath the dignity of a college athlete. That professional football was played on Sundays rendered it antireligious to devout Christians, a failure to observe God's holy day. The major demarcation was class. "By and large," acknowledged one writer, "the line between amateur and professional is mainly a line between the unpaid members of a privileged class and the paid members of an underprivileged class."[46] Yet not everyone who played collegiate football considered himself among the upper crust. The Mahans and Caseys, to take Crimson examples, made it to Harvard despite their societal standing. Harvard readily took them because of Haughton's penchant for winning against Princeton and Yale. Upon leaving, Mahan took the nobler route. He found coaching opportunities, initially at Berkeley. Casey also sought out coaching at Mount Union in Ohio and then closer to his Cambridge stomping grounds, at Tufts University in Medford, Massachusetts. Casey also played for the Buffalo All-Stars, however, a team that boasted a roster of former college greats.[47] Both Horween and Casey, then, had defied Harvard coach Bob Fisher, who had voiced aloud his sincere opposition to the upstart American Professional Football Association. Owing to the cultural caliber of its players, averred Fisher, on the professional circuit the "games are apt to result in all sorts of scraps and arguments." He explained that "this is prevented in college games by the high standard of sportsmanship."[48]

* * *

Professional teams drew from the college ranks to assemble their rosters. Management sought out the All-Americans in direst need of a steep financial boost, beseeching the young men to join their "splendid organization." The professional squads touted the compensation to be earned, exaggerating the point by noting Babe Ruth's hundred-thousand-dollar contract just signed with the New York Yankees.[49] In truth, though, most professional teams did not earn much from ticket sales and had to raise funds from local neighborhood people on the basis that better players would redound to ethnic and local pride. This circumstance alone differentiated the professional game from the college type. The supporters and fans of the professional game (not the wage-earning players, though) were initially much more invested in what sport could do for the people who played and watched it. It was not, at least for a short while before the professional league took off, about the bottom line.

The caliber in the professional ranks still lagged behind the college game. The cynics charged that recruitment of former college stars was not enough to put on a solid athletic performance. Football suited the college schedule. The athletes practiced in the springtime and in the first weeks of autumn before lining up in a game. Rigorous college classes complemented the work ethic, it was alleged, of football preparation. The professionals had no such routine. To the contrary, working men didn't have time to drill or the freedom to lay themselves out during the course of competition. "He does not want to get hurt because he has responsibilities," noted an observer, a regretful referee, of the circumspect professional footballer. "He saves himself as much as he can. He cannot keep physically fit because he is working eight hours a day." Worst of all, the professional's goal was the paycheck rather than pride. His compensation, then, was rendered for able play rather than exceptional performance. "He plays the game for money and gives as little as he can."[50]

The accusations were impossible to confirm. Yet the charges against the professionals appeared believable to the chorus who wished to rid the sports scene of that pay-for-play game. Its most formidable nemesis was Chicago's Amos Alonzo Stagg. Stagg was a Walter Camp protégé. He had learned much from his master: how to coach football and how to cultivate a college culture. In 1892, University of Chicago president William Rainey Harper hired Stagg as associate professor and director of the Department of Physical Culture and Athletics. Stagg insisted that an official academic appointment was an important statement about the place of athletics in a college. Harper agreed. He had hoped Stagg could develop Chicago into a football powerhouse, in line with the type of elite university Harper had aspired to create. "I want you to develop teams which we can send around the country and knock out all the colleges."[51] Stagg delivered, evolving Camp's playbook, leveraging the newfangled forward pass, and bargaining as a member of the national rules committee for regulations that would redound to his team's benefit. Harper's progressive side also insisted that athletics contained within it something for all his students, lessons in sportsmanship and determination.

On some occasions, Stagg revealed too much of his Yale upbringing and stressed winning above all else. Harper tried to mitigate that emphasis but found himself altogether taken with Stagg's quick success on the gridiron. It was Harper who implored Stagg to sometimes stretch the rules on recruitment and to look the other way when Chicago's amateur athletes took side jobs in semipro baseball leagues. Stagg was just as driven to win as Harper was but believed he could do it with honest management of his players.[52]

It was for this reason that Amos Alonzo Stagg felt terribly betrayed by his graduates who took the skills and formation designs that he had developed with them to the professional football ranks. In an open letter published in scores of newspapers, Stagg addressed himself to any and all "friends of college football." He did not believe the owners of the professional teams when they argued that their sport reintroduced virtue into football. Just the opposite, he decried, the pay-for-play league promoted gambling and debauching. Stagg also inferred a "deeper meaning" of "Sunday professional football." He insisted that it was a tramp's game and threatened to undercut the collegiate sport and its leaders who, urged Stagg, inculcate "amateur principles, right ideals, proper standards and wholesome conditions." Stagg made his case that his goal was to produce future generations of "clean, healthy, rightminded and patriotic citizens."[53] His opponents and those who supported them by attending the pro games were committing an act of treason. Theirs was a sedition against football, and against America. Stagg's personal scrapbooks are full of coaches and journalists weighing in on his claims, mostly in agreement with him. Coach Bill Spaulding of Minnesota was one of those who had concurred with the Chicago coach's strong position. Princeton and Pennsylvania officials threatened, in theory at least, to cut off any alumnus who sullied himself with "professional filth."[54] One wonders whether the language of these elites derived from a position on the immigrant working-class men who took the field on behalf of the professional game.

Stagg wasn't through. He conducted inquisitions of his athletes, summoning them to confess their iniquities before him in his office in Chicago's Hyde Park. First, Stagg called Mitt Romney—a cousin-once-removed of the 2012 presidential nominee—to state his business for the Racine Legion. Romney told Stagg that he "did not want to play professional football but that he felt under obligation to pay his debts." He earned $100 per month working for a local bond house, which was not enough to cover his modest bachelor expenses. Romney reported that his superiors had no trouble with him playing professional football, but he nonetheless "played under an assumed name because he did not want to have the University brought into disrepute by reason of his playing." Racine doled out $125 a game to Romney for his quarterback services. After a few games of good playing, reporters revealed Romney's identity, which triggered Stagg's antipathy. Romney was contrite. He swore to Stagg that he had refused to play higher-profile contests against the Bears and Cardinals to avoid shaming Stagg's operations before a more public audience. Romney acknowledged that was not good enough and promised to stay away from the professional ranks, a pledge he could not keep, it turned out, after George Halas offered him a good deal to suit up for the Chicago Bears.[55]

Romney's old teammates also faced severe interrogation. Neither was paid as well as the quarterback, however. Robert Halladay confessed before Stagg. Like his friend, Halladay had bills to pay. He also had a young wife to support. Less repentant than Romney, Halladay did not yield to threats of stripping his college athletic honors. Stagg anticipated this, recollecting how Halladay's attitude, back on campus, had been marked by a "lack of fineness and also positive dishonesty."[56] John Hurlburt was a third fellow summoned to see Stagg. Like the others, Hurlburt played under a pseudonym to protect Stagg. He also needed the cash. Stagg recorded that Hurlburt "said he hated very much to play professional football, but it was a down-right case of necessity, as he was unwilling to call upon his father for help."[57]

Arnold Horween did not need the money as most of these other men did. He played out of conviction. He adored football, the crushing action and the disciplined strategizing. The professional game afforded him an opportunity to learn more about the Midwestern style. How to pass and shift differently than in the sport he had studied in the Haughton system under Bob Fisher. He still respected the Harvard way and, for that reason, did not line up under his own name and carrying the Crimson amateur reputation. Rose Horween was also not keen about her sons associating with a lesser lot of men. One pundit put it that Horween "came from a good family which did not wish to be connected with professional sport any more than Harvard did."[58] Rose Horween was not a bigot, to be sure. But Isadore and Rose had tried very hard to rise among Chicago's better classes of people. It did not sit well with her that Arnold and Ralph associated with a socially demeaning activity, which amounted to another important reason for the emergence of the "McMahon" brothers. She took it on herself to learn of the severe implications attached to the new professional football league and could not allow it to jeopardize all that she and Isadore had worked to achieve in the United States.[59]

The exercise in deception was a futile endeavor. The McMahons could not keep their identities secret. Teammates called on Arnold in the field of play by his real surname. The Middle West sportswriters uninitiated with Harvard football took note of the Cardinals quarterback "called by the players Horween."[60] Others made the connection, perhaps recognizing Arnie beneath his leather football cap. Reporting on the Cardinals game against the Green Bay Packers, the journalists knew about the "Horween brothers, playing under the name of McMahon."[61] The writeups compared the precision in the Cardinal line bucking and formation with the one closely associated with Harvard Crimson football.[62]

The McMahon nom de guerre earned the Cardinals a reputation for recruitment of former college stars who, unlike most of the league, came from "good," well-financed homes. Frederick Montague Gillies, the Cornell All-American, son of a well-heeled steel manufacturing executive, wore the mantle of "C. McMahon," starting in 1923. Duke Dunne was another Cardinal player, a former Michigan standout. Dunne had enrolled at Northwestern Law School and played as "D. McMahon" in order to protect the political reputation of his father, Edward Fitzsimmons Dunne, a former governor of Illinois.[63] Likewise, Johnny Hurlburt sometimes went by "J. McMahon."[64]

Arnold Horween was the Cardinal's best McMahon and the top player behind Driscoll. He and Ralph, in their second season of professional play, were a "big factor in the success of the South Side team."[65] The arithmetic of wins, losses, and ties during Arnold Horween's total tenure on the Cardinals was, from 1921 to 1924, 24-11-1. The Cardinals remained very competitive, among the best of the professional league.

The Cardinals were a rough bunch. In a game against the Bears, Paddy Driscoll "cut loose a knockout punch" at Dutch Sternaman.[66] Driscoll had been knocked to the ground by Sternaman and George Halas and then pushed once more by Sternaman. Driscoll struggled up to avenge himself against the bulkier Sternaman, inciting a skirmish that involved all remaining players, Arnold Horween included.

Arnold Horween's short professional career was a blending of his college experience and the new strategies he had learned in Chicago. As at Harvard's Soldiers Field, Horween had ripped through the line. He was a much-improved dropkicker, and his pluckiness meshed well with the South Siders' brand of football. In the pivotal moments of a contest against the Buffalo All-Stars, the defending champions, the rugged Horween "dug the mud out of his cleats, dropped back to the thirty-one yard line, and drop kicked a perfect goal, giving the Cards the lead."[67] Patty Driscoll showed Horween how to clutch the football and pass it to an open receiver. Arnie also delighted in experimenting with the backward lateral and creative backfield movements that opened the game to new bursts of creativity absent from the playbooks he had memorized back in his dorm room in Harvard Yard.

Horween retired from the Cardinals in the middle of the 1925 season to recover from a miserable bout of influenza.[68] Norman Barry took over the coaching responsibilities and Driscoll resumed the quarterbacking assignment. Horween received a share of the credit for the Cardinal's disputed 1925 championship, a title earned after the NFL's commissioner had disqualified the Pottsville Maroons, a team that in December had handily defeated Chicago. The league found some scheduling irregularities with the Maroons and also wished to honor the Cardinals for a satisfying scoreless tie against the Bears. The South Siders had shut down Halas's newcomer, Red Grange, in the Galloping Ghost's first professional contest. Though no longer employed by O'Brien and the Cardinals, Arnold Horween, still officially referred to as McMahon, had volunteered to assist Barry and Driscoll and "worked over blueprints for a week" to stymie the Bears in Grange's debut.[69]

* * *

American Jews called Arnold Horween by another name. In April 1923, Rabbi Louis Newman probably unknowingly propagated the myth that Arnold Horwitz had dodged antisemitic Harvard admissions censors by applying under the surname Horween.[70] The tale appeared believable because a growing number of Jews had started to Americanize their names after World War I.[71] Newman's purpose was to found a grand college, at a yet-to-to-determined campus in Upstate New York, at which Jews would not be marginalized by admissions departments that exercised antisemitic qualifications to determine acceptable applicants. The best American universities, without much exception, were guilty of this practice in the so-called Tribal Twenties.[72] President Nicholas Murray Butler of Columbia established the Seth Low Junior College in Brooklyn principally to ensure that undesirable students such as Jews attend that school and stay away from Butler's Morningside Heights campus. Princeton and Yale had considered means to eliminate "less-desirable" Jewish immigrants. The worst offender, or at least the most public villain in this matter, was Harvard's top man, A. Lawrence Lowell.

Lowell held very strong views on immigration. He derided immigrants to the very same degree to which he rebuked his fellow Brahmins. Both groups refused to assimilate into the mainstream, he felt, failing to support the American experiment that Lowell believed in and to which he remained, until his death, fully committed. He hated that the wealthy Harvard undergraduates lived among themselves in their upmarket apartments. He upbraided Jews for insisting that they live either off campus as boarders or, when compelled to dwell closer, take up residence in Harvard's Hastings Hall, sometimes called "Little Jerusalem."[73]

There were clear contradictions in how Lowell had carried himself. Before occupying the President's House in Harvard Yard, Anna and Lawrence Lowell lived on Marlborough Street in Boston's Back Bay. Theirs was a neighborhood established in the final decades of the nineteenth century by Brahmins looking to escape from the Irish and other immigrants who had started to overwhelm other parts of Boston. The retreat of these Anglo-Saxon types from the Celtic intrusions anticipated the same settlement patterns around Harvard Yard that Lowell had made one of his chief concerns as Harvard's president. The Boston Brahmins who had fashioned the Back Bay on the Charles River basin purposefully gave their neighborhood streets names such as Berkeley, Clarendon, and Dartmouth to endow their new clime with a flavor of British elitism.[74] At Harvard, however, Lowell observed things differently from others, who more reasonably understood that it was the same patrician sensibilities that dominated both the Back Bay and Harvard College.

Lowell told his Jewish friends that he had no problem with their kind. By this, he meant Jews of German backgrounds who had settled and become socialized in the United States—to his judgment, without difficulty—in the middle decades of the nineteenth century. His issue was with the Eastern Europeans—Jews and non-Jews, for that matter—who refused to conform to his conceptions of palatable American lifestyles. Lowell's concern was for the upkeep of the tenor of mainstream society. "If the huge masses of immigrants coming yearly to the United States can be assimilated within a couple of generations so as to be an indistinguishable part of the population, well and good," wrote Lowell about his immigration position. "If not, the peril to popular institutions is real, for without homogeneity a nation may be great, but it can hardly be a successful democracy."[75]

The guiltiest immigrants in Lowell's ledger were the masses of Russian-born Jews. He observed the effects of these people at Harvard Yard. "Where Jews become numerous they drive off other people and then leave themselves," stated Lowell. This undergirded Lowell's resistance to Harry Wolfson's fulltime appointment at Harvard College. The president feared that Wolfson's scholarship on traditional Jewish texts would become a magnet for the "kinds" of people who could best read them. Lowell was subverted by Lucious Littauer, that active Jewish Harvard alum. Littauer endowed a chair for Wolfson in 1925 and there was not much Lowell could do other than to begrudgingly accept the endowment.[76]

But Wolfson was a drop in the bucket for Lowell at Harvard. In 1922, Jews made up 22 percent of the total Harvard undergraduate population, having more than tripled in size since Charles Eliot had retired in 1909. Eliot had provided deserving Israelites a place at Harvard College. This, despite his caricatures of the Jewish build. With no scientific polling to back himself, Eliot contended that "if you take any representative gathering of, say, a thousand Jews, you will find that they are distinctly inferior in stature and physical development to a similar gathering of representatives of any other race."[77]

Eliot offered these remarks at a gathering of Harvard's Menorah Society. There, he urged his Jewish listeners to do more with themselves than their predecessors had. "Your race has not had a chance to develop physically and mentally as it should," complained Eliot to a group of Jewish Harvard undergraduates. "Now that you have obtained freedom in this country your opportunity has come, and I urge you young men to take advantage of it." Eliot's harsh assessment bristled against the thin skin of American Jews, who had little to offer in response other than both Jews and gentiles were conscripted into European armies and fought beside one another in manly fashion in the theater of war.[78] They also were cautious not to offend, his comments on Jewish physique notwithstanding, a Boston Brahmin who had a strong record, relatively speaking, of allying with their Jewish causes.

Eliot's tough-love approach was good enough to raise the Jewish profile at Harvard College. Lowell, on the other hand, sensing that his predecessor had generated a "Jewish problem" at Harvard, set a limit on the number of Jews to be accepted at his college in order to maintain the school's "character as a democratic, national university, drawing from all classes of the community and promoting a sympathetic understanding among them."[79] Harvard's president was unsure whether the predicament he observed resulted from a supposed Jewish clannishness or a tendency to "form a distinct body, and cling, or are driven, together, apart from the great mass of undergraduates."[80] What he did claim, though, was that segregation by groups was wholly undesirable at his school. He wanted students at Harvard who were interested "not only of book knowledge, but the ideas and traditions of our people."[81]

Lowell installed a rigid quota system to limit unwanted Jews from enrolling at Harvard. He sometimes preferred to call it a project of "race distribution" at Harvard, a phrase he started to use more frequently after Professor Albert Bushnell Hart reported that among the collegians registered for his course in US government, 52 percent of the students were "outside the element" from which the college had "been chiefly recruited for three hundred years."[82] The Harvard College application introduced fields such as Race and Color, Religious Preference, Maiden Name of Mother, Birth Place of Father, and

"What change, if any, has been made since birth in your own name or that of your father? (Explain fully.)"[83] The admissions committee was advised to code applications as J1, J2, or J3. The first indicated that an applicant was conclusively Jewish whereas the last designation was used for a Harvard candidate whose background suggested that the "student might be Jewish." The Lowell plan was very public and drew ire among Jews and Harvard men in general. In April 1923, the Committee on Methods of Sifting Candidates for Admission ruled against Lowell's enrollment scheme. Lowell tried to reassert the quota with some success in 1926. This iteration added a passport photograph to the requirements for admission to Harvard College.[84]

Rabbi Newman's tale about Arnold Horwitz held up as an important counterexample to Lowell's bigoted claims. No one knows whether Newman had fabricated the fiction or had taken the tale as fact from an earlier source. Another incarnation of the myth was recalled much later by a Harvard man who had arrived in Cambridge right after Horween had graduated. This version had it that Arnie Horween had to dine apart from the other members of the football team, segregated because of his religion.[85] Another iteration took pieces from its two predecessors. In the pages of New York's leading Yiddish daily, readers learned that Horween had supposedly changed his name and struggled to gain acceptance from his teammates, having "received the captaincy only with the greatest difficulty."[86] None of this, of course, was true of Arnold Horween's charmed undergraduate experience at Harvard College.

Another account reimagined Horween as a Horatio Alger specimen, that Arnie "had to fight his way to the top."[87] All these legends were patently false, part of a marginalized group's attempt to make much more out of the account than bland facts would allow them to do. These myths were useful tales to tell. They expressed Jewish indignation. In the case of Newman's proposal for a so-called Menorah University, most Jews concluded that it was unadvisable. Their mode of Americanization was to gain access to and cooperate with America's leading institutions. Newman's plan appeared too parochial. Much too Catholic for the sensibilities of America's Jews.[88]

* * *

The pressure among Jews to Americanize was compounded by the rise of antisemitism in the first decades of the 1900s. They interpreted Lowell's animus in this context. The most egregious scene of anti-Jewish violence in this period occurred near Marietta, Georgia. In 1913, twenty-nine-year-old Leo Frank, the administrator of the National Pencil Company in Atlanta, was convicted of the murder of thirteen-year-old Mary Phagan. Many believed the evidence against Frank was not sufficient to determine the Jewish man's guilt. Two years later, Georgia's governor commuted Frank's death sentence to life imprisonment. The affair generated a great deal of commotion in the local and national press, much of the discussion centering on Frank's Jewishness. In June 1915, one rather militant journalist who had provoked much antisemitism went so far as to call for Frank's lynching. That is exactly what transpired. Two months later, a mob of well-to-do men from Mary Phagan's hometown of Marietta abducted Frank from prison. The men drove him to the outskirts of Marietta and hanged him early the next morning.[89]

Antisemitism must be understood in historical context. The barbarism of the Leo Frank lynching was something of an aberration in American Jewish life. The situation in the United States hardly compared to the anti-Jewish violence in some sectors of Europe. Yet rising awareness of American antisemitism made it difficult for some Jews to concede that there was a difference. Rabbi Charles Fleischer of Boston cautioned that "they are after us again." He referred to an outbreak of missionary work in his area that refused to permit Jews to worship their religion in peace. "Even in America," he warned, "there must be a Jew-hunt." The renowned and enraged Reform rabbi compared American missions to Jews to the situation overseas where, Fleischer contended, "the good Christians like, now and then, to slay the bodies of a few Jews."[90]

It also paled in comparison to the horrific treatment of African Americans in the Jim Crow South, but the antisemitic sentiment bespoke a renewed feeling that Jews were "outsiders" in Protestant America. The Christian-led Temperance and Prohibition movements singled out Jews as the proprietors and bootleggers of alcohol and the enablers of loose morals in American life.[91] Jews were constantly on guard to oppose bigots like the radio personality Father Charles Coughlin, who routinely linked Jews to Bolshevism and other movements that Americans considered nefarious. Beginning in 1919, the industrialist and nativist Henry Ford used his newspaper the *Dearborn Independent* to levy outrageous claims about Jews, many of them borrowed from the infamous *Protocols of the Elders of Zion*. Published in Michigan, the newspaper was distributed in many of Ford's automobile dealerships and gained a national readership.

The anti-Jewish nativism can be best illustrated in the realm of immigration. Lowell's Harvard quota was emblematic of the national attempt to exclude Jews. In December 1920, the Committee on Immigration of the US House of Representatives warned about "Russian Poles or Polish Jews of the usual ghetto type." This lot, alleged politicians, were "filthy, un-American and often dangerous in their habits."[92] Along with economic and political fears, these bigoted sentiments—trumpeted by the racist Ku Klux Klan, among others—were manifested in the Immigration Act of 1924. The Johnson-Reed Act, as it was called, revised a temporary order and created a permanent law that virtually halted migration from "undesirable" nations in eastern and southern Europe. A small number of Jews managed to resettle in the United States illegally—another illicit trade for which Jews received outsized blame—but far more were turned away by the new legislation.

President Lowell supported the Immigration Act, as did many Harvard alumni who had founded and belonged to the Immigration Restriction League. Certainly, there were individuals at Harvard who had resisted these positions and policies. Back in 1899, the Harvard philosopher William James had written to a friend that the Boston Brahmins had gotten far too carried away in their Anglo-Saxonism and social stratifications. "If the Anglo-Saxon race would drop its sniveling cant it would have a good deal less of a 'burden' to carry," wrote James. "We're the most loathsome canting crew that God ever made."[93] Upon retirement from Harvard, reading a tract dedicated to the "problems" of immigration, Charles Eliot scribbled into the margins that the "American race," meaning, no doubt, the New England sort found at Harvard, was "dying out because of its own shortcomings—not because of alien admissions."[94] Yet these were the exceptions that proved the rule at Harvard and elsewhere among America's Anglo-Saxon elite classes.

All this raised the volume around American antisemitism in the first decades of the twentieth century. Certain deleterious policies and blatant hostilities like these and the Frank episode bespoke the uncertain place of Jews in American life. They convinced Jews to fight discrimination and acculturate—sometimes through name-changing—at a more rapid pace. Jewish civic freedom fighters stood up to discrimination in the workplace (banking, medicine, and teaching, for instance), housing (restrictive covenants), university admissions, and the public sphere. American Jews established organizations that could properly lobby and represent their interests. The Anti-Defamation League (1913), the American Jewish Committee (1916), the American Jewish Congress (1918), and the National Conference of Christians and Jews (1924) were all founded with some intention of protecting Jewish interests in the United States.[95] Most did not want to fight the Protestant hegemony without meeting the American mainstream halfway.

This was how the image of Arnold Horween was used by American Jews, most of whom stuck to the facts of his athletic achievements. Horween was one of the foremost examples in stories of the "emergence of the Jewish athlete."[96] Together with Michigan quarterback Benny Friedman, Arnold Horween was the "symbol of a new Jewish youth type." The feats of both young men were "extremely important and most significant as indicating a great change in the character of Jewish life in America."[97] The Brooklyn Jewish Center prominently included Horween in its review of "Jewish immortals in football."[98] The Jewish journals in Buffalo and Milwaukee called him their "Jewish boy," although it was very doubtful that anyone in those parts had ever personally met the mythical Horween.[99]

That did not much matter. Without any initiative on his own part, Arnold Horween had become the archetype of Jewish brawn. In 1925, the New York Board of Jewish Ministers held a series of conferences on the role of the synagogue and Hebrew schools. One panelist admitted that there was too much to cover for the sake of his students, and so certain areas of school life had to be shortened for the sake of wholesome Jewish education. With this, Rabbi Norman Salit explained that one such component, physical education, was diminished, much to the chagrin of his pupils. "The physical department may have suffered," Salit conceded. "We may have hampered the development of a future Benny Leonard or Arnold Horween, but the educational work went on undisturbed."[100] The quip makes clear that Arnold Horween was a household name in American Jewish neighborhoods.

Horween was, then, a near-unattainable ideal for Jewish boys. He occupied the rarest of stations as a Harvard football captain and a Rose Bowl champion. By separating Horween from McMahon, Arnold's record remained pristine. He was a model of Americanization, at least as Jews had described their take on this process of acculturation. Horween was the response that American Jews had searched for when Charles Eliot had emasculated their Jewish material. Confronted by a far harsher critic, Jews in Boston, New York, and elsewhere had their symbolic exemplar of Hebrew mightiness. At President Lowell's Harvard, Arnold Horween had penetrated the most exclusive and coveted roles of New England's patrician lifestyle. That it was neither his mission nor his creed to do so made no difference to those who purchased stock in Arnold Horween's ethnic achievements. The only position more sacred was the Harvard presidency or, perhaps even more spectacular, the football coach of the Harvard Crimson.

CHAPTER SEVEN

A "MEMBER OF THE HEBREW RACE" TO BECOME HEAD COACH OF HARVARD?

I am really doubtful if we could expediently invite any member of the Hebrew race to become Head Coach no matter how skillful he might be. There is a settled feeling, apparently very widespread, that we must do something at once to check certain growing influences and that Horween's appointment in the present ticklish situation would be perilous.
—Henry Pennypacker to Fred Moore, February 3, 1926, Harvard University Archives

Bill Bingham and Arnold Horween were brought together by a confluence of circumstances. Their return to Harvard was broadly shaped by President A. Lawrence Lowell's willingness to allow direction of college athletics to be shaped without firm oversight from Harvard's head man. Charles Eliot had played a pivotal role in navigating college sports at Harvard, even though he was hardly pleased with some of the directions it had gone. In contrast, Lowell spent his first years at Harvard's helm without weighing in all that much in football affairs. In the 1920s, however, a variety of forces shook Harvard athletics. The braided narratives that fully merged Bingham's and Horween's stories were mediated by Lowell's stance on sports as well as his much more active role in controlling the flow of outsiders into Harvard Yard.[1] All this, in addition to a heavy fog of nativism clouding the United States at that historical moment, made Horween's return to Harvard something much less than a foregone conclusion. That it happened was contingent on a remarkable series of events.

The first circumstance was Bingham's return to Boston to head up the track-and-field team. His supervision of the Crimson racers had a short run but was a very positive experience. Bingham brought a new spirit to Harvard running. Most observers might have guessed that Bingham's running creed was born out of the vogue Wilsonian belief in Americanization and modernizing the most hapless. Truly, though, he derived it from a renewed devotion to the values inculcated in him during his upbringing in Lawrence. In any case, Bill adopted the motto of "Progress." He preached it. He practiced it. Bill encouraged faster and slower Harvard men to find a place on track and field. Progress, to Bingham, meant openness and opportunity. He looked forward to incremental advancement, modest goals for the sake of inclusion. Bill wanted to make the "novice," in his own words, "feel that he was a part of the Harvard Track Team."[2] Bingham's rejuvenated faith in muscular Christianity—a term no longer in vogue at Harvard or elsewhere—had been repaired since his final racing days. About three hundred Harvard undergraduates reported for the spring tryout in 1921. Not everyone participated in the intercollegiate contests, but they respected Bingham for allowing the chance to compete, even just among themselves. In Bingham's inaugural year, Yale overcame his invigorated Harvard team in the annual May meet, held in Connecticut, but it was "in much closer fashion than many expected."[3]

The feat had earned Bingham high praise, even in defeat. "Good for you, Bill Bingham!" exclaimed a Boston beat writer in congratulation, acknowledging the low bar offered to Harvard track. "The crack Eli team had a hard time beating your fighting athletes. The Crimson did far better than those not close to the men believed they could do."[4] On campus, Bingham collected accolades for making something out of fairly close to nothing. The Crimson football head, Bob Fisher, who was measured by a far severer standard, wrote to Bingham about that good showing in New Haven. "It certainly is a pleasure to know that Harvard is once again in a position on the track so that the competition with Yale amounts to more than a walk-away," noted Fisher in praise. "You surely deserve all the credit in the world for the result of your efforts."[5] Fisher, like most Harvard men, measured success by an individual's or team's proximity to the winner's circle. That Bingham had restored Harvard track to a competitive clip was not fully satisfying. "I do not mean by this that I hold victory unimportant," Bingham shared about his philosophy of sport, an oddity around Harvard Yard at that time. "We want our share, but at the same time we owe to all Harvard undergraduates the opportunity to use our field."[6]

Much more was expected of Bingham in 1922, despite the fact that nearly all his point winners had graduated from Harvard College the prior year. The season that Harvard's runners had endured showed nothing that might have indicated it could stand up to Yale. Pundits had done the math and determined that it would be impossible for Harvard to defeat Yale without claiming the half-mile run, Bingham's old racing length. Yale's Tommy Campbell was the favorite, even though the Elis had overused him all season. "If he runs at all," figured the oddsmakers about Campbell in the half-mile, "he will win over the best that Harvard can show."[7]

Harvard didn't have any athlete specialized in this middle distance. The Crimson's Billy Burke was a long-distance racer whom Bingham was sure to line up against Campbell in place of a more natural fit for that event. "The best that he can hope for," predicted the sportswriters of Burke's chances against Campbell, "is second."[8] In that race, Campbell led by two yards in the very final turn. Somehow, and there was no one who could quite explain how he did it, Burke overtook the Yale flier, crossing the tape ahead of Campbell by an inch or two. Burke's finish provided the Crimson with the overall victory in the dual meet against Yale. The triumph hadn't erased Bingham's shortcomings against Ted Meredith, but it was hailed as a miracle.[9]

Bingham promptly retired from coaching on account of that win-or-else culture that Harvard sport was imbued with. "I knew that my tenure of coaching," Bingham explained, "depended on winning from Yale and if I lost a few meets I should be out."[10] He remembered the shame, conjured in his own mind, upon leaving Harvard Yard at a nadir. He did not want that for himself again and departed Harvard on winning terms. He and Florence had a happy life together and with their two small sons, Bill Jr. and Richard. Bill therefore secured a less precarious occupation importing rubber goods on Boston's Federal Street. He remained a presence at Harvard, serving as vice chairman of the Harvard Athletic Committee. He stayed in very good standing among alumni and students.

* * *

The second circumstance that occasioned Horween's return was a betrayal of Harvard's most ardent Crimson supporters. In October 1925, George Owen Jr. sat among fifty thousand Crimson faithful fans in the shoehorn-shaped Harvard Stadium. Dartmouth was the better football team and had been for several years. Harvard managed to stifle the Dartmouth Green in the opening period, but the Crimson lacked the athletic material to compete with Dartmouth's rugged linemen and quick running backs. Dartmouth scored two touchdowns in the second period, a pair in the third, and another score in the final quarter. Dartmouth won decidedly, 32–9.

No one was surprised. Harvard had suffered a loss against the mediocre Holy Cross College on the prior weekend. That defeat had upended Coach Bob Fisher's campaign to return Harvard to the ranks of football respectability. His squads hadn't taken up residence in those ranks since the time of

Eddie Casey and Arnold Horween. The Crimson might have salvaged a tie against Holy Cross had its captain, Marion Cheek, more accurately floated the ball into the air on the point after touchdown. Holy Cross described their triumph over Harvard as its program's greatest win. To the Crimson, the defeat denoted its mediocrity. It occurred to a goodly number of football fans around Cambridge that Harvard was the very definition of middling. The Crimson had won half of their contests in each of the past two seasons. The loss to Dartmouth and an even more lopsided 36–0 performance against Princeton in November confirmed to Harvard what the Holy Cross defeat had already suggested: Fisher needed to be replaced.

A more playful and impractical solution was to rescue Harvard by reversing the flow of time. "Wouldn't you like to be in there, George?" asked the fan seated beside Owen sometime during the Dartmouth melee. Owen had been a remarkable three-sport star at Harvard. He had come along in the Harvard backfield as an underclassman, beside Arnie Horween. Yet Owen's preferred game was hockey and, in time, he would win a Stanley Cup with the Boston Bruins. His second favorite was baseball. "No, I would not," he replied.[11]

Owen's answer was immediate, brusque, and awkward. It left no room for a response. He didn't care for football and didn't like to watch it either. Owen attended the Harvard-Dartmouth contest because a local newspaper had commissioned him to collect his impressions for an editorial, common collateral income provided to former celebrated Harvard lettermen. It was certainly a far more respectable revenue source than would be derived from moving into the professional game. On that crisp Saturday afternoon, Owen stood out among the thousands of other attending alumni as a former gridiron great. For that very reason, the other Harvard man, bemused by his team's pitiful performance, had turned to Owen for a sense of solace.

Owen's response surely seemed strange to anyone within earshot. George Owen Jr. was a Crimson legend, an All-American fullback remembered for a pivotal punt return against favored Yale on Thanksgiving weekend three years earlier. Owen no longer qualified to suit up and do damage for the Crimson, but it was basic etiquette for someone of Owen's station to offer his services, even as a rhetorical gesture.

His refusal was untoward. His decision to make public his antipathy in the press was a betrayal. "It was the only honest answer I could give," recounted Owen in the pages of a widely syndicated magazine. It was the response, he contended, that any principled, truth-telling sportsman would relate. "I believe quite frankly that the majority of college football players do not enjoy playing the game. There are, of course, a certain number of exceptions, but those are the men, I think, who would enjoy any fight."[12]

Owen's argument was a strident rebuke of the game Percy Haughton and Bob Fisher had nurtured at Harvard Yard: that, aside from the brutes, young men did not enjoy football. They were deceived, contended Owen. College football was stocked with athletes who sought to raise their social profile, win on someone else's behalf, and reach some heroic pedestal that others had imagined for them when they first showed some ability and durability in high school. The game didn't build character and it wasn't any fun. The collegians' participation was a testament to the mindlessness of the sport, their lack of protest evidence that no one would listen to the complaints. "So fickle are the gods of football."[13]

Football's defenders raced to the line to refute Owen's claims. The victorious Dartmouth team issued a pithy statement that their football games "give real enjoyment."[14] Princeton's best players testified that "any one who goes through a hard season without enjoying it just for the sake of social prestige is foolish."[15] Brown's captain suggested that Owen's attitude was perhaps shaped by the indigenous ills of the Haughton system, a regimen of preparation that depended on so much discipline and hard labor.[16]

Everyone agreed that "George Owen put his finger on a sore spot."[17] His bombshell drew the anger of sportswriters, from Grantland Rice to William McGeehan. Most of them found Owen's statement irresponsible. "Gosh," offered one columnist about Owen's antipathy to the gridiron, "it took him a long time to find it out."[18]

Harvard alumni interpreted the Owen episode as a referendum on Harvard's decision two decades prior to disconnect itself from the British traditions of sport. Much had been sacrificed for the sake of winning. Those old enough to recall Harvard football before Percy Haughton reminded their younger peers that "some of us forget that a good sportsman does not plan to win all the time."[19] Several graduates blamed Haughton and Fisher for too much emphasis on Harvard's rivalry with Yale and on other components of winning. Francis Woodman, of the class of 1888, issued a four-column dissertation in the alumni magazine on why football, played Haughton's way, was a "disgrace to American sport."[20] Haughton wasn't to blame, the majority of Harvard alumni insisted. He was a very good coach whose efforts redounded to the school's honor. Some, though, were willing to admit that Haughton was a symptom of a much larger sea change in American life. "The very American, very commendable, and immensely valuable desire to win," contended Roger Derby, class of '05, "has led to the application of methods often in themselves harmful to the sport."[21]

America's top intellectuals joined in. Morton Prince, a founding father of modern psychology, sided with Owen, fearing that "this overvaluation of winning is true to a regrettable degree of all college sports in this country."[22] The writer Upton Sinclair suggested that football reform was beside the point. It represented a more insidious culture. "Boys who have learned to fight football battles will be prepared to command real armies and send millions of their fellow men to a hideous death." The rebuke suggested Sinclair's feelings about sports as well as the recent involvement of the United States in World War I. He pointed his unforgiving finger at the "masters of Modern America," the culprits of capitalist sinning. "Boys who have learned to promote football enterprises will be prepared to organize campaigns to monopolize the necessities of life of millions. Boys who have sat around council tables devising trick football plays will be ready to take their seats at the tables where diplomats plot the strangling of nationalities."[23]

The analogy was apt. In the 1920s, football fans felt that their sport filled an important need. They no longer spoke as much about imbuing values such as courage and Rooseveltian "strenuousness." Certainly, muscular Christianity was out of vogue. They did, however, speak about manliness in its new twentieth-century guise. Football, they alleged, taught about the corporation, how to rise in it and move to the rhythm of Wall Street business life. It was how Percy Haughton and Tad Jones talked to their athletes at Harvard and Yale. Jones, who had a tenderer side than the likes of Haughton or Camp, liked to advise Eli aspirants to "keep your chin up, your chest out, both feet on the ground and play the game of business just as you would play the game of football, hard, clean and square."[24] More and more, masculinity was understood as an ability to provide for a family and was measured by a man's standing at work and in American society. Ensconced in university settings, football spoke to the most privileged classes. By contrast, professional baseball welcomed heterogeneous crowds to its urban parks. In developing its own brand of manhood predicated on self-control and authority, baseball excluded women and African Americans. Yet, these important limitations notwithstanding, baseball was a more egalitarian game.[25] Football was white-collar, a point not at all lost on the American public: "What essentially matters in football is the nice articulation of human beings into a corporation in which each plays his most strenuous part with the neatness and delicacy of wheel or cog or ratchet or piston."[26] The parallel kept football central in the lives of Harvard graduates and raised their ire against George Owen.

Harvard undergraduates still had time for some open-mindedness. Students hosted a debate at the Harvard Union. The program had to be moved from the faculty lounge to the living room to accommodate a thousand spectators eager to rate arguments about the supposed overemphasis on intercollegiate football. Owen turned down an invitation to represent the side of the affirmative, as did another Harvard legend, halfback Eddie Casey. The two three-person squads were composed of men connected to football to some degree. Boston College coach Frank Cavanaugh, a former Dartmouth lineman, unloaded the fieriest ammunition during the two-and-a-half-hour back-and-forth: the "Iron Major" praised football for teaching sacrifice. Cavanaugh castigated Owen, although he refused to enunciate his name aloud as if it were a dirty word, remarking that the whole affair was "brought to the surface by a wonderful name, a man who surprised and disappointed thousands of people by his action." Cavanaugh claimed that the commotion was caused "through someone's stupidity and exhibited a lack of feeling to his college."[27]

Coach Cavanaugh's side initially won the bout by a tally of 204–200 of Harvard undergraduates in attendance. A recount reversed the verdict in favor, this time by a count of 215–205, of censoring football for forgoing fun. The slim decision suggested to insiders and outsiders alike that Harvard athletics might benefit from new management and fresh ideas.

* * *

The sorry state of Harvard football was the third circumstance that brought Horween back to Harvard. The football team had remained in a good position in the three years after the Crimson's Rose Bowl championship. As usual, the Harvard faithful had measured the school's position by whether the Crimson defeated the Elis. The Crimson had done just that. Three times in a row Harvard had vanquished Yale by a cumulative margin of 29–6. This was "our real goal," wrote President Lowell to a friend just before the final bout in that successful streak. "We should, of course, like to win the minor games, but they are not of really great importance."[28] Yet many alumni who also prized the Yale rivalry above all others did not consider Princeton just a minor game. The Crimson had tied or lost to the Tigers in that same timespan. That series of substandard performances had, for some influential graduates, called into question whether Fisher was good enough to command his football forces into gridiron battle.

That evaluation of Bob Fisher was confirmed in the next two years. The Harvard eleven won just as much as they lost or tied. The Crimson continued to lose to Princeton and suffered a rather dismal defeat to Yale in 1924 at the end of a "miserable season."[29] Experts agreed that Fisher, it turned out, wasn't any good at coaching. He had gotten by with splendid players such as Casey, Horween, and Owen and his quarterback, Charles Chauncey Buell. Percy Haughton had been the head coach to recruit most of these men.[30]

The Harvard Athletic Committee had tried to replace Fisher after his squad fell to Yale. The Crimson eleven were the favorites. Babe Ruth, in fact, had "bet five thousand dollars on them Harvards."[31] The Yankee slugger was a regular at the annual Harvard-Yale tilt—"he never gave any inkling as to whether his sympathies lay with Fair Harvard or the Bulldog of Yale"—but this was the lone occasion, by his own admission, that he had placed a wager on the affair, learning a very expensive lesson in the process.[32] It was a very strange game, played in very wet weather. The Crimson had held the Elis scoreless in the first half and managed two field goals to lead at halftime, 6–0. In the second half, the field was muddier and plenty slipperier. The rushers on both teams did their very best to avoid tacklers and the "bogs and lagoons that dotted the field."[33] On two occasions, Harvard men couldn't do that and fumbled the football to Yale, providing the Elis with good fortune and field position. Yale scored two touchdowns in the third period. The Elis added a final score in the fourth quarter. Fisher's Crimson was in no position to put up points and lost 19–6. Bob Fisher resigned. The official reason was to permit him time to concentrate on business. The true explanation was that Fisher had presided over the most "shameful chapter in the Crimson gridiron history."[34]

Harvard targeted Major Charles Dudley Daly to coach the Crimson eleven. Charlie Daly had captained the Crimson in the autumn of 1900 and was a three-time All-American selection of Walter Camp. He played quarterback because he wanted to keep the ball in his arms as long as he could. Daly flourished before the era of the forward pass. In that epoch, it was the quarterback's decision how to call a play and run the offense. No professional coach governed from the sideline before Harvard hired the likes of Bill Reid and Percy Haughton. Daly therefore preferred to call his own number and figured that it worked best to start off with the ball rather than to receive it as a handoff from someone else in that position. Daly extended his football career when he enlisted at West Point. He played and coached the Cadets and then returned to Harvard. In 1905, Bill Reid had beseeched Theodore Roosevelt to appoint Daly to a Boston-based military commission. Roosevelt, a Harvard man and fan, would have liked to agree so that Daly could assist Reid. But Roosevelt could not, explaining that this was William Taft's War Department and Taft's call to make. Taft was in the Philippines and unavailable to issue such a short-notice decision. Further, Taft was a Yale man, and so Reid dropped the issue. Daly, however, resigned from the military a year later and joined Reid's coaching staff.[35]

Harvard desired to bring back Daly—the "Napoleon of football"—to Cambridge once more.[36] In the interregnum, Daly had returned to West Point and earned an extraordinary reputation as the last and most successful coach of the old football type. He preached a regimented approach. Walter Camp had introduced it at Yale, comparing football to battle. In the US Army, Daly did not need to describe it with warlike imagery.[37]

Daly lectured that a "well-rounded attack should have eight running plays, a kick, three passes, and one or two standard deceptions, one of which is the fake kick. Under no circumstances should there be more than these fourteen plays. If the character of the team and its development permit, the number may be reduced."[38] But Daly remained unimpressed by the passing games associated with Stagg and Rockne in the Middle West. In fact, Rockne had been part of the Notre Dame squad that had assaulted Army with an aerial attack and disarmed the Cadets' ground game in 1913, which was Daly's first year as a full-time head coach. Daly's was a quantitative mind and had no use for the guesswork attached to football throwing. "Were it not for the forward pass, the game of football would be more or less a mathematical proposition," wrote Daly. Teams that provided too much energy to passing did so because they had no better, more scientific, means to secure victory against their opponent. "With the forward pass, the element of chance and speculation is tremendously increased."[39] In December 1921, Daly founded the American Football Coaches Association and was behind the group's first resolution that condemned professional football for both the moral worries articulated by Amos Alonzo Stagg and the unscientific style in which the so-called professionals handled their business on the field.[40]

Harvard liked that Daly promised to retain the school's tradition, meaning the Haughton system. The school might have wished for the return of Haughton himself, but he had died in 1924. Just forty-eight years old, Haughton was in the middle of training his new team, the Columbia Lions. Daly was therefore the next best option to retrace Harvard's steps back to the late Haughton. He had emulated his friend's system when coaching Army. The Cadets tended to respond better than most to notions of tradition, in life and in sport.

Daly had asserted tradition as the prime principle for the revitalization of Harvard football in that bygone period. "Harvard has wrested the pre-eminence from Yale by adopting the simple, concentrated, direct attack," he wrote while Harvard was still in that successful stretch. "Yale," by contrast, "has yielded her former glory readily by flirting with various jumping or spread rush lines, queer lateral passing, and other complex formations in defiance of her success and her history."[41] Yale had floundered because it had experimented with what was in vogue rather than remain faithful to a tradition that had worked out for them.

Charles Daly returned to Harvard, but in an overly complicated situation. His commanding officer approved Daly's transfer to Cambridge to assume duties as assistant professor of military science and assistant coach of the football team. The military stipulated that Daly could not serve as head coach, since the responsibilities of that high post might overburden and distract Daly from his military education obligations. Harvard then cajoled Bob Fisher into resuming his position in title only, since the athletic committee had already decided that the "defeated general" ought to be "eliminated."[42]

The arrangement proved to be uninspired. That was the season in which George Owen issued his cantankerous assessment of the Crimson. Harvard had returned to a military-formatted unit under Daly's supervision. Dartmouth routed him. Princeton crushed him, shutting out Harvard, 36–0—with a barrage of long pass plays, to boot.

A pack of Harvard students called for Fisher's ousting because his name was still on the top of the program. They came to shout at Fisher at his home at midnight. "I'm still in the saddle," announced Fisher from his home, awoken by the protestors urging him to respond to reports and the calls for his termination. "Won't you ever learn better? Tell 'em it's bunk, and I'm still in the saddle."[43]

That ordeal moved Fisher to reclaim his position on the Harvard sidelines in actuality. In the final two contests, the Fisher-led Crimson defeated Brown and then finished with a scoreless draw against Yale. The performances might have been sufficient for Fisher to keep his position, but he had had enough of the plight of Harvard coaching. Fisher resigned, even offering to help search for a replacement. Daly had had enough, as well. He was embarrassed by Harvard's playing. He also was distraught that the school administration and its boosters had stepped aside to allow Fisher to reclaim the coaching mantle in the final weeks of the season. Major Daly announced that he would not be a significant individual "in connection with the 1926 coaching plans."[44]

* * *

The fourth and final circumstance that led to Horween's return was President Lowell's frustrations with the administration of Harvard athletics, and football in particular. Since the 1880s, the athletic committee had served as a proxy for the squabbling between the interested parties associated with Harvard sports. Its constitution betokened just how Harvard had weighed the input of these parties. Ten men made up the committee, representing three groups: alumni, faculty, and students. Student involvement was a new thing, but Bingham wanted to guarantee that youth had a say but could not overturn tradition. Dean LeBaron Russell, as chair of the athletic committee since 1907, had for a long time touted "sports for sport's sake." He resigned in 1924 for reasons he preferred not to discuss with the press.[45] In his place,

Lowell installed Henry Pennypacker, Lowell's reliable head of admissions. Pennypacker was loyal. He had defended Lowell's decisions to reduce the number of Jews on campus.[46] He and Lowell were "much disturbed over the Jew Problem at Harvard."[47] Pennypacker was never a bookish man, not at all a scholar like Briggs. He was, however, a sportsman, in his time at Harvard a champion shot-putter. The two men shared an unconditional love for Harvard and its sports.[48]

Neither Pennypacker nor the other committee mainstay, alumnus Fred Moore, could solve the Harvard football mess. Both men had tried to persuade Charles Daly to remain with the Crimson. But Daly had had a dreadful season. Another experience like that, with or without Bob Fisher, was not something that Daly desired for himself. Pennypacker and Moore's committee next sought out Reggie Brown, the scouting genius during Haughton's time. Brown had departed Cambridge a year earlier to work for Ed Robinson and Brown University's eleven. Brown spurned Harvard, choosing instead to remain with Robinson at Boston University.[49] They also courted recent Crimson notables such as Eskie Clark and Charley Buell. Clark declined, understanding that the position would become a "terrific strain upon me."[50] Buell was the search committee's top choice after Daly had removed himself from consideration and, likewise, found the position fraught with far too many political obstacles.

The committee was out of options. Lowell, therefore, sought a new strategy to revive Harvard athletics. In January 1926, Lowell and the Harvard Corporation decided to hire a "suitable man" for athletic director. The corporation specified that the new sports head would hold a faculty position without ordinary voting privileges on academic affairs. He would not get in the way of the college's professors, but neither could the professors position themselves as obstacles to Harvard athletics. Students and alumni remained members of the athletic committee but as advisers, not decision makers. Lowell had summarily detached Harvard athletics from the political thicket whence it was born and hitherto stuck.[51]

Bill Bingham's name was instantly linked to the new position. Since he had left his post as track coach, Bingham had transformed into a proper Brahmin, at least by reputation. His rubber goods accounts had made him into a wealthy man. His business had tripled its value. Several Boston papers published the press release of the search for the athletic director beside a column explaining just why Bingham was the best fit for the role.[52] Bill was the "logical choice," one columnist put it, to fix Harvard sports.[53]

Bingham, even as a private citizen, had remained a part of Harvard athletics. He continued as a member of the athletic committee, though not as active as Pennypacker or Moore. Still, his opinion was sought. Take, for instance, the myriad of reactions to the George Owen affair. Bingham addressed the issue in his hometown in Lawrence. Like everyone else in New England, the good people of that hardworking mill town were piqued by the Owen episode. Bingham had remained Lawrence's favorite son. At a gala to celebrate another successful season for the Lawrence High School eleven, Bill Bingham addressed the gathering. Bingham first rehearsed his origin story, the tale of millhands who had scrounged up the cash to fund him for his trip to the Phillips Exeter Academy and of his mother, Martha Bingham, who had never let him forget his humble beginnings. Then he laid into George Owen's allegations against football.[54]

Bingham, speaking as a quasi-insider, contended that most Harvard men did not share Owen's view. Nevertheless, there was something to be said about the win-or-else attitude that Harvard had absorbed from the outside. Born again, Bingham enlarged on that cultural malady, suggesting that many more Americans had lost touch with what was so precious about athletics in the first place. Turning to the parents in the room, Bill asked whether, "if we grown-ups find it so, are we helping our children any by getting impatient with them because they do not always win all of their games?" He recollected his own upbringing. Aloud and unashamed, Bill recalled no such pressures on him to cross a streak of racing tape before the other runners. His charges from his coach, his pastor, and his parents were to try hard, and then harder the next time. "Athletics properly supervised can do much for our country," preached the World War I veteran to likely a goodly number of other former servicemen in the crowd, "because they foster those traits of character which we like to think are characteristically American." Even if George Owen had been exaggerating his accusations against intercollege athletics, this message of sportsmanship and honor, concluded Bingham, made the entire debate wholly worthwhile.[55]

Bingham's balanced point of view on George Owen Jr. made him just the right sort of candidate for the athletic director position at Harvard. One sportswriter opined that Bingham was "young enough to mingle successfully with the undergraduates in obtaining their slants on things." In that way, Bingham could instill fun and joy in college sport. Bingham also understood the business side and could speak for the faculty and trainers. "He knows the situation from the standpoint of the coaches, having filled such a position himself."[56]

But Bingham declined. "I did not think President Lowell was sympathetic with athletics," Bingham told his friends. Lowell sent for Bingham, demanding that Bill back up his assumptions about the Harvard president.[57]

He explained that his basis was Lowell's silence. Eliot had a long record of opinion associated with football. Lowell had none. It was an open secret that football was big business at Harvard. Few colleges rivaled the windfall Harvard received from the gridiron sport. In 1926, the Crimson eleven had netted $453,000 in revenue for the university. The income covered the expenses for the other, unprofitable, athletic programs, as well as other college departments.

Bingham therefore found it curious that Lowell had never gone on the record on football matters. "I had never heard you speak about athletics," challenged Bingham. "I had never read any article by you on athletics, except to refer to golf as an old man's game."

"I still think golf is an old man's game, and I am entitled to an opinion," responded Lowell. "I have not been sympathetic with our athletic program, because there seems to be no policy; coaches come and go, and we are in a continual confusion of change."

Lowell pledged that the athletic directorship was intended to solve that problem. "I am offering it to you and if you will take it I will not interfere. I will give you sufficient time to work out a policy and I will back you."

Bingham was intrigued. Shrewd counsel from Harvard insiders advised Bill to demand that Lowell offer his allegiance publicly. It wasn't that Bill wished for something to refer to in case Lowell went back on his word. To the contrary, Lowell had a stellar reputation of keeping his promises. Bill did fear the influence of Harvard alumni, however. Once committed to a position in public or in print, Lowell could never recoil from it, no matter the pressure applied on him. Bingham accepted the position on condition that Lowell make some remarks to introduce the new job and its inaugural occupant. Lowell presented Bingham as Harvard's athletic director at a hockey banquet, but most knew to refer to the event as a "Back Bingham" dinner. Before trustees and other interested parties, Lowell announced that "I pledge him my support in fair weather and foul."[58] Then he sat down beside Bill. "I told you, sir," Lowell whispered privately to Bingham, "that if you would take this position I would not interfere and would back you, and I now add that I will be backing you when some of this howling mob in front of you are asking for your scalp."

Bill Bingham's first task was to find a coach for the Harvard eleven. Bill found it a terribly trying endeavor and confided to trusted individuals about the "difficulties of the situation."[59] Several members of the committee suggested that Bill reengage Major Daly or some of the other men who had lately turned Harvard down to assume the football helm. Henry Pennypacker, no longer in full control of Harvard athletics, suggested that Bingham consider a Harvard outsider to fill the vacancy. Bingham and his advisers thought this far too radical a notion. For a long while, it had been reasoned that there was "strong objection on the part of most of our graduates, particularly among football men, to getting an outsider unless we have to, for both practical and sentimental reasons."[60] Bingham was aware of the newness of his own position at Harvard and was not about to strike up a new controversy over bringing in a stranger to Soldiers Field. Pennypacker knew his place and did not protest. Bingham, however, had no viable candidates for one of the most pivotal positions at Harvard.

* * *

In January 1926, Henry Pennypacker announced that he would embark on a four-week tour to improve Harvard's reputation outside New England. Pennypacker planned fourteen stops along his trip. He started out in Pittsburgh, then north to Buffalo, and then onward to Cleveland. He made stops in Cincinnati and Detroit before arriving in Chicago.[61] At each stop, he repeated the goal of his expedition: to extend Harvard's reach beyond the East. "We do not wish to keep Harvard a college made up of New England men," Pennypacker preached, "because we fear it will become excessively provincial."[62] The mission fit Lowell's two reforms about admissions. First, to make things a little uncomfortable for the Boston patricians who had come to think of Harvard as their own social club. Other young men could think as well as the New Englanders, and Lowell wanted them to know that. The other reason to reach the Midwest and further into the United States was that these sections of America were not as densely populated by immigrants, the other group that Lowell hoped to diminish. Of course, there were significant pockets of Catholics and Jews in the American hinterland. Yet these parts were not as heavy with those types as the more usual places like Boston, Philadelphia, and New York, that Pennypacker had typically recruited from.

Lowell had reason to think that his concerns about the Jewish problem at Harvard were starting to resonate better. A month before he had dispatched Pennypacker, Lowell had received a letter from a well-heeled Harvard man who had been struck by his visit to Harvard, his first trip to Cambridge in twenty-five years. The gentleman had attended the 1925 Harvard-Yale game, the one that had almost salvaged Fisher's job. The man was struck with how "Hebrewized" Harvard had become. "They were so obviously everywhere that instead of leaving the Yard with pleasant memories of the past I left with a feeling of utter disgust of the present and grave doubts about the future of my Alma Mater." He had expected such an experience in New York, "where one stumbles over Jews at every step." Boston should have been different. "I cannot but feel that your New England blood must run cold when you contemplate their ever-increasing numbers at Harvard but what I cannot fathom is why you and the other Overseers don't have the backbone to put your foot down on this menace."[63] Lowell responded in agreement, "as I have from many other signs, that the alumni are beginning to appreciate that I was not wholly wrong three years ago in trying to limit the proportion of Jews."[64]

In Chicago, the Harvard men—particularly Harvard Club socialites John Miller and Lawrence Smith—submitted a name to them that appeared to fit Pennypacker's Harvard sermon.[65] Pennypacker relayed the "strong plea made for the consideration of Arnold Horween as Head Coach of the Football or—failing that—as Assistant Coach." Pennypacker rehearsed Horween's credentials at Harvard and as a player and coach for the Cardinals. That he was Jewish seemed like a surmountable situation for Pennypacker, but only because he was misled to understand that Horween was "½ Jewish" and that his mother claimed descent from "Greek nobility."[66] This wasn't the first push for Horween. Malcolm Logan, a former Harvard player, had barked to members of the search committee, "Get Arnold Horween if you can. He's the best of them all if he'll take the job."[67]

Bingham recalled Arnold Horween much better than did Pennypacker. The committee invited Arnie to Boston, but not until Pennypacker returned from his western tour and queried other Harvard men about Horween. By the time he had reached Houston, Pennypacker felt compelled to retract his suggestion. "Since writing you from Chicago," began Pennypacker to Moore, "I have spoken with a considerable number of men in this part of the country and I am really doubtful if we could expediently invite any member of the Hebrew race to become Head Coach no matter how skillful he might be." What Pennypacker meant was that he was now better apprised that Horween was fully Jewish and not at all what people like him described as Aryan. Far less bigoted people in this historical moment also would have used *race* to describe Jews as something different from the American mainstream. It was not just that their prayers and rituals contrasted with those of Protestants. Jews were racially and therefore socially somehow different from white America. No one had pointed this out before Arnold Horween was elected the Crimson's captain. The Harvard head coach, though, was a permanent position and one that commanded a more substantive rank and leadership level. Pennypacker was therefore quick to backpedal from his earlier recommendation. "There is a settled feeling, apparently very widespread, that we must do something at once to check certain growing influences," wrote Pennypacker, alluding to Lowell's revitalized directive to minimize the presence of Jews at Harvard, "and that Horween's appointment in the ticklish situation would be perilous."[68]

Horween traveled to Boston on March 8 to meet with Bingham's committee. He interviewed with an understanding that he was "not a candidate." Horween diagnosed the Crimson maladies. He believed there was too much emphasis on defense and that the team had not been up on recent developments in offense. Arnie believed that practices were far too long and "that no fun could come from such a program."[69]

With that, Arnold Horween was raised to a full-fledged candidate to lead Harvard football. He was Jewish and did not speak about the muscular Christianity that had animated Harvard during a pleasanter epoch. Most others had abandoned it, as well. Instead, Americans in the prosperous 1920s spoke of leisure, adolescence, and fun. They talked about wholesome upbringings and formative experiences before adulthood. Horween invoked all this during his visit to Cambridge. Bingham was very taken by the encounter and liked the fact that Horween was a young man, like Bill, who had a capacity to provoke change. The committee took a vote and unanimously elected Arnie Crimson football coach. Pennypacker did not protest, at least not for the record. Lowell, if he cared, had already given his word not to meddle in Bill Bingham's affairs. Horween stayed in Cambridge a few days longer. He and Bingham "had to eat and talk in the most unusual places because we wanted to work quietly and we did not wish to be seen together."[70]

* * *

That Harvard football had become a disenchanted operation under Bob Fisher did not weaken its place in New England culture. The commotion around the coaching search was symbolic of the position's high rank as a US institution. Before Bingham's decision to appoint Horween to that role, no one had conceived that it could have been dislodged from the Brahmins of Boston's Back Bay and the gilded glitterati of Manhattan's Upper East Side.

On this score, Horween was doubly an outsider. First, he was Jewish. The newspaper reports on his appointment were quick to point out the fact. The lead sentence of the *Chicago Tribune*'s prominently featured article on the hire began "Chicago boy of Jewish descent."[71] The newswire agency United Press syndicated a news report under the headline "Jewish Boy to Head Harvard's Football Team."[72] Other reports were slightly more discrete, describing him in innuendo as the son of Russian immigrants.[73] His detractors were confounded that the Harvard hierarchy could have allowed Horween's ascent. "It is no secret," recalled one insider about the hiring, "that Horween's appointment didn't please the Beacon Street—Park Avenue element among the grads. The clique that supported the old regime would prefer to see a Cabot or a Wendell."[74] More marginalized people such as African Americans approached all this from a very different perspective, indignantly positing that both groups, New England Protestant patricians and well-to-do Jews "drink from the same cup."[75]

Jews applauded it, more than they had six years earlier when Horween was voted captain. "The son of a Russian Jewish immigrant becomes a king of sports," enthused Boston's Jews, "lionized as a brave and daring player, and now sought as mentor of young Harvard aspirants for gridiron honor." The implications of Horween's ascendance was "not only a glowing tribute to his own inherent worth but an eloquent testimony to the rapid Americanization of Russian Jews."[76] Some Jewish weeklies debated just how Jewishly engaged Horween was in his everyday dealings at Harvard or in his hometown Chicago.[77] Most Jews likely did not give Horween's observance that much mind, preferring instead to celebrate the instance as a remarkable moment for America's Jews.

Then there were the onlookers in midwestern outposts, populated by blue-collar workers, immigrants, and their children. They stood by Horween as a symbol of the possibilities of "Americanism." A newspaperman in Moorhead, Minnesota, declared in the editorial columns that "America is still America and the spirit that has made this country great is alive and active. Arnold Horween is going to Harvard as football coach and Arnold Horween is the son of an immigrant. Thirty-four years ago his father landed in this country with nothing except the will to work."[78]

But others judged it far more sinful for Harvard to elect a former professional to the pristine coaching ranks. Their rancor was further enflamed by statements from Cardinals owner Chris O'Brien, who embellished Horween's place in the professional game, claiming Arnold was the "greatest player ever to be identified with professional football."[79]

Foremost was Amos Alonzo Stagg, that self-appointed crusader against the National Football League. Under Stagg's guidance, the football programs in the Midwest had banned ex-pros from coaching. Stagg had campaigned for eastern colleges to follow suit. Some, like Princeton, said they would but there was no official mechanism to canonize commitments to shunning professionals. That Horween was ineligible to join the National Association of Football Coaches because of his earlier professional tenure was of little solace to Stagg. Horween's case signaled the sad fact to Stagg that his "alarm has not extended to the East."[80] Others in Stagg's corner predicted that it was only a matter of time before Harvard would be "overcome with shame and embarrassment by the elevation of Arnold Horween."[81] Another writer negated the whole worthwhileness of the professional game, convinced that Horween, with just that as his coaching background, lacked the experience to refurbish the reeling Crimson squad.[82]

Others did not mind all that much. George Owen, who had one year earlier ignited the Harvard football tinderbox, approved of Harvard's hiring choice: "He knows a lot about modern football tactics." To Owen, Horween stood a good chance of restoring the game for the young men playing it. "He is quiet, and the kind of man who goes ahead and does something without making a lot of talk about it," Owen recalled about his old teammate. "He is the type that is a great example to those under him and I'm certain will turn out to be a most inspiring coach."[83] Yale's Tad Jones agreed that Horween was an "awful nice chap" and "peculiarly well qualified to coach those things so essential to success in football."[84] A letter writer in the Yale student paper, submitted under the nom de plume "Friendly Rival," approved as well, fearing that "Yale men will find no easy task in defeating a Horween-coached team."[85]

All this remained prominently in the background when Bill Bingham and Arnold Horween addressed Harvard on March 11. Three days after arriving for the interview, Horween stood before two hundred students packed into the Harvard Varsity Club. Photographers snapped photographs of Horween flanked by Bingham and other athletic officials. Dozens of staged images appeared in the press, none of them including Henry Pennypacker or Lawrence Lowell.

Bingham introduced the press conference. "The first thing I want to tell you football players is why Arnie Horween was selected as head coach." Bingham appreciated that his decision to tap Horween was seismic, at least in the minds of Harvard traditionalists.[86] The advent of a "Coach Horween" was an unprecedented thing. Haughton had refined football for the Crimson. He did not transform it. The late Haughton had also passed very well for a Boston Brahmin. Of Bob Fisher, much the same could be said. Arnold Horween was different. "There has been a lot of talk about modern football lately, particularly western football progress," Bingham continued. "When the announcement was made that we were bringing a fellow from the West to coach, a lot of the so-called 'old guard' said that we were throwing the rest of the game away. This is not so. Harvard realizes that it has a perfectly good football foundation, but the game is changing in the past few years."[87]

No one seemed to believe Bingham. A reporter recorded the rumors swirling around Harvard Yard: "Harvard using the huddle system! Harvard throwing forward passes; Harvard opening up under a coaching staff composed almost entirely of Westerners. Harvard calling for the first time on two coaches who are not Harvard men! That's the new situation in football

The illustrator of this political cartoon anticipated that the new Bingham-Horween era in Harvard football history would abandon the old Haughton regime. First published in the *Yonkers Herald*, October 13, 1926, 15.

at Cambridge, and it is being watched with intense interest." But certainly, Arnie and Ralph were Harvard men. They were recent alumni and former football standouts. The sportswriter clarified that the Horween brothers were "men from beyond the Alleghanies, men who trace not to the good ship Mayflower, Plymouth Rock, the Pequot Wars, [or] the Boston Tea Party." The Horweens were outsiders whose cultural capital rendered them less American than their forebears. They were "neither Haughtons nor Fishers nor Cabots nor Adamses."[88]

The conditions for Horween's position were somehow different than during his playing days. The Harvard head coaching job was a permanent and prominent role, unlike that of an All-American football captain. It was only with a degree of overstatement that a Hebrew scribe marveled that a "Jewish boy" had been "selected as head coach of the Harvard football activities. This," he surmised, "is one of the most important athletic positions in America."[89] Certainly, the college gridiron landscape had changed; other schools had emerged and usurped the game from the New England universities that had incubated football. But Harvard still loomed large as a result of its antique prominence. Harvard and Horween had also changed in the five years since he had graduated. Lowell had launched his crusade against Jews, particularly those of Eastern European extraction. Horween had made himself vulnerable by joining the professional ranks and excelling in a variation of the sport that valued innovation over custom. In all these ways, Horween stood on the periphery of the mainstream. It troubled many Harvard graduates, but not Bill Bingham. He himself had always felt like an outsider, to some degree or another.

Horween did not speak for that long. He described it as "one of the happiest moments of my life." Then he reiterated Bingham's message. Harvard football was fundamentally strong. It was a program built on tradition, the Haughton system.

Still, there was no denying that Horween had something new to offer Harvard. "Of course, my connection with the game since my graduation from college has been mostly in the middle west," affirmed Horween. "I naturally have imbibed what are considered the modern ideas of that section. What I think worth copying of these phases of western football I will not hesitate to introduce."[90] Bingham grimaced. Horween packed his belongings and departed for Chicago to prepare for a new iteration of Harvard football.

CHAPTER EIGHT

AN HONORABLE FAILURE
AND SATISFACTORY GAME
IN EVERY WAY

You graduates are normal on most subjects, but you are
surprisingly abnormal in your demand for athletic victory.
Your team must always win and after a couple of defeats you
write wild eyed letters to the Bulletin demanding the coach's
scalp. It makes little difference what the circumstances are.
We must always win and in this respect, you are curiously
like the alumni of other institutions.
—William J. Bingham, New England Federation of Harvard
    Clubs, July 23, 1926, Harvard University Archives

The Boston sportswriters were not all that quick to embrace Coach Arnold
Horween. "I regret sincerely that I didn't give Horween credit at the
time," journalist Stanley Woodward remembered, "for having the nerve to do
something new when most of the other coaches were sticking to established
patterns."[1] Woodward might be forgiven, since it was a particularly polarizing
time at Harvard College. There were mixed feelings about Horween and just
about everything else passing through Harvard Yard. To defend Woodward
even more, it is instructive to know that Harvard was a rather inhospitable
place for the newspaper industry. Lawrence Lowell never granted interviews
on the grounds that, to his mind, newspaper reports could only hinder his
school's reputation. Lowell was very proud of the fact that Harvard ranked
first among colleges, no matter how Yale or Princeton might have quibbled
about their own scholastic standing. Chicago, Johns Hopkins, and Stanford
were more fashionable schools to certain members of the avant-garde classes.
Still, that group did not matter to Lowell as much as the members of the so-
called Big Three triumvirate.

Percy Haughton preferred Lowell's policies about the press. He had convinced Lowell that the overemphasis on football that Charles Eliot had decried before Lowell's administration took over was mostly due to the sports scribes. That explanation ingratiated Harvard's president further to Haughton's way of thinking. The Crimson players drilled in closed practices. "Even the president of the college," wrote a former Harvard footballer, "isn't welcome at secret practice."[2] Once, when the University of Michigan Wolverines traveled to Cambridge to face off against the Crimson, Haughton spotted some Boston journalists hiding on the edge of the field. Haughton "chased them out of the park." The stunt surprised Michigan coach Fielding Yost. "Gee," said Yost to Haughton, "I wish I could get away with that out West. If I did that they'd run me out of football."[3] The quip served as an acknowledgment of Haughton's power around Harvard Yard.

The decision to shut out spectators had as much to do with Haughton's fear of enemy scouts as it did with Lowell's patrician snobbishness. The sports scribes found it downright rude, very different from the receptions they received at other colleges. Of course, they understood that those other schools needed the press much more than Harvard did. The poorly built press box at Soldiers Field became a kind of cheering section for Harvard's opponents. The facilities reserved for those disgruntled writers had no restroom until the sportswriters threatened "mass urination on the customers below."[4] Bob Fisher maintained Haughton's stance. "The only way you could get any information was to tag along with Coach Fisher as he walked between the dressing quarters and the practice field."[5]

Horween did not do much to ingratiate himself any better than his predecessors. He maintained closed practices for the Harvard Crimson and offered rather glib responses to the reporters' questions. Then again, that he wasn't Haughton and that he was a part of Bingham's youth campaign made Horween a more pleasing figurehead at Harvard.[6]

Horween dissociated himself from the Haughton system in short order. He brought Jim Brader from the University of Wisconsin to coach the offensive and defensive lines. Ralph Horween, married and enrolled in Harvard Law School, instructed the backs. Arnie had tried to convince Duke Dunne ("D. McMahon") to coach the linemen. Dunne declined, but a year later he came to Harvard to help Horween. Arnie had better fortunes with Fred Gillies ("C. McMahon"), who joined to prepare the varsity squad. Eddie Casey dropped the head coaching job at Tufts to drill the freshman. Eskie Clark was another Harvard man who joined to support Horween, probably at Bingham's insistence to mollify the sensitivities of Harvard graduates. That was an important thing, since Horween maintained that he needed Chuck Carney from the

University of Illinois to coach the wings; that is, the footballers who lined up on the outskirts of the formation, who traditionally blocked for the runners.[7] In Urbana, the wings also sprinted downfield, not yet formally called "wide receivers," to catch a pass.

Carney had learned the football trade from Illini coach Bob Zuppke. The University of Illinois's Zuppke was one of several midwestern coaches to have claimed to be the inventor of the forward pass. Years earlier, Haughton had called on Zuppke to travel to Boston to teach him how to do it. The New England brass was rather stunned by the reports that Haughton had been "prepared to sell off Harvard's traditional set of plays for a popular gimmick run by Middle West hicks." The Harvard alumni did not think that their young men required parlor tricks "picked up in some corner grocery store in northern Michigan," or wherever else Zuppke had traveled in his sojourns.[8]

But Bob Zuppke was a winner, a quality that Harvard had come to embrace. Between 1913 to 1928, the Illini had beaten their opponents in the Big Ten Conference in three-quarters of their games.[9] The forward pass was not the prime reason for the success, not in Zuppke's estimation. He was a "stickler for blocking and tackling."[10] Football had become a form of devotion in Illinois and the rest of the American prairie lands. Zuppke spoke about the sport in deeply religious terms. "Never prophesy a great football future for any back until he has gained his first yard and taken his first bump," was something he liked to say, especially after taking much credit for discovering the star halfback Red Grange.[11] On other occasions, Zuppke, who enjoyed training hearty young fellows, liked to quip that "the Lord is generally on the side of the team with the biggest tackles."[12]

Horween knew Zuppke and his acolytes from Chicago. He liked the idea of bringing some of Zuppke-styled football to Harvard. Foremost was the forward pass. It was totally different from the backward lateral toss that relied on solid blocking and formation assignments. Haughton had used the forward pass at Harvard, although very sparingly. He and Walter Camp believed using it was a principal threat to their style of game, one marked by precision. It changed the quarterback too much. The man in that position was meant to be a kindred spirit of the coxswain, who steers his crewmates toward the finish of a long regatta. The coxswain was never meant to clutch an oar any more than a quarterback, the old guard had it, was tasked to handle a football beyond the simple motion of receiving it from the center and transferring it to another, less-cerebral, man stationed in his backfield.

Regularly charging the quarterback or another player with lunging a forward pass was, to Haughton, a blasphemous way to carry on with the sport. A regular-sized human hand could not grip the heavy and wide football of that time. Michigan's Benny Friedman was an exception, owing to his overly large hands and zealous finger exercises that permitted him to handle a football "as firmly as a pitcher grips a baseball."[13] Most young men resorted to heaving the ball out of their palm, praying that it would glide in the direction they had intended with their inexact toss. Haughton and other coaches who sat on the collegiate rules committees therefore held that the forward pass had no regular place in football and that it was a variation on "basketball techniques," a preferred sport for "high school girls."[14]

The Camp regime did their best to suppress the pass, even after Theodore Roosevelt had insisted, along with the formation of the NCAA, on instituting it to decrease injuries and headbanging, as in the fateful controversies of 1905. The college coaches barred forward passing within twenty-five yards of either goal line. They also decreed that, if the football did not contact an offensive player before touching the ground, it was a turnover; the team on defense, then, claimed possession and transitioned to offense. The rule made the pass too risky except in the most desperate of circumstances. In 1907, an incomplete pass was made less severe, incurring a fifteen-yard penalty rather than a forfeiture of possession. A year later, the committee changed the rule again, deciding that, if an offensive player touched the ball but did not catch it, any defender was eligible to pick it up as a fumble.

The professional ranks were warmer to the pass. Horween quarterbacked the Chicago Cardinals and did a swell job passing to Paddy Driscoll, among others. Driscoll had surrendered the thrower's roll on the Cardinals to Horween because he was more useful, with Arnie on the team, as a halfback. Driscoll was also placated by the fact that he retained input in calling the plays. The pair, along with other teammates, bargained with each other in the presnap huddle. The collective offense then broke to their positions along the line of scrimmage, content with the consensus opinion on how to run the next play. Horween then reached for the football under the center, without any need to call out signs unless he truly felt that the defense had lined up in a manner that anticipated the democratically-agreed-upon play selection.

College coaches such as Camp and Haughton viewed the huddle as a type of sabotage, undermining the quarterback's generalship of the game plan. The other players were meant to rely on the quarterback's coded play calling on the line of scrimmage as a football gospel, whether they approved of the design of their route or not. A close companion testified that "Haughton believed the huddle led to the blind calling of plays and preferred the careful selection of a play by the quarterback after he had called his formation."[15] A fellow coach summed up both Haughton's and Camp's view of the congregating huddle, that it "tends to kill any initiative on the part of the quarterback, thus preventing him from really running the team." That the brief conversation might "permit the team to advise the quarterback about any weaknesses they have discovered" was shoddy strategy and threatened college football's hitherto authoritarian, top-down military form.[16]

Haughton had hated how the huddle democratized decision making just as much as Horween approved of it for the very same reason. Haughton was raised in a rather Republican milieu that sequestered the elites from the working class. He translated that predilection to football. Horween had learned to trust the choices of others from his American-adoring immigrant parents and the progressive teachers who had educated him at Francis Parker School on Chicago's North Side.

The Haughton type was much more ubiquitous among the eastern colleges. It was the very same New England elitism that had reared Harvard-trained economist James Laurence Laughlin, progressives like Louis Brandies notwithstanding. So conspicuous were the politics of conservative pro-banker, unyielding working-class critic that, while teaching at Harvard College, Laughlin prepared an abridgment of John Stuart Mill's *Politically Economy* for his students, rather brazenly, according to one historian, skipping the sections in which Mill lambasted the higher classes for their squelching of "good morals" and their "inequalities for women." Laughlin was therefore sure to delete lines such as Mill's claim of the "total absence of regard for justice or fairness in the relations between capital and labor."[17]

The same sort of teachings was present at Yale College for Camp and others to imbibe. William Graham Sumner, the very first professor of sociology in the United States, considered it a rather futile thing for regular men to assert themselves on the better people. "The truth is that the social order is fixed by laws of nature precisely analogous to those of the physical order," averred Sumner. "The most that any man can do is by his ignorance and conceit to mar the operation of the social laws."[18]

It is certainly the case that Harvard employed its share of liberals such as George Herbert Palmer, a classicist and avowed suffragist. But Palmer was a meek figure, in comparison, say, with Hugo Münsterberg, a bombastic public intellectual and pioneer of applied psychology. Münsterberg, according to one biographer, was a "man with very socially conservative ideas and one with a strong feeling for order and an equally strong sense of duty."[19] The Prussian-born Münsterberg had a very European perspective on classes and social climbing; he was big on the first and very hostile to the second. Münsterberg held traditional-cum-antiliberal views on the intellectual abilities of women. So disparaging was Münsterberg, that his student, William Moulton Marston, creator of the comic heroine, Wonder Woman, based one of his supervillains, Doctor Psycho, largely on Münsterberg and his prejudices against women.[20]

Debate over the huddle was a public item in the sports pages until the rules committee finally dropped it—the debate, not the huddle—in December 1926. The debate had reached that governing group because of a clique of eastern coaches who had disparaged "huddle throttling" as a perturbing innovation.[21] By then, the midwesterners such as Rockne, Stagg, and Zuppke had asserted themselves and were not about to give way to the diminished traditionalists on the East Coast. Horween remained silent on the issue. His silence, however, did little to hide the secrets of his football allegiances, or how his loyalties affixed themselves to the curious ways that football represented several of the pivotal matters of American life.

* * *

Arnold Horween was unsure of Harvard's outcome in his inaugural head coaching campaign in 1926. He had returned to campus in April to drill his prospective athletes and examine the assortment of men at his disposal before football reconvened in earnest later in the autumn. Arnie brought along Eddie Casey, who was still employed as Tuft's football coach. Bill Bingham was away, having traveled with the crew team to Princeton.[22] Almost seventy undergraduates showed up for Horween's first spring practice.

"There will be no one who will be more interested in watching to see what the team will do," jested Horween, "than I will."[23] He was reticent to offer much more than that. He promised not to stray too far from the Haughton system, but his coaching appointments betrayed a different sentiment. He could not do much to deflect the reports that the Haughton philosophy was on the outs in favor of a supposedly vibrant and younger take on athletics in general, and football in particular. The sportswriters, much aggrieved by Haughton's treatment of them, looked forward to rehearsing this trope in their columns.

Someone was required to speak for Harvard amid the transitions. It was Bill Bingham's role to evangelize his "athletics for all" position. His aim was to convert the group he believed mostly opposed to his views. In each speech, he addressed the "alumni problem" at Harvard. He was frank with them. "You graduates are normal on most subjects but you are surprisingly abnormal in your demand for athletic victory," Bingham charged. This is how he concluded one speech: "That day is gone by. We want your counsel, we want your support, but like any other department in the University we intend to make our decisions having in mind at all times the best interests of Harvard University and the undergraduates. Too many of you are likely to think that because conditions were so and so in your day they are the same today."[24] Here is how Bingham ended another football sermon: "Of late, there have been too many graduates trying to run our teams from their offices in Boston. But that day is gone as long as I am director of athletics."[25]

Bingham was congratulated for his "series of heretical utterances."[26] The newer generation of liberal-leaning journalists and even younger undergraduates feted Bingham's audacious declaration. Theirs was the modernist generation that was on occasion emboldened to call out their parents' and teachers' American nativism and rote traditionalism.[27] Some in this rank described themselves as freethinkers and would have counted the youth-touting Bingham among them. Bingham's own boldness tended to increase his self-confidence bolstered by a belief that most alumni wanted someone to repossess football from their untrusting clutches. He continued to blast Harvard graduates at their cherished Harvard Clubs. He admonished them and, as might be surprising, the alums fell into line as Bill Bingham redefined winning at Harvard. "The victory has come for the coach not in what his team has done against an adversary, but in what he has done for his boys." Harvard men continued to applaud Bingham. He, however, stayed incredulous about their adulations. "The graduates will have to stand solidly behind me during a couple of seasons of defeat before I will feel convinced that they are sincerely interested in the welfare of athletics, and not in the mere piling up of victories."[28]

American Jews paid close attention to Bingham's praises. It seemed an antidote to President Lowell's attempt to halt their numbers at America's most prestigious college. Jews were aware of the chance Bingham had taken in resisting the protests against appointing the Jewish Horween as the Crimson's coach. Bill's calls for pluralism, even if he hadn't called it by that designation, was reminiscent of Horace Kallen's declarations for an openness to new voices and contributions in American life.[29]

The Jewish material bequeathed to Horween also appeared promising. The syndicated Jewish columnists took a cue from the Boston journalists who prophesied that, with Horween and halfbacks "Al Miller and Izzy Zarakov, the Harvard football team may be said to possess a distinguished Jewish athletic triumvirate."[30]

Horween paid no mind to these things. The Self-Culture Club that had socialized Rose and Isadore Horween had also made sure that Ralph and Arnie were raised to pay attention to merit rather than race or creed. Once asked to identify his Jewish team members, Horween "admitted that he paid little attention to that." He told the Jewish journalist that the newspaperman could "locate the chaps of our faith as readily as he."[31] The Hebrew press

Bill Bingham and Arnold Horween chatting during football practice in 1928. From the author's personal collection.

would have liked him to do otherwise, indulging to some extent or another in their own fascination with Horween's Jewish background. Horween's very "Jewish" form of Americanization—a member of the American insider elite, armed with Harvard credentials and sports fame—more than satisfied this group. As for his Crimson players, American Jews paid closest attention to Isadore Zarakov. Born in 1903, Izzy lived the Horatio Alger–inspired tale that the well-heeled Horween could never conform to, no matter how badly his coreligionists wished it for him.

Simon Zarakov was a tailor, earning about $2,000 per annum. He had learned the trade in his native Odessa. He was a small-statured immigrant, as was his wife, Sarah. The couple's eldest son, Barney, was a good athlete and a few inches taller than his parents; a credit, they all presumed, to a better diet than the nutrition available to the working classes in Europe.

Izzy Zarakov was something different. He measured five feet, nine inches, a respectable height in that epoch. Izzy cut a slim and sinewy figure, carrying a mass of 150 pounds. At Cambridge Latin High School, the reporters agreed, Zarakov "stands out as one of New England's foremost scholastic athletes." Most newspapers listed him on Boston's all-scholastic teams in baseball, football, and hockey. The last was his finest sport. Hockey harnessed Izzy's agile speed and quick instincts. Baseball did so, too. In football, Zarakov was faster than the other schoolboys, never having to use much more than his normal speed to return a punt or take a handoff and ease past a cluster of approaching defenders.[32] The bottom line was that Isadore Zarakov was one of the most thrilling young athletes in New England or elsewhere.[33]

The reporters also gushed about Izzy's genteel disposition, how well he seemed to fit in among his Boston-born friends. The press offered comment on this aspect of Izzy's modest celebrity because he was "of Hebrew nationality." Despite this, in prose that appears now as backhanded antisemitism, Zarakov had "gained the esteem and popular favor of his mates as well as those he has competed against, by his unassuming manner and clean, sportsmanlike tactics on and off the field of play."[34]

Sarah and Simon Zarakov embraced the attention that their son had attracted, not noticing that it came to him because of how much Izzy appeared to stand in opposition to anti-Jewish tropes. Izzy was destined for sport stardom from birth. According to a legend peddled by his doting mother, Zarakov had used perfect form when he kicked his pillow beyond the rails of his crib as a six-month-old.

On one occasion, the Zarakovs attended a meeting of the Massachusetts Association of Americanization Teachers. There, Charles Eliot, the former Harvard head, gave a talk about educating the classes, irrespective of social privilege. Eliot delivered his discourse—a theme that probably stood out because of much more rigid voices associated with Harvard—and then called on Mrs. Zarakov, singling her family out for their younger son's raised reputation. "We have worked all our lives for the honor our sons might bring us," attested Sarah Zarakov, persevering past her typically broken English, having practiced the short line throughout Eliot's speech. "It is worth it all," she proudly announced. "What is money compared to it? We are satisfied."[35]

Cambridge Latin was not enough to escort Zarakov past Lowell's admission censors at Harvard. Izzy therefore enrolled in Phillips Exeter Academy. He was a decent student and received a conditional acceptance to the New Hampshire prep school, as long as he maintained grades above a C. He did that, except for physics. Exeter overlooked that D because Izzy had proven himself a clever plugger, in school and in sports.

His teachers extolled him. "Zarakov is a young man of fine natural ability who is constantly inspiring. He has a fine character and is a natural leader among boys," wrote one of Izzy's recommenders, very much aware of Harvard's prejudices against the ignoble character of Jews. "I am fond of the boy."[36]

Zarakov's lone year at Exeter in 1922 was sufficient to seek enrollment at Harvard College. Izzy did not try to suppress his Jewishness on the application, and there was no point in hiding it. He selected "Hebrew" under religious preference and his intention to pursue a profession in law, possibly at Harvard. Izzy indicated as well that his father could not afford the tuition. He pledged, however, to pay a hundred dollars each year (about a third of the total tuition) earned from "summer work."[37] Harvard accepted him. Apparently, in the twilight of the Haughton era, Henry Pennypacker's admissions committee was willing to look away from Zarakov's Jewish disposition for the sake of supporting Crimson athletics.

Zarakov continued to play all three of his sports at Harvard. His freshman football team beat the scrubs, that is, the second varsity team, in a scrimmage match, 26–0. He earned a reputation as a "running fool," a moniker that meant something far more positive in 1923.[38] Jews in Boston predicted that Zarakov "will bear watching on the varsity squad next year."[39] Zarakov's facial features were physiognomically eastern European and therefore "Hebraic," to Jewish commentators keeping track of such things. They therefore looked forward to the next iteration of the Jews' "Harvard hero."[40]

Bob Fisher promoted Izzy to his varsity Crimson team in 1924 but ranked him as the fourth-string halfback. The coach did not place him on the field all that much in Izzy's sophomore year. Fisher appreciated Zarakov's speed. Still, the Harvard coaches could not teach him to burrow through the line of scrimmage to use that acceleration after the handoff.[41]

Izzy remained on the bench much of the subsequent year, until the finale. Against Yale, Fisher unexpectedly announced that Izzy Zarakov and Al Miller would start in the backfield against rival Yale. The proclamation brought to bear the social fault lines prevalent in Cambridge. "Harvard has a Beacon Street line and a Salem Street backfield," chided reporters. Useful analogies suggested that the Crimson's Protestant offensive lineman—the "Bradford twins," specifically—took issue with their blocking assignment meant to keep a pair of "runty" Jewish boys upright against the Elis. "In New York this would be the same as saying a Park Avenue line and a Delancey Street backfield. In Chicago it would be equal to saying a North Shore line and a Maxwell Street backfield."[42]

The lineup dynamic did not last too long. Miller was a speedy track and field man, a one-dimensional straightaway runner, ill-suited for a grinding football game. What is more, Miller couldn't block, rendering himself nothing much better than an endangerment to his teammates. Zarakov remained stymied by the defensive wall, unable to break tackles to move forward as he had done against lesser competition at Cambridge Latin and at Phillips Exeter. He twice fumbled the football in the first half of that Yale contest. Fisher replaced both young men in the second half, his last coaching decision in his final game as Harvard's head coach.[43]

The rumor mill had it that Horween hoped to revive Zarakov's football career. After all, Izzy was a rare three-letter man at Harvard, since he played, albeit poorly, in the Harvard-Yale contest. He was the hockey team's very best forward. At third base, he earned honors for hitting for the highest average and for "overall ability." His teammates elected him captain in Izzy's senior year.[44] Everyone agreed that Zarakov would be a dangerous runner if he could cross the scrimmage line. It would have been a terrific tale, and Bingham and Horween both approved of the Zarakov rehabilitation project. Elevating Zarakov would, however, have been tantamount to the patrician privilege system long ensconced at Harvard, but in reverse. Under the new regime, the Harvard Crimson pledged to maintain a culture of unassailable merit.

* * *

Geneva College was Harvard's first challenger under Arnold Horween. Geneva was located in Beaver Falls, Pennsylvania. It had been founded in Ohio by Protestant ministers and moved, back in 1880, to the western section of Pennsylvania, hoping to recruit students from the faithful of Pittsburgh. Almost a half-century later, Geneva's total enrollment was the size of Harvard's freshman class. To solicit better interest, Geneva hired Bo McMillin. McMillin was that shady figure who had turned down Arnie Horween's game-ball gesture and led Centre College in a win against the Crimson the following year. As a professional, McMillin and his Milwaukee Badgers battled Horween's Chicago Cardinals. In 1922, Centenary College in Shreveport, Louisiana, summoned McMillin to coach its makeshift football program.

"Boston liked Bo."[45] To Harvard's chagrin, Boston College booked Bo McMillin's Centenary team before Harvard could extend its own invitation. The Crimson were therefore quick to pounce when McMillin moved to Geneva College, an action that the heads of the Beaver Falls school had surely anticipated when they had courted McMillin.

Aside from McMillin, Geneva was unintriguing. The tradition at Harvard was to schedule an underwhelming opponent to open the season. The purpose was to help refine the players' skills and to spike confidence for the tougher teams on tap. Horween's pregame circumspection about Geneva therefore seemed out of place. "I realize we are meeting the hardest first game competition of any Harvard team in many years," cautioned a worried Coach Horween, "but my team is as far along as can possibly be expected, and I feel that we will make a good showing."[46] Perhaps some read Horween's anxieties as a reaction to Geneva's representative play against Cornell one week earlier. The Ithacans had defeated McMillin's team, 6–0. The low score suggested more about Cornell's misaligned offense than Geneva's defensive prowess, the Bostoners most probably figured.

Such was not the case, and Horween knew it. McMillin had shamelessly confessed that he had brought his "own li'l boys" to Beaver Falls.[47] By this, McMillin meant that he had recruited several of his former Centre teammates to help him win games for Geneva, men who were likely ineligible, like McMillin, when he had suited up for Centre College. Cornell's Gilmour Dobie found out about McMillin's plot and "put up such a scream over Geneva's cast of characters that he shamed Bo into withholding some of the more flagrantly traveled operatives."[48] Cornell's coach's protest was the sole reason the Big Red wasn't smashed in by McMillin's ringers.

Harvard under Horween, on the other hand, "made no protest and took on the whole Geneva aggregation."[49] McMillin's was an intimidating lot, a "gold-jerseyed team of giants." Horween deployed his huddle system against Geneva but did not execute a forward pass until the very end of the contest. Harvard tied the game, 7–7, on a long run in the second quarter but could not muster much offense after that. Horween's charges also missed several long dropkicks.[50] Sensing that he had a handle on the scoring, McMillin ordered his men to ease up on Harvard, departing Cambridge with a respectable 16–7 victory. The uneven bout made at least one sportswriter "giggle," an unbecoming reflex he and other scribes had developed during their cantankerous relationship with Haughton and Fisher.[51]

Beaten and injured, Harvard lost again to Holy Cross a week later. Just four starters from the Geneva debacle led off the match against the Crusaders. Some substitutions were due to injuries. Others, such as Horween's decision to play sophomore quarterback Eliot Putnam instead of the veteran varsity man, Jake Stafford, occurred in order to offer unexpected opportunities to younger and unproven players. Putnam was the speediest back on the Crimson, except for Izzy Zarakov.

On the mend, Horween's team claimed its first victory against William and Mary. The Crimson's best win of the season came against Dartmouth. The most aggressive Boston bookies, offering 2–1 odds in favor of the Hanover squad, suffered a good deal after that game. Harvard's victory arose from a fortunate substitution. Arnie put Henry Chauncey, a kicker, in the game at the opening of the third period to boot a field goal. Chauncey did his work just fine but was of little use other than for drop-kicking. Horween swapped sophomore Arthur French for Chauncey in the final period. He was a former Crimson freshman captain and Worchester Academy sprinter. French bolted through Dartmouth's line and onward to a forty-seven-yard touchdown. French's was the pivotal score in a 16–12 win for Harvard.[52]

French goosestepped with the rest of the Crimson players out of the huddle. Putnam called for the snap and handed it to French, directing the runner to maneuver toward the left of the field with his momentum. French did just that but then reversed. The runner veered away from his interference, almost careering into a tackler. Then French staggered to maintain his balance and dashed to his right. Dartmouth's star, Eddie Dooley, anchored himself to resist French's forward progress. Dooley had had a busy afternoon, and a productive one at that. He drop-kicked a field goal and intercepted a Putnam pass that afternoon. Tackling French was a lesser effort, or it should have been. Instead, Art French slid to his right and Dooley tumbled. No one was left to stop French from broaching the goal line.

Dave Guarnaccia was another source of Harvard's improved play. Like French, Guarnaccia was a handsome sprinter from a Boston neighborhood. George Owen, now soundly a Harvard football supporter, liked the "big, rangy chap." Guarnaccia "runs hard and smoothly, and is never down until firmly tackled."[53] Guarnaccia was almost as quick as French and weighed 155 pounds, a good amount sturdier than his counterpart. "Counterparts" was exactly what the pair amounted to in short order.

Horween discovered Guarnaccia on the second varsity team. Initially, Arnie had figured that his first team fared poorly against the scrub squad because, well, his group wasn't all that good. In practices, however, Guarnaccia glided past defenders, in contrast to Zarakov, and emerged as an able halfback. When Al Miller suffered an injury early in the season, Horween promoted Guarnaccia to the top-tier team and started him in the backfield in the William and Mary contest. Art French joined him there after his long run to vanquish Dartmouth. Allison Danzig of the *New York Times* described

Horween's work as "one of the most remarkable developments football has witnessed."[54]

The decision to insert French and Guarnaccia represented another way Arnie Horween disregarded the older Harvard Brahmin-induced etiquette.[55] Had Percy Haughton or Bob Fisher substituted a better runner for Chauncey, it would have been Izzy Zarakov instead of Art French. Zarakov was the senior member, well respected, and a member of Harvard's most elite societies. In an earlier epoch, Zarakov would probably have been granted an opportunity to replace Miller, not skipped over for a second-stringer like Guarnaccia.

The Jewish press had urged Horween to reestablish Zarakov's place in the Crimson lineup before the William and Mary bout, and again against Dartmouth, and then in preparation for lowly Tufts. That Al Miller, another Jewish footballer, resurged in a romp of the Tufts Jumbos from nearby Medford—he accounted for three of Harvard's ten touchdowns—did not assuage objectors. Zarakov found Harvard glory in baseball during the spring, smashing a bottom-of-the-ninth and two-outs home run to vanquish Yale. The Elis had reclaimed the lead in the top of the ninth inning, so Zarakov's home run— reports alleged that the ball landed in the freshman field and when finally found and tossed into the infield, the bulk of the Yale nine were already in the locker room—was a dramatic affair. In tropes that resembled the exaltations of Bill Bingham during his erstwhile racing career, the Boston sports scribes trumpeted that "Yale may have its Frank Merriwell, but Harvard had its Izzy Zarakov yesterday."[56] Jews likewise relished Zarakov's heroics, all the while noting that it would have been much better had Zarakov been raised on the much grander gridiron stage.[57]

* * *

Bingham and the players were on Arnie's side. It was a firm illustration of the generational divide that did much to account for Horween's polarizing position at Harvard. Bingham "anxiously" issued Horween a contract extension on the grounds that players and students were more excited about football at Harvard than they had been in a long time.[58] Winning was not Bingham's rubric for successful coaching. There were rumors that Harvard trustees were against Bingham's philosophy and pleaded with Lowell to intercede and break his pact with Bingham to leave the latter unimpeded to attend to Crimson matters. No doubt these were New England–soaked men who had opposed Horween's appointment in the first place on the grounds he was neither a Protestant nor a Brahmin. Harvard undergraduates were amazed, remarking that it was a sheer wonder that the Crimson remained competitive with a skeleton roster. They were puzzled "how Horween convinced his players that they had a chance to win."[59] The students in Harvard Yard were forgiving of the Geneva defeat, especially in consideration of McMillin's antics.

Reaching back to an earlier age of American sport, Horween spoke to his charges about manhood. "This is a rough, tough game," he liked to tell them, "and we love it because it is a virile game."[60] The language of muscular Christianity—or in this case, muscular Judaism—had become desacralized. He sermonized about teamwork and about recollecting each teammate's assignment on the field, just in case. Most of all, Horween preached that hard work was a means to good character. Once, during a drill, a Crimson man hit a practice dummy so hard that its springs started to whistle. The footballer nervously stepped away, fearing that the coach would reprimand him for damaging a fine piece of equipment. Instead, Horween smiled and shouted, "Didn't that feel great?"[61] The talk around Harvard about Horween's Crimson units was not framed around winning, although there was, at that point in Horween's inaugural season, much more of it than in the twilight years of Bob Fisher's football tenure. For some, no doubt, Bingham's deemphasis on the accumulation of victories cohered with the sentiments espoused by some of the Harvard instructors about the definitions of success.

American dictionaries first started to link success to the accruing of wealth in the 1890s.[62] Several groups emerged and pushed back against this, specifically the proponents of New Thought and the nascent field of psychology. The two groups had much in common, preaching romantic topics like transcendentalism, metaphysics, and life-affirming healing therapies. Harvard professors were some of the first to offer credence to these modernists. William James believed there was something to the "Gospel of Relaxation" and the "Don't Worry Movement" that the money-minded men of the Boston's Back Bay and New York's Wall Street could not offer.[63] Hugo Münsterberg, while he had unkind things to say about populism, had taken to psychotherapy just as James had taken to the New Thoughters.[64] Both men, who had died before Horween returned to coach Harvard, had generated an enthusiasm for meanings of success separate from financial fortune. Their immediate professorial descendants who toiled in philosophy and the social sciences at Harvard continued to teach about contentment, general wellness, and satisfaction, even as most well-heeled students graduated to join other indoctrinated mammon-worshippers in the temple of American capitalism.[65]

Sport for sport's sake provided perhaps a more relatable outlet for this rogue theology of American success. The notion was patently midwestern.

Amos Alonzo Stagg rued the fact—although he himself was sometimes guilty of it—that the "British play a game for the game's sake; we play to win." Stagg hated that the "doctrine has been carried to outrageous lengths at times and all but killed football."[66] Particularly in the Middle West, the Roaring Twenties, after the melancholy surrounding World War I, was the "Age of Play," an epoch in which young men and women indulged in adolescence, a recently discovered, loosely defined age bracket.[67] Harvard, still enveloped in the spirit of Haughton and caught up in vanquishing Yale and Princeton, had failed to absorb the sentiment of the time.

Horween sought to migrate this "play" culture to New England. Arnie gave credit to his athletes and, like them, shot down winning as a measure of a successful season. "The eleven showed that it is coming along and can fight," explained Horween, "and that is all we can ask at midseason."[68] His players appreciated that. The varsity eleven also noticed that their peers were doing less complaining that the "college's curriculum is so hard," as they had done in the old regime, to excuse poor athletic performances.[69] The newspapermen intuited it also, suggesting, bristling, that Arnie "eradicated the latter-day Fisher cry-baby influence."[70] Bill Bingham reported to Harvard alumni that the footballers had attested that they had "worked much harder and played fiercer this year than a year ago."[71]

Horween had a knack for inspiration. Take, for instance, the Dartmouth game. Eliot Putnam had had an uneven performance against the Big Green. On the one hand, he had scored the game's first touchdown. It was a well-executed deception play: Putnam flipped the football to Guarnaccia, who feigned hesitation before throwing it back to Putnam, who had slipped forward to the goal line. On the other hand, Putnam had shown an unreasonable amount of aggressiveness, opting to run the ball on fourth down rather than punt the football into Dartmouth's territory. In the first half, Putnam rushed unsuccessfully five times on fourth down, returning possession to Dartmouth with very favorable field position.[72]

"I wish he would kick," Horween muttered as Putnam lined up his team. "That is too much of a chance." Nonetheless, Arnie did not remove Putnam, and he forbade the other coaches from accosting him at halftime. Horween's lesson to Putnam during the intersession was quite brief. "Be a little more conservative on your fourth down, Putty, and do not forget there is a foot in football."

Putnam was no more reliable in the second session. He threw arrant passes and almost fumbled away a punt return just before Art French's long scamper. He also called for fourth down runs on three more occasions.

"Now, tell me, why did you always rush on the fourth down?" challenged Horween after the game.

"Well," said Putnam, "I got them back in the huddle," referring to his ten Crimson teammates. "I asked them if they could make it, they said they could and I believed them." Horween smiled. Bill Bingham overheard the short conversation, confirming to him that Arnold Horween had "brought back the spirit or spark."[73]

Others intuited that Horween's modest success, at least for a certain stretch of the season, was attributed in part to better technique and in part to a rejuvenated youth culture. "Horween is teaching them middle western football. He teaches them to go right in and make inquiries the instant the ball is snapped, to learn which way the play is going and dump somebody even if the ball is going the other way," opined one editorialist. "But the technique is not as important as the spirit of the thing."[74]

Horween was ignoring other rules. He had pressed Bingham to break from tradition and cease regularly competing against Princeton each year. Arnie recommended that much more could be gained by exposing Harvard students to Michigan, where the young men play football and "think about things" differently from how they do in the eastern schools. Bingham was intrigued, but both men agreed that the decision ought to be made by the Harvard athletic committee after the close of the football season. In addition, Bingham corresponded with Knute Rockne about a Harvard-Notre Dame game. Both men pressed the other to arrange an "away game" at the other's stadium. Rockne told Bingham that his superiors would permit travel only to an Army game. Bingham complained that his athletic committee made similar demands, severely limiting the travel itineraries of the Crimson eleven. "Because I am new at this position here," Bingham confessed to Rockne, "I know that it would be out of the question for me to propose to the Faculty to alter this rule at present."[75] These discussions represented an invigorated challenge to New England parochialism. The subject was also addressed as the "Yale first" question, suggesting that what ought to matter to Harvard was its final game, "the Game," against Yale.

The so-called Big Three was, by then, a fiction, and Princeton part of a collegiate triumvirate only in its own estimation. Harvard's discussions on whether to part with an annual Princeton tilt threatened to expose the fiction even further. Princeton men were furious that Harvard believed them to be expendable.[76] Yale men tried to broker some peace, but to little avail. Harvard students enjoyed teasing Princeton about old stereotypes, that its ranks were populated by hollow country club personalities, unworthy of rating with the sophisticates of the more substantive New England schools. The football team carried a similar reputation, focused on cheap knocks and illegal maneuvers that called into question Princeton's sportsmanship and the physical safety of its competition.

Horween's former Harvard teammate, Wynant Hubbard, recalled that it was the Tigers' mauling barbarousness and not its football acumen that led to two draws against the Crimson in 1919 and 1920. Hubbard alleged that against Princeton his friends endured "sprained knees and ankles, broken legs, smashed noses, dislocated wrists, scissoring, cursing and filthy language, dangerous kicks and wallops in vital spots, deliberate, constant slugging, kneeing, and scratched and torn eyeballs and eyelids."[77] Hubbard kept a log of casualties Harvard's players suffered in Princeton bouts. The published version of it "set the college sport world on creaking foundations."[78] In 1922, for example, a Princeton player clutched one Harvard footballer's arm and deliberately dislocated his wrist. Another Crimson back, Charley Buell, broke his ankle in the first half. A Princeton defender deliberately crashed onto Buell's exposed ankle while he was attempting a rare forward pass. In 1924, three Harvard players suffered "badly twisted knees." One man fell and broke his leg. Next year, Al Miller, recorded Hubbard, "came out of the game with the clear imprint of a signet ring on his nose."[79]

The excesses were well known and resented in Cambridge. In November 1926, undergraduates prepared an issue of the *Harvard Lampoon* distributed on the Saturday morning of the Crimson-Tigers tilt, reimagining Princeton's players as thuggish pigs, bent on injuring their adversaries.[80]

Harvard was slightly favored in the Princeton game, oddsmakers giving them a 10–9 betting advantage. Princeton won, however, 12–0. The Crimson complained about poor refereeing that led to four Harvard injuries and a miscounting of downs in the Tigers' favor. The most devastating harm was to Dave Guarnaccia's ribcage. The incident occurred on a fourth-down punt. Guarnaccia lined up to block to secure sufficient time for the Harvard kicker. Princeton defenders purportedly had no intent on upending the punter. Instead, they pounced on the more valuable Guarnaccia, crushing two of his ribs and removing him for the remainder of the Harvard-Princeton contest.

After the game, students tore down the goalposts in an unintended co-operation between Harvard and Princeton undergraduates. Harvard men rushed to dismantle the stadium in protest of a cheated game. Princeton loyalists took apart the posts in retribution for an unsavory experience in Cambridge, and for Harvard's threats to discontinue the annual rivalry.[81] Overpowered by the crush of passionate spectators, the police "battled pluckily and pushed the mob back. But it was equivalent to pushing back the Atlantic Ocean."[82] Harvard students later apologized, but not before Princeton officials, on their own terms, discontinued competition between their football team and Harvard's.[83]

Horween remained silent on the whole kerfuffle, but students were enraged. Others, Crimson stalwarts such as Bob Fisher and Eddie Mahan, dismissed it all as "highbrow stuff." What Princeton had bruised and battered more than anything, so these men claimed, was Harvard's collective ego. "If Harvard would do less crying and more hard playing," chastised Mahan, "it would not only win more football games but would occupy the place in the world of sportsmen it deserves."[84] Mahan, a devoted hero of the old guard, explained that Princeton had tried harder than Harvard. His was a call for a return to the late Percy Haughton's system. No one saw fit to investigate the charges of intentional injuring, according to one reporter, because no one was all that sympathetic with the Boston Brahmins of Harvard, "where the Cabots speak only to the Lowells and the Lowells speak only to God."[85] The whole mess must have signaled to both Bingham and Horween that their crusade to change Harvard sports had a long way to go.

The banged-up Crimson eleven struggled through the final two contests of the season, shut out by Brown and then defeated by Yale. The final defeats placed students and alumni at odds. The students adored Horween. Some alumni, forgetting the lessons that Bill Bingham had taught them about sportsmanship, called for Horween's resignation, or at least for forcing Arnie to reinstall Haughton's more traditional playbook.[86]

Horween did not defend the losses, especially the last one to the Elis. "I have no alibis, no excuses, to offer. We played hard, but we lost to a better Yale team." Arnie could not countenance the assumption that Harvard had to beat Yale no matter its talent level. Then Horween extended his subversive rebuttal of the Crimson's priorities. "I enjoyed the game all the way through."[87] A loss to Yale in the Haughton era could never have been described as enjoyable. Bill Bingham was much more forceful about his and Horween's direction. "The Harvard football season of 1926 was perhaps the most disappointing in a number of years from the angle of games won," admitted Bill. "But it was highly successful in regard to the benefit derived to those who played it. It gave the game back to the boys."[88] The newspapers reported that Bill's remarks caused a mild sensation in a variety of Harvard Clubs. Bingham's measure for "success," unaligned with actual winning, could not have computed for that older generation of Harvard faithful.

* * *

The most unorthodox decision Arnold Horween made as Harvard coach was to invite Frank Shaughnessy to campus in March 1927. Shaughnessy, a former Notre Dame footballer, coached the popular McGill University rugby team, as Canada was still beholden to the English sport. Horween hoped Shaughnessy could help the Crimson develop a better lateral strategy. Dartmouth and Yale were also investing in the backward lateral maneuver. Earlier that month, Harvard's Fred Moore had proposed a change to the National Rules Committee. Moore recommended that a backward lateral pass, if dropped by the intended receiver, or if it just missed him altogether, should be rendered a dead ball.[89] According to the regulations current at the time, the bouncing ball on the grass was a fumble, free to any player to pick up and run with.[90]

The rule change was accepted by the majority of coaches, who held that it was good for football to evolve. The risk of lateraling would significantly decrease with the proposed change, to the chagrin of Knute Rockne and a few eastern coaches. Bob Zuppke, however, called it "constructive," and Pop Warner believed it would bring about a "more spectacular game."[91] Yale's Tad Jones agreed with the amendment. Arnold Horween, though it was his idea to suggest the lateral reform to Moore, stayed quiet. His silence was betrayed by the hurried pace in which Harvard looked to get ahead of the pack, even if the lateral rule was soon after curbed and eventually reversed.[92] Horween was eager to see what the new and unorthodox play could do for his team.

Horween offered Shaughnessy a "pretty free hand to experiment," beseeching the Canadian visitor to migrate some of the primordial football game back to his native United States. What he developed was "difficult to master" but "very effective when perfected."[93] The quarterback accepted the ball from the center, as usual, and then delivered it into the clutches of one of the two halfbacks behind him. In addition to them, Harvard lined up another fullback to emerge as the lead blocker.

The innovative step was how that runner developed the play. He and the other halfback could sweep in either direction. The man with possession of the ball moved in coordination with his interference. The empty-handed halfback ventured further outside, toward the sideline. The third back moved along with the pair with an intent to remove the defense's closest tackler from approaching the ballcarrier.

The ball-carrying runner then had to make a decision, just as the opposition penetrated Harvard's blockade and prepared to tackle him. His first possibility was to deliver a "two-hand basketball snap-pass off the shoulder" to his Crimson compatriot. The football had to travel "like a bullet," unusual for a lateral maneuver. Most laterals traveled more gently as an underhanded toss from one ballcarrier to another.

The new rule meant that a miscue of that fast throw merely ended the play and was not ruled as a more dangerous fumble and potential turnover of possession to the defense. The loss of a down on the dead ball ruling was a substantial-enough punishment for poor execution, and so Horween and Shaughnessy made sure that the Harvard men worked to get the timing just right. If the first line of defenders chose to guard the halfback on the outside, the ballcarrier could either run downfield or let down one of his two arms from his shoulder area and attempt a forward pass, sometimes to the quarterback, who had started the play.

The lateral play worked, on the whole, with "conspicuous success," especially with French and Guarnaccia as the pitchmen in the backfield.[94] Pundits considered the Crimson the "dark horse" of the college football scene.[95] By this time, American Jews had forgiven Horween for benching Izzy Zarakov and reinstilled a generous supply of confidence in their kinsman. "Harvard won't go out and clean up the world in the autumn," wrote a reporter for the Yiddish press, "but it will be a stronger outfit than has been seen in Cambridge for years."[96]

Horween's team was a stronger squad than Crimson clubs in the immediate past, but that was not saying all that much. Harvard was mediocre: four wins and three losses on the eve of the 1927 Yale game. It suffered its most crippling defeat on Franklin Field in Philadelphia. The visiting Crimson was favored against Pennsylvania's Quakers, losers of three straight. The Red and Blue led at halftime, 3–0. French played well, and the Harvard eleven reassembled in the third period prepared to overtake the Quaker defense. The opposite occurred. Penn scored three touchdowns and stifled Harvard's offense just as it had managed to do in the opening half: 24–0, Penn.

In the locker room, Horween's eleven were despondent. They had expected to win. The Crimson coach's postgame speech reflected the still-significant distance between him and his players in the matter of win-above-all-else. He directed the football manager to stand outside the room and prevent anyone from entering or leaving. "Pennsylvania won today because they demonstrated that they wanted to win more than you did," announced Horween. The criticism targeted effort, not victory. "This game is now history, and we cannot unmake it. There are many people outside of this dressing room waiting to see a licked Harvard team leave. I want everyone in this room to leave with his head up, his shoulders squared away, and with determination in his heart that we have yet two games to show what this team can do."[97]

Bill Bingham, the rumors had it, had come around to the old ways of Harvard football, that he was no longer impressed with talk of an ever-evolving game and what critics described as athletic hijinks. Further fuel came about from the remarkable performances of Harvard's freshman team, coached by Eddie Casey. Most suspected that Casey would one day take over for Arnold Horween. He boasted a fine Harvard pedigree and always worked along with Arnie and the varsity coaches before the freshmen reported to practice.[98] Casey's yearlings lost in his very first Harvard coaching assignment. For an all-time Exeter great, that it came against Andover was particularly demoralizing.[99] Then that was it. Eddie Casey's Harvard freshman team went unbeaten for the remainder of that 1926 season and did not lose in the next year's campaign.[100]

But Bingham denied that Horween was through.[101] "I have absolute confidence in Horween," declared Bingham. "It is my belief that Harvard football is in much better shape than two years ago, and this opinion seems to be shared by men who have closely followed the progress of the game at Harvard for the last year and a half."[102]

To thwart the speculations, Bingham foregrounded the Yale finale by announcing that Harvard would retain Horween for a third season. The bookmakers had less confidence in the Crimson, placing the odds in the Elis' favor, 10–3.[103] Horween himself gave Yale the edge, lowering the expectations just a fraction, at 3–1 odds.[104] Art French and Dave Guarnaccia had perfected the over-the-shoulder lateral maneuver, but the interference men in front of them hadn't mastered their contribution to the craft. Most disappointing was that quarterback Eliot Putnam had succumbed to a bout of academic probation and missed the entire season to rehabilitate his substandard grades.[105]

The sportswriter Grantland Rice believed that the whole expectation for Horween was unfair, even if measured by the standard of winning. Rice's trenchant reminder was a clear message to the old guard at Harvard Yard who might have unwittingly rewritten its own sacred gospel of Percy Haughton's terrific tenure in New England: "No one can expect Horween and his staff to out-Haughton Haughton." Percy Haughton's teams hadn't scored a touchdown against Yale in his first four seasons, winning in just one of those meetings.[106]

In November 1927, Tad Jones coached his final game for Yale. The Elis capitalized on two very long runs by halfback Johnny Garvey and beat Harvard, 14–0. Horween's men evaluated it as an "honorable failure" and did not display the slightest downcast disposition that was usual after a Yale defeat.[107] No one in the locker room was caught laughing, but neither was any man in tears. "It was a satisfactory game in every way," opined Horween.[108] To outsiders, these terms were peculiar. To Bill Bingham and Arnold Horween, it was another step closer to restoring a forgotten spirit at Harvard College.

CHAPTER NINE

THE CRUSADE TO KEEP
FOOTBALL A GAME

Arnold Horween is so much bigger than victory, his type is
so priceless an asset to the game, particularly in this period
of charges and countercharges, that one cannot but hope that
he will be persuaded once again, some how, to stay in the
pigskin game a little longer before returning to the leather
industry.
—Allison Danzig, "Players of the Game," *New York Times*,
    November 24, 1930, 33

The older Boston Brahmins did not consent to the new ideas about college
football. This, despite the repeat occasions during Arnold Horween's final
seasons when success at Soldiers Field was linked with metrics other than
winning (although there was quite a bit of winning). This lot of privileged
New Englanders were the kind that sardonically remarked how Harvard
had "touched bottom, and the trend henceforward will be upward."[1] In the
summer preceding the 1928 season, alumni detractors gossiped to the newspapers that Horween's tenure was at a harsh end. The determination, it was
alleged "on good authority," was unconditional on the results of the coming
football season. The rumors also placed Eddie Casey into the thick of it, alleging that "virtually all arrangements have been completed whereby Casey
is to step into the head coach's shoes as soon as the whistle blows ending the
Yale-Harvard game in the Yale Bowl this Fall."[2]

Casey was to them a "Second Coming." He understood that Harvard "goes
in strong for Tradition with a capital T."[3] A more sensible man than Horween,
Casey, the patricians believed, "will serve to revive in Harvard football the
true Haughton conception of how the game should be played."[4] That he was
descended from Irish Catholics was an apparently forgivable blemish, as long
as Eddie Casey preached Percy Haughton's football gospel.

This, though, was all conjecture. Eddie had not been engaged in the "undercover talk" at the New York and Boston Harvard Clubs.[5] Casey's inadvertent contribution to the speculation was his freshman squad's sterling win-loss-tie ratio. In two seasons, the Crimson yearlings had posted a 9-1-1 record. His critics from New England's highest class questioned Horween's "failure to produce a winning varsity eleven from the apparently excellent freshman material passed on to him by Casey."[6] They paid no mind to Bingham's calls to revise the criteria to assess success. It was an uncharitable assessment, of course, since Horween had only worked with one of those classes leading into the 1928 season. His defenders appealed for more forbearance:

> Horween's success at Cambridge has not been conspicuous. In the first place, his material has not been anything to crow about. In the second, he was obliged to tinker with a machine left behind by his predecessors that was missing on all cylinders. In the third, he has been handicapped by a pitiless glare of publicity, which has hurt his progress. And in the fourth, he is only entering upon his third season as head coach.[7]

These explanations missed the point. The rotten reason for the so-called Oust Horween Party was a matter of "discrimination," which had "heightened the delicacy of his opponents' whispering campaign." Unrecorded in the newspapers, these were "dirty insults and accusations [that] would hamper the work of the best of mentors."[8] At the bottom of it was an anti-Jewish animus combined with a strong antipathy to immigrants and their children. The animadversion was illiberal, but it was consistent with the tendencies of some of Harvard's most ancient families. The most self-styled progressive individuals around Cambridge, such as LeBaron Briggs, shared with Bingham their feelings of "disgust with the Harvard men who deplored the choice of Horween."[9]

Stories circulated that propounded a particular form of antisemitic trope. The most provocative was a myth about Ralph's and Arnie's residential situation when the brothers had returned to Boston to coach at Harvard. The siblings had reportedly "got into an argument with an apartment landlord about alterations in their apartment at Cambridge." The irate owner evicted them. The Horweens then cabled their father. Isadore Horween wired back: "Buy the building and stop the row."[10] The smear played on an antisemitic vision of underhanded Shylockian-type Jewish business dealings. What was once said about Jews and moneylending in the medieval period was transformed into a modern slur about the newer profile of Jews and urban landlord practices. The account was disseminated in hundreds of newspapers by the

United Press and suggested to readers that Arnold Horween was derived from two unbecoming types in the minds of the Brahmins: the Jews and the newly wealthy.

Bill Bingham tried to repel the insurgents. He brokered with Thomas Lamont, president of the New York Harvard Club, to arrange a gathering of alumni. Lamont and Bingham spoke before Horween did. Their messages were on point, recommending that the Harvard men cease evaluating football on the final score of a Harvard-Yale bout. Since they were usually left out of the newspaper reports and columns, Horween's defenders did not deem it necessary to reprimand those in the audience who harbored and relayed the more offensive statements about Arnold Horween's personal profile.

Arnold addressed the group last, assigning for himself the role of outlining the football scheme for the upcoming season. His part was to discuss football and his position in terms of compromise. He did not harangue too much about good character, nor did he promise victories. He was, however, optimistic about the varsity men because they had been "rolling up 50–0 and 60–0 and 70–0 scores against the scrubs." The backfield led by French and Guarnaccia would remain the Crimson's strongest asset. Its success (a word the alumni interpreted in a very specific way) would be contingent on the development of an untested offensive line.[11] Horween thought that his listeners would be gladdened to learn that he intended to abandon the huddle system, restoring the republicanism of quarterback generalship to the Crimson offense.[12] Horween also announced that Chuck Carney, the Illini-trained footballer, had departed the Crimson coaching staff and was replaced by a Harvard man. Horween provided a happy surprise to the journalists that the Crimson would open practices to the newspapermen. As for the Harvard alumni, Horween's remarks likely did not assuage too much their feelings for him or his college football program. "I thought that the dinner last week was an excellent thing," Lamont wrote to Bingham after the reception. "Certainly, you and Arnold Horween made an excellent impression on all those journalists."[13] Tellingly, Lamont did not relay anything about the state of mind of the Harvard graduates.

The Brahmins had learned from President Lawrence Lowell's inquiry into the "Jewish Problem" at Harvard that, while the sentiment may resonate with many, it was not a popular thing to forthrightly discuss anti-Jewish rules in public. The opposition charily waited for a blunder on the football field, "determined to make a sectarian issue of the matter as soon as an excuse presents itself."[14]

* * *

Arnold Horween posing at a Harvard Crimson practice. His casual dress
contrasted with Percy Haughton's and Bob Fisher's formal attire. Courtesy of Skip
Horween.

The chance for such a revolt was not forthcoming. The Crimson defeated
Springfield 30–0 to earn the Horween regime its first shutout. Captain Art
French scored three touchdowns. He and Dave Guarnaccia showed improvement in their tandem lateral work. Ben Ticknor had elevated his play as a
lineman and sophomore Tom Gilligan proved himself a reliable substitute

for the middle periods when either French or Guarnaccia required a respite from the grind of the playing field.[15]

"Harvard is beating back!" declared the papers after two drab seasons.[16] The Crimson next blanked North Carolina, 20–0. Harvard accumulated its points in the first half and then relieved its starters for the contest's duration. The media announced Harvard's return to football glory. Horween, in one reporter's estimation, had "laid a foundation for a team which may make Harvard forget Percy Haughton."[17] That final clause indicated how misinformed some were about the politics of Crimson football and its relationship to the wider net of Harvard men. Horween was yet unsure how to rate his players. "I would know more about the strength of my team," he told an assembly of reporters while comfortably sipping tea in his office, "if I knew whether North Carolina was any good."[18]

Horween was seen as vulnerable against Army. Betters gave the Cadets 10–6 odds against the Crimson. Army's athletes were older than most college players, a reason that several schools, such as Harvard under Percy Haughton, had dropped the Cadets from their schedules. At a dinner welcoming the military men to Harvard Yard, President Lowell—who still stuck by his pledge to Bill Bingham not to meddle in athletics affairs—joked that "we are all assembled here to welcome the Army from West Point and to wish them as near a victory tomorrow as may be appropriate on the occasion!"[19] Lowell's remark drew laughter because of the obvious mismatch, despite Harvard's early season romps. Army beat Harvard, 15–0. The Cadets outgained the Cambridge collegians on the ground, 275–135 yards.[20]

But the anti-Horween effort was temporarily stymied. The French-Guarnaccia tandem performed much better against Dartmouth. Hanover was favored, but the Crimson held sway with the Big Green. Harvard shut out the Dartmouth offense in the first two periods. The Green made it close with a late touchdown, closing the margin to 12–7. Then French and Guarnaccia had their way with the opposition, lateraling their way in the final minutes to a clinching touchdown: 19–7 Harvard. Then the Crimson vanquished Lehigh University, 39 to 0.

Harvard prepared for Penn, its replacement rival for Princeton. On the first play after the opening kickoff, Guarnaccia drove into the line, choosing to keep the ball rather than sling it behind him to the waiting French. It was the wrong decision. "He came through on the other side, but without the ball." The football had popped out of Guarnaccia's arms and into the bosom of a Quaker player. On defense, Harvard was found guilty of an illegal-use-of-hands penalty, gifting Penn field position a few lengths in front of the Crimson goal line. Two plays later, Penn's Paul Scull barreled over the left side of Harvard's defensive line.[21] It was the lone score of the contest: Pennsylvania 7, Harvard 0. The Crimson then played to a scoreless draw against Holy Cross. Horween's troops lined up without injured fast runner French and the bruising blocker Ticknor in a contest that was mostly overlooked for the looming match with Yale.[22]

It had been a fine season for Harvard, even if it did not reach the high caliber of Haughton's teams a dozen years prior. Of course, in the 1920s, the college game was much more crowded than it had been in earlier epochs. Football had reached all parts of the United States, no longer the sport of the New England elite. It was Notre Dame's decade, even if it shared some of it with Alabama, Michigan, Pittsburgh, and Southern California.

The quality of its team was no solace to Harvard's graduates. On the eve of the New Haven contest, sports scribes started to circulate the opinion that "it has become a generally accepted fact at Harvard that Arnold Horween, head coach of football, will direct the Crimson team for the last time at Yale next Saturday."[23] Wiser men declared that Horween's job was secure as long as Bill Bingham was in charge. The latter group agreed that Horween would indeed depart Harvard Yard but would do so on his own accord, eager to become a steadier business asset for his father's leather manufacturing company.[24] Others alleged that his eagerness to return to Chicago was due to the "gridiron grind, and that he feels that the game he has graced as player and coach is not worth the further expenditure of his energies." What is more, engaging with the entitled Harvard graduates was "one way to grow old ungracefully."[25]

The jostling over Horween at Harvard induced Bingham to redouble his commitment to the football coach and assert that his "confidence in him is now greater than when I asked him to coach in March 1926." Declared Bingham, "If any changes in the Harvard coaching staff are made they will be announced through the Harvard Athletic Association. Neither Mr. Horween nor myself will have anything more to say on the matter."[26] But Bingham's statement was drowned out amid the columns taken up by the more ferocious alumni instigators.[27]

America's Jews were also resigned to their coreligionist's foretold fate. "Unless a couple of miracles are performed before Thanksgiving Day," warned George Joel, "Arnold Horween, coach of the Harvard football team, will have to look for new employment next season." Joel was the American Jewish press's most syndicated sportswriter and was responsible for a multitude of columns that had celebrated Horween and the ascendancy of Jewish brawn. In this instance, however, Joel was solemn. "And so passes the first and probably last Jewish coach of a Harvard football team."[28]

Horween did not comment on the commotion. His attention was directed to preparing for The Game. The odds were with Harvard. Yale had succumbed in three of its previous four contests. It was a rather underwhelming start for Coach Mal Stevens, who had taken over for the retired Tad Jones. Stevens was a somewhat unnatural fit for Yale. Yale was more forgiving of young men of Middle West backgrounds but, like the other New England colleges, preferred not to elevate them beyond supporting roles. If one of them showed promise as a captain or coach, he was eligible only if he had first purified himself in a nearby prep school. Stevens had undergone no such conversion. He was born in Stockton, a small town in the middle of Kansas. Stevens enrolled in Washburn College, in Topeka. There, Stevens lettered in five sports—football, basketball, baseball, track, and tennis—before transferring to Yale to complete his senior year. Stevens played halfback for Tad Jones's prized 1923 Elis. He was tall and lean, and that he did not cut a halfback's figure was something of an understatement. Stevens attended Yale's School of Medicine and earned income aiding Jones as an assistant coach. Stevens also possessed a very pleasant disposition. Bob Zuppke told Stevens that he would "never be a great football coach. You have too kind a face."[29]

Arnold Horween took the Elis quite seriously. Like Horween, Stevens had come to his assignment with a subtle promise to modernize the football program. And like Horween, Stevens struggled to adjust his team in his first season as head coach. All the same, Horween believed that Yale posed a danger should its men pull things together on the gridiron. Horween closed practices again despite the wishes of the newspapermen, fearing that some surreptitious scouts from New Haven might be afoot. Horween did not even disclose the scrimmage lineups, "a daily custom he had religiously observed heretofore."[30] The Crimson also canceled the traditional rally in Harvard Yard to send the footballers off to New Haven. "It was felt," Horween explained through an official statement, "that the rallies did the team no good which could not be obtained through an enthusiastic final practice session."[31]

Harvard was favored against Yale on the cloudy Connecticut autumn afternoon of the match. The offensive line, anchored by Ben Ticknor, played its soundest game of the season. The Harvard interference satisfactorily supported rushers French and Guarnaccia. "Time after time one or the other would lope toward the sidelines with the ball under his arm. Then, as Yale charged in, he would lateral the ball to his teammate, who invariably gained some ground."[32]

The pair amassed some three hundred yards of running on that afternoon. Neither galloped for exceptionally long rushing plays. Instead, they traded chances to punish Yale defenders with powerful spurts. Their aim was to capture a first down and sustain the drive. Once accomplished, "Guarnaccia and French went to work again."[33] Harvard shut out Yale, 17–0.

With that, Bingham and Horween had converted most Harvard alumni to their movement. Only the bitterest graduates were still unredeemable. They charged that The Game had lost its meaningfulness, that Harvard-Yale had been "relegated to a rear seat."[34] The most obnoxious Harvard men, the ones who called him "the Jew Horween," complained that Harvard's "victory over Yale was that of a poor team over a poorer."[35]

*   *   *

Bill Bingham issued a statement directly after the Yale game. "It takes time to build a football system, and I knew that if Arnold Horween were given the opportunity, he would eventually produce a winner. I hope I can induce him to return, for I believe in the offensive type of football which he teaches, and am even more grateful to him for giving the game to the boys."[36] The latter was the important point in Bingham's evaluation. Horween's comments were pithier: "Today's game was a good, clean, hard battle all the way. Harvard played up to our best expectations and turned in by far its best game of the season."[37] Arnie remained silent on his prospects. In a column he wrote for a Boston newspaper after the close of the season, Horween focused on the players. "To my mind Guarnaccia was the outstanding back on the field," he summarized. "Besides having an important part in Harvard's lateral passes, he also ran hard and well." Horween lauded Art French for his sure-handed ball carrying on the gridiron and his leadership off it. "Every one was working for the team, for Harvard, not for themselves."[38]

Horween had other matters to attend to. His family had traveled to the Harvard-Yale game along with his fiancé, Marion Eisendrath, and her close relatives. Marion told a reporter that she had "enjoyed the game immensely but of course that was to be expected."[39] She was the daughter of the late Nathan Eisendrath, the affluent tanner who had approached Isadore Horween at the World's Fair leather exhibit and offered the elder Horween a job. Marion was two years Arnie's senior. She had attended University of Chicago. During the off-season, the pair had been seen together around Chicago quite often during an extended courtship.[40]

The Horween-Eisendrath clan departed New Haven for Scarsdale to visit friends. Their intention was to spend a night in the New York suburb before boarding a train to return to Chicago. The couple had arranged a small wedding—a "quiet affair," planned by Rose Horween—for Thanksgiving later that week.

Bingham followed Horween to Scarsdale. Anxious reporters begged Bingham to relay the contents of their discussion. "I spent a good deal of time talking with Arnold Horween," confessed Bingham. "No definite conclusion on the coaching situation has yet been reached and probably none will be until Mr. Horween has studied his business affairs at first hand and has returned from his wedding trip."[41] Reports in the society columns of the couple's honeymoon location disagreed over whether Florida or Jamaica was their destination.[42]

Bingham was optimistic. The press reported that "reliable sources" had insisted that Horween would return to Harvard.[43] His players vouched for him, probably hoping that Arnie would find them sentimental. "The criticism of Horween is unjust," pleaded James "Red" Barrett, the new Crimson captain. "The public is too willing to offer suggestions, especially the graduates. He is the best coach around. It was very hard for him at first to build up a nucleus around which to form a team."[44]

Arnold Horween returned in January 1929 to the Boston Harvard Club for an official announcement. There, Bill Bingham told a group of four hundred graduates that Horween would be back with the Crimson in the autumn. Bingham read from prepared remarks: "Three years ago it was a fact that few playing football at Harvard really enjoyed it and that conditions were all wrong. Horween, however, succeeded in making his squad find pleasure, not only in the games but also in the workouts."[45] Bingham's statement vindicated the claim George Owen made just before Bill and Arnie took charge of Harvard football. Back then, Bill had felt the pressure to deny Owen's claims, as did most others associated with the Harvard Crimson. Bingham's and Horween's campaign to change the game had given Bill the insight and courage to say something very different about the state of the game during the old regime. Then Horween offered a much briefer statement: "I consider it a great honor to be asked by Bill Bingham to continue as coach of the Harvard eleven. This I wish to do if it were possible and I am glad I can do so."[46]

The undergrads hailed the happy news. The student newspaper had scaled back its commentary on the Crimson team during the past season, siding with Horween and Bingham, and—to the dismay of spirited alumni—opined that far too much pressure had been placed on the eleven by loud and loquacious sources. The Horween decision merited comment because it reinforced that creed. The undergraduate journalists predicted that Horween's return would be "welcomed by all Harvard men who have seen the working out of his influence on the game at Harvard and on the men who play it." Although it did not print it with a capital T, the young men heralded Horween and

Bingham, noting that the duo had "built up a tradition of Harvard football that counts the game as more than the winning of it."[47]

* * *

The new tradition worried about the overemphasis on football. Others decried it as an obsession and framed it in cultish terms. John Tunis admonished that "football is more to sport followers of this country than merely a game. It is at present a religion—sometimes it seems to be almost our national religion."[48] Tunis described the color-coordinated rituals of college men sitting in huge churchlike stadiums listening to the sacred music of the marching bands and hailing their gridiron priests. This "false god," he alleged, had distracted colleges and confused its students, who were no longer able to "distinguish between the things that are of enduring worth and the things that are not."[49] Tunis claimed to have overheard a small boy exclaim that "Yale is a college that has good football teams."[50] The child did not know anything else about the New Haven school. "What Tunis says is true," commented Harvard's A. Lawrence Lowell when asked about the exposé in *Harper's Magazine*. Lowell was hopeful that Harvard had turned a corner. "As you know," he told the magazine's editor, "our trouble comes with the graduates. The undergraduates have a pretty good sense of proportion in these things."[51] The Brahmins of the Back Bay were beside themselves because President Lowell, one of their own, a public figure who had enunciated so many of their other social prejudices, had sided with a millhand from Lawrence rather than with his own societal stock.[52]

They should have known better. Lowell had become very sensitive about overemphasis, sometimes checking Bingham's desire to enlarge Harvard's footprint. Lowell rejected a plan to overhaul Harvard Stadium to accommodate eighty thousand spectators. Lowell had presciently predicted a decline in football fandom in Cambridge. Other universities with higher enrollments had caught up to the New England universities and taken over the college football power rankings and All-American listings. Lowell promised that New Haven's larger Yale Bowl would soon appear much emptier on Saturday afternoons.[53] Instead of enlarging Soldiers Field, he modified Bingham's proposal by agreeing to set up bleachers at the open end of Harvard's horseshoe-shaped stadium, a more modest expansion that increased capacity at the stadium to about sixty thousand. On another occasion, Lowell reassured Bingham that he need not accommodate alumni wishing for better seats to attend Harvard football contests. "The man who refuses to give something over $20,000 to his class committee because he did not like their football seats is probably not of a temperament and attitude that, in the long run, would be likely to be very generous to the University."[54]

More aggressive personalities called for an investigation into football culture on US college campuses.[55] In 1926, the Carnegie Foundation assembled a team to research the state of football. The foundation had published an earlier report on the "condition and administration of college athletics." It had been thin on scholarship, based on a self-reporting questionnaire and relying on the responses from just thirty-three universities. This time, the researchers visited 130 college campuses. Determined to get it right, the Carnegie team spent more than three years conducting interviews and processing its findings.

In October 1929, the Carnegie Foundation produced a report nearly four hundred pages long on the seediness of the collegiate game. The report garnered a "rousing reception in thousands of newspaper columns, speeches in support and in denial, and special articles."[56] The foundation fueled the controversy, holding a press conference, a first time among its myriad research projects. The news competed with the Great Crash on Wall Street. The foundation urged fifty-four of the schools to clean up their football programs. Other colleges had convinced the researchers that they had made some improvement to athletic culture on campus and figured, incorrectly, that more Carnegie Foundation money would further assist in the effort. In all, just twenty-eight colleges were exonerated from any misdeeds for the sake of "gathering a winning team."[57] Yale was among those schools found guiltless. Harvard was charged with a mild misdemeanor. The investigation cited the school for providing student athletes with free food at the concession station in Harvard Stadium.[58] Alumni offered their congratulations to Bill Bingham, suggesting that "it must be a satisfaction to everyone connected with Harvard to realize what little criticism has been made of your management of athletics."[59] Even still, Bingham sought an unofficial acquittal. He summoned a member of the Carnegie Foundation to campus to explain that Harvard was "not as bad as [it] had been painted."[60]

Absolution was a larger issue for Harvard than the serious matters of recruitment corruption and boosterism. Bill Bingham's eagerness for vindication devolved from a quest to revive a bygone epoch of American sport. Bingham was confident that he and Horween had righted the wrongs. The latter's fourth campaign directing the Crimson eleven reinforced that conviction. His fourth was Horween's finest season of leading Harvard football. And winning was not how the pair measured the success of their efforts in the autumn of 1929.[61]

The Crimson opened camp with an intent to further westernize. Horween did not bring back lateral guru Frank Shaughnessy. Art French and Dave Guarnaccia had graduated, and a rule change redefined a muffed lateral as a fumble rather than a dead ball. Horween's new focus was on the forward pass. Arnie had quarterbacked the Chicago Cardinals with an aerial aspect and had hoped to develop the same strategy in the Crimson's offensive game. The timing made sense. A year earlier, Harvard had eliminated the huddle and placed much more authority on the quarterback to make decisions. Horween had also shifted Eddie Casey to the varsity squad to develop the backfield: the quarterback and the halfbacks.[62]

Finally, there was Barry Wood. Wood had captained Casey's freshman team. As a schoolboy in nearby Milton, Massachusetts, Wood had played baseball, hockey, football, and tennis. His idol was George Owen. Wood was determined, like Owen, to make it at Harvard. Wood was 6 feet tall and built on a sturdy frame of 175 pounds. Harvard was glad to have him. Wood was a good student, "consistently maintaining an average of three A's and a B."[63] Horween appreciated that the young man possessed a familiar self-effacing temperament. Wood said of himself that he was equipped with "only the average student's mind."[64] He worked hard at his studies and on the field.

In Wood's sophomore year, Horween promoted the quarterback to the varsity team. He and Casey decided to start Eliot Putnam at quarterback, but the veteran, all understood, held the "narrowest of edges on his rivals."[65] The plan worked well for the first two games: Harvard defeated Bates College and New Hampshire by a combined tally of 83–0.[66]

Army was Harvard's third opponent. The Crimson trailed late, 20–13. The score was particularly devastating, since the Harvard eleven had held a 13–0 advantage at halftime. Captain Chris Cagle had beaten down Harvard, breaking through with three long second-half touchdown runs. In all, Army had rushed for 300 yards, 250 in the final quarters of the tilt. Putnam had had an uneven game and Horween replaced him with Wood. An ungenerous analysis of Putnam's play reported to Horween was that his "quarterback does not possess the slightest knowledge of the rudiments of the game of football."[67] In the first half, "Putty" had completed a long diagonal pass to Dick O'Connell for a touchdown. Putnam, however, missed the extra point attempt and had failed to corral Cagle on several of the Cadet's lengthy gallops. Cagle still overpowered the Crimson defense after Wood took over as quarterback. Cagle's final score, with about three minutes remaining should have clinched it for Army. Harvard turned out to be fortunate that the Cadets missed the point after touchdown.

The Crimson received the subsequent kickoff. Wood lined up his eleven on the Crimson 20-yard line. He then completed a twenty-yard pass to Vic Harding, another substitute player Horween had inserted to "make something of it." The Crimson ran a few lateral plays to reach midfield with about a minute left in the contest. On the next play, Wood's pass was dropped, but the umpires called an interference penalty to advance the scrimmage to Army's 40-yard line. Then the Cadets stuffed the Crimson on two consecutive plays.

Harvard Stadium quieted to an uncomfortable hush. "The game was practically over," recalled Wood. "It looked as if the Army had won. They had stopped our attack in the middle of the field." Wood called for a pass at the lineup. He instructed Harding to run far up the left sideline. "I didn't have the slightest idea I could throw the ball so far, or that anybody could catch it if I did."[68]

Ben Ticknor snapped the ball to Wood. The quarterback immediately retreated backward to avoid the defensive rush. Positioned at midfield, Wood finished counting the seconds Harding would require to reach the goal line. "I bent as far backward as I possibly could, shut my eyes and threw the thing with every ounce of my strength."[69]

Harding was open. The Cadet defense had lined up too close to the line of scrimmage. The speedy footballer accelerated past the coverage and "legged it for all he was worth up the field." Wood's throw sailed fifty yards. Harding caught it a step into the Army goal.[70] Wood tied it with the extra point.

Harvard recovered a fumble on Army's next possession but missed a chance to win on a difficult drop kick. Hardly any of the newspapers reported these final seconds, however. Harvard's comeback was sufficient fodder, for nothing quite like it had ever before happened in the annals of Crimson football.[71]

The balance of the season was satisfactory. Harvard lost to a powerful Dartmouth team. The Crimson shut out Florida, 14–0. Barry Wood recovered three fumbles against the Gators. Then the eleven traveled to the University of Michigan. Harvard played better but suffered some bad breaks and lost the game by 2 points. In Ann Arbor, the journalists reckoned that it was the "thousands of midwestern football fans who saw the Michigan-Harvard football game Saturday [and] learned a great deal about the technique of our gridiron sport from the defeated Harvard team."[72]

That opinion likely struck Bill Bingham, who had brokered an agreement to compete against Michigan because "there is a lot the east can learn from the western universities."[73] Yet editorialists credited Arnold Horween and Eddie Casey with advancing the lateral pass and Wood with a knack for throwing, amounting to combinations and "possibilities which teams and coaches in this section have scarcely realized." That it was the Harvard Crimson representing a progressive style of football was even more astounding. Horween's squad, a newspaper put it, had "nothing in common with the old Haughton-coached teams except eleven crimson jerseys."[74]

* * *

Albie Booth was Yale's "Mighty Atom." The halfback weighed 144 pounds and stood at 5 feet, 7 inches. Other members of the Elis could outsprint Booth. No one could outhustle him, however. He reminded pundits of the agile Eddie Casey. Booth had a penchant for shifting and spinning. "He made tacklers look foolish, and, at times, drove them into an insensate rage."[75] Born in New Haven, his family was not part of the Yale elite. Booth's father was a foreman in the Winchester firearms factory. Albie possessed a fine and favorable disposition. Booth chose to attend Yale, making him an even better version of the Frank Merriwell myth than Bill Bingham, who had spurned Yale for Harvard.

In New Haven, Booth captained the freshman Elis in baseball, basketball, and football. With some collateral disrespect for the athletes who lined up with Walter Camp, Albie Booth was touted as the "most exciting, the most crowd pleasing of all Yale football players."[76] Now that Camp had died, in March 1925, Yale was perforce more open to change. Mal Stevens gushed whenever others spoke or asked about the sensational halfback. To make the most of this fortuitous running sensation, Stevens hired Adam Walsh, captain of Notre Dame's undefeated 1924 team, to coach the offensive line. Walsh anchored the "Seven Mules" whom Rockne assigned to block for his "Four Horsemen." Walsh was the first non-Yale man to coach the Bulldogs. The affront, as in the politics of Stevens's earlier appointment, had been mitigated by Bingham's earlier Horween experiment at Harvard. Mal Stevens wasn't trying to push the outside of the envelope, although he did learn how the "down curves in Yale's football chart overemotionalized the Old Blues."[77] Stevens required Walsh to instruct the Elis' bigger men how to push defenders out of Booth's running lanes.

Albie Booth and Barry Wood had a shared football destiny. Captain Wood's Harvard yearlings had defeated Captain Booth's Yale freshmen a year prior, 7–6. Like Wood, Booth started the season as a substitute. Stevens figured that Booth had the better advantage over the defense once the opposition had to replace its exhausted starters with second-string scrubs. Like Wood, Albie Booth was placed in the starting lineup because of a masterpiece performance against Army, one week after the Cadets' fateful draw at Harvard Stadium.

Against Yale, Army was holding a 13–0 advantage. The Elis claimed the lead on two Booth touchdowns. For the second score, Albie received a handoff on fourth down just a yard in front of the Cadet goal line. The sophomore phenom "flung himself over the seething scrimmage for the touchdown": 14–13, Yale.

Booth secured the game for the Elis on a punt return. He gathered the long kick on Yale's 30-yard line. His blockers did as Walsh had commanded them. Each interferer laid out a serviceman as Booth scrambled downfield. Yale's Tuffy Phillips dropped the last defender, Captain Chris Cagle, who watched the final stretch of the play lying on the grassy field. Albie sprinted forward, eluding each defender, sometimes more than once, until he reached the Army goal line. It was an "incredible piece of open-field chicanery that had the Bowl in an uproar."[78] Booth scored all the Elis' 21 points on that October afternoon at the Yale Bowl. He had carried the football thirty-three times and totaled 223 yards. After the punt return score, the "stands rose and greeted him in one resounding ovation."[79]

Harvard and Yale awaited the season finale at Soldiers Field. It was the first varsity meeting between the respective schools' football prodigies, Barry Wood and Albie Booth. "The hotel situation is worse than any Boston has seen in years," reported the newspapers. "The manager of one leading hotel said today that he had turned down nearly 500 applications for reservations and most of the hotels have been booked solid for two weeks and more." Harvard and Yale graduates had made it a point to solicit seats for "the Game." They were "sensing one of the greatest games these two have turned in in their history, and they are not missing the chance of seeing it."[80]

Bettors agreed that Harvard held a slight advantage over Yale. The reason was that Barry Wood was fresher than Booth. Horween had relieved his starters in the Holy Cross game a week earlier. The scrubs fared just fine in a 12–6 win over the Crusaders. In contrast, Yale required Booth's stalwart services for their prior matchup against Princeton. Booth did the job but was bruised up during the Elis' shutout of the Tigers.[81]

Horween assembled his eleven after Harvard won the coin flip. His message lacked the fierceness of the pregame rituals orated by Percy Haughton and Tad Jones. "Now, fellows," said Horween. "It's your game. Go out and play it!"[82] It was a frigid and blustery afternoon that slowed down the game considerably. But both Booth and Wood delivered on the expectations. All scores occurred in the second period. Wood directed a lateral attack for a touchdown drive. He also kicked a field goal from a very sharp angle at Yale's 15-yard line. Positioned at quarterback on this occasion, perhaps for symmetry purposes, Booth threw a touchdown before the close of the period, although Yale missed the extra point attempt. 10–6, Harvard.

The main difference in the first half was a blocked drop kick. Booth lined up for the field goal on the Crimson's 25-yard line. Harvard defenders surged into the Yale backfield. Booth delivered the kick, but it was blocked upon deployment by the fierce defensive rush. After the game, a reporter queried Horween whether he believed it was his gamesmanship and substitution decisions that had helped Harvard's "good psychology" against Albie Booth. Horween paused for a moment and then smiled: "But it was better psychology to block his kick."[83]

The game was decided directly after the halftime intermission. Booth stood at the Yale goal line to receive the kickoff. He was anxious and started to move before securing the football in his arms; he fumbled. Then he picked it up and composed himself. He surveyed the field. His generalship instincts caught on and his confidence increased. The Yale interference formed a barricade on his left, the side Albie preferred to start his run. He galloped forward, gaining speed.

Everyone in Harvard Stadium watched as Booth sidestepped in search of a seam to wriggle through for a decisive score. The spectators remained silent, stunned by the "heart-pumping drama" of the annual affair. "Harvard must stop Booth to win," cried a Crimson cheerleader to the Cambridge student box.

Booth found a crease as he passed the Yale 30-yard line. He countered right and then spun past a slower Harvard man. He adjusted for a moment to regain his stride, seeing no one between him and the Harvard goal. Booth did not, however, sense the Harvard breach on the left side of him. Ben and Bill Ticknor, Harvard's hulky linemen, broke through the Yale wall. Bill, the younger Ticknor brother on the Crimson roster, reached for Booth from behind. He just barely grasped Booth by his "billowy blue sweater." Booth came within "inches of making the greatest run ever known on any football field."[84]

Grantland Rice figured that had Ticknor not grabbed him at the Yale 35-yard line, Albie Booth would have "run 95 yards for a touchdown and would also have won the most dramatic game of football ever played."[85] All the same, Ticknor had upended Booth, who was too much of a sportsman to agree with some journalists that it was all the fault of a leg injury sustained against Princeton. Neither team scored for the remainder of the game. "The

Goliath had done his work and David's pebble had not hit its mark."[86] 10–6, Harvard.

Two weeks later, Grantland Rice reflected once more on the condition of Horween and Harvard football. This time, no one had called for the coach's resignation. "Arnold Horween turned out a smart, high powered Harvard football team for the stretch this season and it was only natural that Harvard would want him back." Rice was taken by Horween's demeanor and the way Harvard's head man had so profoundly redefined success within his sphere of influence, a circle of New England's most influential. "Horween has the knack of making his squad like football."[87] With earlier iterations of Harvard and Yale in mind, Rice said of Horween that he "doesn't believe in any driving, high pressure systems, but goes at things with more serenity than many coaches show. He has tried far as possible to keep football a game and not a substitute for war."[88] It was altogether apparent that Horween's greatest success was convincing Harvard that football was just a game.

CONCLUSION

In December 1930, two thousand women and men packed into the Harvard Club in Boston. Three weeks earlier, Captain Ben Ticknor had read aloud a petition signed by every Crimson player to convince Arnold Horween to remain with Harvard football. The young men at Harvard believed that Horween represented their view of sport and wanted to keep having fun at it. Victories were accumulating too. The Crimson had beaten Yale for a third straight time. "The lateral pass won the game for us," declared Coach Horween. The maneuver helped the Crimson runners break through the Eli defensive line. The very threat of it provided Barry Wood with a "wide-open channel down the centre of the field for the forward passes."[1] Horween's planning had paid off again. That, Ticknor explained, was not the real reason Horween was needed around Harvard Yard. Arnie had been "pretty much overcome" by the gesture but objected that he needed to return full-time to his work at the leather factory in Chicago.[2] Ticknor's squad relented. The dinner in Boston was designed to fete Horween's achievements and welcome his successor, Eddie Casey, to the helm of Harvard football.[3]

Thomas Lamont chaired the gala event. At it, Barry Wood was elected captain and Bill Bingham delivered the keynote remarks of the evening. Bingham reflected on Horween's appointment. "We wanted to win football games—yes, a thousand times yes—because we believed the real amateur spirit was the expectation of victory." Bingham, anticipating Franklin Delano Roosevelt, recalled that a "new deal was necessary, and clearly a new era had dawned." Bingham praised Horween, saying his greatest gift was that "he loved the game of football and made the boys love it."[4]

When Casey took over for Horween, there were no suspicions that Eddie would return the Crimson to the Haughton system. Casey had helped architect the more open and liberal program with Horween and was not about to dismantle it. Casey invoked Horween's messages and even lauded him to the members of the Jewish Maccabee Association in Boston.[5]

Casey's Harvard teams were overall very good. In his first three seasons, the Crimson eleven posted a 15-7-2 record. Casey's varsity beat Yale in two of three meetings during that span. Like all college football programs, Harvard suffered a steep decline from the Great Depression. In the United States overall, football attendance fell by 25 percent. Interest in football never waned for very long, however, and the crowds started to repopulate in even larger numbers by the mid-1930s.[6] College football underwent a revival in almost every section of the United States. The Northeast was an obvious exception. Harvard, Princeton, and Yale never did recover. Even in Horween's final season, sports scribes had started to refer to other regions as football meccas. With considerable bias, a journalist in Los Angeles described the University of California at Berkeley, Stanford, and the University of Southern California as the "Big Three."[7] Harvard refused to keep pace with other universities and offer scholarships strictly for athletic abilities. That policy became the defining characteristic of the Ivy League once it was officially formed in 1954. The formation of this football guild was the final step in more or less removing the New England's Big Three from the national college football scene.

In Harvard Yard, undergraduates appeared to be at peace with the new reality. In a more mellowed state, Harvard and Princeton mended its relationship and renewed its annual tilts. In 1934, during Casey's final season, a challenging one for the Crimson, it had been apparent that Harvard did not stand much of a chance to defeat Yale. After the Elis' first touchdown, the Harvard band, prepared for the inevitable, revealed a banner that read "Who Gives a Damn?" The band unveiled a second poster declaring "Who the Hell Cares?" after Yale's second score. In the final minutes, Yale stopped a long Harvard drive. The good-humored band leaders then uncovered a final sign that bigheartedly proclaimed, "Nuts."[8]

The relaxed disposition reflected broader currents of change in Cambridge. In October 1933, Harvard elected James Bryant Conant to succeed President Abbott Lawrence Lowell. Conant was a brilliant chemistry professor. He was a Harvard man but, by his own admission, made "no claim to being a proper Bostonian." Conant grew up a poor kid, a fact made very well known when the newspapers reported that "Harvard had crowned a commoner." Even as the head of Harvard, Conant gave off an aura that was "not noticeably Republican."[9] In his first report to Harvard's board of overseers, Conant sounded much like Horween and Bingham when he recommended that the college "should attract to our student body the most promising young men throughout the whole nation." To do so meant the college had to "keep the way clear for the gifted youth of limited means."[10]

In that context, no one made much of Eddie Casey's plebeian background when he started to run the Crimson. Casey coached Harvard for four years, followed by a single season stint with the Boston Redskins. Eddie and Anna Casey had a good life. They remained in Boston and raised a daughter, Janice. Casey directed the Boston branch of the National Youth Administration and was principal of Coolidge Junior High School in Natick. Eddie died in July 1966. Father Charles Mahan, Eddie's brother, helped officiate the funeral. His brother Eddie was among the Harvard football men seated to pay their last respects to Eddie Casey of Natick's East Street.[11] Casey was elected to the College Football Hall of Fame in 1968.[12]

* * *

Arnold Horween had departed Harvard in good spirits. "It was a lot of fun," he told a reporter just before leaving Cambridge.[13] Back in Chicago, Horween took over the leather company from his father, just as Isadore had wanted it. Arnie served as president of Horween Leather Company from 1949 until he retired in 1984. Ralph left the daily work in the tannery to pursue an influential career in law. Military leather did not prove the boon it had been for Isadore. Instead, Horween turned to the business side of sports. His old friend George Halas, owner of the Chicago Bears, was eager to improve the aerodynamics of modern football. He believed that one of the better ways to accomplish that aim was to experiment with narrower footballs. In April 1940, Halas convinced his fellow owners to make Wilson Sporting Goods, a Chicago outfit, the NFL's official supplier of footballs. Wilson required plenty of leather to produce prototypes for Halas's Bears players to practice with. Horween's company provided the leather to Wilson and has continued to supply it.[14]

Arnie and Bill maintained a close correspondence. In difficult times, Horween liked to remind Bingham to "have faith in the principles for which we have always stood."[15] Bill visited Arnie and Marion whenever Harvard matters took him to Chicago. Arnie traveled routinely to Boston for business and made it a point to see Bingham. Each year, Arnold made sure to send Florence Bingham a leather handbag for the holidays. In return, Bill graciously reserved football tickets for Horween and his son, Arnie Jr., whenever they found themselves in Cambridge, usually for The Game against Yale. Arnie Jr. later attended Harvard and played football for the Crimson eleven.

Horween stayed in contact with coaches and players for the remainder of his life. With Barry Wood, Arnie gossiped about Harvard football and followed his protégé's research in microbiology at Johns Hopkins University. In Baltimore, Wood liked to boast to Horween about the Colts professional football team. He once commented to Arnie that the "town here went crazy" after Baltimore defeated the New York Giants in the 1958 NFL championship, a contest dubbed the "greatest game ever played."[16] Wood proudly wore Arnie's cordovan leather footwear. "I'm so spoiled now that all I can wear is Horween shoes."[17] In later stages, both men took an interest in each other's grandchildren.

Arnold Horween died in August 1985.[18] Ralph outlived his younger brother by a dozen years. Over a hundred years of age, Ralph was singled out as the NFL's oldest living player, the last of the first generation of professional footballers.[19]

The short-term impact of Horween's work is captured in the reporting of local and national newspapers cited throughout this book. The long-term influence is harder to measure. Certainly, the strong American culture of winning has persisted and at times dominated. The 1936 publication of Dale Carnegie's *How to Win Friends and Influence People*, one of the all-time best-selling books (perhaps the very best-selling self-help manual), is an indicator of how powerful winning and a certain definition of success has become in American life. For a long while, the Jewish press liked to reminisce about the "halcyon days of the Arnold Horween regime."[20] At the time of Horween's retirement, Jewish journalists took some solace in the fact that Benny Friedman, the All-American Michigan quarterback, still served as backfield coach for Yale.[21] Friedman's position, though, was far below Horween's station at Harvard. Yet other Hebrews emerged to compete and then overtake Horween as the finest exemplars of Jewish brawn. In fact, in the column beside the write-up of Horween's impending resignation from Harvard, a Jewish newspaper in Los Angeles reported that "Henry Greenberg, the slugging first baseman of the Raleigh club of the Piedmont League, has been recalled [to the Majors] by the Detroit Tigers."[22] With the aid of better audio and visual technology, Hank Greenberg became the next darling sports hero in the American Jewish world. The elevated status of professional sports in the 1930s and "Hammerin' Hank's" pursuit of Babe Ruth's home run record redounded to Greenberg's Jewish celebrity, compelling a number of scouts to "hunt for the next Jewish star."[23] Greenberg's fame as well as Harvard's recession from the sporting arena eclipsed the football adventures of Arnold Horween.

Bill Bingham finally made it to the Olympics. Back in 1912, Bill had ceded that opportunity to Ted Meredith, unaware that his generosity helped launch his rival's collegiate running career. The high point of Meredith's running was his University of Pennsylvania tenure. He continued racing and even coached a bit after serving in World War I but never returned to his prior form at Pennsylvania. In some measure, it was in their postcollegiate careers that Bill Bingham finally bested Ted Meredith. In 1936, Bingham was appointed chairman of the USA Track and Field Committee. It was his role to select the runners to represent the United States in the contentious Olympiad in Berlin. He was "limp" with excitement after a tryout on New York's Randall's Island. There, Bingham watched Jesse Owens win the 100- and 200-meter runs and the broad jump. Owens, Bingham said with pride, was the best of the ten "fine negro athletes" his squad proudly sent to compete in Hitler's Germany.[24] Bingham's commitment to fairness and "athletics for all" proved pivotal in breaking the color barrier in US sports.

Bill Bingham served as Harvard's athletic director until 1951. He stayed active in retirement and passed away in September 1971.[25] After the Harvard-Yale game in 1929, a friend wrote to Bill, offering that "sticking to Arnie in 1927 was one of the finest things that you have done as Director of Athletics."[26] Bingham's response is not preserved in the archives. I would like to imagine that Bill responded that the decision was no different from so many others he had made in his lifetime. His position on sportsmanship was at times an unpopular creed, one that Bingham himself had forgotten during the tail end of his racing career. In the end, Bill Bingham made it the defining attribute in a lifetime given to sport and all that it had come to represent in American life. It was a choice that sprung from deeply held values and the conviction that the center can be influenced by those on the periphery, along the sidelines.

NOTES

INTRODUCTION

1. In some ways, then, this point of departure mirrors the case made in Michael Oriard, "Football, Cultural History and Democracy," *Journal of Sport History* 29 (Summer 2002): 241–49. From a sociological perspective, it was made much earlier in David Riesman and Reuel Denney, "Football in America: A Study in Culture Diffusion," *American Quarterly* 3 (Winter 1951): 309–25.

2. "Harvard Grads Cheer Horween at Dinner Here," *Chicago Tribune*, April 18, 1926, 1.

3. Dominic A. Pacyga, *Chicago: A Biography* (Chicago: University of Chicago Press, 2009), 150–82.

4. On the history of Jews and sports, see Peter Levine, *Ellis Island to Ebbets Field: Sport and the American Jewish Experience* (New York: Oxford University Press, 1992). See also Frederic Couple Jaher, "Antisemitism in American Athletics," *Shofar* 20 (Fall 2001): 61–73.

5. Jerome Karabel, *The Chosen: The Hidden History of Admission and Exclusion at Harvard, Yale, and Princeton* (Boston: Houghton Mifflin, 2005), 77–109.

6. Harold S. Wechsler, "An Academic Gresham's Law: Group Repulsion as a Theme in American Higher Education," *Teachers College Record* 82 (1981): 575–76.

7. Jim Cullen, *The American Dream: A Short History of an Idea that Shaped a Nation* (Oxford: Oxford University Press, 2003), 59–131.

8. See, for example, Susan Ware, *Game, Set, Match: Billie Jean King and the Revolution in Women's Sports* (Chapel Hill: University of North Carolina Press, 2011).

9. Norman Hapgood, "Schools, Colleges and Jews," *Harper's Weekly*, January 22, 1916, 79.

10. "Harvard's Inquiry Starts on 4 Lines," *New York Times*, June 24, 1922, 20.

11. "'Good Old Hah-vahd' to Have Its Day," *Chicago Tribune*, June 4, 1911, 13.

12. "Horween Says He'll Keep Old Harvard Plan," *Chicago Daily Tribune*, March 12, 1926, 21.

13. Sarah Imhoff, *Masculinity and the Making of American Judaism* (Bloomington: Indiana University Press, 2017), 1–30.

14. On the inglorious beginnings of the NFL, see Robert W. Peterson, *Pigskin: The Early Years of Pro Football* (New York: Oxford University Press, 1997), 13–21; and John Eisenberg, *The League: How Five Rivals Created the NFL and Launched a Sports Empire* (New York: Basic Books, 2018), 81–93.

15. "Horween to Stick to Harvard System," *New York Times*, March 12, 1926, 12.

16. "Harvard Grads Cheer Horween at Dinner Here," *Chicago Daily Tribune*, April 18, 1926, A2.

17. "Harvard Club of Chicago," *Harvard Alumni Bulletin*, April 29, 1926, 873.

18. Susan E. Hirsch, "Ethnic and Civil Leadership in the Progressive Era: Charles H. Wacker and Chicago," *Journal of American Ethnic History* 35 (Summer 2016): 5–6.

19. Jessica Cooperman, *Making Judaism Safe for America: World War I and the Origins of Religious Pluralism* (New York: NYU Press, 2018), 1–11.

20. Charles Fountain, *The Betrayal: The 1919 World Series and the Birth of Modern Baseball* (New York: Oxford University Press, 2015), 1–11.

21. Scholars have a propensity for using Harvard as a site for testing historical change. See, for example, Richard Norton Smith, *The Harvard Century: The Making of a University to a Nation* (New York: Simon and Schuster, 1986); Morton Keller and Phyllis Keller, *Making Harvard Modern: The Rise of America's University* (New York: Oxford University Press, 2001); George Howe Colt, *The Game: Harvard, Yale, and America in 1968* (New York: Scribner, 2018).

22. See Jane Leavy, *Sandy Koufax: A Lefty's Legacy* (New York: HarperCollins, 2002), 167–94; Mark Kurlansky, *Hank Greenberg: The Hero Who Didn't Want to Be One* (New Haven, CT: Yale University Press, 2011), 1–15.

23. Steven Elliott Tripp, *Ty Cobb: Baseball and American Manhood* (Lanham, MD: Rowman and Littlefield, 2016), 293–353.

24. Mark F. Bernstein, *Football: The Ivy League Origins of an American Obsession* (Philadelphia: University of Pennsylvania Press, 2001), 143–69. See also Raymond Schmidt, *Shaping College Football: The Transformation of an American Sport, 1919–1930* (Syracuse, NY: Syracuse University Press, 2007), 82–107.

25. Perhaps the best historical survey on college football is John Sayle Watterson, *College Football: History, Spectacle, Controversy* (Baltimore, MD: Johns Hopkins University Press, 2000). See also John J. Miller, *The Big Scrum: How Teddy Roosevelt Saved Football* (New York: HarperCollins, 2011).

26. See, for example, Michael Oriard, *Reading Football: How the Popular Press Created an American Spectacle* (Chapel Hill: University of North Carolina Press, 1993); Kate Buford, *Native American Son: The Life and Sporting Legend of Jim Thorpe* (New York: Knopf, 2010).

27. Julie Des Jardins, *Walter Camp: Football and the Modern Man* (New York: Oxford University Press, 2015); Ray Robinson, *Rockne of Notre Dame: The Making*

of a Football Legend (New York: Oxford University Press, 1999); Robin Lester, *Stagg's University: The Rise, Decline and Fall of Big-Time Football at Chicago* (Urbana: University of Illinois Press, 1999); Jeffrey J. Miller, *Pop Warner: A Life on the Gridiron* (Jefferson, NC: McFarland, 2015); Dick Friedman, *The Coach Who Strangled the Bulldog: How Harvard's Percy Haughton Beat Yale and Reinvented Football* (Lanham, MD: Rowman and Littlefield, 2018).

28. Marcia Graham Synnott, *The Half-Opened Door: Discrimination and Admissions at Harvard, Yale, and Princeton, 1900–1970* (Westport, CT: Greenwood, 1979), 3–25.

29. Ronald A. Smith, "Winning and a Theory of Competitive Athletics," in *Sports and the Humanities: A Collection of Original Essays*, ed. William J. Morgan (Knoxville, TN: University of Tennessee, 1980), 44–50; Smith, *Sports and Freedom: The Rise of Big-Time College Athletics* (New York: Oxford University Press, 1988), 3–12. For Smith's more recent treatment of the subject, see Smith, "The Lost Battle for Gentlemanly Sport, 1869–1909," in *The Rock, the Curse, and the Hub: A Random History of Boston Sports*, ed. Randy Roberts (Cambridge, MA: Harvard University Press, 2005), 160–77.

30. Particularly on Yale's sports culture, see Robert J. Higgs, "Yale and the Heroic Ideal, Götterdämmerung and Palingenesis, 1865–1914," in *Manliness and Morality: Middle-Class Masculinity in Britain and America, 1800–1940*, ed. J. A. Mangan and Hames Walvin (Manchester, UK: Manchester University Press, 1987), 160–75.

31. James Bryce, "American Revisited: The Changes of a Quarter-Century," *Outlook*, March 25, 1905, 738.

32. See Henry D. Sheldon, *Student Life and Customs* (New York: D. Appleton, 1901), 53.

33. Bruce Barton, *More Power to You: Fifty Editorials from Every Week* (New York: Century, 1917), 189.

34. "Some Tendencies of Modern Sport," *Quarterly Review* 199 (January 1904): 150.

35. Ibid., 141.

36. "From a Graduate's Window," *Harvard Graduates' Magazine*, December 1905, 218.

37. "Professional Coaching," *Harvard Graduates' Magazine*, September 1903, 32.

38. Ronald A. Smith, *Pay for Play: A History of Big-Time College Athletic Reform* (Urbana: University of Illinois Press, 2011), 34–51.

39. On the consumerism of college football, specifically in the 1920s, see Mark Dyreson, "The Emergence of Consumer Culture and the Transformation of Physical Culture: American Sport in the 1920s," *Journal of Sport History* 16 (Winter 1989): 261–81.

40. There is a significant literature on the various processes and strategies of Americanization. For good summaries of this material and the arguments, see Russel A. Kazal, "Revisiting Assimilation: The Rise, Fall, and Reappraisal of a Concept in American Ethnic History," *American Historical Review* 100 (April 1995): 437–71;

Gary Gerstle, "Liberty, Coercion, and the Making of Americans," *Journal of American History* 84 (September 1997): 524–58; William R. Hutchison, *Religious Pluralism in America: The Contentious History of a Founding Ideal* (New Haven, CT: Yale University Press, 2003), 111–38.

41. James R. Barrett, *The Irish Way: Becoming American in the Multiethnic City* (New York: Penguin, 2012), 76. On the failed attempt to forge a more integrated process of Irish Catholic Americanization, see Jay P. Dolan, *In Search of American Catholicism: A History of Religion and Culture in Tension* (Oxford: Oxford University Press, 2002), 99–117.

42. Steven Steinberg, *The Academic Melting Pot: Catholics and Jews in American Higher Education* (New Brunswick, NJ: Transaction, 1974), 59–74.

43. See Lloyd P. Gartner, "Temples of Liberty Unpolluted: American Jews and Public Schools, 1840–1875," in *A Bicentennial Festschrift for Jacob Rader Marcus*, ed. Bertram Wallace Korn (New York: Ktav, 1976), 157–89.

44. See Jonathan D. Sarna, "The Cult of Synthesis in American Jewish Culture," *Jewish Social Studies* 5 (Autumn 1998–Winter 1999): 52–79.

45. Eric L. Goldstein, *The Price of Whiteness: Jews, Race, and American Identity* (Princeton, NJ: Princeton University Press, 2006), 1–7.

46. Charles S. Bernheimer, "Jewish Americanization Agencies," *American Jewish Year Book* 23 (1921): 84–111.

47. Philip Gleason, *Contending with Modernity: Catholic Higher Education in the Twentieth Century* (New York: Oxford University Press, 1995), 22–32.

48. "Add Your City to the List," *Notre Dame Scholastic*, December 11, 1920, 186–87.

49. Patrick R. Redmond, *The Irish and the Making of American Sport, 1835–1920* (Jefferson, NC: McFarland, 2014), 5–33.

50. Schmidt, *Shaping College Football*, 108–30; Murray Sperber, *Shake Down the Thunder: The Creation of Notre Dame Football* (New York: Henry Holt, 1993), 207–22.

51. *Brooklyn Tablet* quoted in *Notre Dame Football Review*, 1919, 12. On Catholics at non-Catholic universities, see Kathleen A. Mahoney, *Catholic Higher Education in Protestant America: The Jesuits and Harvard in the Age of the University* (Baltimore, MD: Johns Hopkins University Press, 2003), 110–50.

52. Gerald R. Gems, "The Prep Bowl: Football and Religious Acculturation in Chicago, 1927–1963," *Journal of Sports History* 23 (Fall 1996): 284–302.

53. Gerald R. Gems, "Negotiating a Native American Identity through Sport: Assimilation, Adaptation, and the Role of the Trickster," in *Native Athletes in Sport and Society: A Reader*, ed. C. Richard King (Lincoln: University of Nebraska Press, 2005), 1–21.

54. Patrick B. Miller, "To 'Bring the Race Along Rapidly': Sport, Student Culture, and Educational Mission at Historically Black Colleges during the Interwar Years," *History of Education Quarterly* 35 (Summer 1995): 111–33.

55. Stephen Hardy, *How Boston Played: Sport, Recreation, and Community, 1865–1915* (Boston: Northeastern University Press, 1982), 137.

56. Russ J. Cowans, "Fritz Pollard Made an Impression," *Chicago Defender*, Janu-

ary 18, 1958, 24. For more on Pollard, see John M. Carroll, *Fritz Pollard: Pioneer in Racial Advancement* (Urbana: University of Illinois Press, 1998).

57. Michael Hurd, *Black College Football, 1892–1992: One Hundred Years of History, Education, and Pride* (Virginia Beach, VA: Donning, 1998), 27–31.

58. "Wilberforce May Stop Roger Williams with Aerial Attack," *Chicago Defender*, October 22, 1921, 10.

59. Frank Young, "Howard Must Bolster Up to Win from Lincoln on Nov. 30," *Chicago Defender*, November 25, 1922, 10.

60. Jon Butler, *Becoming America: The Revolution before 1776* (Cambridge, MA: Harvard University Press, 2000), 1–7.

61. Allison Danzig, "Players of the Game," *New York Times*, November 24, 1930, 33.

62. Jeffrey E. Mirel, *Patriotic Pluralism: Americanization Education and European Immigrants* (Cambridge, MA: Harvard University Press, 2010).

63. William J. Bingham, "Arnold Horween," *Harvard Alumni Bulletin*, December 18, 1930, 395.

CHAPTER 1. THE (CINDER) PATH
TO A BETTER LIFE

1. "The Competition at the Boston College Indoor Meet," undated, box 3, Bingham Scrapbook, William J. Bingham Diaries and Scrapbooks, HUM 387, Harvard University Archives, Cambridge, MA. [Hereafter cited as Bingham Scrapbook, with box no., and with page no. and date, where given.]

2. Nathaniel J. Hasenfus, *Athletics at Boston College*, vol. 1 (Worcester, MA: Heffernan, 1943), 2.

3. Katrina Irving, *Immigrant Mothers: Narratives of Race and Maternity, 1890–1925* (Urbana: University of Illinois Press, 2000), 126–27n27.

4. "Lawrence Amateur Athletes Rank with Country's Best," undated, box 3, Bingham Scrapbook.

5. Stanley Woodward, *Paper Tiger: An Old Sportswriter's Reminiscences of People, Newspapers, War, and Work* (New York: Atheneum, 1963), 88.

6. Robert J. Higgs, *God in the Stadium: Sports and Religion in America* (Lexington: University Press of Kentucky, 1995), 189–207.

7. "Local Boys to Compete," undated, box 3, Bingham Scrapbook.

8. "Relay Team Lowers Guards' Track Mark," *Boston Post*, February 16, 1908, 14.

9. "Bingham to Lead Y.M.C.A. Team," undated, box 3, Bingham Scrapbook.

10. Tom Derderian, *Boston Marathon: The History of the World's Premier Running Event* (Champaign, IL: Human Kinetics, 1994), 44.

11. Clifford Putney, *Muscular Christianity: Manhood and Sports in Protestant America, 1880–1920* (Cambridge, MA: Harvard University Press, 2001), 45–72.

12. Bingham's biographical details are scattered throughout his scrapbooks at Harvard University Archives. Some of the more substantive accounts include "Bingham

Makes Good at Exeter," undated, box 4, Bingham Scrapbook; "William J. Bingham: Records Held by Bingham," undated, box 4, Bingham Scrapbook; and "Varsity Captains of Teams in the Bix Six," undated, box 5, Bingham Scrapbook.

13. "Varsity Captains of Teams in the Big Six," undated, box 5, Bingham Scrapbook.

14. Maurice B. Dorgan, *History of Lawrence, Massachusetts: With War Records* (Cambridge, MA: Murray, 1924), 39–48.

15. Donald B. Cole, *Immigrant City: Lawrence, Massachusetts, 1845–1921* (Chapel Hill: University of North Carolina Press, 1963), 79–80.

16. Bill Cunningham, "Track and Field Marshal," *Collier's*, August 15, 1936, 26.

17. "With Song and Joke and Athletics," undated, box 3, Bingham Scrapbook.

18. Michael S. Kimmel, *Manhood in America: A Cultural History* (New York: Oxford University Press, 2006), 80–104.

19. "Bill Bingham a Self-Made Man," *Boston Globe*, December 12, 1915, 56.

20. Theodore Roosevelt, *The Strenuous Life: Essays and Addresses* (New York: Century, 1905), 1.

21. "Big Squad Out for Track Team," undated, box 3, Bingham Scrapbook.

22. "Bingham to Lead Y.M.C.A. Team," undated, box 3, Bingham Scrapbook.

23. Tom McCabe, "Career of Bill Bingham, Harvard Track Coach, Reads like a 'Frank Merriwell,'" undated, box 6, Bingham Scrapbook.

24. Ibid.

25. Ibid.

26. "Citizens Drag Welton," *Boston Globe*, August 7, 1908, 5.

27. "America's Path Was Rocky One," *Boston Globe*, August 6, 1908, 14.

28. Ibid.

29. On Sheppard at the Olympics, see Don Holst and Marcia S. Popp, *American Men of Olympic Track and Field: Interviews with Athletes and Coaches* (Jefferson, NC: McFarland, 2005), 77.

30. "Melvin Sheppard Beaten by Crowd," *Boston Globe*, January 25, 1908, 4.

31. "Bingham Talks to Track Team Men," undated, box 4, Bingham Scrapbook.

32. "Fine Competition at the Boston College Indoor Meet," undated, box 3, Bingham Scrapbook.

33. "William J. Bingham," undated, box 3, Bingham Scrapbook. Parks were a newfangled notion at this time. See Stephen Hardy, *How Boston Played: Sport, Recreation, and Community, 1865–1915* (Knoxville, TN: University of Tennessee Press, 2003).

34. "Bill Bingham Leads Harvard Cheers While Bob Plays Halfback for Yale," undated, box 5, Bingham Scrapbook.

35. Robert Pruter, *The Rise of American High School Sports and the Search for Control: 1880–1930* (Syracuse, NY: Syracuse University Press, 2013), 22–44.

36. "History and Statistics of the Intercollegiate," *Harvard Illustrated*, June 1, 1916, 340.

37. See J. E. "Ted" Meredith, *Middle Distance and Relay Racing* (New York: American Sports, 1925), 15–124. This volume, by Bingham's rival at Harvard, is a superb

manual and captures the attitudes and trends in racing in this historical period. Many of the paragraphs here are based on Meredith's book.

38. "Athletes' Faces Show Do or Die Spirit," undated, box 5, Bingham Scrapbook.

39. "Harvard Sends Forth Class of 1908," *Boston Globe*, June 25, 1908, 8.

40. Paula S. Fass, *The Damned and the Beautiful: American Youth in the 1920's* (Oxford: Oxford University Press, 1977), 124.

41. "Harvard Sends Forth Class of 1908."

42. Ibid.

43. Morris A. Bealle, *The History of Football at Harvard, 1874–1948* (Washington, DC: Columbia, 1948), 174–78.

44. "Commencement," *Harvard Graduates' Magazine*, September 1908, 67.

45. Brian M. Ingrassia, "Public Influence Inside the College Walls: Progressive Era Universities, Social Scientists, and Intercollegiate Football Reform," *Journal of the Gilded Age and Progressive Era* 10 (January 2011): 59–88.

46. *Blacks at Harvard: A Documentary History of African-American Experience at Harvard and Radcliffe* (New York: NYU Press, 1993), 129.

47. Cole, *Immigrant City*, 17–26.

48. Ibid., 27–41.

49. Mark A. Noll, *A History of Christianity in the United States and Canada* (Grand Rapids, MI: William B. Eerdmans, 1992), 360–62.

50. "Athlete Bingham Given a Purse," undated news clipping, 1908, box 3, Bingham Scrapbook.

51. Bingham's method is outlined in many reports, including "Harvard Relay Team Finishes Two Inches Ahead of Tech's," *Boston Globe*, January 24, 1915, 15.

52. Oliver Wendel Holmes, *Elsie Venner: A Romance of Destiny*, vol. 1 (Boston: Ticknor and Fields, 1861), 13–19.

53. Barbara Miller Solomon, *Ancestors and Immigrants: A Changing New England Tradition* (Cambridge, MA: Harvard University Press, 1956), 5.

54. Cunningham, "Track and Field Marshal," 26.

55. Ibid.

56. "Athlete Bingham Given a Purse," undated, box 3, Bingham Scrapbook.

57. "Commencement," *Harvard Graduates' Magazine*, September 1908, 71.

CHAPTER 2. WINNING ISN'T EVERYTHING, BUT IT IS SOMETHING

1. Dennis Clark, *The Irish in Philadelphia: Ten Generations of Urban Experience* (Philadelphia: Temple University Press, 1973), 24–37.

2. I received information on Bingham's ancestry from his closest surviving relative, a daughter-in-law, Jinsie Scott Bingham. I am grateful to her for sharing her memories on August 16, 2018, and for supplying key documents to reconstruct the early information in this chapter.

3. Lawrence M. Crosbie, *The Phillips Exeter Academy: A History* (Exeter, NH: Phillips Exeter Academy, 1923), 214.

4. Myron R. Williams, *The Story of Phillips Exeter* (Exeter, NH: Phillips Exeter Academy, 1957), 15.

5. "Bingham and Mahan Will Enter Harvard," undated, box 4, Bingham Scrapbook.

6. Many of the details of Bingham's experiences at Exeter are derived from stray lines in his scrapbooks held at the Harvard archives and from Bill Cunningham, "Track and Field Marshall," *Collier's*, August 15, 1926, 26, 36.

7. Victor M. Haughton, "Thanksgiving Tide," undated, box 3, Bingham Scrapbook.

8. Williams, *Phillips Exeter*, 76.

9. Steven B. Levine," "The Rise of American Boarding Schools and the Development of a National Upper Class," *Social Problems* 28 (October 1980): 63–94.

10. Frank H. Cunningham, *Familiar Sketches of the Phillips Exeter Academy and Surroundings* (Boston: James R. Osgood, 1883), 334.

11. John L. Taylor, "A Memoir of His Honour Samuel Phillips, LL.D.," *North American Review*, July 1858, 129.

12. "Academy Hymnal," undated, box 3, Bingham Scrapbook.

13. Williams, *Phillips Exeter*, 74–84.

14. "Bingham Makes Good at Exeter," undated, box 4, Bingham Scrapbook.

15. Richard P. Borkowski, "The Life and Contributions of Walter Camp to American Football" (PhD diss., Temple University, 1979), 188.

16. Francesco Duina, *Winning: Reflections on an American Obsession* (Princeton, NJ: Princeton University Press, 2011), 193.

17. Mortimer Jerome Cohen, *The Annals of America*, vol. 1 (Chicago: Encyclopaedia Britannica, 1968), 320.

18. Richard Weiss, *The American Myth of Success: From Horatio Alger to Norman Vincent Peale* (New York: Basic Books, 1969), 27.

19. Jeffrey Louis Decker, *Made in America: Self-Styled Success from Horatio Alger to Oprah Winfrey* (Minneapolis: University of Minnesota Press, 1997), xxiii.

20. Charles H. Cooley, *Personal Competition: Its Place in the Social Order and Effect upon Individuals* (New York: Macmillan, 1899), 173.

21. Richard M. Huber, *The American Idea of Success* (New York: McGraw-Hill, 1971), 187.

22. Oliver Wendell Holmes, *The Autocrat of the Breakfast-Table: Every Man His Own Boswell* (Cambridge, MA: Riverside, 1891), 20.

23. Richard Hofstadter, *Age of Reform: From Bryan to F.D.R* (New York: Vintage, 1955), 213.

24. James R. Mock and Cedric Larson, *Words That Won the War: The Story of the Committee on Public Information, 1917–1919* (Princeton, NJ: Princeton University Press, 1939), 240–41.

25. Mary Shaw, "Producing a Play on a Shoestring," *Saturday Evening Post*, July 8, 1911, 10.

26. E. Boyd Barrett, SJ, *The Will to Win: A Call to American Boys and Girls* (New York: P. J. Kenedy and Sons, 1917), 64.

27. J. A. Zahm, *Evolution and Dogma* (Chicago: D. H. McBride, 1896), 385.

28. Miller, *Big Scrum*, 175–204.

29. Roger R. Tamte, *Walter Camp and the Creation of American Football* (Urbana: University of Illinois Press, 2018), 311–16.

30. Axel Bundgaard, *Muscle and Manliness: The Rise of Sport in American Boarding Schools* (Syracuse, NY: Syracuse University Press, 2005), 52–83.

31. "Principal Amen of Phillips Exeter on Pres Eliot's Arraignment of Football," *Boston Globe*, February 5, 1905, 5.

32. Ibid.

33. Ibid.

34. "The Phillips Exeter Academy," 1911, box 4, Bingham Scrapbook.

35. Williams, *Phillips Exeter*, 78.

36. Horace Bushnell, *Work and Play; or, Literary Varieties* (New York: Charles Scribner, 1864), 12.

37. Ryan Swanson, *The Strenuous Life: Theodore Roosevelt and the Making of the American Athlete* (New York: Diversion, 2019), 154.

38. Endicott Peabody, "The Ideals of Sport in England and America," *American Physical Education Review* 19 (April 1914): 283.

39. Peabody, "Ideals of Sport," 278.

40. *Life at Phillips Exeter* (Exeter, NH: Phillips Exeter Academy, 1913), 5.

41. Williams, *Phillips Exeter*, 89.

42. Ibid., 79.

43. On the losing streak and the formation of the Exeter-Andover rivalry, see Fred H. Harrison, *Athletics for All: Physical Education and Athletics at Phillips Academy, Andover, 1778–1978* (Andover, MA: Phillips Academy, 1983), 76–101.

44. "No Gymnasium," *Exonian*, April 6, 1878, 2.

45. "Important Meet Is Proposed," *Chicago Tribune*, March 2, 1902, 19.

46. "Gymnasium," *Exonian*, January 31, 1880, 1.

47. "Outdoor Training," *Exonian*, May 1, 1901, 2.

48. Crosbie, *Phillips Exeter Academy*, 242.

49. *Marshall Newell: A Memorial Volume for His Classmates and Friends* (Boston: Lamson, Wolffe, 1898), 3–6.

50. Ibid., 49.

51. Samuel A. Munford, "John Paul Jones—All-Round College Man," *Outing*, September 1913, 715–20.

52. "Faculty Shield Meet," *Exonian*, February 24, 1909, 1.

53. "Exeter First in Big School Meet," undated, box 3, Bingham Scrapbook.

54. "Bingham a Star," undated, box 3, Bingham Scrapbook.

55. Weiss, *American Myth of Success*, 11.

56. "Inquiry Business Meeting," *Phillipian*, February 21, 1912, 6.

57. "Track at Exeter under Connors," *Exonian Supplement*, February 8, 1922, 2.

58. "Capt. Track Team at Exeter," undated, box 4, Bingham Scrapbook.

59. "Bingham in Olympic Race," undated, box 4, Bingham Scrapbook.

60. "Remarkable Times Made in Stadium," undated, box 3, Bingham Scrapbook.

61. "Andover Triumphs Again," *Phillipian*, June 1, 1909, 5.

62. "'Bill' Bingham Speaks at Meeting at Y.M.C.A.," undated, box 6, Bingham Scrapbook.

63. Ibid.

64. "Andover Triumphs Again," 1.

65. "The Biography of George Connors," *Exonian Supplement*, February 8, 1922, 1.

66. "William J. Bingham," undated, box 4, Bingham Scrapbook.

67. "Yale Yearlings Humble Harvard in Dual Games," undated, box 4, Bingham Scrapbook.

68. "Andover Beats Exeter, 49–47," undated, box 3, Bingham Scrapbook.

69. "How 'Bill' Bingham Broke the Record," undated, box 4, Bingham Scrapbook.

70. "Harvard Secures Bingham," undated, box 4, Bingham Scrapbook.

71. "How 'Bill' Bingham Broke the Record."

72. Ibid.

73. Laurence M. Crosbie, "Alumni Notes," *Bulletin of the Phillips Exeter Academy* 12 (September 1911): 46.

74. Ibid.

75. "Bingham's Election Pleases Hundreds of Local Admirers," undated, box 4, Bingham Scrapbook.

76. The Gregory Family to Bill Bingham, May 3, 1912, box 4, Bingham Scrapbook.

77. "Capt. Track Team at Exeter," undated, box 4, Bingham Scrapbook.

78. Tom McCabe, "Career of Bill Bingham, Harvard Track Coach, Reads like a 'Frank Merriwell,'" undated, box 6, Bingham Scrapbook.

79. "The Speaker," undated, box 4, Bingham Scrapbook.

80. Ibid.

81. McCabe, "Career of Bill Bingham."

82. Ryan K. Anderson, *Frank Merriwell and the Fiction of All-American Boyhood: The Progressive Era Creation of the Schoolboy Sports Story* (Fayetteville: University of Arkansas Press, 2015).

83. Burt L. Standish, "Frank Merriwell's Rival," *Tip Top Library*, May 9, 1896, 6.

84. Ibid.

85. Gilbert Patten, *Frank Merriwell at Yale* (Philadelphia: McKay, 1903), 257–58.

86. "Varsity Captains of Teams in the Big Six," undated, box 5, Bingham Scrapbook.

87. "Address of President Charles W. Eliot, LL.D," in *Exercises at the Centennial Celebration of the Founding of Phillips Exeter Academy* (Exeter, NH: William B. Morrill, 1884), 63.

88. "Bingham Opinions," undated, box 6, Bingham Scrapbook; see also Frank A. Merrill to William J. Bingham, January 4, 1916, box 6, Bingham Scrapbook.

89. "New Additions," *Exonian*, May 1, 1912, 1; "Harvard Secures Bingham," undated, box 4, Bingham Scrapbook.

CHAPTER 3. AMERICANIZATION, THE JEWISH TAKE ON SUCCESS

1. On Horween Leather Company and its connection to sports, see Richard Lara, "'It Was in the Water': Chicago's Leather Industry, 1886–1917" (PhD diss., University of Delaware, 2019), 77–93. The biographical information on Rose and Isadore Horween is drawn from this dissertation as well as a lengthy interview by the author with Skip Horween in the Horween Leather Company's offices in Chicago on June 9, 2017, and a recording of an interview conducted by the author with Ralph Horween on February 20, 1990. Chaim Motzen provided me with valuable census data.

2. Norman Bolotin and Christine Laing, *The World's Columbia Exposition: The Chicago World's Fair of 1893* (Urbana: University of Illinois Press, 1992), 110.

3. Alexander Watt, *The Art of Leather Manufacturing, Being a Practical Handbook* (London: Crosby Lockwood, 1885), 2.

4. Louis Wirth, *The Ghetto* (Chicago: University of Chicago Press, 1928), 195–240.

5. The document still hangs in the Chicago offices of the Horween Leather Company.

6. Skip Horween, interview, June 9, 2017.

7. Philip P. Bregstone, *Chicago and Its Jews: A Cultural History* (Chicago: Philip P. Bregstone, 1933), 92–93.

8. Moses Rischin, *The American Gospel of Success: Individualism and Beyond* (Chicago: Quadrangle, 1965), 12–14.

9. Albert Nelson Marquis, *Who's Who in Chicago and Vicinity* (Chicago: A. N. Marquis, 1936), 485.

10. A. F. Gordon to Isadore Horween, May 13, 1918, Horween Leather Company Private Collection, Chicago, IL.

11. "Standish Singers Best," *Boston Globe*, June 2, 1915, 9.

12. Marie Kirschner Stone, *The Progressive Legacy: Chicago's Francis W. Parker School (1901–2001)* (New York: Peter Lang, 2001), 135–87.

13. Ronald Kronish, "John Dewey and Horace M. Kallen on Cultural Pluralism: Their Impact on Jewish Education," *Jewish Social Studies* 44 (Spring 1982): 135–48.

14. Skip Horween, interview, June 9, 2017.

15. "Miss Cooke," Morning Exercises, September 21, 1915, box 4, folder 24, Flora Juliette Cooke Papers, Chicago History Museum, Chicago, IL.

16. "The Hebrews," Morning Exercises, September 22, 1915, box 4, folder 24, Flora Juliette Cooke Papers.

17. *Parker Record* (1916), 24.

18. Ibid., 15.

19. Ibid., 28.

20. Ibid.

21. Lester, *Stagg's University*, 72.

22. Stone, *Progressive Legacy*, 183–84.

23. "Play as Fundamental in Education," *Francis W. Parker School Year Book: The Social Motive in School Work*, June 1912, 33.

24. "One More for Parker Highs," *Chicago Tribune*, January 26, 1913, C3.

25. Gerald R. Gems, *Windy City Wars: Labor, Leisure, and Sport in the Making of Chicago* (Lanham, MD: Scarecrow, 1997), 96–97.

26. "The Football Finale," *Parker Weekly*, November 23, 1914, 1.

27. "Athletics," *Parker Weekly*, May 8, 1915, 1.

28. *Parker Record*, 15.

29. Ibid., 56.

30. Samuel Eliot Morison, *Three Centuries of Harvard, 1636–1936* (Cambridge, MA: Harvard University Press, 1936), 417.

31. "News Notes," *Parker Weekly*, December 14, 1914, 2.

32. Thomas Hughes, *Vacation Rambles* (London: Macmillan, 1895), 176.

33. Theodore Roosevelt, *A Compilation of Messages and Speeches: 1901–1905*, ed. Alfred Henry Lewis (Washington, DC: Bureau of National Literature and Art, 1906), 644–45.

34. Oliver Wendell Holmes, *Speeches* (Boston: Little, Brown, 1896), 63.

35. Alar Lipping, "Charles W. Eliot's Views on Education, Physical Education, and Intercollegiate Athletics" (PhD diss., Ohio State University, 1980), 242.

36. *Reports of the President and Treasurer of Harvard College, 1903–1904* (Cambridge, MA: Harvard University, 1905), 22.

37. Higgs, *God in the Stadium*, 116.

38. Smith, *Harvard Century*, 44.

39. Miller, *Big Scrum*, 95–109.

40. Des Jardins, *Walter Camp*, 126.

41. Smith, *Harvard Century*, 44. On Roosevelt's use of this term, see Swanson, *Strenuous Life*, 195–96.

42. Ibid., 33.

43. "The Football Buried in the Delta," *Boston Advertiser*, September 4, 1860, 1. See also Morton Prince, "History of Football at Harvard," in *The H Book of Harvard Athletics, 1852–1922*, ed. John A. Blanchard (Cambridge, MA: Harvard Varsity Club, 1923), 334–42.

44. Bealle, *History of Football at Harvard*, 17–29.

45. Elting E. Morison, ed., *The Letters of Theodore Roosevelt: The Years of Preparation, 1868–1898* (Cambridge, MA: Harvard University Press, 1951), 20.

46. Ronald A. Smith, "Harvard and Columbia and a Reconsideration of the 1905–06 Football Crisis," *Journal of Sports History* 8 (Winter 1981): 5–19. See also Miller, *Big Scrum*, 175–204.

47. John T. Bethell, *Harvard Observed: An Illustrated History of the University in the Twentieth Century* (Cambridge, MA: Harvard University Press, 1998), 31.

48. "Football Differences," *New York Times*, September 30, 1906, 8.

49. Nathaniel S. Shaler, "The Athletic Problem in Education," *Atlantic Monthly*, January 1889, 83.

50. George Santayana, "Philosophy on the Bleachers," *Harvard Monthly*, July 1894, 187.

51. Michael Oriard, *Sporting with the Gods: The Rhetoric of Play and Game in American Culture* (Cambridge: Cambridge University Press, 1991), 188.

52. Craig Bruce Smith, *American Honor: The Creation of the Nation's Ideals during the Revolutionary Era* (Chapel Hill: University of North Carolina Press, 2018), 2–3.

53. Ibid., 232–36.

54. Kim Townsend, *Manhood at Harvard: William James and Others* (New York: W. W. Norton, 1996), 17–29.

55. David Q. Voigt, *America through Baseball* (Chicago: Nelson-Hall, 1976), 3–25.

56. W. R. C. Latson, "The Moral Effects of Athletics," *Outing*, December 1906, 389.

57. Des Jardins, *Walter Camp*, 161.

58. Latson, "Moral Effects of Athletics," 391.

59. Morris Joseph Clurman, "The American Game of Football: Is It a Factor for Good or for Evil?" *Medical Record* 79 (January 7, 1911): 19.

60. *Reports of the President*, 20.

61. "Encouraging Athletics," *New York Observer and Chronicle*, December 13, 1894, 642.

62. "Favor Revision of Rules," *New York Times*, November 27, 1905, 5. See also Scott McQuilkin, "Brutality in Football and the Creation of the NCAA: A Codified Moral Compass in Progressive America," *Sport History Review* 33 (May 2002): 3–4.

63. Tobias Schanfarber, "News and Views," *American Israelite*, December 10, 1903, 1.

64. Tobias Schanfarber, "Chicago Hebrew Institute," *American Israelite*, May 27, 1909, 1.

65. Joseph Lee, *Play in Education* (New York: Macmillan, 1915), 335.

66. Frederic L. Paxon, "The Rise of Sport," *Mississippi Valley Historical Review* 4 (September 1917): 167.

67. Charles F. Thwing, "Football: A Game of Hearts," *Independent*, November 3, 1898, 1261.

68. Charles F. Thwing, "The Ethical Functions of Foot-Ball," *North American Review*, November 1901, 630. For other Christian condemnations, see Andrew Doyle, "Foolish and Useless Sport: The Southern Evangelical Crusade against Intercollegiate Football," *Journal of Sport History* 24 (Fall 1997): 317–40.

69. Bealle, *History of Football at Harvard*, 58–62.

70. Bliss Perry, *Life and Letters of Henry Lee Higginson* (Boston: Atlantic Monthly Press, 1921), 536.

71. For just one indicator of the entrenchment of football at Harvard, consider that in the 1890s Waldron Kintzing Post's well-read stories of undergraduate life at Harvard depicted the outsized popularity of football and the efforts that students put into it to generate manhood and loyalty. See Waldron Kintzing Post, *Harvard Stories: Sketches of the Undergraduate* (New York: G. P. Putnam's Sons, 1893), 293.

72. K. F. Brill, "The Failure of Football," *Harvard Illustrated Magazine*, June 1910, 289.

73. Ira N. Hollis, "Football," *Harvard Graduates' Magazine*, March 1903, 351.

74. Louis P. Benezet, *Three Years of Football at Dartmouth* (Concord, NH: n.p., 1904), 182–83.

75. Josiah Royce, *Race Questions, Provincialism and Other American Problems* (New York: Macmillan, 1908), 286.

76. Henry Beach Needham, "The College Athlete," *McClure's Magazine*, June 1905, 127.

77. David L. Westby and Allen Sack, "The Commercialization and Functional Rationalization of College Football: Its Origins," *Journal of Higher Education* 47 (November–December 1976): 643.

78. Des Jardins, *Walter Camp*, 198.

79. Harford Powel, *Walter Camp, the Father of American Football: An Authorized Biography* (Boston: Little, Brown, 1926), 112.

80. Smith, *Sports and Freedom*, 141, 148.

81. Walter Camp and Lorin F. Deland, *Football* (Boston: Houghton Mifflin, 1896), 266–68, 278–83.

82. Casper Whitney, "The Sportsman's View-Point," *Outing*, January 1905, 495.

83. Henry Cabot Lodge, *Speeches and Addresses, 1884–1909* (Boston: Houghton Mifflin, 1909), 293.

84. "The New Year at Harvard," *New York Daily Tribune*, November 9, 1878, 3.

85. Henry Adams, *The Education of Henry Adams: An Autobiography* (Boston: Houghton Mifflin, 1918), 19.

86. Ibid., 348.

87. Joseph Bucklin Bishop, *Theodore Roosevelt and His Time: Show in His Own Letters*, vol. 2 (New York: Charles Scribner's Sons, 1920), 110–11.

88. George W. Pierson, *Yale: A Short History* (New Haven, CT: Yale University Press, 1979), 57.

89. Allen L. Sack, "Yale 29–Harvard 4: The Professionalization of College Football," *Quest*, January 1973, 26.

90. Charles Francis Adams, *An Autobiography* (New York: Russell and Russell, 1916), 190.

91. "From a Graduate's Window," *Harvard Graduates' Magazine*, December 1905, 218.

92. See editorial columns in *Harvard Advocate*, December 8, 1905, 75.

93. F. Santayana, "A Glimpse of Yale," *Harvard Monthly*, December 1892, 92.

94. Ibid., 95–96.

95. Needham, "College Athlete" [June 1905], 124.

96. Ibid.

97. Lewis Sheldon Welch and Walter Camp, *Yale: Her Campus, Class-Rooms, and Athletics* (Boston: L. C. Page, 1899), 519.

98. "Blue above the Crimson," *New York Herald*, November 25, 1894, 4.

99. Arthur S. Link, ed., *The Papers of Woodrow Wilson*, vol. 8 (Princeton, NJ: Princeton University Press, 1970), 47.

100. For example, see "West Point to Play Cornell in Future," *New York Times*, November 12, 1906, 8.

101. "Honors for Matthews," *Boston Globe*, December 27, 1904, 5.

102. On Matthews and Yale, see Bernstein, *Football*, 73.

103. Needham, "College Athlete," *McClure's Magazine*, July 1905, 271–72.

104. Burton Alan Boxerman, "Lucius Nathan Littauer," *American Jewish Historical Quarterly* 66 (June 1977): 500.

105. Lucius Littauer to Harvard Varsity Club Executive Committee, September 27, 1913, box 10, folder 110, Papers of Lucius N. Littauer, Harvard University Archives, Cambridge, MA.

106. "College Foot-Ball," *New York Times*, November 3, 1881, 8.

107. Nitza Rosovsky, *The Jewish Experience at Harvard and Radcliffe* (Cambridge, MA: Harvard University Press, 1986), 1–7.

108. Libby Garland, *After They Closed the Gates: Jewish Illegal Immigration to the United States, 1921–1965* (Chicago: University of Chicago Press, 2014), 14–42.

109. Alfred Jospe, "Jewish College Students in the United States," *American Jewish Year Book* 65 (1964): 131.

110. Stephan F. Brumberg, *Going to America, Going to School: The Jewish Immigrant Public School Encounter in Turn-of-the-Century New York City* (New York: Praeger, 1986), 52–94.

111. Leo W. Schwarz, *Wolfson of Harvard: Portrait of a Scholar* (Philadelphia: Jewish Publication Society of America, 1978), 20–21. See also Joseph S. Stern Jr., "Harvard and Cincinnati," *Queen City Heritage* 45 (Winter 1987): 23.

112. Philip Gleason, "American Catholic Higher Education: A Historical Perspective," in *The Shape of Catholic Higher Education*, ed. Robert Hassenger (Chicago: University of Chicago Press, 1967), 27–28.

113. Nathaniel S. Shaler, "European Peasants as Immigrants," *Atlantic Monthly*, May 1893, 649.

114. F. Scott Fitzgerald, *This Side of Paradise* (New York: Charles Scribner's Sons, 1921), 52.

115. Charles W. Eliot to George A. Bartlett, July 22, 1901, Letter Book no. 92, box 158, Records of the President of Harvard University, Charles W. Eliot, 1869–1930, Harvard University Archives.

116. Daniel Greene, *Jewish Origins of Cultural Pluralism: The Menorah Association and American Diversity* (Bloomington: Indiana University Press, 2011), 14–34.

117. Synnott, *Half-Opened Door*, 11–12.

118. "May Jews Go to College?" *Nation*, June 14, 1922, 708.

119. Bernard M. L. Ernst, "The Greek Letter Societies and the Jew," *American Israelite*, November 3, 1904, 1. On Jews, sports, and intermingling at Yale, see Dan A.

Oren, *Joining the Club: A History of Jews and Yale* (New Haven, CT: Yale University Press, 1985), 24–37, 77–78.

120. Fass, *Damned and the Beautiful*, 142.

121. On this characterization, see "From a Graduate's Window," *Harvard Graduates' Magazine*, March 1897, 342.

122. Alfred A. Benesch, "The Jew at Harvard," *New Era*, February 1904, 58.

123. W. Cameron Forbes, "The Football Coach's Relation to the Players," *Outing*, December 1900, 339.

124. Edward R. Bushnell, "The Jew as an Athlete," *American Hebrew*, November 1905, 876.

125. "Jews as Athletes," *American Israelite*, August 18, 1904, 6.

126. Oscar Handlin, *The Uprooted: The Epic Story of the Great Migrations That Made the American People* (New York: Grosset and Dunlap, 1951), 251–53.

127. "Literary Notes," *American Hebrew*, August 18, 1893, 508; "Minor Mention," *Jewish Messenger*, October 16, 1896, 5.

128. "Personal and Social," *American Israelite*, November 9, 1893, 2.

129. "Correspondence," *American Israelite*, November 10, 1904, 3.

130. "The Fighting Jew," *American Israelite*, January 4, 1906, 1; "The Jewish Athlete," *American Hebrew*, November 27, 1908, 109.

131. "A Crimson Victory," *American Israelite*, December 16, 1897, 1.

Chapter 4. Winning for Winning's Sake

1. Synnott, *Half-Opened Door*, 48.

2. Julie A. Reuben, *The Making of the Modern University: Intellectual Transformation and the Marginalization of Morality* (Chicago: University of Chicago Press, 1996), 121–22.

3. Henry James, ed., *Charles W. Eliot: President of Harvard University, 1869–1909* (Boston: Houghton Mifflin, 1930), 141.

4. "Opening Day at Harvard," undated, box 4, Bingham Scrapbook.

5. "All Natick Honors Capt. Eddie Mahan," *Boston Globe*, January 12, 1915, 9.

6. Woodward, *Paper Tiger*, 116.

7. "Edward Mahan, 83," *Boston Globe*, July 24, 1975, 49.

8. Roger Birtwell, "Greatest Football Player Who Ever Lived," *Boston Globe*, January 15, 1967, A3.

9. *H Book of Harvard Athletics*, 463.

10. Joe D. Willis and Richard G. Wettan, "L. E. Myers, 'World's Greatest Runner,'" *Journal of Sport History* 2 (Fall 1975): 93–11.

11. Bainbridge Bunting, *Harvard: An Architectural History*, ed. Margaret Henderson Floyd (Cambridge, MA: Harvard University Press, 1985), 116–23.

12. *H Book of Harvard Athletics*, 481.

13. Frank A. Merrill to William J. Bingham, January 4, 1916, box 6, Bingham Scrapbook.

14. Smith, *Harvard Century*, 72–74.

15. "Bill Bingham Is President," undated, box 4, Bingham Scrapbook.

16. Ibid.

17. "Harvard's 'Pooch' One of the Famous Natick Athletic Group," *Boston Globe*, April 22, 1928, A21.

18. "W. J. Bingham Was Winner," undated, box 4, Bingham Scrapbook.

19. "Records of the Class," *Harvard College Class of 1916*, vol. 3, ed. Wells Blanchard (Cambridge, MA: Harvard University, 1922), 31.

20. "Yale Yearlings Humble Harvard in Dual Games," undated, box 4, Bingham Scrapbook.

21. Ibid.

22. "Why Should Wilkie Be Allowed to Eat at Travers Island," *St. Louis Star and Times*, November 6, 1915, 8.

23. "Athlete and Class President," undated, box 4, Bingham Scrapbook.

24. Ibid.

25. "Bingham and Meredith as Finishers," undated, box 5, Bingham Scrapbook.

26. James C. Curran, "Training the World's Half-Miler," *Illustrated Outdoor World and Recreation*, December 1912, 36, 55.

27. Kenneth D. Hay Jr., "Immortal of Cinderpath," *Everybody's Weekly*, April 20, 1947, W-16.

28. Ibid.

29. Ibid.

30. Ibid.

31. Arthur Daley, "When Meredith and Sheppard Were Olympic Rivals," *New York Times*, December 31, 1943, 20.

32. "Dickeys Take in Athletes," undated, box 5, Bingham Scrapbook.

33. Morison, *Three Centuries of Harvard*, 423–25.

34. "Bingham Praised by Coach Pooch Donovan," undated, box 5, Bingham Scrapbook.

35. "Harvard Relay Runners Make New World Record," undated, box 5, Bingham Scrapbook.

36. Ibid.

37. "Cornell Lands the Track Meet," undated, box 5, Bingham Scrapbook.

38. Harvard Alumni Association to Bill Bingham, May 12, 1914, box 5, Bingham Scrapbook.

39. Briggs to W. J. Bingham, May 13, 1914, box 5, Bingham Scrapbook.

40. Amos R. Wells, "Won by an Inch," undated, box 5, Bingham Scrapbook.

41. "Bingham from Scratch Captures 220-Yard Run," undated, box 5, Bingham Scrapbook.

42. "Harvard Easy for Yale in Dual Meet," undated, box 5, Bingham Scrapbook.

43. Casper Whitney, "The Sportsman's View-Point, *Outing*, January 1904, 475. Whitney was referring to "Professional Coaching," *Harvard Graduates' Magazine*, September 1903, 32.

44. Whitney, "Sportsman's View-Point," 475.

45. Ibid., 496–97.

46. Ibid.

47. Morison, *Three Centuries of Harvard*, 406.

48. For college coaches' salaries in this period, see Smith, *Pay for Play*, 66.

49. "'Bill' Reid Is on His Way East," *Boston Globe*, December 31, 1904, 1.

50. Ronald A. Smith, *Big-Time Football at Harvard, 1905: The Diary of Coach Bill Reid* (Urbana: University of Illinois Press, 1994), xxi-xxiv.

51. Casper Whitney, "Amateur Sport," *Harper's Weekly*, May 20, 1899, 512.

52. Smith, *Big-Time Football at Harvard*, 22. On Reid's concern for his relationship with the Harvard College faculty, see "Football Differences Prolong Big Meeting," *New York Times*, September 29, 1906, 4.

53. Smith, *Big-Time Football at Harvard*, 162.

54. See, for instance, John Sayle Waterson, *College Football: History, Spectacle, Controversy* (Baltimore, MD: Johns Hopkins University Press, 2000), 56.

55. Smith, *Big-Time Football at Harvard*, 300–301.

56. Ibid.

57. Casper Whitney, "The View-Point," *Outing*, January 1906, 496.

58. Smith, *Big-Time Football at Harvard*, 323–25.

59. "Joshua Crane Jr. to Be Head Coach," *Boston Globe*, March 15, 1907, 7.

60. Ibid. See also "News of All Branches of Sport," *Boston Globe*, January 10, 1908, 4.

61. William H. Edwards, *Football Days: Memories of the Game and of the Men behind the Ball* (New York: Moffat, Yard, 1916), 352.

62. Friedman, *Coach Who Strangled the Bulldog*, 111–28. See also Percy D. Haughton, *Football and How to Watch It* (Boston: Marshall Jones, 1922), 197.

63. See, for example, "Mr. Haughton's Address to the Football Men," *Harvard Alumni Bulletin*, March 29, 1911, 397.

64. Morison, *Three Centuries of Harvard*, 414.

65. Walter Camp, *Walter Camp's Book of College Sports* (New York: Century, 1901), 48.

66. Walter Camp and Lorin F. Deland, *Football* (Boston: Houghton, Mifflin, 1896), 101.

67. "British vs. American Foot Ball," *Yale Courant* 19, November 29, 1882, 75–76.

68. Haughton, *Football*, 23.

69. Harry von Kersburg, "Coaches and Coaching," in Bealle, *History of Football at Harvard*, 438.

70. Ibid.

71. "How Harvard Prepares," *Baltimore Sun*, January 22, 1916, 11.

72. Ronald A. Smith, *The Myth of the Amateur: A History of College Athletic Scholarships* (Austin: University of Texas Press, 2021), 35.

73. "Plans like Napoleon," *Baltimore Sun*, December 5, 1916, 10.

74. "'Very Satisfactory,' Says Pres Eliot," *Boston Globe*, November 22, 1908, 12.

75. Friedman, *The Coach Who Strangled the Bulldog*, 13.

76. "Brown Should Give Harvard Hard Game Today," *Boston Globe*, October 23, 1909, 5.

77. Kersburg, "Coaches and Coaching," 446.

78. Grantland Rice, *The Tumult and the Shouting: My Life in Sport* (New York: A. S. Barnes, 1954), 199.

79. Haughton, *Football and How to Watch It*, 210–11.

80. P. D. Haughton, "Football Coaching," *Harvard Alumni Bulletin*, June 7, 1916, 685.

81. Edwards, *Football Days*, 354.

82. Ibid.

83. "Cornell Wins the Track Honors in the Stadium," undated, box 5, Bingham Scrapbook.

84. "Bill Bingham of Harvard Says Wyoming Cowboys Root for Braves," undated, box 5, Bingham Scrapbook.

85. "Finishes in Two of the Harvard-Cornell Races and Alma Richards Winner of Three Firsts," undated, box 5, Bingham Scrapbook.

86. "Harvard Relay Team Loses by Scant Inch," *Boston Globe*, February 20, 1915, 4.

87. Ibid.

88. "Bingham and Meredith as Finishers," undated, box 5, Bingham Scrapbook.

89. "How Points Were Scored at Harvard-Cornell Meet," undated, box 4, Bingham Scrapbook.

90. "Bingham and Meredith as Finishers."

91. Bill Barron to Bill Bingham, undated, box 5, Bingham Scrapbook.

92. Grantland Rice, "Sporting Capitals," *Boston Globe*, September 16, 1915, 7.

93. On the football downturn at Yale, see Des Jardins, *Walter Camp*, 248–68.

94. Thomas G. Bergin, *The Game: The Harvard-Yale Football Rivalry, 1875–1983* (New Haven, CT: Yale University Press, 1984), 62–94.

95. "Prayer Helped Yale," *New York Times*, November 26, 1907, 10.

96. Eddie Casey, "Razzing Opponent Popular," *Boston Post*, October 17, 1920, 95.

97. Eddie Casey, "Football Crisis Eve of Big Game," *Boston Post*, October 3, 1920, 43.

98. Eddie Mahan, "Percy Haughton and Harvard's Golden Era," in *Oh, How They Played: The Early Days of Football and the Heroes Who Made It Great*, ed. Allison Danzig (New York: Macmillan, 1971), 217.

99. "Memorial to Percy D. Haughton Unveiled at Soldiers Field," *Boston Globe*, November 20, 1927, A31.

100. Mahan, "Percy Haughton," 218.

101. "Lessons of the Game," *Boston Globe*, November 27, 1911, 4.

102. Friedman, *Coach Who Strangled the Bulldog*, 59.

103. Ibid., 195–96.

104. "How Harvard Prepares," *Baltimore Sun*, January 22, 1916, 11.

105. Ibid., 196.

106. Edwards, *Football Days*, 345.

107. Ibid., 318.

108. Ibid., 346.

109. R. E. McMillin, "Harvard Mass Meeting Cheering Raises the Roof of Union as Haughton Speaks," undated, box 6, Bingham Scrapbook.

110. "Brother of Bill Bingham," undated, box 6, Bingham Scrapbook.

111. "Crushing of Shevlinism Benefit to Football," undated, box 6, Bingham Scrapbook.

112. "Bill Bingham Leads Harvard Cheers While Bob Plays Halfback for Yale," undated, box 6, Bingham Scrapbook.

113. Ibid.

114. "Haughton Defers Drive," *New York Times*, October 20, 1915, 12.

115. "Harvard's Superb Machine Gives Yale's 11 Players Worst Beating in the Blue's 41 Years of Football," *Boston Globe*, November 21, 1915, 1.

116. "Cheer Mahan and Haughton," *Boston Globe*, November 21, 1915, 19.

117. "Winning Combination," undated, box 5, Bingham Scrapbook.

118. LeBaron Russell Briggs to William J. Bingham, June 4, 1915, box 5, Bingham Scrapbook.

119. John W. Hallowell to William J. Bingham, June 3, 1915, box 5, Bingham Scrapbook.

120. Harvard Alumni Association editor (unnamed) to Bill Bingham, June 3, 1915, box 5, Bingham Scrapbook.

121. "Bingham Raps Crew System at Harvard," undated, box 6, Bingham Scrapbook.

122. Ibid.

123. "Bill Bingham a Self-Made Man," *Boston Globe*, December 12, 1915, 56.

124. Ibid.

125. Louis F. Post, "Success in Life," *The Fra*, July 1909, 96.

126. "Mahan Is Defeated for Honor," undated, box 6, Bingham Scrapbook.

127. Robert Edgren, "Meredith, Greatest of Runners," *Boston Globe*, June 11, 1916, 65.

128. Herbert Reed, "The Amateur Sportsman," *Town and Country*, June 10, 1916, 31, 44.

129. Thomas W. Lamont to Bill Bingham, October 22, 1915, box 6, Bingham Scrapbook.

130. "Harvard Class Day More Brilliant than Ever," *Boston Globe*, June 21, 1916, 1.

131. Howard Valentine, "Bill Bingham Is Through," *New Castle News*, June 16, 1916, 21.

132. Ibid.

133. "Bingham Lost to Team as He Is Going Away," undated, box 6, Bingham Scrapbook.

CHAPTER 5. FOOTBALL, THE ULTIMATE WARGAME OF LIFE

1. "The Worth of a Star," *Marion* (Ohio) *Star*, November 15, 1915, 8.

2. "Current Sporting Gossip," *Hartford Courant*, December 1, 1910, 16; and "Live Tips and Topics," *Boston Globe*, June 27, 1911, 6.

3. "101 to 0 Score by Natick High," *Boston Globe*, October 13, 1911, 15.

4. "Natick Adds 74 to Its Total, Which Is Now 282," *Boston Globe*, October 19, 1911, 8.

5. "Exeter Captain to Enter Harvard," *New York Times*, January 22, 1915, 12.

6. "Andover Is Defeated by Exeter," *Phillipian*, November 12, 1913, 1.

7. "Crimson Wins on Brothers Field," *Phillipian*, November 14, 1914, 1.

8. "Exeter and Andover Meet in Annual Game Next Week," *Boston Globe*, November 7, 1914, 4.

9. "Cradle of Gridiron Heroes," *Altoona Tribune*, December 21, 1921, 8.

10. Roger Birtwell, "H's Eddie Casey Joins Hall," *Boston Globe*, December 4, 1968, 65.

11. "Points of View," *Catholic Advance*, November 28, 1903, 1.

12. Ellis Lucia, *Mr. Football: Amos Alonzo Stagg* (South Brunswick, NJ: A. S. Barnes, 1970), 37.

13. Mark S. Massa, *Catholics and American Culture: Fulton Sheen, Dorothy Day, and the Notre Dame Football Team* (New York: Crossroad, 1999), 203.

14. "Boston College," *Brooklyn Tablet*, November 22, 1919, 4.

15. "To Divide Harvard Squad," *New York Times*, September 12, 1916, 8; "Harvard Class Selections," *Boston Globe*, October 25, 1916, 6.

16. Morison, *Three Centuries of Harvard*, 407.

17. Townsend, *Manhood at Harvard*, 106.

18. Huber, *American Idea of Success*, 75.

19. Henry Aaron Yeomans, *Abbott Lawrence Lowell, 1856–1943* (Cambridge, MA: Harvard University Press, 1948), 70.

20. Ibid., 20.

21. Ibid., 88.

22. Morison, *Three Centuries of Harvard*, 445–48.

23. A. Lawrence Lowell to Arthur T. Hadley, December 9, 1909, box 3, folder 88, President Lowell's Papers, 1909–1914, UAI.15.160, Harvard University Archives, Cambridge, MA [hereafter, Lowell Papers].

24. Arthur T. Hadley to A. Lawrence Lowell, May 31, 1910, box 3, folder 88, Lowell Papers.

25. Yeomans, *Abbott Lawrence Lowell*, 38.

26. "Get into the Game," *Daily Illini*, September 22, 1921, 4.

27. "Why Varsity Athletics?" *Daily Illini*, April 5, 1921, 4.

28. Lowell to Hadley, December 9, 1909.

29. Bunting, *Harvard*, 116–23.

30. Yeomans, *Abbott Lawrence Lowell*, 337.

31. Ibid., 336.

32. Louis M. Lyons, "The World's Wise Men," *Boston Globe*, August 14, 1936, 18.

33. "Harvard Goal Line Crossed," *Boston Post*, September 20, 1916, 9.

34. "Secret Work for Harvard Next Monday," *Boston Herald*, September 14, 1916, 7.

35. "Eddie Casey Star at Cambridge in Game in Which the Harvard Eleven Beats North Carolina by 21 to 0 Score," *Boston Post*, October 15, 1916, 13.

36. Eddie Casey, "Forward Pass Players Scarce," *Boston Post*, October 14, 1920, 21.

37. "Eddie Casey, 72, Star at Harvard," *New York Times*, July 28, 1966, 33.

38. "Eddie Casey Known as 'the Crimson Crash,'" *Hartford Courant*, November 22, 1916, 16.

39. "Casey of Harvard Is a Great Player, but No Mahan," *Washington Post*, November 5, 1916, S2.

40. Eddie Casey, "The Backfield Threat," *Boston Post*, October 20, 1920, 18.

41. "Scrubs Hold Varsity to 16," *Boston Globe*, September 29, 1916, 6.

42. Casey, "Backfield Threat," 18.

43. "Harvard Finds Itself," *Baltimore Sun*, October 15, 1916, 29.

44. "Harvard Is Facing a Supreme Ordeal," *New York Times*, September 3, 1916, S2.

45. "Haughton Defers Drive," *New York Times*, October 20, 1915, 12.

46. "Brickley with Drop Kickers," *Boston Globe*, October 1, 1915, 6.

47. "Poor Old Harvard," *Bridgeport Times*, September 25, 1916, 9.

48. "Harvard Beats Cornell at Every Angle, 23 to 0," *Boston Globe*, October 29, 1916, 1.

49. Evan Stone, "Give Praise to Horween," *Chicago Tribune*, October 30, 1916, 15.

50. "Eddie Casey of Harvard Weighs Only 155 Pounds," *Oregon Daily Journal*, November 19, 1916, 20.

51. "Live Tips and Topics," *Boston Globe*, November 14, 1916, 7.

52. "Crimson Conquers the Tiger on a Field Goal by Horween," *Washington Post*, November 12, 1916, S1.

53. "Harvard and Brown," *Brown Alumni Monthly*, December 1915, 123.

54. "Mighty Harvard a Victim of Brown," *New York Times*, November 19, 1916, S1.

55. Tim Cohane, *The Yale Football Story* (New York: G. P. Putnam's Sons, 1951), 204.

56. Ibid., 200.

57. "Innovations in Eli Football Practice," *New York Times*, September 10, 1916, S4.

58. "Crimson Offers No Alibi," *New York Times*, November 27, 1916, 12.

59. "Crowd of 77,453 Sees Triumph of Elis, 6–3," *Chicago Tribune*, November 26, 1916, A1.

60. Arthur Duffey, "Comment on Sport," *Boston Post*, November 27, 1916, 11.

61. Eddie Casey, "Football Improves with Age," *Boston Post*, November 19, 1920, 25.

62. Percy D. Haughton, "Haughton Tells How Yale Beat His Team," *Boston Globe*, November 26, 1916, 17.

63. "Harvard Practice Begins Tuesday," *New York Times*, August 21, 1919, 24.

64. Cohane, *Yale Football Story*, 208.

65. Grantland Rice, "Harvard's Outlook," *New York Tribune*, February 8, 1917, 14.

66. "Cum Bob's Sporting Talk," *Daily Commonwealth*, November 1, 1916, 3.

67. "Harvard Freshman a Heavyweight Team," *Boston Globe*, October 23, 1916, 7.

68. "Harvard Cubs Beat Eli's, 21–6," *Boston Globe*, November 19, 1916.

69. "Should Conciliate Brown," *New York Herald*, November 23, 1916, 14.

70. L. S. Mayo to Arnold Horween, March 9, 1917, Arnold Horween Student File, Harvard University Archives, Cambridge, MA.

71. "To Stake All on First Half," *Los Angeles Times*, December 31, 1919, III, 1.

72. "War a Cloud over Harvard Athletics," *New York Times*, March 25, 1917, S1.

73. Ibid.

74. Morison, *Three Centuries of Harvard*, 460.

75. "Ralph Horween on Naval Patrol," *Chicago Tribune*, April 3, 1917, 11.

76. "Football Prospects Dark," *New York Times*, June 3, 1917, 31.

77. "Resent the Name 'Informal,'" *Boston Globe*, October 28, 1917, 54.

78. John J. Hallahan, "No Dearth of Good College Game Today," *Boston Herald*, October 27, 1917, 13.

79. "Empty Stadium Looks Down on Martial Scenes," *Boston Globe*, May 13, 1917, 51.

80. "No Harvard-Princeton 'Informal' Game," *Princeton Alumni Weekly*, November 7, 1917, 138.

81. G. E. Johnson, "A Defense of Intercollegiate Athletics," *Harvard Graduates' Magazine*, June 1918, 584–85, 588.

82. "News and Views," *Harvard Alumni Bulletin*, June 20, 1918, 729.

83. "No Varsity Games for Yale, Coach 'Tad' Jones Says," *Boston Globe*, October 6, 1917, 4.

84. "University Football Team Not to Play Championship Games," *Yale Daily News*, October 26, 1917, 1.

85. "Harvard Shows Way to Dean," *Boston Herald*, October 17, 1917, 4.

86. "Big Three Likely to Play Football," *New York Times*, March 31, 1918, 29.

87. "Harvard Beats Soldiers in Bitterly Fought Game," *Boston Herald*, October 21, 1917, 2.

88. "Leo Leary Enrolls Horween and Woods," *Boston Globe*, November 21, 1917, 7.

89. Walter Camp, "Foot Ball at the U.S. Naval Training Stations," in *Spalding's Official Foot Ball Guide*, ed. Walter Camp (New York: American Sports, 1918), 89.

90. Arnold Horween to L. S. Mayo, November 19, 1918, Arnold Horween Student File, Harvard University Archives, Cambridge, MA.

91. "War Football," *New York Times*, November 23, 1919, S1.

92. Chris Serb, *War Football: World War I and the Birth of the NFL* (Lanham, MD: Rowman and Littlefield, 2019), 151–72.

93. William H. Wright, "Come On, Yale!" *Outing*, November 1919, 94.

94. "Haughton May Not Coach," *New York Times*, March 20, 1919, 10.

95. Bealle, *History of Football at Harvard*, 230–31.

96. John Hallahan, "Harvard's Football Warriors Honored," *Boston Globe*, February 4, 1920, 7.

97. "Harvard to Have Strong Back Field," *New York Times*, September 7, 1919, 90.

98. Athletic Committee Minutes, vol. 2, March 13, 1919, Harvard University Archives, Cambridge, MA.

99. "Harvard's Eleven Begins Practice," *New York Times*, September 3, 1919, 25.

100. "Harvard Regulars Drilling on Plays," *New York Times*, October 22, 1919, 14.

101. Bealle, *History of Football at Harvard*, 228–31.

102. "Harvard and Yale Are Building Well," *Nashville Tennessean*, October 26, 1919, B3.

103. Eddie Casey, "Football Crisis Eve of Big Game," *Boston Post*, October 3, 1920, 43.

104. Eddie Casey, "Bulldog Tenacity in Games," *Boston Post*, November 7, 1920, 57.

105. "Late Rally Ties Game for Harvard," *New York Times*, November 9, 1919, S1.

106. "Princeton Defies Odds and Holds Rival to Draw in Massive Gridiron Struggle," *Daily Princetonian*, November 10, 1919, 1.

107. "Look to Haughton to Teach Winning Punch," *Boston Globe*, November 18, 1919, 8.

108. "Harvard Faces Problem," *New York Times*, November 11, 1919, 14.

109. "Arnold Horween in Fullback Berth," *Boston Globe*, November 18, 1919, 8.

110. Ibid.

111. William D. Sullivan, "Up-to-Date Harvard Football a Winner," *Boston Globe*, November 23, 1919, 1.

112. Eddie Casey, "Football, the Inside Game," *El Paso Herald*, November 30, 1920, 10.

113. "Easy Athletes," *Pilot*, October 28, 1916, 5.

114. Michael Oriard, *King Football: Sports and Spectacle in the Golden Age of Radio and Newsreels, Movies and Magazines, the Weekly and the Daily Press* (Chapel Hill: University of North Carolina Press, 2001), 34–36.

115. "Notre Dame University News," *Catholic Tribune*, December 20, 1919, 4.

116. Skip Horween interview, June 9, 2017.

117. "Horween Brothers Triumphed for Harvard," *Jewish Advocate*, November 27, 1919, 1.

118. J. Joseph Hutmacher, *Massachusetts People and Politics, 1919–1933* (Cambridge, MA: Harvard University Press, 1959), 92.

119. "Cambridge, Mass.," *Reform Advocate*, December 6, 1919, 428.

120. "Chicago Boys Are Football Heroes," *Sentinel*, December 12, 1919, 5.

121. "The Week in Review," *American Hebrew*, December 19, 1919, 165.

122. "Jewish Brawn," *Jewish Monitor*, December 12, 1919, 2.

123. D. M. Bates to A. Lawrence Lowell, October 6, 1923, box 175, folder 6, Lowell Papers.

124. A. Lawrence Lowell to D. M. Bates, October 9, 1923, box 175, folder 6, Lowell Papers.

125. Rube Samuelsen, *The Rose Bowl Game* (Garden City, NY: Doubleday, 1951), 10.

126. Ibid., 1–17.

127. Ibid., 25–26.

128. Ibid., 18.

129. Ibid., 1–9.

130. The diplomatic details of the 1920 Rose Bowl can be found in Samuelsen, *Rose Bowl*, 25–32.

131. Thomas W. Lamont to Walter Camp, January 17, 1920, reel 11, HM 137, Walter Chauncey Camp Papers, Yale University, New Haven, CT.

132. Samuelsen, *Rose Bowl*, 26.

133. "Harvard Cancels the Pasadena Trip," *Boston Globe*, December 7, 1919, 18.

134. Samuelsen, *Rose Bowl*, 25–26.

135. Hugo Bezdek to A. A. Stagg, February 3, 1916, box 24, folder 4, Amos Alonzo Stagg Papers, Hanna Holborn Gray Special Collections Research Center, University of Chicago Archives, Chicago, IL [hereafter, Stagg Papers].

136. Hugo Bezdek to A. A. Stagg, January 3, 1917, box 24, folder 4, Stagg Papers.

137. Samuelsen, *Rose Bowl*, 24–25.

138. C. N. McArthur to Walter Camp, November 24, 1919, reel 11, HM 137, Walter Chauncey Camp Papers, Yale University, New Haven, CT.

139. Keith Kane, "The Pasadena Trip," *Harvard Graduates' Magazine*, March 1920, 466.

140. Tamte, *Walter Camp*, 256–60.

141. Lester, *Stagg's University*, 103.

142. Rice, *Tumult and Shouting*, 194.

143. Melville E. Webb, "When East Meets West on Gridiron," *Boston Globe*, December 14, 1919, 41.

144. This and other quotations are derived from undated clippings and public relations materials found in "Football General Folder, 1919," box 3, HUD 10000, Harvard University Archives, Cambridge, MA.

145. W. D. Sullivan, "Crimson Working in Wyoming Town," *Boston Globe*, December 24, 1919, 1.

146. W. D. Sullivan, "Harvard Has a Long Drill," *Boston Globe*, December 27, 1919, 5.

147. "Gov. Coolidge's Victory Message to Harvard," *Boston Globe*, December 29, 1919, 1.

148. "Harvard Football Team Begins Final Drive for Game with Oregon at Pasadena Thursday," *New York Times*, December 28, 1919, S3.

149. Samuelsen, *Rose Bowl*, 28.

150. Ibid., 29.

151. Eddie Casey, "The Surprise Attack," *Charlotte News*, November 22, 1920, 15.

152. Ibid.

153. Lucia, *Mr. Football*, 93.

154. "Harvard's Crimson Triumphs over Oregon by 7 to 6," *Chicago Tribune*, January 2, 1920, 15.

155. "Harvard Eleven Defeats Oregon by Point Margin," *New York Times*, January 2, 1920, 1.

156. Harvard Downs Oregon 7–6 in Thrilling Game," *Boston Herald*, January 2, 1920, 10.

157. "Glad Footballs Given to Heroes," *Boston Herald*, February 4, 1920, 17.

158. Burt Whitman, "Criticism of Harvard Grid Players Unjust," *Boston Herald*, January 22, 1920, 15.

159. "Harvard Downs Oregon 7–6."

160. Ibid.

161. Ibid.

162. "To Radiate Football Contests," *New York Times*, October 12, 1924, 15.

163. "Joy at Harvard Club," *New York Times*, January 2, 1920, 12.

164. "The Harvard-Oregon Football Game in Pasadena," *Literary Digest* (January 17, 1920): 114.

165. Ibid.

166. Ibid.

167. "Harvard Players Elect Football Leader Today," *Boston Herald*, January 20, 1920, 11.

168. "Football and Union," *Boston Globe*, January 2, 1920, 12.

169. "Brilliant Eddie Casey Hangs Up Gridiron Suit," *Boston Herald*, January 15, 1920, 1.

170. "'Eddie' Casey Takes a Bride," *Boston Globe*, September 15, 1921, 7.

171. Bernstein, *Football*, 116.

CHAPTER 6. HORWEEN VERSUS MCMAHON AND THE RISE OF THE NATIONAL FOOTBALL LEAGUE

1. Burt Whitman, "Arnold Horween Chosen Harvard Gridiron Leader," *Boston Herald*, January 21, 1920, 11.

2. "Captain Horween," *Harvard Crimson*, January 21, 1920, 1.

3. "Horween Harvard Captain," *Daily News*, January 21, 1920, 17.

4. "Arnold Horween," *Harvard Class Album, 1920* (Cambridge, MA: Harvard University Press, 1920), 190.

5. "Arnold Horween Chosen to lead Harvard Eleven," *Yale Daily News*, January 21, 1920, 1.

6. Isadore Horween to E. R. Gray, April 7, 1920, Arnold Horween Student File.

7. E. R. Gray to Arnold Horween, April 16, 1920, Arnold Horween Student File.

8. "The Week in Review," *American Hebrew*, February 20, 1920, 44.

9. "The Jew in Athletics," *Modern View*, January 30, 1920, 4.

10. "St. Joseph's Association Dines," *Boston Globe*, February 5, 1920, 2.

11. "Jewish Varsity Athletes," *Menorah Journal* 2 (October 1916): 262.

12. "Is It Breakdown Down?" *Jewish Monitor*, January 23, 1920, 8.

13. "Who's Who in College Athletics—1920," *American Hebrew*, December 3, 1920, 68.

14. See David E. Kaufman, *Jewhooing the Sixties: American Celebrity and Jewish Identity* (Waltham, MA: Brandeis University Press, 2012), 49–98.

15. Sidney S. Cohen, "Who's Who in College Athletics—1920," *American Hebrew*, December 3, 1920, 68.

16. Isadore E. Brown, "Another Member of 'Who's Who in Athletics,'" *American Hebrew*, December 17, 1920, 171.

17. W. D. Sullivan, "Harvard, in Last Ditch Pull-up, Battles Princeton to 14–14 Tie," *Boston Globe*, November 7, 1920, 19.

18. Watterson, *College Football*, 147.

19. "Harvard's Wonderful Team," *Nashville Tennessean*, October 24, 1920, A2.

20. "Centre College Astonishes Harvard and Reverses Defeat Handed It by Crimson Last Year," *Los Angeles Times*, October 30, 1921, I9.

21. Burt Whitman, "Indications that H-Y Game Will Be Replete with Varied Forwards," *Boston Herald*, November 17, 1920, 14.

22. W. D. Sullivan, "Buell and Capt. Horween Kick Harvard to Victory over Desperate Yale, 9 to 0," *Boston Globe*, November 21, 1920, 19.

23. Ibid.

24. "Find Talisman at Harvard," *New York Times*, December 3, 1920, 12.

25. "Eckersall Names All-American Team," *Chicago Tribune*, December 12, 1920, A1.

26. Jack Cavanaugh, *The Gipper: George Gipp, Knute Rockne, and the Dramatic Rise of Notre Dame Football* (New York: Skyhorse, 2012), 214–44.

27. "Auto in Ditch, Girl Is Dying?" *St. Joseph's Gazette*, August 21, 1911, 2.

28. "Records of the Class," *Harvard College Class of 1916*, vol. 3, ed. Wells Blanchard (Cambridge, MA: Harvard University, 1922), 31–32.

29. "Wed Here before He Goes to France," *St. Joseph's Gazette*, May 30, 1917, 10.

30. Ibid.

31. "Football Men Good Aviators," undated, box 6, Bingham Scrapbook.

32. "Harvard Athlete Saw the Germans Bomb Hospitals," *Churchman* 117 (March 23, 1918): 395.

33. "Records of the Class," 30.

34. "Bill Bingham Goes Back to Harvard," *Paris Morning News*, August 22, 1920, 5.

35. "Harvard Picks Bill Bingham for Big Job," *Boston Globe*, August 12, 1920, 8.

36. "Arnold Horween May Play 'Pro' Football," *Washington Times*, February 16, 1921, 15.

37. Joe Ziemba, *When Football Was Football: The Chicago Cardinals and the Birth of the NFL* (Chicago: Triumph, 1999), 20.

38. Ibid., 3–28.

39. L. G. Edwardson, "Son of Immigrant Comes Out of West to Coach Crimson," *Boston Globe*, March 14, 1926, B1.

40. Irv Kupcinet, "Jewish Greats of Sportsdom," in *The Sentinel's History of Chicago Jewry, 1911–1961*, ed. J. I. Fishbein (Chicago: Sentinel, 1961), 95.

41. Ziemba, *When Football Was Football*, 116.

42. Rudolf Ganz, *Jew and Irish: Historic Group Relations and Immigration* (New York: Waldon, 1966), 103.

43. "Fighting Joe," *American Israelite*, September 23, 1887, 9.

44. "Boxers with Queer Names," *New York Sun*, June 5, 1904, 25.

45. "Nationalities of Fighters," *New York Sun*, November 27, 1904, 10.

46. Paul Weiss, *Sport: A Philosophical Inquiry* (Carbondale: Southern Illinois University Press, 1969), 192.

47. "Eddie Casey May Join the Buffalo Team," *Buffalo Times*, October 6, 1920, 16.

48. "Harvard Frowns on Paid Football," *Boston Globe*, February 5, 1920, 5.

49. W. P. Dudley to George Hartong, February 26, 1921, box 24, folder 9, Stagg Papers.

50. "Concerning the Financial Success or Failure of Professional Football Games," December 3, 1925, box 24, folder 9, Stagg Papers.

51. Lester, *Stagg's University*, 19.

52. Ibid., 17–18.

53. "Stagg, Maroon Coach, Condemns 'Pro' Football," *Chicago Tribune*, November 2, 1923, 28.

54. Scrapbook 170, 29–95, box 212, Stagg Papers.

55. "The Visit of M. A. Romney," November 8, 1923, folder 9, box 24, Stagg Papers.

56. "The Visit of R. T. Halladay," November 12, 1923, folder 9, box 24, Stagg Papers.

57. "The Visit of John B. Hurlburt, November 13, 1923, folder 9, box 24, Stagg Papers.

58. Bill Henry, "Observations," *Los Angeles Times*, March 14, 1926, A8.

59. Richard Goldstein, "Ralph Horween, 100, the Oldest Ex-N.F.L. Player," *New York Times*, May 29, 1997, D19.

60. "Chicago Wins over Buffalo in Sunday Professional Football Feature," *Chicago Tribune*, November 6, 1922, 25.

61. "Bays Go Down to Defeat at Hands of Cardinals," *Green Bay Press-Gazette*, October 16, 1922, 10.

62. Ibid.

63. Tim Tyers, "NFL's Oldest Living Player Once Had Ruse," *Arizona Republic*, May 7, 1996, D2.

64. Howard Roberts, *The Story of Pro Football* (New York: Rand McNally, 1953), 256.

65. "Cardinals and Bears Meet to Settle Claims," *Rock Island Argus*, November 30, 1922, 14.

66. "Cards Whip Bears, 6–0, for City Pro Title," *Chicago Tribune*, December 1, 1922, 21.

67. Hugh Fullerton, "Drop Kick Gives Cardinals Win over Buffalo by 9 to 7," *Chicago Tribune*, November 6, 1922, 25.

68. "Wilfrid Smith, "Cardinals 2 Weeks Away," *Chicago Tribune*, December 16, 1947, 37.

69. Ibid., B10.

70. Louis I. Newman, *A Jewish University in America?* (New York: Bloch, 1923), 13.

71. Kirstein Fermaglich, *A Rosenberg by Any Other Name: A History of Jewish Name Changing in America* (New York: NYU Press, 2018), 25–44.

72. John Higham, *Strangers in the Land: Patterns of American Nativism, 1860–1925* (New Brunswick, NJ: Rutgers University Press, 1955), 264.

73. Yeomans, *Abbott Lawrence Lowell*, 166.

74. Solomon, *Ancestors and Immigrants*, 60.

75. Marcia Graham Synnott, "A Social History of Admissions Policies at Harvard, Yale, and Princeton, 1900–1930" (PhD diss, University of Massachusetts, 1974), 203.

76. See Paul Ritterband and Harold S. Wechsler, *Jewish Learning in American Universities: The First Century* (Bloomington: Indiana University Press, 1994), 92–123.

77. "Physical Culture for the Jews," *New York Observer*, January 9, 1908, 62.

78. "Dr. Eliot on Jewish Physique," *American Hebrew*, December 27, 1907, 207.

79. Oliver B. Pollak, "Antisemitism, the Harvard Plan, and the Roots of Reverse Discrimination," *Jewish Social Studies* 45 (Spring 1983): 112—22.

80. Wechsler, "Academic Gresham's Law," 575—76.

81. Karabel, *The Chosen*, 89.

82. Solomon, *Ancestors and Immigrants*, 204.

83. Ibid., 94.

84. Karabel, *The Chosen*, 108.

85. Anthony Netboy, *The Memoirs of Anthony Netboy: A Writer's Life in the 20th Century* (Ashland, OR: Tree Stump, 1990), 57.

86. J. Melitz, "The Truth about Jewish College Athletes at Last," *Forvert*, May 2, 1926, 4.

87. "Son of Russian-Jewish Immigrant to Coach Harvard Football Team," *Jewish Advocate*, March 11, 1926, 1.

88. Zev Eleff, "'The Envy of the World and the Pride of the Jews': Debating the American Jewish University in the Twenties," *Modern Judaism* 31 (May 2011): 229–44.

89. Leonard Dinnerstein, *The Leo Frank Case* (Athens: University of Georgia Press, 2008), 136–47.

90. Charles Fleischer, "On 'Converting the Jews,'" *Boston Advocate*, January 11, 1907, 1.

91. Marni Davis, *Jews and Booze: Becoming American in the Age of Prohibition* (New York: NYU Press, 2012), 104–35.

92. Libby Garland, *After They Closed the Gates: Jewish Illegal Immigration to the United States, 1921–1965* (Chicago: University of Chicago Press, 2014), 38.

93. *The Letters of William James*, vol. 2, ed. Henry James (Boston: Atlantic Monthly Press, 1920), 88.

94. Solomon, *Ancestors and Immigrants*, 187.

95. See Stuart Svonkin, *Jews against Prejudice: American Jews and the Fight for Civil Liberties* (New York: Columbia University Press, 1997), 1–10.

96. Lawrence Perry, "The Emergence of the Jew as Athlete," *American Hebrew*, April 22, 1921, 648.

97. "Benny Friedman, Symbol of a New Jewish Youth Type," *Wisconsin Jewish Chronicle*, October 23, 1925, 4.

98. Paul G. Goldberg, "Jewish Immortals in Football," *Brooklyn Jewish Center Review* 16, November 1935, 11.

99. "The Jew and Physical Strength," *Wisconsin Jewish Chronicle*, March 31, 1922, 4; and "The Jew and Physical Strength," *Buffalo Jewish Review*, April 7, 1922, 3.

100. Norman Salit, "The Synagogue Center: Practical Operations," in *Problems of the Jewish Ministry*, ed. Israel Goldstein (New York: New York Board of Jewish Ministers, 1927), 124.

CHAPTER 7. A "MEMBER OF THE HEBREW RACE" TO BECOME HEAD COACH OF HARVARD?

1. On the concept of "braided narrative," see David Hackett Fischer, "The Braided Narrative: Substance and Form in Social History," in *The Literature of Fact: Selected Papers from the English Institute*, ed. Angus Fletcher (New York: Columbia University Press, 1976), 109–33.

2. William J. Bingham, "Harvard Track Today," *The H Book of Harvard Athletics*, 482.

3. Melville E. Webb Jr., "Boston College Wins the Eastern Meet—Sullivan the Star," *Boston Globe*, May 15, 1921, 1.

4. "Live Tips and Topics," *Boston Globe*, May 16, 1921, 8.

5. R. T. Fisher to William J. Bingham, May 17, 1921, box 6, Bingham Scrapbook.

6. Bingham, "Harvard Track Today," 484.

7. "Harvard Has a Chance but It Is a Slim One," *Boston Globe*, May 7, 1922, 41.

8. Ibid.

9. Melville E. Webb Jr., "Burke Defeats Yale's Stars as Harvard Captures Meet," *Boston Globe*, May 14, 1922, 1.

10. Yeomans, *Abbott Lawrence Lowell*, 338.

11. George Owen Jr., "Football—Pleasure or Grind?" *Independent*, November 7, 1925, 520.

12. Ibid.

13. Ibid., 521.

14. "Owen's Views on Football Disputed by Best Players," *Boston Globe*, November 16, 1925, 8.

15. "Love Football for Game Itself," *Boston Daily Globe*, December 13, 1925, A53.

16. "Owen's Views on Football Disputed by Best Players," *Boston Globe*, November 16, 1925, 8.

17. "Drudging College Gladiators," *Independent*, November 21, 1925, 571.

18. "Waits Two Years and Says Game Is No Good," *Atlanta Constitution*, November 27, 1925, 16.

19. R. S. Hale, "What Percentage of Victories?" *Harvard Alumni Bulletin*, November 26, 1925, 264.

20. Francis Call Woodman, "American Football—a Protest," *Harvard Alumni Bulletin*, November 26, 1925, 261.

21. Roger Derby, "From Another Player," *Harvard Alumni Bulletin*, November 26, 1925, 263.

22. Morton Prince, "Hand Back the Game to the Boys!" *Forum* 76 (December 1926): 834.

23. Upton Sinclair, "Killers of Thought," *Forum* 76 (December 1926): 841.

24. "Tad Jones Tells Boys to Play Business Game like Football," *New York Times*, April 29, 1926, 31.

25. Michael S. Kimmel, *The History of Men: Essays in the History of American and British Masculinities* (Albany: State University of New York Press, 2005), 61–72.

26. "Baseball and Football," *Nation*, December 1, 1920, 610.

27. "Football Reform Advocates Score," *Boston Daily Globe*, December 3, 1925, 21.

28. A. Lawrence Lowell to Thomas W. Slocum, November 19, 1923, box 175, folder 6, Lowell Papers.

29. Bealle, *History of Football at Harvard*, 257.

30. "Harvard to Name 1925 Coach Today," *New York Times*, December 12, 1924, 27.

31. Rice, *Tumult and Shouting*, 108.

32. Tom Meany, *Babe Ruth: The Big Moments of the Big Fellow* (New York: Grosset and Dunlap, 1947), 151.

33. Ibid., 260.

34. "Details of Fisher's 'Retirement' Bared," *San Francisco Examiner*, February 8, 1925, 1.

35. "Tackles Are in Great Demand," *Boston Globe*, September 30, 1907, 5.

36. Swanson, *Strenuous Life*, 32.

37. Des Jardins, *Walter Camp*, 269–87.

38. Charles D. Daly, *American Football* (New York: Harper and Brothers, 1921), 56–57.

39. Ibid., 132.

40. "Coaches Protest Professionalism in College Game," *San Francisco Chronicle*, December 28, 1921, 10.

41. Ibid., 57–58.

42. Fred W. Moore to Lothrop Withington, January 17, 1925, box 4, folder "Football 1925–1926," HUD 10000, Harvard University Archives, Cambridge, MA.

43. "Here's New Tip That Harvard Seeks New Coach," *Chicago Tribune*, November 11, 1925, 27.

44. "Daly Also Retires as Harvard Coach," *New York Times*, November 26, 1925, 29.

45. "Personalities and Events," *American Educational Digest*, April 1925, 378; "Harvard to Find the Parting Hard," *Boston Globe*, March 30, 1924, 18. Briggs retired as Harvard dean a year later to "return to his literary work." See "Dean Briggs Leaves His Harvard Post," *Boston Globe*, February 25, 1925, 22.

46. "Says Harvard Has Democratic Spirit," *Boston Globe*, March 24, 1922, 15.

47. Synnott, *Half-Opened Door*, 142.

48. "Pennypacker Heads Harvard Athletics," *Boston Globe*, November 25, 1924, 23A.

49. "Robinson and Brown Signed to Coach B.U.," *Boston Globe*, April 3, 1926, 1.

50. Eskie Clark to F. W. Moore, February 20, 1926, "Football 1925–1926," box 4, folder "Football 1925–1926," HUD 10000, Harvard University Archives, Cambridge, MA.

51. Melville Webb Jr., "Harvard to Appoint Athletic Director," *Boston Globe*, January 14, 1926, 1.

52. Ibid.

53. George C. Carens, "Bingham Is Logical Choice as Harvard's New Sports Director," *Boston Evening Transcript*, January 14, 1926, 8.

54. "Bingham Makes Staunch Plea in Defense of School Athletics," undated, box 6, Bingham Scrapbook.

55. Ibid.

56. Carens, "Bingham Is Logical Choice," 8.

57. The following substance and quotations in this episode are derived from Yeomans, *Abbott Lawrence Lowell*, 339.

58. "Harvard Head Backs Bingham," undated, box 6, Bingham Scrapbook.

59. Langdon P. Martin to William J. Bingham, November 26, 1928, box 1, folder 3, William J. Bingham Correspondence, Harvard University Archives, Cambridge, MA.

60. Fred W. Moore to Gerald Wendt, January 21, 1925, box 11, folder 1, Harvard Athletic Association Records, UAV.170.95.2, Harvard University Archives, Cambridge, MA.

61. "Pennypacker Starts Tour of Harvard Clubs," *Boston Globe*, January 19, 1926, 4.

62. "Pennypacker Tells New Harvard Aims," *Boston Globe*, January 29, 1926, 17.

63. Karabel, *The Chosen*, 105–6.

64. Ibid., 106.

65. "Horween Says He'll Keep Old Harvard Plan," *Chicago Tribune*, March 12, 1926, 21.

66. Henry Pennypacker to Fred Moore, January 26, 1926, box 11, folder 1, Harvard Athletic Association Records, UAV.170.95.2, Harvard University Archives, Cambridge, MA.

67. "Harvard, under Horween, Regaining Place in the Sun," *Brooklyn Daily Times* November 14, 1928, A1.

68. Henry Pennypacker to Fred Moore, February 3, 1926, box 11, folder 1, Harvard Athletic Association Records, UAV.170.95.2, Harvard University Archives, Cambridge, MA.

69. William J. Bingham, "Arnold Horween," *Harvard Alumni Bulletin*, December 18, 1930, 395.

70. "Horween to Stick to Harvard System," *New York Times*, March 12, 1926, 12.

71. "Horween, Chicagoan, to Lead Harvard," *Chicago Tribune*, March 11, 1926, 15.

72. See, for example, "Jewish Boy to Head Harvard's Football Team," *Republican and Herald*, March 30, 1926, 7. A few newspapers changed the United Press's headline, but most did not.

73. "Arnold Horween Named Head Coach at Harvard," *Boston Globe*, March 11, 1926, 13.

74. George Trevor, "Horween at the Crossroads," *New York Sun*, December 31, 1927, 24.

75. "A Jew Coach," *Chicago Defender*, March 20, 1926, A1.

76. "Harvard's Head Coach," *Jewish Advocate*, March 18, 1926, 4.

77. Charles H. Joseph, "Random Thoughts," *Jewish Criterion*, April 2, 1926, 8.

78. "Americanism," *Moorhead Daily News*, March 26, 1926, 2.

79. "Horween, Chicagoan, to Lead Harvard."

80. Amos Alonzo Stagg and Wesley Winans Stout, *Touchdown!* (New York: Longmans, Green, 1927), 297.

81. "In the Press Box with Baxter," *Washington Post*, March 25, 1926, 15.

82. Mike Kelley, "Harvard Taking Long Chance That Horween Will Succeed," *Washington Post*, March 30, 1926, 15.

83. "Arnold Horween '21 is Appointed Coach of Crimson Gridiron Forces for Next Fall," *Harvard Crimson*, March 11, 1926, 1.

84. "T.A.D. Jones Prophesies Horween's Return to 'Fundamental Harvard Football System,'" *Yale Daily News*, March 16, 1926, 2.

85. Ibid.

86. "Horween Greets 200 Men at Harvard Grid Meeting," undated, box 6, Bingham Scrapbook.

87. "Horween to Stick to Harvard System."

88. Daniel M. Daniel, "Arnold Horween, New Football Coach at Harvard, Has All Eyes on His Ideas," *Yonkers Herald*, October 13, 1926, 15.

89. "Arnold Horween Achievement," *Modern View*, March 26, 1926, 12.

90. Ibid.

CHAPTER 8. AN HONORABLE FAILURE AND SATISFACTORY GAME IN EVERY WAY

1. Woodward, *Paper Tiger*, 105.
2. Kersburg, "Coaches and Coaching," 435.
3. Rice, *Tumult and Shouting*, 198.
4. Woodward, *Paper Tiger*, 101.
5. Ibid., 100.
6. Ibid.
7. Melville E. Webb Jr., "Arnold Horween Names Assistant Coaches for Harvard Football Team," *Boston Globe*, August 27, 1926, A1.
8. A. M. Hjort, "Others' Opinions," *Daily Illini*, December 4, 1921, 4.
9. Maynard Brichford, *Bob Zuppke: The Life and Football Legacy of the Illinois Coach* (Jefferson, NC: McFarland, 2008), 34.
10. Walter Eckersall, "Bob Zuppke Builder of Great Backs by Stressing Blocking," *Chicago Tribune*, October 5, 1925, 25.
11. Brichford, *Bob Zuppke*, 57.
12. Ibid.
13. Benny Friedman, *The Passing Game* (New York: Steinfeld, 1931), 22.
14. Tamte, *Walter Camp*, 227.
15. Lothrop Withington, "Percy Haughton and Harvard's Golden Age," in *Oh, How They Played the Game: The Early Days of Football and the Heroes Who Made It Great*, ed. Allison Danzig (New York: Macmillan, 1971), 220.
16. Sol Metzger, "Coaches Disagree on Huddle Value," *Brooklyn Daily Eagle*, October 28, 1826, 26.
17. Merle Curti, *The Growth of American Thought* (New York: Harper and Brothers, 1943), 639.
18. William Graham Sumner, *The Challenge of the Facts and Other Essays*, ed. Albert Galloway Keller (New Haven, CT: Yale University Press, 1914), 37.
19. Joan Baird Steindorf, "Hugo Münsterberg's Report on America" (MA thesis, Stanford University, 1955), 134.
20. Jill Lepore, *The Secret History of Wonder Woman* (New York: Vintage, 2014), 24–32.
21. "Navy Grid Head against Huddle," *Baltimore Sun*, December 4, 1926, 14.
22. "Horween Arrives for Spring Drills," *New York Times*, April 24, 1926, 12.
23. "Harvard Abandons Haughton's Ways," *New York Times*, October 1, 1926, 21.
24. William J. Bingham, speech delivered to the New England Federation of Harvard Clubs, July 23, 1926, box 3, folder 1, Bingham Papers.
25. William J. Bingham, speech delivered on January 18, 1927, box 3, folder 1, Bingham Papers.
26. "Director Bingham's Philosophy," undated, box 6, Bingham Scrapbook.
27. Christine Stansell, *American Moderns: Bohemian New York and the Creation of a New Century* (Princeton, NJ: Princeton University Press, 2000), 1–8.

28. "Harvard's Future Athletic Policy," undated, box 6, Bingham Scrapbook.

29. Matthew J. Kaufman, *Horace Kallen Confronts America: Jewish Identity Science and Secularism* (Syracuse, NY: Syracuse University Press, 2019), 169–89.

30. "In the Limelight of Sport," *Jewish Advocate*, October 28, 1926, 3.

31. Harry Glantz, "Our Own Athletics," *B'nai B'rith Messenger*, October 24, 1930, 10.

32. Frank Gafney, "'Izzy' Zarakov Is All Around Star," *Boston Post*, December 20, 1920, 15.

33. "Cantabs Tie with Newton," *Boston Post*, November 21, 1920, 21.

34. Ibid.

35. "Young Jew Is Chief Factor in Harvard Football Victories," *Wisconsin Jewish Chronicle*, December 14, 1923, 7.

36. L. L. Cleveland to C. N. Greenough, April 13, 1922, Isadore Zarakov Student File, Harvard University Archives, Cambridge, Massachusetts.

37. Undated application to Harvard College, Isadore Zarakov Student File.

38. "Harvard Will Have Stellar Man in Izzy Zarakov," *Bridgeport Telegram*, November 9, 1923, 4.

39. "More Zarakov," *Jewish Advocate*, November 8, 1923, 2.

40. "A Harvard Hero," *Wisconsin Jewish Chronicle*, July 1, 1927, 4.

41. "Gridiron Notes and Gossip," *Hartford Courant*, September 27, 1924, 11.

42. Westbrook Pegler, "Harvard Torn by Social Factions," *Washington Post*, November 20, 1925, 15.

43. Melville E. Webb Jr., "Wonderful Defense of Inspired Harvard Team Balks Yale Drive in Scoreless Game," *Boston Globe*, November 22, 1925, 20.

44. "Zarakov Gets Double Honor," *Boston Globe*, February 10, 1926, 13.

45. Woodward, *Paper Tiger*, 101.

46. "Horween Expects Fiercest Opening Contest in Years," *Harvard Crimson*, October 2, 1926, 1.

47. Woodward, *Paper Tiger*, 102.

48. Ibid.

49. Ibid.

50. Allison Danzig, "Harvard Humbled by Geneva, 16 to 7," *New York Times*, October 3, 1926, S1.

51. Woodward, *Paper Tiger*, 103.

52. Ford Sawyer, "Stadium Throng in Delirium of Joy," *Boston Globe*, October 24, 1926, B1.

53. George Owen Jr., "Harvard's Air Game Developing Rapidly," *Boston Globe*, October 19, 1926, 14.

54. Allison Danzig, "With Slagle Back, Princeton Sharpens Claws for Harvard," *New York Times*, November 5, 1926, 18.

55. Allison Danzig, *The History of American Football: Its Great Teams, Players, and Coaches* (Englewood Cliffs, NJ: Prentice-Hall, 1956), 106.

56. "Picked Up on Soldiers Field as Izzy Zarakov Belted Yale," *Boston Globe*, June 23, 1927, 10.

57. George Joel, "Zarakov of Harvard," *Jewish Advocate*, June 30, 1927, A1.

58. "New Contract Is Offered Horween," *Washington Post*, November 3, 1926, 17.

59. "The World Wags," *Harvard Crimson*, October 26, 1926, 2.

60. Bingham, "Arnold Horween," 395.

61. Ibid., 395–96.

62. Weiss, *American Myth of Success*, 98.

63. William James, *The Varieties of Religious Experience: A Study in Human Nature* (New York: Modern Library, 1902), 93–94.

64. Hugo Münsterberg, *Psychotherapy* (New York: Moffat, Yard, 1909), 346.

65. William Matthews, *Getting on in the World; or, Hints on Success in Life* (Chicago: S. C. Griggs, 1883), 327.

66. Stagg and Stout, *Touchdown*, 57.

67. Robert L. Duffus, "The Age of Play," *Independent*, December 20, 1924, 539–40.

68. "Harvard Regulars Have Light Drill," *New York Times*, October 26, 1926, 33.

69. Benjamin H. Dibblee to Richard Derby, November 1925, box 11, folder 1, Harvard Athletic Association Records, UAV.170.95.2, Harvard University Archives, Cambridge, MA.

70. Woodward, *Paper Tiger*, 105.

71. William J. Bingham, speech, January 18, 1927, box 3, folder 1, Bingham Papers.

72. Ibid.

73. Ibid.

74. Westbrook Pegler, "Horween Proves Ability," *Los Angeles Times*, October 27, 1926, B1.

75. William J. Bingham to Knute Rockne, August 23, 1926, box 13, folder 45, Director of Athletics Papers, 1909–29 [1908–1931], University of Notre Dame Archives, Notre Dame, IN.

76. Marcia G. Synott, "The 'Big Three' and the Harvard-Princeton Football Break, 1926–1934," *Journal of Sports History* 3 (Summer 1976): 190–91.

77. Wynant Davis Hubbard, "Dirty Football," *Liberty*, January 29, 1927, 43–44.

78. George Currie, "Hubbard Defends Charges, Adds One from Own Experience," *Brooklyn Daily Eagle*, January 27, 1927, 2A.

79. Hubbard, "Dirty Football," 44.

80. Synott, "Big Three," 188–202.

81. James R. Harrison, "Princeton Defeat Harvard by 12 to 0, Third Year in a Row," *New York Times*, November 7, 1926, S5.

82. Ibid., S1.

83. Synott, "Big Three," 195–96.

84. "Mahan Comes to Defense of Roper," *Boston Globe*, January 26, 1927, 23.

85. Bill Cunningham, "Crimson Refused to Accord Tigers Equal Rating with Yale, Says Cunningham," *Brooklyn Daily Eagle*, January 30, 1927, 2C.

86. Ibid.

87. "Coach Arnold Horween Praises Fighting Spirit Which Pulled Yale Out of Long Losing Slump," *Yale Daily News*, November 23, 1926, 1.

88. "Bingham Declares Football a Success," *New York Times*, October 5, 1927, 22.

89. Robert F. Kelley, "Football Goal Posts Set Back Ten Yards," *New York Times*, March 6, 1927, S1.

90. Ibid.

91. "Football Coaches Disagree on Backward-Pass Ruling," *Washington Post*, March 9, 1927, 15.

92. David M. Nelson, *Anatomy of a Game: Football, the Rules, and the Men Who Made the Game* (Newark: University of Delaware Press, 1994), 495.

93. Herbert Orin Crisler and Elton Ewart Wieman, *Practical Football: A Manual for Coaches, Players and Students of the Game* (New York: Whittlesey House, 1934), 130.

94. Allison Danzig, "Harvard Offense Crushes Vermont," *New York Times*, October 2, 1927, S1.

95. Allison Danzig, "Harvard Outlook Considered Bright," *New York Times*, September 30, 1927, 21.

96. Jack Kofoed, Listening In," *Forvert*, September 4, 1927, 13.

97. "Football and the Ideal Coach," *Pennsylvania Gazette*, January 3, 1931, 195–96.

98. Melville E. Webb Jr., "Casey Outstanding in Harvard Ranks," *Boston Globe*, November 21, 1928, 16.

99. "Passes by Andover Trip Crimson Cubs," *Boston Globe*, October 10, 1926, B20.

100. "Harvard Freshmen Cheer Team to Face Yale Cubs," *Boston Globe*, November 11, 1926, 22.

101. "Bingham Declares Football a Success," *New York Times*, October 5, 1927, 22.

102. "Harvard Has Faith in Horween System," *Washington Post*, October 27, 1927, 15.

103. James R. Harrison, "Yale and Harvard Will Clash Today," *New York Times*, November 19, 1927, 11.

104. Westbrook Pegler, "Harvard May Whip Yale, but Horween Sets the Odds at 3–1," *Chicago Tribune*, November 18, 1927, 24.

105. "Ineligibility Jinx Ousted at Harvard," *Boston Globe*, July 7, 1927, 22.

106. Grantland Rice, "Horween Faces Big Task," *Boston Globe*, November 17, 1927, 22.

107. "Harvard Is Satisfied with Results of Game," *New York Times*, November 20, 1927, S6.

108. "T.A.D. Jones Praises His Last Eleven's Offense," *Yale Daily News*, November 21, 1927, 6.

CHAPTER 9. THE CRUSADE TO KEEP FOOTBALL A GAME

1. John Kieran, "The Battle of Boston," *New York Times*, February 10, 1928, 21.

2. Malcolm Roy, "Eddie Casey to Coach Harvard Football Machine after 1928," *Yonkers Herald*, August 14, 1928, 16.

3. Clay Cotter, "Horween Victim of Haughton Regime," *Brooklyn Daily Times*, October 24, 1928, 11.

4. Roy, "Eddie Casey to Coach."

5. "Fuller, Line Coach, Boomed for Jones's Job," *Standard Union*, September 24, 1928, 16.

6. "Eddie Casey's Frosh Elevens Pride of Harvard's Football," *Yonkers Herald*, November 21, 1928, 15.

7. George Currie, "Horween Now at Critical Point of His Career as Harvard Football Coach," *Brooklyn Daily Eagle*, September 27, 1928, 27.

8. Harry Glantz, "Our Own Athletics," *B'nai B'rith Messenger*, November 30, 1928, 11.

9. Briggs to Bingham, October 24, 1926, box 1, bolder 4, William J. Bingham Correspondence.

10. George Kirksey, "Coach Arnold Horween Responsible for Best Team Harvard Has Put on Gridiron in Last Five Years," *Brooklyn Citizen*, November 14, 1928, 9.

11. "Arnold Horween Must Build New Line at Harvard," *Hartford Courant*, September 18, 1928, 13.

12. George Currie, "Harvard's Line Untried Quantity but Backs Are without Price," *Brooklyn Daily Eagle*, October 2, 1928, 27.

13. T. W. Lamont to William J. Bingham, October 8, 1928, box 1, folder 2, Bingham Correspondence.

14. "Fuller, Line Coach."

15. "Harvard Crushes Springfield, 30–0," *New York Times*, October 7, 1928, S2.

16. Kirksey, "Coach Arnold Horween Responsible."

17. Heyman Zimel, "The Great God Football," *Forvert*, October 7, 1928, 15.

18. Westbrook Pegler, "Harvard Hints It Has a Team," *Chicago Tribune*, October 19, 1928, 25.

19. "More than 1500 at Football Smoker," *Boston Globe*, October 20, 1928, 11.

20. Melville E. Webb Jr., "Cadet Corps and Colorful Crowd of 53,000 See Erring Crimson Lose to Army, 15–0," *Boston Globe*, October 21, 1928, A1.

21. Robert F. Kelley, "Penn Team Upsets Harvard by 7 to 0," *New York Times*, November 11, 1928, S1.

22. "Harvard Passes Up Scoring Chance, Tied by Holy Cross," *Chicago Tribune*, November 18, 1928, A5.

23. "Rumor Eddie Casey Will Coach Harvard," *Morning Call*, November 21, 1928, 18.

24. "Horween to Retire, Trumbull Believes," *Boston Globe*, November 21, 1928, 16.

25. Murray Robinson, "Crimson Coach to End Career with Eli Game," *Standard Union*, November 14, 1928, 14.

26. "Horween to Keep Post, Chief States," *Atlanta Constitution*, November 21, 1928, 16.

27. See, for example, "Dr. Wilce Mentioned to Succeed Horween," *Boston Globe*, November 27, 1928, 24.

28. George Joel, "Jewish Coach Out at Harvard," *Sentinel*, November 2, 1928, 14.

29. Cohane, *Yale Football Story*, 249.

30. "Harvard Coach in Break with Scribes," *Philadelphia Inquirer*, November 21, 1928, 21.

31. "Traditional Yale Rally Abolished," *Harvard Crimson*, November 19, 1928, 1.

32. Bealle, *History of Football at Harvard*, 278.

33. Ibid., 279.

34. Westbrook Pegler, "Harvard-Yale Game Relegated to a Rear Seat," *Chicago Tribune*, November 19, 1928, 27.

35. Larz Anderson, "In This Year of Grace," 28, Larz Anderson Typescript Journals Collection, vol. 2 (1929), Society of the Cincinnati, Washington, DC.

36. "Bingham's Faith in Horween Justified," *Boston Globe*, November 25, 1928, A30.

37. "Harvard Played Its Best, Says Horween," *Boston Globe*, November 25, 1928, A30.

38. Arnold Horween, "Harvard Team Wins Praises of Horween," *Boston Globe*, November 26, 1928, 21.

39. "Harvard Coach Weds Thursday," *Standard Union*, November 26, 1928, 79.

40. "Horween's Wedding to Be Thanksgiving," *Boston Globe*, November 27, 1928, 25.

41. "Horween's Status Still Is Withheld," *New York Times*, November 27, 1928, 36.

42. Walter Eckersall, "Horween Mulls Harvard Bid as Rumors Point to Wilce," *Chicago Tribune*, December 5, 1928, 31.

43. Ibid.

44. "'Red' Barrett, Captain-Elect of Harvard Elevens, Comments upon Important Football Problems," *Yale Daily News*, December 12, 1928, 7.

45. "Stadium Will Not Be Enlarged Next Year," *Boston Globe*, January 6, 1929, A20.

46. "Coach Horween to Retain Post," *Boston Globe*, January 12, 1929, 1.

47. "Horween's Return," *Harvard Crimson*, January 12, 1929, 2.

48. John R. Tunis, "The Great God Football," *Harper's Magazine*, November 1928, 743.

49. Ibid., 746.

50. Ibid.

51. A. Lawrence Lowell to Frederick L. Allen, October 17, 1928, box 258, folder 145, Lowell Papers.

52. "To Honor Crimson Football Players," *Boston Globe*, December 18, 1928, 23.

53. "Will Not Enlarge Harvard Stadium," *New York Times*, January 7, 1929, 35.

54. A. Lawrence Lowell to William J. Bingham, October 13, 1928, box 1, folder 2, Bingham Correspondence.

55. Schmidt, *Shaping College Football*, 217–33.

56. Howard J. Savage, *Fruit of an Impulse: Forty-Five Years of the Carnegie Foundation, 1905–1950* (New York: Harcourt, 1953), 157–58.

57. Howard J. Savage, *American College Athletics*, Bulletin No. 23 (New York: Carnegie Foundation, 1929), 240.

58. "Soldiers Field Concessions Now Out of Hands of H.A.A.," *Boston Globe*, October 24, 1929, 33.

59. Thomas W. Lamont to William J. Bingham, October 25, 1929, box 1, folder 3, Bingham Correspondence.

60. "Dr. Savage Speaks in Harvard Union," *Boston Globe*, October 25, 1929, 44.

61. Ibid.

62. "Four Assistants to Horween Named," *Boston Globe*, April 5, 1929, 1.

63. Bill Cunningham, "As a College Hero Sees It," *North American Review* 229, May 1930, 530.

64. Ibid.

65. William R. King, "Harvard Likely to Start Season with 11 Veterans," *Washington Post*, September 21, 1929, 18.

66. Bealle, *History of Football at Harvard*, 279.

67. Barry Wood, *What Price Football: A Player's Defense of the Game* (Boston: Houghton Mifflin, 1932), 93–94.

68. Cunningham, "As a College Hero Sees It," 533.

69. Ibid., 533–34.

70. Melville Webb Jr., "Harding Grabs Pass in Dusk for Touchdown, Wood Kicks Goal to Give Harvard 20–20 Tie," *Boston Globe*, October 20, 1929, A21.

71. Ibid.

72. "Something New under the Sun," *Chicago Tribune*, November 18, 1929, 14.

73. "Harvard Seeks to Learn West's Sport Methods," *Chicago Tribune*, March 6, 1928, 21.

74. "Something New under the Sun."

75. Cohane, *Yale Football Story*, 253.

76. Ibid., 254.

77. John McCallum, *Ivy League Football since 1872* (New York: Stein and Day, 1977), 107.

78. Cohane, *Yale Football Story*, 258.

79. Ibid.

80. "Snow-Fall Tinges Scene at Harvard," *New York Times*, November 22, 1929, 33.

81. Cohane, *Yale Football Story*, 258–60.

82. Cunningham, "As a College Hero Sees It," 532.

83. "Horween Parries Praise," *New York Times*, November 24, 1929, S5.

84. Grantland Rice, "Freak Tackle Halts Albie Booth," *Atlanta Constitution*, November 24, 1929, B8.

85. Ibid., B1.

86. Melville Webb Jr., "Drive of 83 Yards for Touchdown and Wood's Second Period Field Goal Win for Harvard 10–6," *Boston Globe*, November 24, 1929, A21.

87. Grantland Rice, "The Sportslight," *Boston Globe*, December 12, 1929, 30.

88. Ibid.

CONCLUSION

1. "Lateral Pass Won, Declares Horween," *New York Times*, November 23, 1930, S5.

2. "Horween's Return Asked by Players," *Boston Globe*, November 23, 1930, 30.

3. "Harvard Men Honored at Dinner in Boston," *New York Times*, December 13, 1930, 26.

4. Bingham, "Arnold Horween," 395.

5. "Boston Maccabees Plan Athletic Night Thursday," *Jewish Advocate*, August 4, 1931, 6.

6. Watterson, *College Football*, 181–82.

7. Braven Dyer, "'Big Three' Well Fixed," *Los Angeles Times*, September 1, 1930, A10.

8. Albert H. Barclay, "Yale, 14—Harvard, 0," *Yale Alumni Weekly*, November 30, 1934, 258.

9. Smith, *Harvard Century*, 108–9.

10. James B. Conant, *My Several Lives: Memoirs of a Social Inventor* (New York: Harper and Row, 1970), 129.

11. "Sports Figures at Funeral of Eddie Casey," *Boston Globe*, July 30, 1966, 8.

12. Marcia G. Synnott, "Eddie Casey," in *Biographical Dictionary of American Sports*, ed. David L. Porter (Westport, CT: Greenwood, 1995), 396–97.

13. Charges Bartlett, "Horween Says He's off the Gridiron for Good—This Time," *Chicago Tribune*, November 26, 1930, 21.

14. Barbara Rolek, "Horween's Leather Bound by Tradition," *Chicago Tribune*, October 27, 2003, sec. 4, p. 1.

15. Arnie Horween to Bill Bingham, January 14, 1941, box 17, folder 2, Harvard Athletic Association Records, UAV.170.95.2, Harvard University Archives, Cambridge, MA.

16. Barry Wood to Marion and Arnold Horween, December 29, 1958, W. Barry Wood Jr. Collection (unsorted), Medical Archives of the Johns Hopkins Medical Institutions, Baltimore, MD. For the description of this championship game, see Richard Crepeau, "The Greatest Game Ever?" in *Replays, Rivalries, and Rumbles: The Most Iconic Moments in American Sports*, ed. Steven Gietschier (Urbana: University of Illinois Press, 2017), 94–103.

17. W. Barry Wood to Arnold Horween, March 16, 1967, W. Barry Wood Jr. Collection.

18. "Arnold Horween," *Chicago Tribune*, August 7, 1985, C15.

19. "Former Pro Horween Hits 100," *Washington Post*, August 4, 1996, D5.

20. Howard J. Richard, "Here's Howie," *Jewish Advocate*, September 9, 1938, 6.

21. George Joel, "The Year in Sport," *Jewish Exponent*, September 11, 1931, 27.

22. Harry Glantz, "Our Own Athletics," *B'nai B'rith Messenger*, October 3, 1930, 10.

23. Tom Meany, "Terry Reaps Reward of McGraw Hunt for Jewish Star," *Sporting News*, September 30, 1938, 3.

24. George Currie, "Owens Leading the Parade as Strongest Threat," *Brooklyn Daily Eagle*, July 13, 1936, 6.

25. "W. J. Bingham—Harvard's First Athletic Director," *Boston Globe*, September 8, 1971, 41.

26. Edward H. Bradford to William J. Bingham, November 29, 1929, box 1, folder 3, William J. Bingham Correspondence.

INDEX

ZEV ELEFF is president of Gratz College and professor of American Jewish history. His books include *Authentically Orthodox: A Tradition-Bound Faith in American Life.*

The University of Illinois Press
is a founding member of the
Association of University Presses.

———————————————

University of Illinois Press
1325 South Oak Street
Champaign, IL 61820-6903
www.press.uillinois.edu